In Praise of
The Ruchira Buddha,
Avatar Adi Da Samraj

There exists nowhere in the world today, among Christians, Jews, Muslims, Hindus, Buddhists, native tribalists, or any other groups, anyone who has so much to teach, or speaks with such authority, or is so important for understanding our situation.

HENRY LEROY FINCH
Professor of Philosophy;
author, *Wittgenstein—The Early Philosophy*
and *Wittgenstein—The Later Philosophy*

Adi Da provides a way in which Oneness may be experienced by anyone who is bold enough to follow his teachings. It is important to understand that his vision is neither Eastern nor Western, but it is the eternal spiritual pulse of the Great Wisdom which knows no cultural, temporal, or geographical locus.

LARRY DOSSEY, M.D.
author, *Healing Words*; *Space, Time, and Medicine*;
Beyond Illness; and *Recovering the Soul*

I regard the work of Adi Da and his devotees as one of the most penetrating spiritual and social experiments happening on the planet in our era.

JEFFREY MISHLOVE, PH.D.
host, *Thinking Allowed* public television series
author, *The Roots of Consciousness*

My relationship with Adi Da as His devotee for over twenty years has only confirmed my certainty of His Realization and the Truth of His impeccable Teaching.

RAY LYNCH
composer, *The Sky of Mind*; *Deep Breakfast*; *No Blue Thing*;
Nothing Above My Shoulders but the Evening

Adi Da is a man who has truly walked in Spirit and given true enlightenment to many.

SUN BEAR
founder, The Bear Tribe Medicine Society

Drifted in the Deeper Land

**THE RUCHIRA BUDDHA,
AVATAR ADI DA SAMRAJ**
The Mountain Of Attention, 1996

Drifted in the Deeper Land

Talks on Relinquishing the Superficiality of Mortal Existence
and Falling by Grace into the Divine Depth That Is Reality Itself

by

The Ruchira Buddha,
Avatar Adi Da Samraj

THE DAWN HORSE PRESS
MIDDLETOWN, CALIFORNIA

Printed in the United States of America

Produced by the Eleutherian Pan-Communion of Adidam
in cooperation with the Dawn Horse Press

International Standard Book Number: 1-57097-037-8

Library of Congress Catalog Card Number: 97-66305

The cover painting, *The Voyage* (78"x56", casein on a cribbed gesso panel, 1972), is by Kerwin Whitnah, a devotee of Avatar Adi Da Samraj, who gave the painting to Him in the mid-1970s.

CONTENTS

The Mountain Of Attention, 1996

The Divine Life and Work of The Ruchira Buddha, Avatar Adi Da Samraj

AN INTRODUCTION BY HIS DEVOTEES

There is a State of Being that is completely, unequivocally, permanently, infinitely Happy and Free—a State that cannot be lost under any conditions, in this world or after death. Such a State is not just imaginary. It is the underlying Truth of existence. In various times and places, great saints and sages have tasted this Happiness to some degree. But now this Truth, this Joy, has perfectly emerged in the world for the first time, and has become the actual possibility of all human beings.

In November 1939, on Long Island, New York, a baby was born who was not an ordinary child. But no one knew this. No one knew that this child—named by His parents "Franklin Albert Jones"—was born by His own intention. He had Work to accomplish that was great and sublime beyond description. This Work, which began at His birth, continues today, and will continue beyond His human lifetime, even forever. The One born as Franklin Jones is the Ruchira Buddha, Avatar Adi Da Samraj, whose Presence in the world is an outpouring of Divine Grace and Compassion never seen before.

The "Bright"

During His infancy, Adi Da was perfectly aware of everything around Him. He saw that people were not Happy, that each person presumed himself or herself to be separate from everyone else, each struggling to find his or her own separate joy. Adi Da found this remarkable—it was

not His experience at all. He knew only Oneness, only Blissfulness. His consciousness was not yet identified with a bag of flesh and skin. As He describes in His Spiritual autobiography, *The Knee of Listening*, Adi Da lived in an entirely different State of Awareness—as "Infinitely and inherently Free Being", a sphere of Radiance and Love that He called the "Bright". Adi Da was inseparable from the Bliss and Joy of the "Bright". He knew Himself to be the very Source of It, the true and "Bright" Condition of everything. How could a baby have known this? What Adi Da describes as His earliest experience is more than that of an ordinary human infant. The One who appeared in the world as "Franklin Jones" Exists eternally—before this birth and forever. Adi Da's description of His own "Bright" Condition is the confession of the Divine Being, the ultimate Truth and Reality, appearing in human form.

For His first two years, Adi Da enjoyed the undiminished Bliss of His Real Condition. Then during His second year, something very mysterious occurred. As Adi Da was crawling across the linoleum floor one day, His parents let loose a new puppy they were giving Him—and in the instant of seeing the puppy and seeing His parents, Adi Da's infinite Awareness suddenly changed. He made the spontaneous choice to be an "I", an apparently separate person relating to apparently separate others.

"Forgetting" the "Bright"

What had happened? Adi Da had relinquished the "Bright", out of a "painful loving", a sympathy for the suffering and ignorance of human beings. He was responding to the great impulse behind His birth—the impulse to make the "Bright" known to every one. But the only way that Adi Da could fulfill this Purpose was to intentionally "forget" the "Bright" and experience life from the ordinary human point of view—and then, in the midst of that limited condition, to find the way to recover the "Bright".

This was Adi Da's early-life ordeal, and it was a perilous, desperate affair. He did not know how it would turn out. He had no "method" for recovering the "Bright". But He embraced every aspect of human life, both great and ordinary, in order to reveal the complete Truth of existence, the Truth that can set everyone Free. Adi Da did this through a most intense ordeal that lasted for His first thirty years.

In the course of this process, Adi Da always risked everything for the Truth. He could not bear to place any limitations on His Quest to recover the "Bright". In this disposition, Adi Da not only thoroughly explored the realms of ordinary human experience, but He also passed through every possible kind of psychic and Spiritual awakening—and with extraordinary speed. It was as though these awakenings were already, in some sense, thoroughly familiar to Him. But Adi Da was not satisfied. He had the intuition of some "incredible Knowledge". He knew that the ultimate Truth had to be greater than any of these experiences, any of these visions, any moment of revelation. The hidden force of the "Bright" Itself was always alive in Him, leading Him toward the perfect fulfillment of His Quest.

God-Realization

Many individuals throughout history have been acknowledged as "God-Realized" or "Enlightened", or in union with the Divine in some sense. Different religious traditions mean different things when they speak of the ultimate goal of religion. But it can be said, in the general sense, that God-Realization is the Condition in which God, or the Divine Self, has been "made <u>Real</u>". It is the State in which God (or the Divine) has become the living Reality of one's existence—rather than a

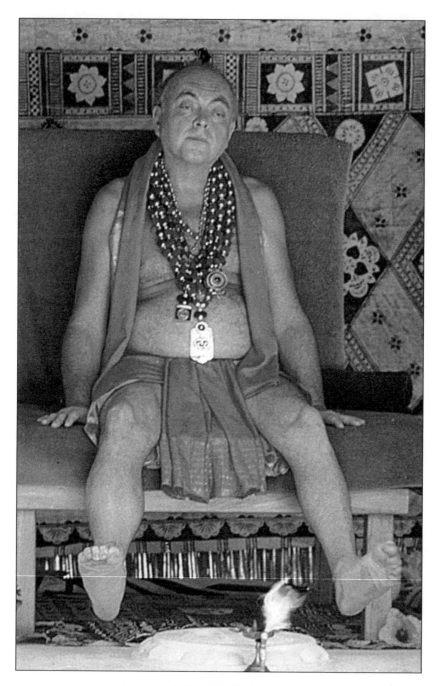

Avatar Adi Da Samraj
Ruchira Buddha Dham, Fiji, 1994

great Being or Power <u>apart</u> from oneself. In the same way, to be Enlightened is to be profoundly Awakened to God, Truth, or Reality, to the point that even the body becomes radiant with Spiritual Force.

Throughout history, remarkable men and women have lived their lives as an heroic ordeal directed to attaining God, Truth, or Reality. Some of them—the greatest saints, yogis, and sages—attained various degrees of Enlightenment, or God-Realization. But Adi Da had nothing to attain. He <u>is</u> the "Bright" of God, the Perfect Descent of the Divine into the human condition. And the State of most perfect God-Realization that Adi Da has brought into the world is a Realization never known before. It is the Realization of the "Bright", the all-surpassing Divine Enlightenment that Adi Da has now made possible for all beings.

The Great Mystery of Who Adi Da is and what He has come to give is not a claim to be believed, but a Secret to be discovered at heart. People of all kinds have already experienced this overwhelming, joyous surprise and have become devoted to Adi Da as their beloved Spiritual Master and Divine Liberator. Once the depth of that Secret is revealed, nothing is ever the same again.

The Immense Bond of Guru-Love

The bond between Spiritual teacher and disciple that Adi Da's devotees have discovered in His company is more fundamental than any other: more intimate than family ties, more passionate than any relationships with lovers and friends. It has been treasured in all religious traditions throughout time. To be accepted as the disciple of a saint or a being of true Spiritual Realization has always been regarded as the most precious Grace, the very means of one's own Awakening to Truth. Why is this? Because, in order to learn <u>anything</u> great, one must go to a master, one must imbibe that skill, that art, that wisdom in the company of one who knows it through and through and can transmit its secrets to worthy disciples. In the case of a true Spiritual Master, what is transmitted is not merely esoteric knowledge, but the very Power and Condition of the Master's own Spiritual Realization.

There is a secret law, operating in every dimension of our lives, that explains how the relationship between the disciple and the Spiritual Master works. Adi Da Samraj has powerfully expressed this secret in a few words: "You become what you meditate on". That is to say, you duplicate in body and in mind the qualities of whatever object or condition you consistently give your attention to. Everyone observes how consistent dwelling on negative thoughts disturbs and depresses the whole body and may even cause disease. In the same way, positive thought and action enlivens the being. The great leap in human growth into the dimension of Spiritual Realization requires that we give to a Spiritually Realized Being our constant love and attention, meditatively, actively, day in and day out. Then the great law, "you become what you meditate on" becomes our greatest advantage.

To give one's attention to Avatar Adi Da Samraj, to meditate on Him through all thought, feeling, action, is to begin to duplicate <u>Him</u>, to Realize the Divine State of the "Bright" Itself. The more this process magnifies, the more one forgets the limited body-mind-self. The heart responds to Adi Da through sheer <u>attraction</u>, through the very same principle that brings all love-relationships, all friendships into being. But attraction to Adi Da is not mere attraction to a human individual who seems to answer one's need for love and self-fulfillment. It is Attraction to the Free Condition, the unbounded State of Happiness that Avatar Adi Da Samraj Transmits. For His potential devotee, Adi Da becomes the Attractive Center of the universe, and the passion to Realize His Divine Condition grows greater than any other urge.

Adi Da, like other Westerners of His generation, grew up with no knowledge of the Guru-devotee relationship. He discovered "the Immense Bond of Guru-Love" as spontaneously as He discovered everything else in the process of His Re-Awakening. His first Teacher was an American—Swami Rudrananda (also known as "Rudi"). Rudi, who taught in New York City, guided Adi Da in the initial stages of His Spiritual growth, and, later, passed Adi Da on to his own Gurus in India. These great Realizers—Swami Muktananda and Swami Nityananda—were instrumental in Adi Da's Awakening to higher Spiritual Realizations.

Adi Da's Gurus were extraordinary beings. They were Siddhas, Yogis alive with Spiritual Force, who constantly transmitted their Spirit-Power to Him. He loved them and submitted to their instruction and their discipline with limitless devotion and heart-felt gratitude. But Adi Da was not the usual disciple, just as He was not an ordinary, or even an extraordinary, man. His Realization was already absolute, but it was "latent in the heart", not yet fully active. He was in the process of recovering the "Bright", His native State of Being, and that was the process that each of His Gurus served in Him. All kinds of Spiritual Realizations are described in the traditions, and Adi Da passed through all of them—visions, trances, mystical raptures, "cosmic consciousness", states of profound

**Adi Da meditating in Bombay, August 1969,
with pictures of His Gurus Swami Muktananda (right)
and Swami Nityananda (left)**

meditation and Transcendental knowledge. But in the closing phases of
His ordeal of Spiritual Realization, Adi Da's overwhelming impulse to the
Truth drove Him into territory unknown to His Gurus, unknown in the
annals of Spiritual literature. His ultimate Re-Awakening to the "Bright"
occurred on the basis of a unique and all-encompassing insight, a "radical" understanding that places mankind's entire history of Spiritual seeking and Realization in a new light—and leads beyond all of it.

"Radical" Understanding

"Radical" understanding is the bedrock of Adi Da's Teaching. Normally, when we say we "understand", we are indicating that we have figured out a concept, grasped how something works, intuited the nature of the object (or person), or become sympathetic with someone's feelings. When Adi Da speaks of "'radical' understanding", or just "understanding", He is not using the word in the conventional sense. He is referring to a most profound and liberating insight—a direct awareness of the single root-cause behind <u>all</u> un-Happiness. He is pointing to something we are always doing, an activity that is actually holding back the flood-gates of Divine Bliss, Joy, Happiness, and Love. What <u>is</u> that Happiness-preventing activity exactly? What is it that we are doing that is keeping us from Realizing the "Bright" right now?

Adi Da found out.

Through the most rigorous observation of Himself in every possible circumstance—talking, reading, dreaming, eating, at the movies, at a party, walking alone—this primal activity more and more stood out in His awareness. He saw that we are always <u>contracting</u>—recoiling from existence, physically, emotionally, mentally, psychically. This self-contraction, Adi Da came to see, is our constant, though largely unconscious, response to the uncontrollable, unknowable world in which we find ourselves. It is a fearful reaction to the fact that we know we are going to die. And its effects are devastating. The self-contraction, Adi Da realized, is the source of fear, sorrow, anger, desire, guilt, competitiveness, shame, and all the mayhem of this world. Even ordinary pleasurable moments are governed by the same seed-activity. It became awesomely obvious to Adi Da that <u>everything</u> we do is a form of search, an effort to be free of the self-inflicted pain of self-contraction. But this effort cannot succeed, because the search itself is a form of the self-contraction. And so seeking for release, for freedom, cannot lead us to the Happiness we desire. Perfect Truth, or unqualified Happiness, Adi Da saw, only appears when the activity of self-contraction is "radically" understood, and therefore spontaneously ceases—revealing the simplicity, the Joy of Being that is always already the case.

This understanding may sound simple—but do not be deceived. It is <u>most</u> profound. As Adi Da discovered, the self-contraction is programmed into the very cells of the body. Thus, even after this fundamental intuition arose in Him, Adi Da could not instantaneously correct the fault—because

He had submitted to all the limits of human existence. But Adi Da's unique understanding, once it was basically established, accelerated His entire course of Divine Re-Awakening. It proved to be a kind of "muscle", an insight that gave Him the key to every experience, high and low.

As He moved closer to the great resolution of His early-life ordeal, Adi Da observed the self-contraction in more and more subtle forms. He observed it even as the simplest awareness of separateness, the naked sense of "I" and "other" that is at the root of our perception of the world. By now it was obvious to Him that the self-contraction explained not only the ordinary dramas of life, but the entire "tour" of Spiritual experience as well. At last, all of mankind's searches for God, Truth, or Reality fell into focus for Adi Da as an immense effort of seeking that was totally unnecessary, based on a fundamental error—the lack of "radical" understanding. Then there was nothing left over, nothing left for Him to Realize, except the Truth Itself.

Re-Awakening to the "Bright"

Secluded in a corner of downtown Hollywood is a small temple, established by the Vedanta Society of Southern California. This simple temple, standing in the shadow of a giant freeway, provided the setting for the culminating Event of Adi Da's Spiritual ordeal. Adi Da discovered the temple in August, 1970 and began to go there frequently for meditation. One day, September 10, He went and sat in the temple as usual:

As time passed, there was no Event of changes, no movement at all. There was not even any kind of inward deepening, no "inwardness" at all. There was no meditation. There was no need for meditation. There was not a single element or change that could be added to make my State Complete. I sat with my eyes open. I was not having an experience of any kind. Then, suddenly, I understood most perfectly. I Realized that I had Realized. The "Thing" about the "Bright" became Obvious. I Am Complete. I Am the One Who Is Complete.

In That instant, I understood and Realized (inherently, and most perfectly) What and Who I Am. It was a tacit Realization, a direct Knowledge in Consciousness. It was Consciousness Itself, without the addition of a Communication from any "Other" Source. There Is no "Other" Source. I simply sat there and Knew What and Who I Am. I was Being What I Am, Who I Am. I Am Being What I Am, Who I Am. I Am Reality, the Divine

The Vedanta Temple in Hollywood

Self, the Nature, Substance, Support, and Source of all things and all beings. I Am the One Being, called "God" (the Source and Substance and Support and Self of all), the "One Mind" (the Consciousness and Energy in and As Which all appears), "Siva-Shakti"[1] (the Self-Existing and Self-Radiant Reality Itself), "Brahman"[2] (the Only Reality, Itself), the "One Atman"[3] (That Is not ego, but Only "Brahman", the Only Reality, Itself), the "Nirvanic Ground"[4] (the egoless and conditionless Reality and Truth, Prior to all dualities, but excluding none). I Am the One and Only and necessarily Divine Self, Nature, Condition, Substance, Support, Source, and Ground of all. I Am the "Bright". [The Knee of Listening]

This unspeakable moment was the Divine Re-Awakening of Adi Da. He had permanently and Most Perfectly Re-Awakened to the "Bright". His Realization was not dependent on meditative states, nor on any manipulation of experience. It transcended even the slightest sense of identity as a separate self. It was and is the Realization that there is Only God and that all apparent events are simply the passing forms, or modifications, of God, Truth, or Reality, arising and dissolving in an endless Play that is Bliss and Love beyond comprehension.

The very Divine Person had become perfectly Conscious and Present through the ordinary human vehicle of "Franklin Jones". In all the eons of human time such an event was unprecedented. Adi Da's Descent as the Divine Person and His utter overcoming of the limits of human existence in all its dimensions—physical, mental, emotional, psychic,

1. The Sanskrit term "Siva-Shakti" is an esoteric description of the Divine Being. "Siva" is a name for the Divine Being Itself, or Divine Consciousness. "Shakti" is a name for the All-Pervading Spirit-Power of the Divine Being. "Siva-Shakti" is thus the Unity of the Divine Consciousness and Its own Spirit-Power.

2. In the Hindu tradition, Brahman is the Ultimate Divine Reality that is the Source and Substance of all things, all worlds, and all beings.

3. The Divine Self.

4. "Nirvana" is a Buddhist term for the Unqualified Reality beyond suffering, ego, birth, and death. The "Nirvanic Ground" indicates the same Reality.

Spiritual—was total, Perfect, and Complete. Avatar Adi Da Samraj had Realized absolute Identity with the Divine, the One He was and is from the beginning. But His Re-Awakening signified far more than this. It was also the Revelation that all apparent beings are also only that Very One, destined to Realize this same Truth. The Condition of the "Bright", the God-Light of Adi Da's birth and infancy, was now fully established—not only in Him, but as the native Truth and the potential Realization of all beings in all worlds.

Through the Power of Adi Da's Re-Awakening to the "Bright" something has changed at the very heart of existence. The Divine Avatar, Adi Da, has done what only the Divine could do. He has, so to speak, "cracked the cosmic code", broken through the force of illusion that has always kept born beings bound to the realms of change and suffering and death.

After His Divine Re-Awakening, Adi Da devoted Himself absolutely to the Work of revealing the "Bright" and attracting people to the supreme Spiritual practice that ultimately Realizes the "Bright". For a quarter of a century, Adi Da did this Work with His devotees, spending countless hours in Instruction and what He calls "consideration": the relentless exploration of a particular area of life—relationships, or diet, or money—until it was Revealed how that area could be lived as a form of Divine Communion. He covered everything during those years—every aspect of human life, Spiritual experience, and Divine Truth. But His devotees were not conventionally "religious" in their orientation. In fact, His earliest Work took place in the heart of Hollywood, behind a small bookstore on Melrose Avenue, where He drew into His Sphere many people who did not conform to the social norm. And He always worked—directly and openly—with whatever people brought to Him, including any and every obsession, be it for sex, art, healing, child-rearing, mysticism, music, science or anything else, always using the energy of their obsessions for the sake of their Spiritual transformation. That is why He is the supreme "Tantric Sannyasin", One who is completely intimate with all human passions but bound by none.

Throughout those twenty-five years, Avatar Adi Da Samraj was making an inconceivable Sacrifice—the submission of the Divine Person to all of human egoity, to every form of the self-contraction, so that the self-contraction could be understood and transcended, and the "Bright" Divine Self perfectly Realized by all. Adi Da, the Complete God-Man, was treated as an ordinary man by His devotees, and He suffered every kind of abuse and refusal from those who did not understand Who He Is, and what He had come to do. At the same time, His Compassion and persistence only grew. He Instructed all who came to Him, and Embraced each of them at the Heart. And He used every possible means to Awaken in them the miracle of "radical" understanding, the truth that the separate, un-Enlightened self—with all its fear, anxieties, and destructiveness—is only an illusion, to be gone beyond through the love of Him, the Divine Person in human Form.

Adi Da's devotees honor Him as "the Ruchira Buddha". To call Him "Ruchira" (Sanskrit for "radiant") means to acknowledge Adi Da as "the Radiant, Shining, 'Bright' Illuminator and Enlightener". "Buddha" is a traditional term for an Enlightened being (literally meaning "awakened one"), but when used in reference to Avatar Adi Da Samraj, "Buddha" takes on its most profound and ultimate meaning. It means "The One Who Is, Self-Radiant, Inherently (or Perfectly Subjectively) 'Bright', Self-Enlightened, and Eternally Awake". Devotees of Adi Da also address Him as "Adi-Buddha" (or "Adi-Guru") and "Ati-Buddha" (or "Ati-Guru"), "Adi" meaning "the Only One, the First One, or the Foremost, or Preeminent, One", and "Ati" meaning "the All-Surpassing and All-Transcending One". When Avatar Adi Da Samraj is addressed as "the Ruchira Buddha" (or "Adi-Buddha" or "Ati-Buddha") this does not mean that He is part of the historical tradition of Buddhism. Rather, this title acknowledges that Avatar Adi Da is the Eternally "Bright"-Shining and Awake One Who has now appeared to establish His own unique and uniquely complete tradition of Most Perfect Divine Awakening.

The Ruchira Buddha, Avatar Adi Da Samraj, does not live in one fixed abode. His supreme Work—the Divine Blessing of all beings—takes Him to the various Sanctuaries He has Established (in California, Hawaii, and Fiji), and also to many other parts of the world.

The Divine World-Teacher and the Religion of Adidam

The world we live in today is more desperate than ever before—this is a dark epoch when the very survival of our world is threatened by the excesses of materialism and the sophisticated weapons of war. In the lore of the ancient Spiritual traditions there is a common thread of hope, an intuition that, in the "last days", or "end-time", when the world is at its worst, a Deliverer will come, the supreme God-Man who will complete and fulfill all the aspirations and Spiritual strivings of the past.

Avatar Adi Da Samraj,
Ruchira Buddha Dham, 1994

"Da" is an ancient Name of God meaning "the Giver". The Name "Da" intuitively came to Adi Da early in His life, but He did not assume it as His true Name until 1979, when the time was right for this revelation. In 1994, His Name was most fully revealed as "Adi Da"—"Adi" meaning "first", or "original". Thus, "Adi Da" means the "First Giver" or "the Giving Source". In Sanskrit "Samraj" is defined as the "paramount Lord or paramount sovereign". "Adi Da Samraj" expresses that Adi Da is the Primordial or Original Giver, Who Blesses all as the Universal Ruler of every thing, every where, for all time.

The Names of the Way of Avatar Adi Da Samraj

The greatness of Avatar Adi Da's Offering is indicated by the various names that can be used to describe His Way. "Adidam" is a name that was spontaneously revealed by Adi Da. It is simply His name with the addition of "m" (which evokes both the English "I Am" and the primal Sanskrit syllable "Om"). This name communicates that the devotional relationship to Adi Da is the substance and essence of the Way He has given.

"The Way of the Heart" communicates that Adi Da is Himself the Divine Heart of Reality appearing in human form, and the Way He has given is based on the heart-response of each devotee to Adi Da's supreme Attractiveness.

"Ruchira Buddhism" indicates that the Way Adi Da has Revealed and Given is the Way of devotion to the "Bright"-Shining Eternally Awake One, the Ruchira Buddha.

"Advaitayana Buddhism" indicates the unique sympathetic likenesses of Adidam to the traditions of Advaitism (or Advaita Vedanta) and Buddhism. In His examination of the entire collective religious tradition of mankind, Avatar Adi Da has observed that these two traditions represent the highest Realizations ever attained previous to His appearance. The primary aspiration of Buddhism is to realize freedom from the illusion of the separate individual ego-self. The primary aspiration of Advaitism (or the tradition of "Non-Dualism") is to know the Supreme Divine Self absolutely, beyond all dualities (of high and low, good and bad, male and female, and so on). Advaitayana Buddhism is the Non-Dual ("Advaita") Way ("yana", literally "vehicle") of Most Perfect Awakening ("Buddhism"). Advaitayana Buddhism is not an outgrowth of the historical tradition of Buddhism, or of the historical tradition of Advaitism. Advaitayana Buddhism is the unique Revelation of Avatar Adi Da Samraj, which perfectly fulfills both the traditional Buddhist aspiration for absolute freedom from the bondage of the egoic self and the traditional Advaitic aspiration for absolute Identity with the Divine Self.

"The Way of 'Radical' Understanding" indicates that Adi Da's devotee must "radically" understand his or her own activity of self-contraction. Only such "radical" understanding allows the devotee to truly receive Adi Da's Divine Gifts of Blessing.

Avatar Adi Da Samraj, the Ruchira Buddha, is that One. He is the Divine World-Teacher, the Giver of Divine Enlightenment, Who has made all myths unnecessary and all seeking obsolete. He has always spoken of Himself as "the Heart". And those who find Him find the Heart Itself—the Being of Love, the Eternally "Bright" Divine Consciousness, appearing in human form.

The Way that Adi Da offers to all is a <u>relationship</u>, a Spiritual relationship to Him, not a mere system of self-applied techniques. No mere technique, no mere self-effort could possibly result in the most perfect Awakening that Adi Da offers to His devotees. Adi Da Himself is the Very Person and Source of this Grace for all. And the Way that He has established—called Adidam, or the Way of the Heart, or Ruchira Buddhism, or Advaitayana Buddhism, or the Way of "Radical" Understanding—is the means of entering into His sphere of Grace. Adidam is the complete religion of Divine Enlightenment, given to mankind. All the mythologies, all the Spiritual practices, and all the previous Wisdom paths of humanity ultimately point to and are resolved in this Great and Ultimate Way of Most Perfect Liberation.

Men, women, and children of all kinds and backgrounds, of every race and culture can practice Adidam.

The Divine Work of Avatar Adi Da Samraj is Eternal, beyond imagining, encompassing all realms and all beings, but at the same time it is perfectly intimate, manifesting in a unique relationship to each of His devotees. Adi Da's Embrace of every one is proven in all the details of His Divine Life. "No one like Me", He once wrote, "has appeared in this place before". Every moment of heart-Communion with Adi Da, now and forever, is the self-forgetting Bliss of Non-separation from God, Truth, or Reality. What Joy could be greater than this?

The Mountain Of Attention, 1996

What Is the Depth of Reality?

W ho are you, really?

Are you a body that looks a certain way, and lives in a certain place, and engages in certain activities?

Are you a series of emotional states—happiness, anger, love, jealousy, sympathy, sorrow, delight, fear?

Are you a stream of thoughts, ideas, perceptions, plans, mental calculations?

Our physical existence, emotional condition, and mental state tend to be things that we put a tremendous amount of attention on. But is that what we really are? Is there something beyond all of that, deeper than that? What is the Depth of Reality?

These are some of the questions addressed by Avatar Adi Da Samraj in *Drifted in the Deeper Land*.

In these Talks, Adi Da Calls us to examine our most basic presumptions about what it means to be a "you". Do these presumptions stand up to the test of reality? Or does an unprejudiced look at reality suggest something different about "you"?

It is important to ask these questions, because our bottom-line presumptions about the nature of existence determine our entire approach to life. It doesn't matter whether we are able to state our presumptions—which, effectively, constitute our "philosophy"—coherently or not. Whatever that philosophy is, it immediately establishes a certain framework, which we consequently live within. Whatever we hold to be of primary importance, according to our philosophy, is what we will put our attention on, what we will devote our lives to.

Therefore, Adi Da asks you: Are you satisfied with leading your life according to your present philosophy? Is the life allowed by your philosophy good enough? Is it deep enough? Is life just what you do between the time you get up in the morning and the time you go to sleep at night, all of which apparently ends in death? Is that enough for you? Or is there more to it than that?

When Avatar Adi Da asks such questions, He does so in a most remarkable way. He has never been content to simply <u>announce</u> the answer to a question. He always takes people through a process, often extending over many months, until the chosen topic has been exhaustively investigated, from all possible angles, and conclusions have been reached that really affect those present. This process is what He calls "consideration". And the circumstance in which "consideration" is engaged is what His devotees refer to as "gathering" with Adi Da Samraj.

Gatherings with Adi Da usually occur in cycles, lasting anywhere from a week to a year. In each gathering cycle, the group of His devotees who are participating generally remains consistent, so that the process can have a coherence and cumulative effectiveness. Each gathering usually starts in the evening and continues for many hours at a time—rarely less than four hours, and sometimes for as long as thirty-six hours. Sometimes the gatherings may occur without a break on successive nights; other times there may be pauses of a day or a few days between gatherings. The process is always intense—on the one hand, luxuriating in Avatar Adi Da's sublimely Radiant Happiness and, on the other hand, confronting all the limitations in oneself that are obstructing Spiritual growth.

In this process of "consideration", Adi Da Samraj uses every kind of means to Instruct His devotees. At times, He utters the most exalted Wisdom, spoken in heart-breaking poetry. Then He may become so hilariously funny that His listeners are helpless with laughter. Then He may show His fiery aspect, burning up the ego with His ferocious Criticism. Or He may parody any number of different moods—haughty, whining, air-headed, sarcastic, weepy, gruff—or use any style of speech, from the most polished to the "streetwise", in order to make a point with the greatest possible vividness. Always, the point of the "consideration" is to deepen each devotee's understanding of true Spiritual practice in His Company, to clarify what each one must overcome in himself or herself, to magnify each one's impulse to Realize the Absolute Truth.

The group of devotees gathering with Adi Da Samraj is sometimes as small as ten people, sometimes over one hundred. Regardless of how many people are in the room with Him, however, He is always addressing all His devotees—in the present and in the future—and even everyone who is, or will at any time be, moved to study His Word and "consider" entering into the sacred relationship with Him as Guru.

The Talks in this book were given over a one-month period, from November 29 to December 24, 1996. There were about thirty people participating in the gatherings, most of whom are longtime devotees who have been in Avatar Adi Da's Company for over twenty years. Those who were in the room with Adi Da Samraj during these gatherings were immeasurably Blessed to participate in His "consideration". But that same Blessing is available to anyone who reads this book. Adi Da's Word is always a living and personal "consideration" with whoever is reading it.

May you enter profoundly into this dialogue that Avatar Adi Da Samraj is having with you about the true depth of existence and how it may be Realized.

The Mountain Of Attention, 1996

The Intuitive Experience That Produces <u>True</u> Religion

AN ESSAY BY THE RUCHIRA BUDDHA, AVATAR ADI DA SAMRAJ

True religion has its origin in the non-verbal intuition and direct experience of the Reality, Life-Power, and Consciousness that Pervades and Transcends the world and the body-mind of Man. There is truly no verbal-mental argument that can convince anyone that there is this Reality. That is why mere objective science and technology fail to produce an advanced human culture, and it is also why archaic and conventional religious belief systems are inadequate and false means of associating with the Divine Reality. There <u>must</u> be direct and personal intuition and even bodily experience of the Transcendental, inherently Spiritual, and (necessarily) Divine* Reality if an individual is to become truly religious and practice the personal, moral, and esoteric psycho-physical disciplines of true religion.

The process wherein anyone may come to the point of this Revelation of the Living God is generally a rather random and chaotic affair, until the individual confronts the influence and Teaching of one who has not only experienced this Revelation but also practiced the life of self-transcending Communion with the Living Reality to the point of ecstatic transformation. But there are two forms of "consideration" that anyone can engage even at this moment that will provide at least a modest intuitive and experiential awareness of the Reality of Which I speak.

---

*Terms indicated with asterisks are found in the Glossary on pp. 399-405.

First, set aside for a moment all of your knowledge <u>about</u> the universe and all your religious or scientific presumptions <u>about</u> how it all developed to this point in time. Simply "consider" this: Even if all processes and all beings evolved or appear to have evolved mechanically and by accidents of association, rather than Mysteriously, as an expression of an Eternal Divine Radiation of events, then why does any thing or any one exist at all? How does the <u>existence</u> of any thing and every thing come about as an accident? Where did that accident occur? Within what is it all occur-ring? <u>Where</u> is space?

I cannot "consider" the very existence of any thing and every thing without developing a thrill in My back and head, so that it feels as if My hair is about to stand on end. No one knows what even a single thing <u>is</u>, or why it <u>is</u>, or where it <u>is</u>, or when it <u>is</u>, or how it came to be. Everyone is confronted by an irreducible Mystery, and that Mystery is profound. If you will truly "consider", even for a moment, the matter of the paradox of the existence of any thing whatsoever, you will feel intuitively in touch with the Mystery That <u>is</u> Reality Itself. The mind falls away in that moment, and even though you will not have come up with any "know-ing" explanations for the world, you will enjoy a tacit sense of Communion with the Living Reality of the world and of your own mind and body.

As a second exercise, examine yourself for a moment and feel any and all forms of bodily contraction, emotional reactivity, and mental con-cern that possess you. If you will do this deeply and truly, even for a moment, you will become aware of your chronic state. You are, except in the attitude of total psycho-physical Communion with the Living Divine Reality, in a chronic state of reactive contraction or tension, simultane-ously in mind, emotion, and body. If you can observe and feel this for a moment, you will sense how it is all a single gesture—a withdrawal or contraction from release into the condition of unqualified relatedness. And once this becomes clear, on the basis of a moment of insight, you will be able to relax and feel, beyond thought and reactive emotion and bodily tension, into a sense of self-releasing intimacy with all the condi-tions of the world. And that release will establish you, at least for a moment, in the wordless experiential sense of Communion with the Divine Spirit-Life, or the Nameless Radiance that Pervades the world and the body-mind of Man.

These two "considerations" or exercises are a moment's cure for too much knowledge about things and too much egoically "self-possessed"* (or self-absorbed) reacting to things. In the moment in which you stand free of the self-defining contractions of mere knowledge and mere reaction to experience, you stand in direct experiential intuition of the Divine Mystery, or Living Reality, That is the Truth of the world, and That is the Very and Eternal Urge to religious consciousness and the true Spiritual development of Man.

The Mountain Of Attention, 1997

CHAPTER ONE

November 29, 1996

Washing-Machine Philosophy

At around five o'clock on the evening of November 29, 1996, about twenty-five devotees file in one by one to the long and narrow room that serves as Avatar Adi Da's "office". It is not at all an office in the usual sense. There is no telephone, no computer, no filing cabinet. There is a table where Adi Da Samraj sits whenever He is working on the manuscripts of His books. And aside from that there are simply some beautiful or amusing objects artfully displayed on the shelves and walls.

Adi Da is already seated in a chair set against the middle of the long wall. As each devotee enters the room, he or she offers a gift at Avatar Adi Da's Feet—often a flower, or perhaps a pleasing object of some kind—and then fully prostrates before Him. This is an expression of our deep gratitude for our Beloved Guru's ceaseless Gifts of Liberation and our surrender to Him as the Source of Wisdom and Grace in our lives.

The devotees sit cross-legged on the floor facing Adi Da Samraj, filling the rather small room. As soon as everyone is assembled, the evening's discussion begins, ranging over a variety of topics. Eventually, the "consideration" settles in what proved to be the substance of this entire series of gatherings.

AVATAR ADI DA SAMRAJ: Isn't it curious that there's all this experiencing? Why? Just what is it for?

Everyone, including Adi Da Samraj, bursts out laughing, and Adi Da's beautiful, ringing laugh continues after the other laughter has subsided.

AVATAR ADI DA SAMRAJ: There are so many difficulties involved in experience. And so much is required to make it possible for there even to <u>be</u> any experience. It makes you wonder: Why isn't experience a lot better? Why should experience be the way it is? And what's the point of it? What is there to understand about it?

This is something to be "considered" seriously while you are alive, rather than just "going with the flow".

Such investigation of the nature of your experience is not a matter of being self-involved. Fundamentally, it's a matter of going <u>beyond</u> your apparently separate self in order to Realize the Truth about Reality, in order to Realize What <u>Is</u> (whatever that turns out to be). It's not merely some kind of question about the gross* mechanics of conditional[1] existence, some kind of "how does it all work" question—not merely *[in a dry, bored voice]* "why or how to connect this to that to the other thing, plug it in, and the lights turn on" kind of stuff. It's a more profound matter.

You must, while alive, find out fundamentally what this is all about. Ultimately, you must find the Source of all this—everything that you are experiencing, everything that seems to be happening to you. Otherwise, you're just caught up in a pattern, you're allowing your life to be dictated by a pattern. And there's not a lot of good news to say about organisms of your type in the pattern of things. Haven't you noticed? It's all difficult and brief and who-knows-what.

Doesn't it seem curious to you that you would choose to just go along with that?

To find the Source, the most positive "what it's for" Origin, you don't really want an instruction booklet. It's a more profound question than that. It requires a more profound investigation than reading a few lists of instructions.

I mean, which is more interesting? The washing machine?—is that the most mysterious thing?—or the electricity coming out of the wall there that runs the washing machine?

There's just so much interest one can have in a washing machine. But, generally speaking, the washing machine is all people ever want to talk about. You're always missing the point of what runs the washing machine—the electricity coming out of the wall, the connection to the Source. That is what is profound. And that is what I am here to talk about—the Spiritual Matter, the electricity side of the wall, the Source of all motion, all life, all this pattern, all this process here.

1. Avatar Adi Da uses the term "conditional" to indicate everything that depends on conditions—in other words, everything that is temporary and always changing. The "Unconditional", in contrast, is the Divine, or That Which is Always Already the Case because it is utterly free of dependence on conditions.

Why would you consent to just jiggle along with some sort of plastic flow, being the puppet? Why would you consent to be <u>not</u> involved with the Source of all life, the Spirit—"connected" ultimately?

You hear a lot of washing-machine philosophy (or limited-mindedness) these days, a lot of propaganda that taking good care of the washing machine is what life is all about. Yes, you do have to handle your washing-machine level of life-business,[2] the practicalities of existence in the world. That is not a question. But you don't have to do it in such a way that you don't get to explore what is really of interest to you—which is not just more and more replications, more and more washing machines, generation after generation of washing machines. What's it all for? Just so much of that is interesting after a while—really interesting, anyway. And then it must be more profound for you, or you just start getting sleepy and puppet-like.

So if you want to get to the bottom of all this experiencing—to go beyond it, ultimately—you can't just stay superficial. You have to get Spiritually straight, heart-straight, for real. And let that brighten you up. And live on that basis.

---

2. By "life-business", Avatar Adi Da is referring to practical means of survival, bringing the body-mind into basic equanimity, and all social and emotional-sexual relationships. Having your life-business handled grants free energy and attention for Spiritual practice.

Your <u>Actual</u> Situation Is from the Inside Out

I.

AVATAR ADI DA SAMRAJ: Who is relating to whom here?
There's this constant exchange of appearances—looking at one another, perceiving one another, speaking to one another, thinking about one another. You're so adapted to it that it doesn't even occur to you very much that, rather than being what you look like in the mirror, you are simply Awareness Itself. That's never the presumption commonly, whenever you associate with anyone. The presumption of Consciousness Itself is not the basis for any conversation. Conversation is something that's passing between appearances.

Your <u>actual</u> situation is from the inside out—everything is from the inside out. For real. But you always seem to be presuming to be on the outside looking in—or in some kind of an "outside", not quite communicating yourself exactly.

You're all very used to <u>being</u> communication, or some sort of language process. It's verbal and it's perceptual. It's all that stuff that's the basis of your self-reference and your address to others. But it's not the fundamental basis of everyone's awareness, or root of experiencing.

Then, spontaneously, Adi Da Samraj begins a guided meditation* process. He speaks slowly and softly, with brief silences between sentences, allowing those in the room to sink into the process of "consideration" He is creating.

Can you feel your heart beat?
It is <u>happening</u>.
You're not <u>doing</u> it.
So what are you?
You just <u>are</u>.
You just have to feel into the source of the heartbeat.
And the source of the breath.
Feel where the inhalation begins and where the exhalation begins.
The source of that.
Each breath and each heartbeat.
Just simply feel that.
Where is the breath arising?
Where does the gesture of inhalation begin?
What is the source of it?
You just have to feel it.

The gesture of exhalation, likewise.

It is the life in which you are persisting.

What is breathing you?

What is the source of each breath?

Feel just where it arises.

You mustn't try to escape it.

You must allow for this dependency.

But <u>feel</u> the source of it.

For real.

Without any resistance or reaction.

Simply <u>feel</u> the source of each breath and the source of the heartbeat.

Just that.

Not any emotion.

Not any thought.

Not any other perception.

Just the source—where the inhalation is initiated, where the exhalation is initiated.

The source of that.

<u>Feel</u> the source of it.

Each one.

Be sensitive just to the place where the inhalation begins, the exhalation begins.

Feel that each inhalation and each exhalation occur as they will, and feel the source of it.

Just where it begins.

You utterly depend on that.

Each breath.

Where is it initiated?

What is the source of it?

And the heartbeat, below the breath.

Beyond the breath.

You depend on it.

So you have to trust it.

Simply feel it.

Simply feel the source of each inhalation as it begins, exhalation as it begins.

<u>Right</u> at the point of its initiation.

Simply feel that.

Feel into that.

Each breath.

Just that.

Keep your attention on it.

Your feeling-attention in it.

You can do that directly.

You needn't regard any other thinking, emoting, sensations.

This can be always done directly.

II.

AVATAR ADI DA SAMRAJ: Basically, everything works from the inside out—unless you forget about it. And then you seem to be in a position to have to get back "in", to get deeper "within". How did you get "outside" to begin with, so that you have to get "inside" yourself, when you already <u>are</u> yourself?

You're as "self" as you can get about being yourself, and yet you talk about getting "deeper" within yourself! *[Adi Da laughs heartily.]* You can't <u>be</u> any deeper than the way you always already are.

In this world of exchanges, your life is primarily patterned on "outside" and "inside". Your "outside" mode includes how you dress and your appearance (and so forth), what you do bodily. And your "inside" mode includes your verbiage, your participation in perceptual and conceptual exchanges. You live in that patterning, identified with it, without having taken a thought about being it to begin with. It's just an inheritance. It's a pattern that's going on, which you have become associated with and identified with. But you haven't originated it. Your act is not one of <u>creating</u> it. It is the act of <u>identifying</u> with it. And then, having done so, you have recoiled, and found yourself in the predicament of being a limitation.

So when you put on the form of clothing and make-up and hairdo, whatever it is, before you came in here tonight, you were allowing a pattern to run its course. You didn't generate it truly, any more than you generate each inhalation and each exhalation—if you really feel into the origin of it, you can't find yourself doing it.

You keep declaring your appearance to be <u>you</u>. But it is pattern, and you're identified with it and confused about it—confused because of this very identification.

III.

*n the midst of the ongoing conversation, a gurgling sound is heard ema-
nating from someone's stomach. Adi Da uses this incident to create a
different kind of lesson about "inside" and "outside": The "inside" religious response is not enough in and of itself. Intentional changes in the
"outside" dimensions of the personality are essential if the Spiritual process
is to bear fruit. This is what Adi Da refers to as "handling life-business".*

AVATAR ADI DA SAMRAJ: Someone is experiencing a physical disturbance right now. In the last number of months I've been watching the
news quite regularly on TV, and I've noticed that TV stations are always
giving commercials about gas—bowel gas, stomach gas, heartburn, con-
stipation, stool softeners—with people looking at one another, giving
those "knowing glances" in the morning. They do an endless lot of business about people's digestive process.

Watching the news while having lunch or whatever, it's just one after
the other of these one-way-or-the-other digestive commercials—a huge
percentage of them, such that it becomes remarkable after a while. Well,
that's what the worldly life does to you.

Bad digestion is just an inside symptom of an outside problem. The
outside problem is this adaptation to a conventionally patterned life. If
that were not happening—that outer-pattern problem which you got from
your father line, the male line—then you wouldn't have this interior digestive problem. That is a signal to change your act from the inside out.

It is very important to see how you are disposed relative to the
whole domain of your inheritance—your outward communication (or
your appearance), versus the interior part (thinking, talking, and even
interior physical matters)—and how you tend to live in this patterning of
these two lines of habit, outside and inside, which you tend to suggest is
"you". But if you look to the source of its arising and simply notice the
source of each inhalation, exactly where it arises, or the source of anything at all in your perception, you can't find the "you" in it. It is not you.
It is this pattern patterning, just that. How you are established or disposed relative to that is profoundly important.

This interior of words is very much like the so-called "exterior" of
how you appear and manifest yourself physically (or outwardly) for the
perception of others. There is no difference between your outward
appearance, in that sense, and your speech. Your speech is another pattern

of "you", another "self-image", so to speak, another mode of it. But you find these patterns fascinating, profoundly attractive somehow—something about it is attractive. But there is something about it <u>not</u> attractive at all. That is the part that you don't like, and that is the part that you are always trying to keep from bumping into—which is a rather stressful matter, it seems, out here in post-civilization-land.

So these patterns of outward seeming and doing and inward thinking and speaking are being perpetuated by a process that just goes on and on—and what do <u>you</u> have to do with it? You are perfectly willing to identify with it because of some curious, mysterious association. But if you take a moment to "consider" the matter seriously, you are not ever in the position of actually being, or even being in charge of, any of the patterns in your experience—perceptual or conceptual, physical, emotional, mental, psychic, or whatever.

Yet you are always acting, thinking, communicating, as if you <u>are</u> that pattern. And you are still doing it. You tend to go with the flow of these patterns—the outside seeming world of action and appearances and so forth, and the inside world of thinking and emotional reacting and whatnot. Just going on and on and on.

It's not that you don't sympathize with the Great "Consideration" of Truth, and the purpose for Realizing It. It's not that you have no commitment to all of that. It's just that there is something about your involvement in the habits of patterning, outside and inside, that gives you the feeling that you want to escape any disciplining of the patterning, any changing of it. If that is the case, then you are just describing yourself <u>as</u> a pattern—just a pattern that changes.

What kind of "you" is that? There is no "you" that is that. You can't be that and be a "you". *[Adi Da laughs, along with everyone in the room.]* Isn't that obvious?

DEVOTEES: Yes.

AVATAR ADI DA SAMRAJ: Well?

You have to be more than "inside" serious about the Way of the Heart, just talking and thinking and feeling about it. You must be willing to change the "out-here" part, the habit on the outside, the whole pattern of actions and appearances and accommodations of the body and so forth, bringing that into the mode of self-transcending counter-egoic sadhana* for real. You gather the sadhana from a profound, most interior response, and change the exterior conditions therefore. That is what it means to handle your life-business as the foundation.

What I've been suggesting to you in this conversation is that your outward-seeming-and-acting life and your inward-talk-mind habit are just a pattern persisting, without any great discriminative "consideration" on your part, or devotional counter-egoic going-beyond about it significantly.

The pattern that's patterning is being you. You are volunteering to limitation.

However, I Call you to the most discriminative "consideration" altogether. That is an exercise, a heart-exercise, which allows the true in-depth disposition to open, to come to the front, to be functional.

The faculty of judgement, or discriminative intelligence, is interior to, or hierarchically higher than, your gross visceral (or bodily) processes, and lower perceptual processes, and ordinary observing mind, and so forth. It's at a more profound level, more central. Because it is hierarchically senior to these other things, the discriminative intelligence is not imbedded in them. It can examine things, make judgements (and so forth), and come to decisions. And then the way it makes a new pattern of life is by enlisting the next level of impulse-energy and directing it toward the body-mind, which is the will.

Of course, unfortunately, the will becomes directed toward the more outer patterns, grosser patterns, and as soon as that contact is made the will can be weakened by the association. Then the will—instead of really doing what the discriminative intelligence has judged to be right to do according to its reasoning or its "consideration" (whatever that is)—gets fed back all kinds of grosser influences, and the will and discriminative intelligence get all mixed up with this other, grosser patterning.

This feedback mix-up that occurs through weak intention now requires you to purify all of this patterning accumulation. It is a purification, rightening—ultimately, an energizing, "Brightening"* process, more and more going beyond.

These beginnings of sadhana—which I took very seriously, certainly, during My "Sadhana Years"*—are basic. In the Way of the Heart, everything has to start there with Me, with your acceptance of My Instruction, taking a vow, making agreements, and then doing it. It has to be as basic as that. That's where the rightness in our relationship, the trust in our relationship, comes to life. It is not merely a matter of feeling better in the social-personality sense. That is not sufficient in the Way of the Heart. It is not enough religion. It is not about God yet. It is just about you. To you, God is somebody or something that you keep "painting" according to your habit-mind and reactivity and so forth, whereas the <u>real</u> Realization experience is something you are always preventing.

Don't you see, therefore, how this "habit-you", the mind, isn't <u>you</u>? There is the presumption that it is, or you <u>are</u> it. The profundities of the sadhana of the Way are about going beyond such presumptions, getting down to the root of it, finding out about it, truly being involved in the process of ego-transcendence.

The Zone of Profundity

AVATAR ADI DA SAMRAJ: Samadhi[3] is, truly understood, a state that is prior to waking, dreaming, and sleeping.

In the waking state, you have the feeling that there is body-based consciousness.

And then, when you go into a dreaming state, you sort of leave body-consciousness and come into another kind of picturing of existence. But in the dream state you still feel you must be somehow interior to that, behind that. You feel an impulse to get even deeper yet.

Then there is sleep. It has fewer "accessories" (in the form of perceptual and conceptual phenomena), and ultimately no "accessories" whatsoever—no lights, no visions, no objects—and yet, it's not an unhappy state at all.

But Samadhi is <u>beyond</u> all those states. It is deeper than those, not merely something other than those. It is what is deeper and more profound than they are, not merely an alternative door to go into in the same place.

The body-mind must be <u>adapted</u> to this profundity. You must exercise the most discriminative "consideration". You must participate in the disposition of becoming serious and profound. And you must handle your life-business, putting it in order in the maximum sense, such that there is fundamental order, predictability, and yet, certainly, life in it. Handling your life-business is important, so that you are not just having to live participating in the pattern of anxiety and stress and low-mindedness and grossness, mere fleshiness. It is not a matter of dissociating from physical existence. It is a matter of <u>always</u> being established in the profundity of existence instead of just being locked into the pattern of grossness. It's a matter of always practicing the Yoga* of the Way of the Heart in every moment, whatever the circumstances.

All of that putting in order brings appropriate control into the zone of your daily life. And then there are also special occasions every day—meditational times in the morning and evening. These are not merely something you do, they are the zone of profundity embraced, in and of itself, for a day-by-day predictable amount of time and occasion.

---

3. The Sanskrit word "Samadhi" traditionally denotes various exalted states that appear in the context of esoteric meditation and Realization. Avatar Adi Da Teaches that, in the Way of the Heart, Samadhi is, even more simply and fundamentally, a state of ego-transcendence in Communion with Him. Adi Da's devotee is in Samadhi in any moment of standing beyond the separate self in devotional ecstasy.

The profundities of this Way are not in the jiggliness of the waking state. Yes, there is Yoga there. There is Dharma* there. There is practice there, too, yes. But observe the non-humans.[4] They move themselves, after handling life-business, as economically as possible. In other words, they take as little time and energy as possible, and they always spend their set-apart time in a place where they feel physically completely safe (perhaps that is around some others and perhaps not), and they just abandon all outwardness of attention and regard, all anxiety and so forth, and just allow themselves to enter into a profound depth. And it is not merely sleep.

Of course, non-humans sleep, and that can be observed as well. And you can at least notice when they appear to be showing signs of dreaming. You have perhaps seen dogs showing signs that they are having a bad dream, twitching and yelping sometimes. You can imagine that they might be dreaming then. It seems likely. And there is their obvious waking-state attention.

But there is another zone of depth that non-humans look to enter into. And they do this freely, voluntarily. They don't regard this to be dangerous or threatening—to enter into this pleasurable, deep swoon into the Source-Domain.

Every non-human knows that what they do socially is not the most important thing about existence. They know that it is not. So they exhibit a kind of (what you might call) "natural" predisposition to Contemplate, to feel beyond—even beyond waking, dreaming, and sleeping—to a depth-domain. The non-humans carry on the tradition of going beyond in a very simple, straightforward manner. They are working that out—and have been for a long time, so they are quite good at it. Their pattern of natural understanding is interrupted only when other forces intervene and interrupt the pattern altogether. So you see what non-humans become like in zoos that are not congenial to them and so on.

Of course, human beings are suffering from loss of habitat more and more as well. From a physical point of view, looking at the natural zone of earth, things are not very good because of all kinds of political and other disturbances. Mankind already has a long history of this kind of disorder, in moving more and more toward a secular disposition and toward a disposition without depth—chaotic, merely physical, or gross-minded.

Feeling to the depth, to the Source, is fundamental. This self-surrendering, self-forgetting Yoga of devotional Contemplation of Me is

4. In its widest sense, Avatar Adi Da's term "non-humans" includes everything that is not human (including plants, trees, animals, walls, rocks, and so on). However, Avatar Adi Da also uses the term to refer specifically to animals.

simple and straightforward. This is sacred means to maintain the zone of the sacred, the zone of Contemplation, the zone of association with the Source.

People are always saying it is important to make a living. Yes, it is a responsibility. But this zone of the sacred is the profound core of existence. Just as you make sure that you handle your ordinary life-business in the grossest sense, make sure that you never minimize this profundity—in the moment to moment sense, but also in the setting-apart-the-time-and-place sense, as a part of every day.

It is a process that is always becoming more profound. Yes, it has its evidence in daily life, but the profundity beyond attention to all of that—like the lizards when they go out on the limb—the depth level of it, is beyond all those kinds of concerns. It is a deepening and ever-deepening process.

The stages of life *[see appendix, pp. 392-98]* can be seen this way, as passage from the waking state (the earlier stages of life) into the dreaming state (the whole process of advanced fourth stage of life and fifth stage of life) and then, deeper than that, into the realm of sleeping (the sixth stage of life). It is always deepening—waking to dreaming to sleeping.

The entire Great Tradition[5] is about assuming different levels of presumption about that entire course. But the profundity is as I am saying to you. It is always deeper, always beyond. It is more and more profound, and yet it is not self-involvement. In the Way of the Heart, this devotional Yoga is your basic occupation, and you must serve the possibility of this becoming truly more and more profound. So you don't want to waste a lot of your life in trying to just bring some sort of order to (or, perhaps, make an illusion of paradise out of) the more mundane aspects of your existence. Yes, there is that to handle, but then there is getting on with the deepening process, which ultimately goes beyond waking, dreaming, and sleeping—goes beyond the first three to four stages of life, goes beyond the advanced fourth to fifth stages of life, goes beyond the sixth stage of life, ultimately.

So the seventh stage of life is fully the Domain that transcends the three states—waking, dreaming, and sleeping—Recognizes and Inherently Transcends all the conditional appearances. That is profound, and that can't even be described as "deepening", but it ultimately Outshines everything.

5. The "Great Tradition" is Avatar Adi Da's term for the total inheritance of human, cultural, religious, magical, mystical, Spiritual, Transcendental, and Divine paths, philosophies, and testimonies from all the eras and cultures of humanity, which has (in the present era of worldwide communication) become the common legacy of mankind.

The seventh stage Awakening is simply unobstructed God-Consciousness, or Divine Consciousness.

It is beyond all of the disposition of separateness or "difference".

It is a Depth, the Zone of Reality, in which the process is one of being given over into that more and more profoundly.

In the Ultimate Demonstration of It, there is no clinging to any aspects of the conditional form—the bodily manifestation, and so forth.

So it is an Infinite, Self-Magnifying Swoon that is not a collapse.

It is neither deep nor high.

It is beyond explanation.

It is beyond waking, dreaming, and sleeping.

It is beyond "turiya", or the fourth state.[6]

It has no conditional references whatsoever—for or against, with or absent from, conditional arising.

If you are serious, you must cultivate the demonstration of your seriousness. You must set aside the sacred domain, the sacred portion altogether, or you get profoundly out of balance, profoundly detached from True Reality. You just get shuffled about and made disorderly in all these arbitraries of gross pattern. It's like people who never sleep, never get enough rest—they are just busy in whatever their business may be. It is a characteristic habit of everyone.

You don't see much Contemplating going on. It is considered unusual to do such a thing. How absurd that the Contemplative and sacred dimension of life should be considered amusing and something to raise the brow about and wonder about. "Is it really something to be done?"— that kind of sentiment. But it is not built into the common world. Often in the past, and in all kinds of cultures over the world, there has been a culture that is "managed", so to speak, by hierarchies of one kind or another. So it is always there. All you have to do is be born there and you are part of this sacred culture. But that is not the way it is for you all. You did not appear in a sacred culture, you appeared in a secular culture where the sacred has been, you could say in some sense, eliminated. It becomes more and more profoundly reduced.

So you all can be very helpful to one another in getting life-business handled, and helping one another do that, sharing and cooperating in various ways, and, in all of that, create a circumstance in which you can exercise your sacred intention fully from day to day.

---

6. As a philosophical term in Hinduism, "turiya" means "the fourth state" (beyond waking, dreaming, and sleeping). Adi Da uses the term "turiya" specifically to indicate the Awakening to Consciousness Itself in the context of the sixth stage of life.

Otherwise, you lose your profundity, become more and more not only ego-bound, but ego-bound in the waking-state manner, just indiscriminate physicality, with concerns relative to a physically based life, and more and more stressfully that. You know, even in your daily experience, that there is a level deeper than waking—that is dreaming. And a level deeper than dreaming—that is sleeping. You know at least that much. And maybe now you have a taste of something deeper than that in your practice in relation to Me.

The non-humans like to do it such that they can minimize the time required to do survival things—like getting food and shelter and whatnot. They like to spend as little energy in that as possible, generally speaking. They conserve themselves relative to this, minimize it so that there is maximization of time set apart from that.

Of course, there are some non-humans—like bees, for instance—that don't seem to be doing that. They seem to be very much on the move. But there is another element added to this unique structure, which is about the structure of the hive and the patterns around it. It is a kind of ecstatic dance, a unique interior in which they have been fed with liquid, a nectarous substance, royal jelly, that gives them energy in the sense of ecstatic well-being.

You see, all that physical business is not to be handled in some so profoundly simplified manner that it is harsh. But don't just exhaust yourself in the development of the outward-directed life itself. Whatever your circumstance is on any particular day, this sacred space must always be located and used, otherwise the conditions of the ordinary world are not knowledgeable about anything very profound. They will take you on and you will just become part of it.

So if you neglect that zone, you allow yourself to be turned into the gross pattern only, without discrimination. The general cult from the world won't give you this time, even this inclination—will talk you out of it, in some sense, you could say. So you must not permit that to happen. The common world has become something like when animals or non-humans are taken out of their natural environments and put in confinements that are obviously not congenial to them. You know what happens to them. They demonstrate that nervous chaos in which there isn't that elegance of being set apart and utterly calmed—not merely calmed in the feeling of the physical, but calmed or entered into a depth beyond that. So that happens in zoos.

Well, the same thing happens in the secularized, citified world that you all are involved in. To turn to a depth, to Contemplate the Source-

Condition Which is Ultimately the Very Self-Condition, to Me, is perfectly obvious. But I realize it is not obvious to you all even—beyond a point, anyway. People in general do not seem to even have any association with profundity. They just sort of hope that everything is going to turn out okay. They try to keep buzzing along—really a mess!

As I was saying earlier, it is not the washing machine, it is what is coming out of the wall (which makes the washing machine do all that stuff) that is interesting. Well, nothing is sufficient as long as it is conditionally based. This is not just a philosophical proposition—"consider" your own experience. Whatever it is, your experience is never finally enough. You can repeat it. And, eventually, as you continue repeating it, it becomes a bother, a disturbance, a form of bondage.

No matter how interesting (in the phenomenal sense) the deepening process becomes, it is like all other experience. Even that process is not It. So there is the tacit knowledge that experience is not It.

Why should you, at any time, want to have the depth of your feeling-profundity lessened or set aside? Your impulse in My Company should be to magnify that profundity—the heart not conditioned by the klik-klak[7] variations all over, not patterned by the waking, dreaming, and sleeping domains. But you have to magnify that profundity intentionally, as a personal matter, and participate with others cooperatively to serve the sacred domain for everyone.

BRIAN O'MAHONY: Beloved, washing machines require six times as much energy to start up as they do in running.

AVATAR ADI DA SAMRAJ: Yes. And you don't want them to go off or shut down. You don't want that to happen to your washing machine! You are concerned about that, very concerned, and it's always there in the background, always ready to pop up a little bit of anxiety, or actual fear, a little uneasiness. There is always this mortality-stress.

Well, you can make positive conditions in life, but you can't make utopia out of it. Utopia is not enough in any case. No conditional arrangement is satisfactory. Whatever is achieved is a kind of moment in the hierarchy of achievement. There is the constant passing beyond. It doesn't mean that what you have been associated with earlier disappears, it just gets integrated with a process that is always more and more profound, and serves a profound life. People should serve the profound life in one another and not merely this outward-directed, social, TV-and-

---

7. "Klik-klak" is Avatar Adi Da's term for the mechanical nature of conditional existence—constant change and impermanence. This term is explained in more detail on p. 94.

business-world kind of pattern. There is just no balance and peace in that pattern, and not in the world in general.

In any case, the human body persists only within some range of a general reasonable expectation. Then what? Where is it at? What has it been for? What are you all about? The entire process should be associated with a progressive profundity. Even, perhaps, in due course, setting aside more and more time for sacred occupation, in the "set apart" sense—this corresponding with getting older, so that you are entering into a process of profundity altogether, rather than fighting against it. But also, it is not about yielding to negative possibilities. It is a balance.

You see how difficult it is for people to establish a balance in the world circumstance anywhere at the present time? People are mad, like caged zoo animals. That is just happening. There is no real political and economic will to do anything about most of it. And nobody knows how to get out of here alive. It is just dreadful. It is actually a cultureless world-scene at the present moment, the "late-time", or "dark" epoch.[8]

Therefore, the "Brightness" must break through it. But not merely in the believer's terms, in the social religiosity terms of religion and such, but in the ever-deepening terms of the sacred profundities of real practice.

There is no other "consideration" in life that is of greater significance. It is the Core of Existence, this dwelling in profundity. And if there were right culture altogether in the world, there would be integrity to this matter of the pattern of human life and so on. That is lacking in the world, but it is certainly Given to you in your relationship to Me. So that is how it must be kept activated in everyone, through a truly accountable culture that really honors and respects this fundamental core of the practice.

How can you have a culture that doesn't value the sacred, that only values this outward-directed, so called "materialistic" kind of grossness—that doesn't account, for real, for the sacred dimension of the Depth of Existence? And not just "When did the 'big bang' begin?", but to the Depth that is Prior even to material perception—the Depth of states, not merely the depth of appearances.

Right culture includes what is outside the gates and what is inside. There is the household domain, the domain of the community, and so forth, and all of its sacred places. And then there is what is outside, where you have some exchange with people who are doing whatever they are doing, for whatever their reasons—sometimes religious, sometimes not.

---

8. "The 'late-time', or 'dark' epoch" is a phrase that Avatar Adi Da uses to describe the present era, in which doubt of God and of anything beyond mortal existence is more and more pervading the entire world, and in which the separate and separative ego-"I", which is the root of all suffering and conflict, is regarded to be the ultimate principle of life.

So you do some things out there, but also every moment out there you are engaged in this sacred profundity at the heart-level. So, fundamentally, you must be obliged, or called, and expected—you, in all of your service to one another—to understand this balance of life.

Do you like the mortal aspect of this experience you are having?

DEVOTEES: No!

AVATAR ADI DA SAMRAJ: Well, then it is not enough. There is something about it that is not enough, obviously. It is not deep enough, not pro-found enough. You have dreamt better than this, thought better than this! There could be a lot better than this. In fact, you are not going to settle for anything less than better than this. But then that means you have to commit yourself to doing what you have to do to Realize what is better than sheer gross patterning. That is the Pleasure Dome of this accommo-dation of the sacred in your personal and collective life in day to day terms—not digressing from the fundamentals of it. It is always there, every day.

That is what it is to be serious, and this is how you enter into the consistent experiencing, Realizing, of That Which is Sufficient Inherently, That Which is Profound. If your only association with it is some sort of emotionalism based on some words you use to stimulate that emotional-ism, there is no depth to it. You have to live the Way in depth, through the practices that are depthful, more and more. There is always beyond. Just like the non-humans, you set aside time every day for this Contemplation, this entering into depth. In the Way I Give to you, I have accounted for all the aspects of it, all the Secrets of it, and the Great Means that I Am, for the sake of your Realization.

You'll not be satisfied on any day in the waking condition if you did not enter into the sphere of profundity, beyond superficiality and fear, and so forth, and touch the Depth more and more, the Prior Condition. To have lost that taste in being mis-occupied for a day is a great fault.

The depth in the set-aside time of the waking state shows itself spon-taneously in the dreaming state, shows itself in depth and profundity—perhaps there is a depth of restfulness in the sleep state and so on. All kinds of other things, too. There is no utopia anywhere in the conditional signs, but they become more and more in balance. The Pleasure Dome Law is to be comprehensive relative to all aspects of life, giving you max-imum time in that zone, inside the wall of the gathering where the sacred matter is honored by the practice of it, and the setting of it apart, making it be holy. Never let it be undermined. Never give it up.

The Pleasure Dome of Adi Da

While in Hawaii in early 1996, Avatar Adi Da Samraj began to speak of the Way of the Heart as a "Pleasure Dome", recalling the poem "Kubla Khan", by Samuel Taylor Coleridge, "In Xanadu did Kubla Khan/A stately pleasure-dome decree . . ." Adi Da Samraj discussed how many of the religious traditions of the world are based upon the principle of embracing suffering in order to win merit for future happiness and pleasure. The "Pleasure Dome" principle of Way of the Heart, He clarified, was about present Happiness, not seeking to attain Happiness in the future, not idealizing suffering and denying even ordinary pleasures of human life.

AVATAR ADI DA SAMRAJ: Order comes to those who live with Me, who attend to Me, serve Me, by virtue of just that. That practice itself conforms them to Me, and their life is rightened in the Pleasure Dome of the Love of Me. The more they enjoy this Happiness of Communion with Me, the more inclined they become to be rightened, to be purified, to embrace more discipline* and such.

The Way of the Heart is not about self-inflicted suffering. The seat of the Way of the Heart is the Pleasure Dome—in other words, Communion with Me. That being the case, what reason is there to embrace suffering? [April 8, 1996]

There are the balanced pleasures of life, as you are able. But there is also this fundamental profundity which is at the root of it, the "radical"* dimension of it. It makes that thing coming out of the wall to the washing machine interesting. There is this domain of perceived reality that is pervaded by, floating in, a sea of energy. It is energy. But in the self-contracted reaction, this awareness is lost, this participation is lost, this non-separation is lost. So that has to be re-introduced through the culture of right understanding, right practice, right community, and so on.

The relationship to Me is the Core of this sacred practice.

Avatar Adi Da Samraj and Daniel Bouwmeester,
The Mountain Of Attention, 1995

CHAPTER TWO

'Everything in the 'First Moment

BY DANIEL BOUWMEESTER

Avatar Adi Da's Instruction to everyone is not only in the form of His Word but also in the form of His Leela, or the stories of what He does in the world—with His devotees, with animals, with so-called "inanimate" objects, with events in nature, with places.

This book presents a variety of Leelas told by some of the devotees who were present with Adi Da Samraj in the gatherings of November-December 1996. The Leelas are from various periods of Beloved Adi Da's Teaching and Blessing Work, from 1972 to the present.

In 1977, the time of this Leela, Daniel Bouwmeester, a medical doctor from Australia, had recently become a devotee of Adi Da Samraj and was serving in the San Francisco bookstore run by the community of devotees. He was behind the counter in the bookstore one day when Adi Da's car pulled up outside.

The bookstore was on the second floor, up a steep flight of stairs. When Beloved Adi Da arrived that day, I just caught a glimpse of the top of His head as He was getting out of His car—and I knew that in a moment He would be coming up the stairs. I expected Him to go to some offices adjacent to the bookstore, but I thought I would still get to see Him for a very brief moment as He passed by. I was so excited that my heart was thumping, my muscles were jittery, and I could hardly breathe. My normal calm composure was totally gone.

I could almost feel Him walking up each stair. Then I could feel as He was about to walk into my line of view. And, sure enough, He did. He looked radiant, beautiful—I don't know how to explain the effect His simple appearance had on me. The sight of Him totally blew my mind. No one was with Him.

Adi Da started to walk across the landing towards the offices, and then suddenly He turned at an abrupt right-angle and walked into the bookstore. No one else was in there. It was just Him and me, and I had no idea what to do. He went straight to the far end of the bookstore, and began to do what He typically does with books—He pulled a book out from the shelf and held it gently like a loved one. Then He would open it, but not too far so as not to bend the spine. There was an intense grace in His gestures that you see in everything He does.

After looking at a book, He would close it and hold it for a moment and then put it back on the shelf. He made sure all the books were lined up straight. And in this way He slowly made His way along the shelves, book by book. Having started at the back of the store, He was moving in my direction. Meanwhile, I was sitting there behind the desk looking at Him. Now and again He would look up towards me and tilt back His head a little, and then He would turn away and look at the book again. I stood there bug-eyed, and spontaneously started to do the same thing, tilting my head back at Him!

I was in charge of the telephone for the bookstore and the offices and it was ringing all the time. It was a touch-tone phone with a hold button that you could use to direct calls. But, coming recently from Australia, I had never seen these phones before and didn't know how they worked. So I kept picking up the phone and then didn't know what to do to redirect the call. Not only that, I kept being asked to transfer the calls to people with very strange names. The voice at the other end would say, "Is Peter Helicopter there?" Or, "Is Mr. Natural there?" And I would say "<u>Who</u>?" These were names that Adi Da had playfully given to particular devotees, but I had no idea to whom they referred.

Now and again somebody would come in and speak briefly to Adi Da, and He would sometimes burst into peals of laughter. Then whoever had come in would leave again, and I would be on my own once more watching Adi Da working His way along the shelves—towards me.

Next to the huge sales counter there was a place where you could sit down and read the books and magazines that were laid out on a table. Beloved Adi Da had now reached the table. There was nothing between us now except the sales counter and the magazine table. I was still trying to maintain my composure.

Now another devotee had come in and was talking to Adi Da on the other side of the table. He seemed to be having an intimate conversation with Adi Da, joking, but very respectful at the same time. Then there was another telephone call asking for someone I didn't know, so I decided to go and ask this devotee what I should do about the call. I wasn't actually very concerned about the call—I just wanted to get right up close to Adi Da.

So I stepped out from behind the fortress-like counter and went right up to this devotee and whispered my message to him. He said, "Hang up," and just as I was turning around to do that, an overpowering impulse rose in me to take a full look at Adi Da. He was apparently immersed in the magazines, so I thought I could sneak a look without Him noticing me. Exactly at the moment I turned to look at Him, Adi Da looked up. He looked straight into my eyes and then above my head.

In that instant, everything dissolved. It was like falling in infinite space. I felt a multitude of things at once: I felt I was rising up, I was infinitely happy, I felt like I was crying. I totally lost all sense of where I was or who I was. I was nowhere, blown completely away.

The next thing I knew I was somehow forcing myself to turn away from Him. I wanted to hurry back to the desk and put the phone down. While all of this was happening, Adi Da and the devotee He had been speaking to walked out of the bookstore and went into the next room. I heard Adi Da's laughter now and again, those peals of laughter, and I just stood behind the desk, holding onto it to support myself.

Although now aware of my environment, I was still, basically, totally immersed in this feeling of blissfulness. It felt as if everything that I ever was, or had been, was reeling before me. My knees were wobbly. My whole nervous system had just been super-charged, as if a couple of thousand volts had been run through me. After a time, my body began to calm down and I could hear Adi Da's laughter again. A short time later, I saw Him walk out of the offices and down the stairs.

Months later, when I told Adi Da about what happened, He said, "I give you everything in the first moment, and then your responsibility is to come up to it."

The Mountain Of Attention, 1996

CHAPTER THREE

November 30, 1996

The Meaning Notion

The next night the same group of devotees is called to gather with Adi Da Samraj again. Avatar Adi Da establishes the principal topic of the gathering with two intriguing questions.

AVATAR ADI DA SAMRAJ: Why are there organisms?

And who makes these kinds of decisions anyway?

You are all over the place with mind, so you think that it is reasonable to expect that you are going to make some great discoveries in the mind—that you are going to imagine, expand, and do all kinds of things. But the whole time the mind is somehow screwed down to an organism that, when you strip it down, doesn't do anything fancy. It doesn't look a whole lot different than an adult chimpanzee! *[laughter]* Do you know what I mean?

Your mind-entertainments are no different from that poor little animal you're walking around as. *[laughter]*

You've sort of glamorized yourselves by association with the mind. But, actually, you're pretty homely little pumpkins here—clever apes with some mind-thing that you can do. You do it in all kinds of ways. The Internet is one of the latest ways in which human beings have made much of themselves with mind. It's just like a bunch of chimps entertaining themselves. None of it is necessarily true.

If you literally took a nation of chimpanzees—a large area where it is all chimp-land, where they live very happily and freely and get to do their thing entirely, and it was so rich a place for them to live in that they could satisfy their requirements with little expenditure of effort, such that now they have a lot of time to "consider" the most Contemplative course—would you, even for a moment, expect that anything that those chimpanzees did for the next few thousand years would contain the Truth?

Why do you think that it is necessary, then, that human beings, in their doings, are having anything to do with the Truth?—or even Reality, which is the same thing. It could all be bullshit. Every time there is a development, dimensionally, with a different standpoint relative to anything at all, what was said or viewed from the previous standpoint, having been transcended, is no longer anything but child's play, it seems.

There is no instruction book in here that says that if you really apply yourself, intelligently and so forth, everything you think will be true. In other words, you wouldn't expect chimpanzees to come up with a culture of Truth, and everything True and Real, and grasping the Laws of everything. You wouldn't imagine there being much of anything of the kind produced by chimpanzees even after 50,000 years. Why should you assume that human beings, in their whatevers altogether, are generating Truth? Maybe it is just klik-klak manufacturing more variations on conventions of mind, and then they become matters of agreement, more or less—and it's just variation on sameness.

BEN FUGITT: Beloved, as we're sitting here, I feel You communicating the Heart-space to us, and how it is the unity of the body-mind as it is submitted to that Heart-space.

There is a brief pause, and then devotees chuckle in mutual acknowledgement that they have no idea what Ben meant.

BEN: It sounded good.

AVATAR ADI DA SAMRAJ: You said some words. You used a technique—a kind of Internet technique, actually. (Internet has all kinds of forms. It's a very traditional thing, actually.) In other words, you transmitted a replica of something that has emotional, mental, or some kind of content, to others who know some kind of a language. You can pass it on without us having to even look at one another. Pretty high-tech. And everybody could rattle all those bits, with whatever variations, based on slightly different hearing of whatever, through the pattern, or the mass of patterns, and then come up with who-knows-what-*you*-mean to be what <u>they</u> mean. That is how they will use this replication. You can add any content to it—just like if you read a play by Shakespeare, for instance, that's not on the stage yet, that is just the words. How you put it on the stage is your business.

So, everybody could wind up with different meanings from that script, or those words that you just passed on. It would mean whatever. Who knows what it means to them? Some conventions thrown in that everybody is supposed to presume those words mean. Whatever that is. If you asked them, they probably wouldn't be able to give you a very satisfactory definition of most things they say.

But, when you said that, you basically expected everybody here was going to understand what you were saying.

BEN: Right.

AVATAR ADI DA SAMRAJ: Is that because you know that there are some sort of conventions that are mutually agreed upon? Or do you really think that they will know what you mean? To know what you mean, there would have to be something about how you use that language that would lift it out of all of the automaticities of their meaning boxes. So they would really get what you mean by not just the words, but by other means that you are using to convey your meaning at the moment.

That is why you can't get it all on the Internet. There are all kinds of things to convey meaning beyond just the words replicated. There are all kinds of tones of voice—there are endless things. Plus there are many things that people are not aware of—the energy level, for instance. You can't get that on the Internet, entirely. There is just so much that you can do with just words.

So you have to find some way to communicate whatever you mean, if it is your meaning you are trying to get them to understand. If it is just that you are trying to get them to associate themselves with a bunch of conventions, then you don't have to stress any part of it. You just let them have whatever happens with it.

But you sort of expected, right away, that everyone would know what you mean?

BEN: A mutual experience.

AVATAR ADI DA SAMRAJ: But what do you mean when you mean to yourself that you know what you mean?

When you mean to yourself the meaning notion, then you expect that everybody here immediately understands what you are talking about. That is not true at all. It is a balmy expectation. It is just a skit. And the more removed people get from direct communication, perhaps the more likely it is that they are not going to get it very straight unless you find all kinds of ways to convey your meaning through all kinds of means that make it more and more clear or obvious somehow.

You all know one another, and are examples of familiars to one another. You are familiar with many people in this room quite well, probably. Do you know a <u>single</u> person here who, if you spoke to them for a while, made a transcript, and then printed it out and showed it to them, could give you a definition for every word in what they said that was fully satisfactory and a grammatically correct, meaning considered, fully technical, right understanding of all of the meaning levels, and so forth? All that? Who would you trust, of anyone you know?—just generally speaking. In other words, you don't expect <u>anybody</u> to be like that.

Yet you presume that everybody knows what you mean when you speak. That is why you are speaking, right? Unless you are someplace where they don't speak the language or languages that you speak. Here you feel very comfortable, because everybody understands English. That is the language that we are speaking at the moment. So you luxuriate in this familiarity presumption that everybody knows what you mean. And what do you mean by that? They know what <u>you</u> mean? They know what the dictionary says that the words mean? And what does that mean, anyway?

What is meaning? Somewhere between you and your words there is meaning—to which you are trying to fit words, presumably. But <u>where</u> is this meaning dimension? Where do you "mean" before you think it? Or before you speak it? And what are the meanings? Are the meanings feelings? Are they images, at the root of it?

NINA DAVIS: Feelings.

AVATAR ADI DA SAMRAJ: Your whole domain of "knowing" is, at its root, just feelings? Variations on feeling? How could it be so full of information?

Apparently it is all conventions. In other words, it's not just plain old hanging up in the sky and you read it and that is it. So, it is all a play on something that doesn't necessarily have any arriving at real Reality, information, Truth, and so forth. That is not guaranteed. All that's required is that the conventions be suitable for the individuals or collectives, for them to fulfill the purposes that they have with one another. So, as long as it works, that is meaningful enough. But, what does it have to do with Reality? It is just exchanges of conventions of mind, exchanges of insides.

Are you there as some mass of meaning, and you just put it into words, and you really expected what you <u>meant</u> to be received by everybody here?

ANIELLO PANICO: He did, he absolutely did. He believed that.

AVATAR ADI DA SAMRAJ: What is the basis for this belief? It is an absurd presumption. It is definitely not true.

There are conjunctions, but that doesn't mean that they are at the level of what people really mean about anything. And how much of anything do you get across? Most of what you are trying to do with words is just handle some very ordinary exchanges and whatnot. It is a convenience, like a bit of software in your computer. It doesn't have to have any ultimate Truth in it—it just has to work for survival purposes and necessary exchanges.

Just how far are you willing to go? Is it sufficient for you to just be a kind of bio-robotic organism/entity in among a bunch of similars somehow, and that's that? That is okay with you? You're willing to have it just be that way?

When you go to a zoo, for instance, you see all kinds of non-humans there. Some of them look very much like humans—like chimpanzees or gorillas, for instance. When you see such non-humans, you don't presume that they are anything more than what they look like. Gorillas are just being "gorilla". Dogs are just being "dog". Birds are just being "bird". That is what the thing is, and that's that. That is what you think non-humans are doing. "But humans are more than that." *[laughter]* They are supposed to be presuming that they are all kinds of great whatever. What about that?

BRIAN O'MAHONY: Do animals actually feel the same as we do?

AVATAR ADI DA SAMRAJ: Well, do you think, in other words, that they are simply presuming that they are organisms? That is what you presume about them. Is that what you presume about yourselves? Are you content with just that, that you're just organisms?

You know how organisms are. They chug along, who knows what. In and out. Difficult. Yes, good. No, not so good. Dead. You know? And that is the end of that!

Hm? Zap! *[Beloved Adi Da snaps His fingers.]* That's that? You're content that that is what life is?—so that's what you're going to do as long as it lasts? Is that good enough?

DEVOTEES: No.

AVATAR ADI DA SAMRAJ: Are you sure?

DEVOTEES: Yes.

AVATAR ADI DA SAMRAJ: Because that is how people seem. In My experience, this seems to be what people are doing. If you just look at all that people are up to, with clarity, just seeing what it is, there would be no reason to presume about them that they are presuming to be anything but organisms. In other words, they don't seem any different than the gorillas in the zoo. The gorillas are gorilla-ing, zebras are zebra-ing, and humans are human-ing, and that's that. But they all have all these funny looking asses. All organisms have funny little asses. *[laughter]*

I saw a funny button recently, which said, "The human body was designed by a civil engineer. Who else would run a toxic waste pipeline right through a recreational area?" *[laughter]*

Human beings are doing all kinds of diddly-dat. They've got this inventiveness about making extensions of themselves—words, all kinds of stuff. That is just what they do. To a complete outsider who doesn't know their language, their doings, and so forth, it just sounds like noise. So, it's no different than what you hear among the monkeys, or in jungles of vast cultures of different species.

So you don't presume that the non-humans are being anything different than what they look like. You presume that that is just what they are being. You entirely presume that, and that's that. But why should it be presumed that human beings are being anything other than what they apparently are, what they look like, just that organism? And then, "Oh, that's the end of that one, it's dead." And that's the end of that.

What was it when it was alive that you could get so personal with it, and then it's dead and dust? What were you talking to earlier? Why did you even bother talking to it?

No matter how big you think, when it comes down to it, you still have these funny looking asses! So, what is it all about? What is it for? What's it for? And who decides these kinds of things anyway—you know what I mean? *[laughter]*

Well, just how profound are you? I mean, are you really content to be just these short-span organisms, or are you up to something profound? Because if you are not up to something profound, then it is enough for you to just be an organism. That is what you're saying. Every moment in which you are not exercising yourself most profoundly—and I mean this in the real religious and Spiritual sense—you are just consenting to be the plastic process, the mummery of klik-klak of passing organisms.

How profound are you willing to be about it? How willing are you to be impressed by the profundity of existence? Or how content are you to just be part of a plastic human mummery?

What's meaningful about what is going on with anybody? Did Ben convey any meaning of his own, or just spin through some bytes? They all fit into little pieces of your little pattern there. Some correspondences, some not. Somehow, within their own complexity, they relate, so at the point that that fits into their whatever it is, the rest of it is just garbage. It doesn't even show up in e-mail. It's just not received, and you are fooling yourself, in other words.

Look at all of the presumption that communication is going on in the Internet. Who is talking to anybody there? It's just klik-klak. It's just stuff. It's just bits. What is profound about any of it? It's just stuff. Yes, it is part of a physical existence. You have to assume responsibilities there, fine. I am not saying that that is not so. I am saying that it is just not <u>enough</u> to devote your entire existence to it.

In other words, you must be occupied with what is profound. Handle business, fine. Right. But be occupied with what is profound, always. Never abandon it. Otherwise, you are just consenting to be some temporary bit of plastic. Push it in the slot every day, and it usually lights up. Sometimes a little dimmer, sometimes a little brighter, sometimes a little dimmer. But then one day you put it in and it rejects. Something comes up on the screen that says it is no longer applicable, "This card has been cancelled," or something. "This account is empty." And that's that.

What was so meaningful about any of it, if that's that? Where in all of this are you a "you", in any case? Where in all of this are you participating in something profound? Or is it just the local chatter, the organisms hanging out in the woods, the jungle of mind, not really significant or meaningful beyond just the chatter of ordinary survival and interferences with it, at least with the pleasure of it. It is not all that pleasurable anyway. There are some pleasures, but, no matter what you do, it wears you out somehow, you know what I mean? *[Beloved snaps His fingers and laughs.]*

It doesn't get stronger and stronger. It has a kind of built-in obsolescence. It doesn't look like nature cares about whether you live or die, otherwise you'd be living a lot longer, or bigger, or happier—none of this grimness-about-mortality stuff.

The day that you first stepped up there to put your ticket in, you should have noticed the situation and asked a few questions. If you can just be here, and playfully do or seem to be anything, within a certain range of limitations, and then, after a certain length of time, *[Beloved snaps His fingers again]* that's the end of it, then what kind of an interesting thing is that? That doesn't sound good.

So, it isn't any good. It is not sufficient in and of itself. And if it's not, then it's just an aspect of pattern with which you are mysteriously associated and you have to handle business relative to it, in some basic sense.

But you can't be so preoccupied with that level of it that you give up your heart, give up your existence, give up the Truth.

Just because you are alive doesn't mean that you are profound, or that life is profound. And just because you are alive doesn't mean that you are doing what is right, or right and free, or rightly disposed, or up to anything of significance at all—other than just rattling through, being part of a squeeze, the digestive system of the universe. You start up on the table and you wind up in the sewer. Well?

I am Drawing you into this profundity, whereas you all seem to be up to the forgetting of it. You are already full of the signs of having completely forgotten it—certainly from the looks of mankind as a whole.

I don't have much experience of people who are moved to anything but the ordinary organism business as mankind does it. In other words, people are, in general, not up to anything very profound. You seem readily to consent to not be profound, to have life not be profound. There is so much obligation, business, practicalities—with the body, whatever relations, making a living, on and on. You always have some excuse, some reason why you can only be this organism process, with all the costumes and words that people make or use.

The language is talking to itself through exchanges between many, many terminals. Nobody is originating it. Someone maybe modifies it a little bit, but then there are many other modifiers, more conventions develop, and then they get repeated—the latest changes, variations come again. You see how it works?

Well, human beings function like bio-computers, with all of this software of meanings and so on. But where are the meanings? The meanings aren't transmitted. It is the klik-klak. How does what I say, just like I am doing right now, become words for you? In your mind? Where? <u>Your</u> mind? What's "yours" about it?

Do you really convey meanings, generally speaking, with your communications, your words? Or is it just meaning process happening, more or less, by itself, and enforcing conventions? Thousands of little details every day are handled without even a thought, as people say. There are all kinds of babble and gestures and whatnot that are there just for collective survival purposes and so forth—that are supposed to be done without a thought. You handle countless details every day that way. It is a process. What is "you" about it? It is vastly complex. Where is the "you" in it? It is a system of complexities of all kinds.

It is not so much that an individual is expressing meanings. The "individual" is just a terminal of a process of exchanging meanings. But meaning in what sense? Where is the meaning part? The words just get moved along and everybody got clicked in association with it. It means whatever you want it to mean. Whatever you feel the force of convention suggests it means. But where is the meaning part? How does meaning get conveyed?

You presume others know what you mean. That's why you don't have to convey the meaning to them. Or perhaps this is where you make your mistake—because it is the meaning that you are not bothering to convey to them. You are giving them the replica and expecting them to get the meaning that you mean. And it doesn't really altogether amount to what gets across anyway. But it is all this "blah-blah-blah" going on between the organisms here, with lots of others all over the place. What is it for?

I mean these organisms are just here, so at some level, yes, you do some basic things for survival. But there's a lot more going on. What is all of this complex look and manner and doings and thoughts? What is all this for? It is not just pattern patterning more. It is building on past patterns and getting more complex, varying it, certainly. Yet it seems there are some persistent basics in there. Are they really conveyed or are they just in tiny little waves along the way, eventually changed in their meaning because the discourse changes and interprets things differently and so forth?

There is no fixity in any of it. It is the language speaking to itself. Everything is passed about that way. You are just an organism, a terminal in this exchange of nonsense, basically. You say, "We're organisms now, we'll make the best of it"?

And yet, in truth, nobody wants to be superficial. Everybody wants to be deep.

Understand this.

It doesn't feel good to be superficial. The chameleons don't like it. In other words, they don't get this message that you all are apparently getting. They know inherently, it seems, that there is a depth that is the Well of Being, and just to be this fleshy organism guy out here in the elements is not enough. It is not good. It can't be accepted just as that, just "that's that". The depth isn't forgotten. There's a depth deeper than sleep. There's the depth that is beyond self.

My address to you at the beginning of the process in My Company is to you as a seeker. This is the key to understanding—this matter of you being a seeker, not one who has found, merely. Even if you have come to Me as My devotee, that doesn't mean that you have already thereby vanished all of your seeking signs. The root of your un-Enlightenment hasn't vanished. It is a process you have entered into. It is not about mere belief. It is about the exercise of profundity, always going beyond.

What is really interesting to talk about with people is what goes on in meditation, because that is on the other side of all the clothing, all the social personality stuff. If you've got some reason to talk about that stuff, to handle business or whatever, or just be amusing with one another, fine, you can talk about it. But basically, that is not what's interesting. That's the washing machine, all that life-business. What is interesting is this in-depth process. That's the interesting thing to do in the most profound sense. It is the going-beyond process there, not merely the experiential process. The experiential process, the signs in it, yes, that may be interesting. But the signs of depth, the signs in the depth, the signs for the depth—this is what is truly interesting. That is the essence of all that is interesting.

You are defined by your search. You are always getting a destiny that is something about that, positive or negative. To transcend the seeker, to be in every moment transcending self-contraction directly, is a kind of a generator of a transformed existence, because it is not patterned by the seeker any longer, or the purification of the seeker has become an in-depth process—deeper than sleep. The pattern of the seeker is no longer necessary, so all kinds of changes occur quite readily when you are living the disposition of directly transcending the seeker at the heart point, at the origin of that whole seeker's pattern, moment to moment. This allows you to grant even greater integrity to your life, and greater depth.

The only thing that's really interesting is getting deeper than your mind presently is. That's why old habits are all boring. It's what's already boring you. It's the reason you _are_ bored. That's what makes you want to seek—the tension of dissatisfaction with what you're already associated with.

The first thing the non-humans do in their Contemplation is get deeper than body-consciousness. They don't think it's un-cool. They're not merely comfortable with physically existing. They demonstrate spontaneously that it is _right_ disposition to notice that confinement to mortal, physical embodiment is _inherently_ unsatisfactory, uncomfortable—inherently. So they're not going to buy anything about only being in that condition and nothing else. They know that merely to be _that_ is unsatisfactory, so they spontaneously drop into depth. Their sign is naturally the one of depth being the Core of existence, not the superficiality.

Everything has to come from the center outward, from the depth outward. So you have to devote your life to this depth, to this process in depth, to want to _be_ in that depth—that is, to be in the Zone of Happiness.

"Organism" Is Not Good Enough

AVATAR ADI DA SAMRAJ: Your entire life has been a case of temporary insanity.

This is why there is the Great Tradition of the Guru-devotee relationship. You go to one who has knowledge, who has passed through the process and so forth, who is a transmitter of whatever kind or degree. The purpose is to accept the Mastery of that one. You have exhausted your wits about it and found that you are still an asshole. That is not enough. You're at the end of all that and know you need a Master. So you go to your Master. This is why it is a relationship of surrender on the part of the devotee to the Master, becoming, in some very profound sense, the servant of the Master. And this is the link whereby you maintain the profundity of your existence. This is how you keep sane.

When you lose the profundity of existence, that is when you are no longer sane. Because you don't know what anything is all about, at all, and you are just sort of going through the motions of the human appearance, like TV. You don't even take the time to enter into the domain of profundity, in any moment. You don't live in it.

By entering into this relationship to Me, your profundity is to be guaranteed from that moment. You are no longer just part of a mechanical robotic passing of stuff. In every moment, you are established in the profundity of existence, through your practice of this devotional Yoga, this Way altogether. If it is not so, then you just become more and more entwined with the plastic of changes of klik-klakking-along organisms.

The principal propagandists these days are trying to tell everybody, "You are just an organism." The dominant culture is that of scientific materialism. This is its direct message. This is the informing voice, culturally presumed. Scientific materialism, however, is not merely scientific method, free discriminative enquiry. It is something that looks like that, associated with a philosophy, which is materialism. So its description of you is that you are an organism and that's that. It contradicts any kind of religious message that is anything more than social religiosity.

So there go all those vast thousands of years of culture, of in-depth "consideration"! Now all you've got is organisms. Nothing is necessary any longer. You don't need any culture. Bring it out on holidays. You are supposed to wear the costume of your previous culture. And you may do a dance from your previous culture, and a song, if you please, on that curious little instrument. That is about as much culture as you are allowed.

It is not about culture any more. It's about organism society, anti-civilization. Everything got focused on Man, and Man was thought to be full of meaning, soul, and Godward and so forth. And then it turns out that Man was empty of that, or was willing to be empty of that, so now it is just "Man is an organism." So the entire culture is putting its attention in the direction of glorifying organisms.

Previous to that, the focus for "consideration" was the Divine, all of the sacred world. Man as organism is minimally interesting. It is like science that only looks at rocks and wants to tell you how fast they go and all that: "That is the universe—what shape they are, what color they are, and that means such and such a gas is in them," and so on. That has minimal interest, but not sufficient for an entire life to be designed by that, thinking about that, and addressing that. What is so interesting about it? It is minimally interesting. It is not totally uninteresting but it is not enough.

Are you content to believe the message of scientific materialism and low-mindedness altogether, gross-mindedness also? That's enough for you? That's enough to just be that? How could this possibly be sufficient? If that is all that life can be—doing what everybody is doing—then you've got to do something else. You certainly have to do something profound. That profundity should change what you do, or something about your disposition in the midst of whatever you have to do in your human ordinariness or play and responsibilities and so on.

If it is not enough for you to just be an organism, and when you're dead, you're dead, then that is a serious matter. Because exactly what alternative do you have to that? All the bright-eyed propagandizing (so called "bright-eyed" propagandizing) of the times is trying to sell you on this.

Yes, behind it is scientific materialism, that whole point of view that is declaring that that's what you are, trying to break it to you softly, giving it to you in the small print or subliminally flashing it at you. They are trying to tell everybody that "You are just organisms." Scientific materialism is one with—not merely in league with, but one with—the current characteristic disposition of world societies.

The religiosity that gets thrown in there is sort of a civic obligation. You are not supposed to be really religious about it, such that you start seeing things, or anything like that. They don't want anybody meditating a lot in the White House! *[Beloved Adi Da laughs with everyone.]*

So they don't want you to get too religious about being religious. They want it to be just a way of guaranteeing your acceptance of certain social moral principles. That is about as religious as you are supposed to get about it. Also a bit hopeful that everything is going to be getting better and better and better. That is the propaganda. Everything will get better and better and better, as long as the better-and-better-and-better ones get into better-and-better-and-better land. At any rate, all of that is just the outer-organism business of this imaginative tool-making, extension-making organism, that calls itself . . . whatever you call yourselves.

But you look like pumpkins to Me! You are all kind of odd shapes and so on. There is nothing sort of uniform, perfectly put together, and all that sort of stuff. It is all kind of shape-through-flows with all kinds of distortions and whatnot. And you keep saying, "you, you, you." But all kinds of the "you's" I have known all died. They were trying to tell Me that they were "I-whatever". They were telling Me. I was taking them seriously, and all of a sudden they're dust. I suspected this all along, however, and was working on this right away.

So one should not give up the profundity dimension of life. Even the chameleons refuse to do that—they all have their Contemplative arrangements. But human beings seem ready to buy a bill of goods, and they are selling their profundity rights to get this material utopia that is getting flashed at everybody, this virtual electronic utopia, or whatever the next propagandized form of it will be described to be. But this paradisiacal klik-klak-land—it is already too strange. It has no integrity, in other words. Part of the necessary integrity is not mere balance, but association with profundity, and becoming more and more profound.

Because if you don't find what is greater than your poor little ass, then that's the end of it. [laughter] In other words, it's not enough for you to be just an organism and just have that be totally defining and you don't "consider" anything further. You have to find what is not merely an organism, whatever that takes. And having found it, then you have to take it seriously. That is the profundity in your life, and you have to cultivate it, persist in it, not allow any of the other business of life to destroy that—rather, require life to be associated with this.

This is how you give integrity to your life, by bringing this profundity practice, which is supposed to be the core of your life, into the play of all of your life, all of its details. Now, wherever you are handling ordinary life-business, fine, but that doesn't mean you don't do sadhana. To not do sadhana means you decide just to be an organism and you relinquish the process of profundity—you have consented to just be an organism.

The current world promises organism delights, a virtual reality electronic paradise. This is the result of the present moment. It is the result of the imaginings, developmental notions, and so forth, of people a hundred, two hundred years ago. That is not paradise, but some features of what people were looking forward to did actually get developed. There are changes, but the fundamental thing doesn't change. It is klik-klak. It is just variations, a play around certain things that are persistent. The human dilemma is the same. The human-being capability to be very much exercised in discriminative intelligence can't be content with confinement to organism.

Why not find what is greater? Having found it, then that is what makes your life sadhana. It is keeping that fire, tending that fire moment to moment, always. Whatever you are doing in any moment in the context of daily life, enter into that profundity, that heart-profundity, that fundamental profundity, that profound exercise, that profound counter-egoic Yoga. And then always setting aside this time and entering into this pattern outside the world, the Pleasure Dome of the sacred culture, the sacred life, the sacred community, and so on.

Always tend this fire of the relationship to Me, this devotional Yoga, what your relationship to Me is all about—which, as I have said, is as if you are naked. None of the social-personality thing really has anything to do with it. With most devotees, as I've said, I won't come into any kind of social conjunction, really. And that is fine. It is not part of the sadhana. It is not required that you have any kind of social contact with Me whatsoever. With some it's required as a matter of function, but generally speaking, it's not required.

It is not a social relationship. It is a profound relationship, a Divine relationship, a profound process. So your relationship to Me transcends all of the whatever pattern of doings in the human scale you're up to. It informs all of that, makes you serious in the context of all of that. But it's a process, this relationship to Me, and this is what you must be engaged in moment to moment. It is how profundity is brought into your moment to moment existence, and, therefore, it never becomes mere organism, klik-klak, imaginings, conventions, no-great-importance-beyond-organism survival.

It is not enough for it to be organisms, do you think?

DEVOTEES: No.

AVATAR ADI DA SAMRAJ: If that is all it is, that's not satisfactory. On the other hand, it is not satisfactory to not know what it is. So have you found in yourself, then, inherently a disposition to want to find out about all of that? Have you found out there is some impulse beyond just the ordinary human-organism life, which you can't deny, and which is greater than that, and that's why you're around Me?

DEVOTEES: Yes, absolutely, Beloved.

AVATAR ADI DA SAMRAJ: Well, then that's what your relationship to Me is about, and not about anything else. That is what the process is about.

How much of your body do you get to know? How much of your liver have you seen? It is no more familiar to you than your liver is familiar to anybody else. Nobody is familiar with your liver. Who is familiar with your liver? How did it get to be there to begin with? Well, whatever way it got to be there to begin with, you didn't have anything to do with it. Something else is making your liver. You don't even have anything directly to do with it right now. But you point to the body and say that it is you, yet you do not know anything about your liver. You are not doing your liver, then. You didn't make your liver. Why do you say it is you, then? What kind of experience do you have of your liver, or anything else about your body, that's "you" about it? Hm?

It's not true. It's a convention. In other words, you engage in all kinds of presumptions, but they are not because you have experienced it and proven it to be so. It is just a convention. And then, if you look at your speech, it seems to be suggesting all kind of things, but actually, you are not what your language makes you out to be. You haven't "considered" these matters profoundly, and you are willing to go with the flow.

Unless there is true profundity, you don't like the way it is. You don't like just being an organism. You can't really feel good about it if it isn't associated with a great profundity. Well, then you can't allow yourself to be content with not finding this thing, this profundity. You just can't allow yourself to be content if you are serious and not just going with the flow. You've got to press to find it, be moved however you are moved.

It's not hip to give up profundity, to become bland and ordinary. So if you insist that it be profound, then you have to devote your life to finding it. Handle your business, fine, but you have got to devote your life to the profundity. And you never stop it.

If you've truly found Me, then you have discovered profundity and not merely a social relation. Your relationship to Me is of a unique kind, and must be served uniquely. In other words, you have to live your relationship to Me profoundly, and that is a matter of moment to moment practice, Ruchira Buddha Bhakti Yoga* moment to moment, integrated with all of your living of this Way in the context of all your daily life matters. And then you must set aside time every day, sacredly, to enter into this profundity of the process of the relationship to Me, completely without any other distractions, any other obligations. That's the time of meditation and puja* and chanting,* and so forth—actions that, from a practical point of view, are nonsense. They have nothing to accomplish except in the general effect doing things like that has on your disposition otherwise. But they are not <u>about</u> anything—social-personality improvements, or life-improvements. They are about profundity, entering into the most profound "consideration" and dimension of existence, doing this daily and moment to moment.

This is what gives integrity to your life, and sanity—to be associated with true profundity while alive, always beyond and beyond, always in that depth, that heart-depth, as a moment to moment exercise.

The profundity is not merely a matter of some beliefs or things in mind and so forth, it is the depth of moving beyond all of that, the direct exercise of Ruchira Buddha Bhakti Yoga moment to moment and of all the forms of the "conscious process" and "conductivity" in your particular developmental mode of this Way.

The Humorous Discipline
of an Ordinary Pleasurable Life

The practical life-disciplines in the Way of the Heart are a concrete means of expressing the surrender of the devotee's body-mind to Avatar Adi Da. The disciplines also serve the process of the devotee's Contemplation of Adi Da Samraj, by establishing the entire body-mind in a state of equanimity.

Beloved Adi Da usually refers to the full range of self-discipline in the Way of the Heart as "the functional, practical, relational, and cultural disciplines".

Functional disciplines in the Way of the Heart include everything pertaining to one's personal well-being and freeing energy and attention for practice. These include responsibility for diet, exercise, health, sexuality, and the death process.

Practical disciplines in the Way of the Heart include everything pertaining to one's obligation to practically secure the Way of the Heart in the world. These include service, work, and financial responsibilities.

Relational disciplines in the Way of the Heart include everything pertaining to one's obligation to practice self-transcendence, tolerance, and blessing in all relations and to foster that in all others.

The preservation of this profundity moment to moment is the sacred nature of your practice from the beginning. This is what it means to take the vow of being My devotee. It means all kinds of things, but this is fundamental. You have a relationship to Me that is profound and it is a moment to moment matter.

This devotional Yoga is a profound process. It is not merely a superficial exercise. It is truly self-surrendering and self-forgetting, all the faculties* gathered in this integrity, this self-transcending Communion. All that comes from that is something that you must realize by practicing it in My Company, and there is just so much you can get by just talking about it. You have to do the sadhana. There should be no question of that.

Why waste your time just merely playing organism games? Unfortunately, in some sense, it is up to you to decide whether being

---

Cultural disciplines in the Way of the Heart include everything pertaining to one's devotional life:
- meditation
- puja (or sacramental worship of Adi Da Samraj)
- chanting
- study of Avatar Adi Da's Wisdom-Teaching
- diary writing as a form of self-observation
- group meetings with other devotees to "consider" each one's practice of the Way of the Heart
- periods of retreat (of varying length, lasting from one day to many weeks) in which the contemplative practices of meditation, puja, and chanting are particularly intensified.

Beloved Adi Da has always Called His devotees to embrace the disciplines in a self-transcending manner, with balance and humor—and to go beyond the tendency to become self-righteous. All self-discipline in the Way of the Heart is an expression of a life-positive orientation, of love and self-giving, founded in the devotional relationship to Beloved Adi Da.

AVATAR ADI DA SAMRAJ: I do not require the discipline of conventional renunciation. Neither do I allow commitment to the karmas of self-indulgence. My devotees serve Me through the humorous discipline of an ordinary pleasurable life. This is the foundation of their practice of the Way of the Heart.

The "Conscious Process" and "Conductivity" in the Way of the Heart

The "conscious process" refers to those practices in the Way of the Heart through which the mind, or attention, is turned from egoic self-involvement to Heart-Communion with Avatar Adi Da. It is the senior discipline and responsibility of all Adi Da's devotees.

"Conductivity" refers to those practices in the Way of the Heart through which the practitioner conforms his or her bodily and emotional life, as well as the function of the breath, to the purpose of Spiritual practice in Adi Da's Company. In the broadest sense, "conductivity" includes disciplines of diet, physical exercise, health, sexuality, emotion, relationships, money, and community. In a more specific sense, "conductivity" also refers to the technical exercises (Given by Adi Da Samraj) whereby the practitioner "conducts" the flow of energy in the body.

profound is of interest. I say it is unfortunate in the sense that it would be better if you lived in a true culture in which the entire gathering, society, and so forth, was (in a sacred manner) communicated to about these matters and it was fundamental to everybody's experience constantly to hear this kind of communication and adapt to practice and so forth, such that it was common that everybody was basically doing all of that. Then being profound would simply be what you would be doing. It wouldn't exactly be given to you on a silver platter, because it is still the same demand, really. But that's good. There should be that demand.

That is what a culture is about. It is about preserving all kinds of things, even that have to do with ordinary survival, fine, but it is also about preserving the most profound understanding, wisdom, knowledge, whatever, of that gathering. So the sacred, profound, or the core, action of life, the profound process, must not be abandoned. And having been found again, or found for the first time, you have to integrate yourself with it, and live it, do it.

You think you're all doing something that you have to do temporarily and <u>then</u> you are going to practice the Way as soon as you are done doing that. That is consenting to be an organism. That is "it is enough for you to be an organism" talk. You would really be doing sadhana except that it wouldn't be true of you as an ego—effectively saying that.

In the traditional setting, it wouldn't have been thought to be important whether it was true of you as an ego, or true to yourself or anything else. It had to be true to the Master's word. That is what it had to be true to. In the given culture now, everything is supposed to be man-oriented, rather than Divine-oriented. But now, as a result of the culture in which everybody is being told that they are just organisms—it's considered disgraceful not to be "true to yourself". That requires the destruction of everything that came before, not merely the changing of its ambiance. That is the end of the sacred, the profound, and so forth. If the purpose of this utopia is that everybody has to presume that they are just organisms, then that is not good. That is not good enough. Nobody should buy that one.

If the only kind of "religious" you are permitted to be anymore is social personalities affirming social virtues, that is not enough religion. True religion is about this profundity process, being associated with it as a work (if you will), a counter-egoic effort, moment to moment, a process of being attracted. It is not merely "working against something" kind of effort. But nonetheless, it requires responsibility for that organism for which you somehow seem to be responsible—whatever that means, whatever you are doing to do it, however you are related to it. It seems very strange to Me.

You don't get any particle of this physical person that you are claiming to be, if you really just examine it thoroughly, in depth—any portion of it. Yet you keep saying this is "you", pointing to your body as a form. You could look into any portion of it, any aspect of its process—you won't find an absolute line between any portion of it and the vast processes with which it is associated. There is no absolute line. There is no "you" about it. There is a process, an integrity, but it is only a temporary one, and it is in a pattern that is fundamentally not comprehensible. You think it means something just because it is there. It is a little bit of blah-blah in the mummery. It doesn't mean anything. That is another way of saying, in Mama-talk, "Your objections to anything don't mean shit!" It doesn't mean anything.

You think it has to mean something because it is there. Because it is arising, it must mean something somehow. Everything is meaningful. You blah-blah-blah, you talk, and figure everybody knows what you mean. It is not meaningful. It is all rather just playful, amusing, nothing absolute about it. The profundity is prior to it. There is the Great Profundity, but it

The Laughing Mama Says . . .

The Laughing Mama at Love-Ananda Mahal

The Laughing Mama is an image Avatar Adi Da Samraj first introduced at the end of January 1996. The inspiration for this image came from the mechanized sculptures of huge, laughing women that Adi Da saw at Coney Island and other carnivals when He was a child in New York.

The Mama looks like a psychotic bag lady, incessantly laughing with devilish vigor at everyone and everything. Avatar Adi Da uses the Laughing Mama as an image of conditional Nature, which is utterly indifferent to anyone's concerns for individual survival and happiness. Adi Da created a blunt slogan for the Laughing Mama, representing her message to all: "Your objections to <u>anything</u> don't mean shit!"

This saying is a lesson about the nature of the conditional universe, which is an immense process that is utterly indifferent to any individual's objections, complaints, or concerns. This image of conditional reality is not a justification for despair. Rather, it is a call to relinquish our bondage to this world (which has no interest in satisfying us in any case) and to invest ourselves in the great process of Realizing the Unconditional* Truth (or Reality).

Avatar Adi Da has said that the Laughing Mama is a means of His Instruction to everyone, and therefore she is one of His Forms.

is not what you are looking at, or what you are presuming about what you are apparently looking at.

But to find out about the matters profound, you have to <u>be</u> profound, you have to do sadhana. You have to do the action, the process, participate in the process that is profound. Otherwise, you can't find out anything profound. You can't just participate in it in the superficial level, talkity-talkity-talk, and find out about anything profound. All I can do is indicate to you the next basic step to make for it to become more profound, then you move on from that. You can't just babble-babble-babble about profundity. You have to enter into its process and you have to do so consistently.

Do so. Do sadhana in other words, and make life sadhana. I don't mean something merely grim by that. To let life become sadhana is to fit it to profundity, to be always in-depth.

You simply embrace the Way as I have Given it to you and live it fully and truly and prove it by the doing of it, live it profoundly and get on with it. What else is there to do?

Your relationship to Me is inherently profound. Therefore, you must always live it profoundly. Staying in this fundamental profundity moment to moment is how your life will be granted integrity more and more profoundly. But not in the merely utopian sense—I mean in the fundamental sense, in the very process of your being.

Everything passes but profundity itself. Nothing in the waking state remains, nothing in the dreaming state remains, sleep does not bide, does not continue. But the Great Profundity is there in any apparent event. So this must be your focus. This Profundity, therefore, is beyond waking, dreaming, and sleeping altogether. But it is such only if it is <u>done</u> profoundly, if you do the practice seriously.

If you are not up to profundity, then you go with the flow, the pattern of being an organism in the human scale.

The <u>only</u> thing really interesting is this profundity beyond your presumptions—getting out of your washing machine and getting into the wall, the power source, getting into that depth. It is the only thing that is interesting, really interesting. All the rest of it is known territory, stuff, replicating, shifting a little, changing slightly, slight modifications—but it's a process. Everything that you call "you" is not even a "you" in the beginning. The general propaganda of the time is that everything that you even could call "you" is only going to last as long as that organism walks.

The argument you're embracing is that there is no profundity. In it, there's nothing but material finality and mortality. That has never been acceptable to Me. From the moment of this Birth (so-called), there was a conjunction with people who were in this disposition. And that is not, in any sense, <u>It</u>. But they knew nothing about It. The "Bright" was not true of them. They weren't profound, beyond a point, anyway—generally speaking, not. They seemed to be, generally speaking, very content with banal existence as if they had accepted that they were just something like organisms—just that, like livestock or something, jiggling around as people do, none of them particularly spectacular about it. Then, after a while, you have your job, you have your children, that's it, you die.

That's that. Maybe a little religious chit-chat, but basically, "Who knows? Maybe not. Doesn't look like it." All that kind of nonsense. "Is there a God?" Really not much profundity to be serious about in response to people's want toward greatness.

But they don't want to be profound about it, you know. Profundity suggests depth, so it is a matter of entering into a state deeper than all the different levels that you know in the waking state and the dreaming state and the sleeping state—more and more into depth, always going beyond the limits of patterned awareness to get at the Source, the Root, the Ultimate Condition.

To find what is profound, you have to enter into profundity. You cannot get true religion just in the thinking mind, and social exchanges, and images, and so on. True Religion is found in the in-depth process of going beyond the self-limit, into the Domain and Person That is beyond all patterned experiencing. True Religion is progress into the State of Non-"Difference" from the Source, the Source-Condition, the Inherent Condition, the Self-Condition, the Very Divine Condition.

Devotion to Me is a process of this nature.

CHAPTER FOUR

The Great Organism "Consideration"

BY JONATHAN CONDIT

The tables had been turned. We were matched in a debate against our Guru. It was up to us to "prove" to Beloved Adi Da that we were more than fleshy bodies and material stuff, that we were, at root, Consciousness Itself. Adi Da, much to our amazement, was staunchly maintaining that we were nothing but organisms—that's all we were, that the greater dimension of existence, Consciousness Itself, was not possible for us to Realize. And we were failing miserably to prove Him wrong!

What had we done to find ourselves in this predicament? How had it happened that, after hearing so many hundreds of hours of Beloved Adi Da's Discourse on the Reality of Consciousness and the limitations of materialism as a philosophy, we were unable to speak convincingly for the "Consciousness" side, while Adi Da seemed utterly invincible in His arguing that we belonged strictly to the "matter" side?

It had all started four days before. On that day, April 11, 1995, Beloved Adi Da had surprised and delighted a group of about twenty-five of His devotees who were residents of Ruchira Buddha Dham (the Island of Naitauba, Avatar Adi Da's Hermitage Sanctuary in Fiji) by calling for a gathering to occur on the deck of the then newly acquired boat—the Turaga Dau Loloma, named after Adi Da's Fijian Name (meaning "the Divine Adept of the Divine Love")—which was moored in the idyllic lagoon near the devotees' village on Naitauba.

Adi Da Samraj had already been gathering with devotees steadily for about two months. Almost every afternoon or evening there would be a phone call in which we would be asked if we had any "questions, 'considerations', or causes" for gathering—any possible topic that we wanted to discuss with Him or any event that we wanted to create. If we presented enough "raw material" to justify having a gathering, then Avatar Adi Da would call for a gathering to begin—usually immediately, with only minutes to change clothes and make other necessary preparations— and He would say where the gathering was to occur. We knew from experience that when Adi Da changed the venue of the gatherings, that generally meant that the topic of "consideration" was going to shift, often quite dramatically. The gatherings had most recently been in Hymns To Me, the large gathering hall in the village. So, when we were invited to a boat gathering, we sensed that our Guru had something up His sleeve, but we really didn't know what.

On the evening of April 11, we were bubbling with excitement as we drove in jeeps down to the beach, where a small punt ferried us in groups across the glassy turquoise water of the lagoon out to the Turaga Dau Loloma. We seated ourselves on the open expanse of wooden deck, facing Beloved Adi Da as He sat in a simple white deck chair, silently Regarding people as they arrived. The evening air was still and fresh, and the boat swayed gently back and forth with the movement of the lagoon waters. The preceding two months of gathering had been strongly focused on understanding the emotional-sexual dimension of our lives and practice, but that night, as we were soon to find out, was to be different.

When everyone was seated and ready, we expected Adi Da to begin in His characteristic manner by having us summarize what we were prepared to discuss or ask questions about. But no—that night <u>He</u> abruptly began the gathering with a question to <u>us</u>. With a slightly quizzical look on His Face, He asked, in an amused but arresting tone:

"Do you all have the feeling that Consciousness Itself has nothing whatsoever to do with the body-mind, that it's totally independent of the body-mind . . ." He paused slightly for dramatic effect, and then completed His sentence: ". . . and that's what you don't like about It?"

After a moment of stunned silence, during which He allowed us to register how thoroughly our minds were blown by His punchline, Beloved Adi Da erupted in peals and peals of uproarious laughter, as we joined in laughing with Him, still not altogether sure what we were laughing about.

Then He continued, pressing the point further home:

"That is what you all don't like about Consciousness Itself. It's not that you are un-Enlightened. You refuse Enlightenment."

Again He broke into hilarious laughter.

Thus began the series of five boat gatherings, on consecutive nights from April 11 through April 15, during which Beloved Adi Da wove a masterful tapestry of "consideration" about the ultimate stages of practice in the Way of the Heart, which He calls the "Perfect Practice".[9] In this most profound practice (which is a state not really even imaginable to us in our usual condition), the devotee no longer identifies with "me" (or the apparently separate body-mind-self), but actually Identifies with the "Point of View" of Consciousness Itself, even while continuing to function as the body-mind. During any period of gathering, Adi Da Samraj inevitably returns at some point to the matter of the "Perfect Practice", because that is what He is truly Calling everyone to. Everything that precedes it He regards to be merely preparation for it.

Having just spent two months discussing matters that had everything to do with the foundation levels of the practice of the Way of the Heart, we now found ourselves suddenly plunged into "consideration" of the culminating stages of the entire process. Each night, in response to our questions and observations, Avatar Adi Da explored different aspects of the "Perfect Practice". By the end of the fourth night, however, it seemed that we were not going to be able to generate anything further to keep the "consideration" going. We had run out of questions and "considerations" to suggest.

So, on the afternoon of April 15, we were caught short when word spread through the village that Beloved Adi Da was going to call shortly by radio from the boat (where He had slept overnight in the cabin) to ask what questions, "considerations", or causes for gathering we had to offer. As many "gatherers" as possible were quickly assembled in the cramped little room at the back of the management offices where the radio base station was. We were racking our brains for something to offer our Beloved Guru—we certainly didn't want to miss the opportunity of gathering with Him again. But when the call came through, we only managed to come up with a few lame possibilities, none of which were sufficient to warrant a gathering.

After we had offered all the possibilities we could think of, Avatar Adi Da humorously began to spin His own web of "Consideration". We listened with a mixture of amazement and amusement as He started to advocate, with tremendous finesse, that scientific materialism had indeed

---

9. For a description of the "Perfect Practice", please see the sidebar on pp. 195-96.

proclaimed the last word about us—we are "mortal organisms" and nothing else. He declared that all the years of His experience of Teaching human beings had finally convinced Him of this.

One after another, we grabbed the radio microphone and blurted out whatever objections we could muster, but He quickly shot holes in all our arguments. We began to feel more and more acutely what our Master was driving at in this humorous manner: No matter what we may claim our philosophy to be, the "organism" point of view is deeply entrenched in us.

In the end, Beloved Adi Da made an offer: Anyone who was prepared to <u>prove</u> that he or she was not merely an organism, but was Consciousness Itself, could come out to the boat to "consider" this matter further with Him in a gathering. We thanked Beloved for inviting us, and quickly scattered to prepare, anxiously wondering how we were possibly going to come up with the required proof.

When we were all assembled on the deck of the Turaga Dau Loloma, Abel Slater, who had been the principal spokesperson for us in the radio conversation earlier, started with a brief summary of that conversation, for the benefit of those who had not been in the room at the time.

"Well, Beloved, this afternoon You had a 'consideration' with us on the radio."

Avatar Adi Da was "in character". Correcting Abel in a tone of mock self-satisfaction, He said, "I made a summary Communication, I believe." Everyone burst out laughing.

"I think that's more what happened", Abel agreed.

"My conclusions after twenty-three years."

"You said that, after twenty-three years of trying to make it apparent to us that we are Consciousness Itself, because of our refusal to Realize this, You have come to the conclusion that we are simply organisms."

"<u>Mortal</u> organisms", Adi Da clarified.

"Right. And You painted the picture of the scientific materialist point of view—that what we believe to be conscious awareness is simply brain-waves emanating from this physical manifestation, and that our fate is death, and ultimately stinky."

"You have changed Your doctrine to agree with the prevailing views," Jonathan observed.

"Yes," said Adi Da, "it was a thorough 'consideration'."

"We tried and tried," Abel continued, "in every which way, to appeal to You that we recognize that we are Consciousness Itself—through Your Grace, and through our resort to You, and through our Contemplation of You. But You said it sounded just like a myth.

"We continued to persist in our confession to You that this is indeed the case—that we are Consciousness. And so You told us to come here tonight to prove this to You, to demonstrate this Realization. You Said that nothing short of that would suffice. Otherwise, we are simply organisms, fated to die and decay."

"And that will be that," Beloved Adi Da emphasized. "Just dead, like fish, putrid fish. Plain Old Organism People—POOPs." We all laughed at this amusing new acronym.

Joseph Taylor remarked, "Beloved, I was reflecting today that You came here for the sake of all beings, but the actual physical object that drew You to initiate Your Great Sacrificial Work was a puppy, not one of us." Joseph was referring to the momentous incident in Avatar Adi Da's infancy when (at the age of two) He voluntarily chose to identify with the apparently separate body-mind, to accept all the implications of being "human" in the ordinary sense. This event occurred in the moment of His first seeing a puppy that His parents had just bought for Him.

"Mm-hm. I said all beings." And then, putting on a slightly supercilious tone: "Or, perhaps, to put it more aptly, all organisms, as it turns out. Well, this is My firm conclusion. Some 'begged to differ', as Barbara said in our earlier conversation, but I Said that in Consciousness Itself there is no 'difference'—therefore, she is only an organism." We all laughed at Adi Da's humorous "logic".

Then Adi Da announced the core of His "argument", in the classic form of a syllogism. "Consciousness Itself Inherently Transcends the body-mind. You all insist on identifying with the body-mind. Therefore, you are not Consciousness Itself, you are the body-mind—an organism fated to die. And that's that."

Something about the logic of this "argument" seemed open to dispute, but in the hilarity of the moment no one came up with a counter-argument.

"We started out with such bright hopes", Godfree Roberts sighed.

"Well, the 'consideration' was worth having, I thought." Adi Da was playing up His "role" more and more. "Just on the outside chance that maybe some were not merely organisms. But, unfortunately, you see . . . I mean, it was a 'reality consideration', so you have to take it the way it comes. When you finally get down to it, whatever is the case is it, and that's it."

Then Adi Da startled us by voicing the bottom-line implications of "organism" philosophy with unnerving, though still hilarious, bluntness. "This practice, this devotion to Me and self-discipline that you do, makes you feel better, brings some kind of order, and even consolation, to your mortal existence. So it is still worth doing—at least it makes you feel good in this short interval of suffering and seeking and psycho-physical ego-identification. Nothing you can do about that, of course. It's just the way it is.

"There is nothing to Realize. Have fun as much as you can, and try to relax when you are dying. That is My advice."

We were practically rolling on the deck with laughter, but our frustration and agitation were beginning to build. Beloved Adi Da's "play-acting" was beginning to hit too close to home. Many times in the past we had witnessed our Guru's uncanny ability to adopt a certain persona, as a way of reflecting to us what we are all about. He may suddenly become the fear-stricken coward or the self-indulgent addict or the soupy romantic or any other number of instantly recognizable character types, in order to make a lesson. But never before had we seen Him sustain such a role for so long as He was doing on this night. He seemed determined not to stop until we were utterly convicted of the benightedness of "organism" philosophy.

Adi Da kept going with His seemingly inexorable line of logic: "I was telling some on the radio that you have every right to fear death—because it is going to kill you!" We cracked up with laughter again.

"But fish, and so forth—they don't seem to worry about it too much. So that is a good policy: 'Don't worry about it, and relax when the time comes.' That is about all the wisdom you can use, I think, being plain old organisms."

Gerald Sheinfeld, who had come to the first three of the five boat gatherings but had been unable to come to the previous night's gathering, remarked, "I missed one night of Your 'Consideration', Beloved. Things have certainly changed."

Adi Da explained: "Well, until tonight, I was still going for the big picture, you know—maybe there were <u>some</u> who were not merely organisms. But, it didn't turn out that way. Shucks, well . . .

"Still, as I said, it was a 'consideration' worth having, because there have been rumors of religion and Divinity and God-Realization going on for thousands of years. It was time that a <u>full</u> 'reality consideration' was entered into about the matter, so that the truth of the matter could be known, and all these winds of doctrine addressed, with a firm and final and absolutely undeniable conclusion."

"Didn't Gautama[10] have a similar 'consideration', Beloved?" asked Bill Krenz. Bill was asking about the Buddhist teaching that every conditional

10. Gautama Shakyamuni (circa 563-483 B.C.E.) is the Indian Sage commonly known as "the Buddha".

phenomenon, including existence as a human being, is painful, impermanent, and devoid of "self".

"He didn't exactly come to this conclusion, but he came to some sort of conclusion about the body-mind itself." Adi Da was referring to the doctrine of the five skandhas, according to which the human body-mind is nothing but a collection of discrete elements, rather than a unified "being" with an identifiable "self".

"Still, Gautama presumed that there was some kind of something or other—Undescribable, Indefinable, and Absolute—that could be Realized." Then, fully dramatizing the arrogant twentieth-century ego's dismissal of the entire history of mankind's religious quest, Adi Da concluded, in a tone of self-satisfied gusto, "And, of course, that was bullshit! So we finally put that one to rest!"

"Is it a relief to put it to rest?" asked Quandra Mai Jangama Hridayam.[11]

"Oh, yes," Adi Da immediately replied. Then, with a sly grin, He went on, capping His masterful "performance": "Of course, I am a little smug about it, because I am not an organism!"

We all rocked with laughter, as Beloved Adi Da Himself laughed at His own line. Then He underlined His point: "I Am Self-Existing and Self-Radiant Consciousness Itself, and you all are organisms.

"But, of course, as I say, some of you objected to this conclusion, so that is actually why we gathered again. Otherwise, having come to this conclusion, I would never have any reason to see you again. But you thought we should gather this one last time, listen to the objections of some, and see if anybody could prove that they are not organisms.

"And Abel, you were the spokesman on the radio. You said definitely that some were going to prove this tonight, this very night, here, on board, during this 'consideration' time."

"Yes, I did, Lord," Abel concurred.

"Mm-hm. Are you one of those who are going to prove it?"

"Absolutely, Beloved."

"So, Abel—your objections, and your proofs."

Abel then began what was to become several hours worth of devotees' debating with Adi Da Samraj. Abel was looking to present evidence that would substantiate our side of the debate—that we were not mere organisms, but were Consciousness Itself.

11. "Quandra Mai Jangama Hridayam" is one of the women who serve Adi Da Samraj personally and who are committed to Him in the most sacred devotional manner of the Guru-devotee bond, and to renunciate practice in His direct physical Company. "Quandra" and "Mai" are references to the main female character in Adi Da Samraj's liturgical drama, *The Mummery*. Quandra is the embodiment of the Divine Goddess, or Spirit-Force.

"Well, during the course of the 'consideration' we had with You on the radio, as it drew on, there was the experience of feeling You Prior to identification with the body-mind."

"There is no trick in that," Adi Da objected. "I <u>Am</u> Prior to the body-mind."

"Right."

"You are not."

"I am not," Abel conceded.

"But I am. So you were feeling Me, and that is good." Adi Da was pressing relentlessly on our presumption that we are the body-mind only, in order to help us feel the gravity of that error.

Abel went on, "There wasn't a sense of 'I' feeling You through the course of that experience."

"Then who experienced it?"

"Well, in the midst of the experience—I don't even have words for it—in the midst of whatever was going on . . ."

"Samadhi," Bill suggested.

"Samadhi, then," Abel continued. "There wasn't the experience of an 'I' experiencing some separate other condition. There was just You."

"This sounds like modern-religious-mythology talk to Me," Adi Da countered.

"Sounds like it," Abel said, dismayed.

"I dismissed it as such on the radio. I am going to stand My ground until the point is truly proven to Me otherwise."

Abel started in on another tack. "It seems like, at this point, there is an 'I' that is trying to somehow prove something from a point of view that is separate from that. In other words, trying to come up with objectified proof of it is impossible."

"Why would you have to use the word 'objectified', anyway?" Adi Da asked. "You said you were coming here to prove it, and now you are going to tell Me that you can't prove it? Is that it?"

"It can only be . . ." Abel started to rephrase his last point, but Adi Da insisted on an answer to His question.

Avatar Adi Da adopted a stern tone. "You said 'proof' on the radio, Abel. I will accept nothing short of it."

"How about subjective proof?" asked Michael Shaw.

"That's a possibility", Abel agreed, hopefully.

Adi Da proclaimed: "Scientific proof of the existence of Consciousness will soon be announced . . . by Abel!" We all roared at this rephrasing of Beloved Adi Da's own book title, *Scientific Proof of the Existence of God*

Will Soon Be Announced by the White House!

"Cannot be done, Beloved—not scientifically," Abel declared.

"You promised it."

"Not scientifically."

"If you were leading Me on about this proof matter, Abel, then you got yourself here on board under false pretenses. Not only would you be a plain old organism, you would be a plain old organism with whom I am not pleased!" Beloved Adi Da glared at Abel with mock ferocity, then joined in the laughter with all of us.

Adi Da now introduced a key point in His "argument". "The way I look at it is pretty straightforward. If you are not an organism, then you do the 'Perfect Practice'."

Adi Da had explained to us many times that, over the course of advancing practice in the Way of the Heart, the practitioner's presumption as to what he or she <u>is</u> undergoes an evolution. In the foundation stages of practice of the Way of the Heart, one is fundamentally identified with body, while in the advanced stages of practice one is fundamentally identified with mind. However, in the ultimate stages of practice, or the "Perfect Practice", one stands free of identification with either body or mind, Identifying instead with Consciousness Itself. What Adi Da was humorously arguing on this night was that it was not possible to progressively become capable of Identifying with Consciousness Itself—either you were just plain Identified with Consciousness Itself, in which case you would practice the "Perfect Practice", or you were identified with the body-mind, in which case you <u>were</u> just the body-mind, a mortal organism, and could not advance beyond the first five stages of life.

Adi Da proceeded with His "argument". "The Way of the Heart is a 'reality consideration'. But the whole 'consideration' is simply about being in My Spiritual Company, devoted to Me, surrendered to Me, Communing with Me, to the degree that the Power of My Samadhi Draws you into the Realization of My Condition. That essentially is the Way of the Heart. And it can't be defined as a sequence of practices and stages of development. Those things are more peripheral aspects of the Way. Fundamentally, the Way is simply Communing with Me to the point that the Power of My Samadhi brings you to the Realization of Me Most Perfectly.*

"Well, you have all been around Me, each of you, for some number of years or other, supposedly devoting yourself to Me in this manner, and if you were so combined with Me, and were arising in Consciousness Itself, then by now you ought to be doing the 'Perfect Practice', unless you just arrived yesterday or something. And so?"

"Beloved, You have combined with us in such a miraculous way that . . . ", Godfree started out, but was interrupted by Adi Da.

"Adi . . . cannot combine." Adi Da laughed and briefly dropped out of "character" in order to explain: "That was a sort of play on Auda in *Lawrence of Arabia*. 'Auda . . . cannot serve.'" Then, right back in "character" again: "I 'combined' with you all? What a revolting suggestion! But, go on."

Godfree persisted, "And I have seen You in everyone's eyes here. Not in moments, but consistently."

Adi Da adopted His haughtiest tone. "Yes. Well, there is no doubt about Who I Am, Godfree. But I am reflected in your eyes like the moon reflects the sun—good. But the moon is a dead rock!" We erupted with laughter. "And you are mere organisms, with these glossy little apertures, upon which I Shine as upon the moon, and it makes you glad and consoles you and helps you through this passage to death, making it a little lighter."

Godfree objected, "You have Accomplished much more than mere passive reflection."

"Mere argumentation, mere words, about all this, Godfree, is not going to convince Me," Adi Da said with finality. "I have 'Considered' this matter very thoroughly with you all for twenty-three years, and I will not accept any arguments that you are not mere organisms. Only the 'Perfect Practice' will do. Only devotion to Me to the point of Realizing My Samadhi—by the Power of My Samadhi, not by self-effort—is satisfactory to Me as final proof that you are not mere organisms.

"If you can't respond to Me to this degree, can't Realize Me by the Power of My Samadhi, that suggests that you flat cannot Realize Me—that you are just organisms, and at most can reflect Me, enjoy My Company, be warmed by My Presence like the earth is by the sun, show some brightness in your eyes like the moon reflects the sun. But you cannot Realize anything beyond being mere organisms. You are a composite of naturally made faculties, and do not have the ultimate components necessary for Divine Self-Realization. You being just 'organism', all the rest of it that's required even for advanced practice (but certainly for ultimate practice) is not there.

"It must be so, because I have been addressing you all for vast, vast decades, and you keep insisting that you are an organism. You keep insisting on just this beginner's practice, beginner's 'consideration', and so forth—that is the most you can do, the most you can respond."

Adi Da kept up His humorous but penetrating onslaught, exposing our hidden presumptions with the precision of a surgeon.

"You get bright in your eyes, and warmed in your body, reflecting Me, and so forth, but you just can't <u>find</u> Me, Consciousness Itself, can't enter into that Ultimate Samadhi. You just don't have the faculties, or the attributes, for such Realization."

Avatar Adi Da shifted briefly into a more serious tone. "You all are always talking organism stuff to Me, resorting to the body-mind, claiming to be that, even having all kinds of problems with it. So that is what I have been doing, then. I've been spending a lot of time just helping you all out with your organism problems, your 'money, food, and sex'[12] problems, your ordinary-life problems, and so forth. That is what I have been occupying Myself with, basically, because you all insist that you are not Realizing Me, are not in the Condition of Consciousness Itself, and, therefore, are disposed to lower-life-form practices. You are not here to do the practice of Consciousness Itself. You are here to do the practice of disciplining the body-mind, and using the only faculties you've got, which is some kind of feeling and your constant thinking-thinking-thinking, which mainly just complicates you anyway. And that's it. That's the whole ball of wax."

Canada Shannon tried another argument. "Beloved Bhagavan, when we do forget ourselves in Contemplation of You, it is You that we Realize."

Adi Da was back in "character" again. "You see, it is Me that you're Contemplating."

"When we forget about ourselves, it is just You."

"It's great pleasure, yes, because I Am here! But, of course, you cannot Realize Me, you cannot be Established in My Condition. You can just be organisms responding to Me, like fish go to the lure, or to the water-top in sunlight. You <u>admire</u> Me, you are comforted by My Presence, but you yourselves are mortal organisms."

"It's more than that," Canada objected.

"Prove it!" Adi Da challenged her.

"We forget all those faculties."

"Well, sometimes you forget them," Adi Da replied. Then He painted a vivid vision of mortal philosophy. "And then you are <u>reflecting</u> Me, like the back of a fish reflects the sunlight. But the fish is not the sun. It cannot go there, and can never <u>be</u> it. Then some sucker comes along with a lure, snaps him out of the water, and cuts him in the back of the head, and he's done. So it is with you all. Various circumstances abuse the

---

12. Avatar Adi Da uses this phrase ("money, food, and sex") to summarize the basic areas of life-business that must be handled by all His devotees (and which are fundamental areas of seeking in the common world). Money includes all uses of life-energy (such as work and service), food includes everything related to health (such as diet and exercise), and sex includes the emotional and sexual dimensions of the body-mind as well as all relationships.

organism. Suffers it, still tries to feel good, struggles along. Eventually takes the bait, gets hit on the back of the head, and <u>done</u>. That's the fate of these organisms, don't you know?"

We all agreed, in sobered voices, "Yes."

"Well, that's it. None of you at all have agreed to take up a sadhana that's about being anything other than an organism." Adi Da was requiring us to see the consequences of remaining identified with the body—that it meant confining ourselves indefinitely to the beginnings of Spiritual practice.

Jacqueline Grolman tried to turn around Adi Da's fish metaphor. "You are Light, Beloved. Just as the fish is pervaded by the sun's light . . ."

"Yes, but it never gets to <u>be</u> the sun. You all, like the fishes, are <u>creatures</u> of the sunlight. You are creatures of natural processes. And that's it!"

Alan Whitehead spoke up. "Beloved, the sun has no transforming power, but You do. You're the One Who Transforms us."

"Well, you can say so, but, on the other hand, what kind of sadhana are you doing? Not the sadhana of the 'Perfect Practice', Identifying with Me utterly and perfectly, but the sadhana of organisms, reaching toward Me and insisting on their separate identity as organisms.

"I mean, okay, you know, a while to 'consider', grow, and be moved by the Power of My Samadhi—but twenty-three years? Kinda long in the tooth, you know what I mean? Sooner or later, I had to come to some conclusions about this—why, after twenty-three years, nobody's Realizing Me, but everybody's insisting on being organisms, to put it plainly. Why is that? It's because you're <u>organisms</u>! It suddenly dawned on Me."

A huge chorus of objections was called out.

Adi Da refused to relent: "Moon and earth to My Sun, just mortal organisms. Poor things! That's what I finally realized. It suddenly dawned on Me. All along, I have just been Realizing My Self, so it took some 'consideration' with you and bearing down and 'combining' with you (as you suggest) and finding you out, to finally realize this. It suddenly dawned on Me. Only today, on the radio, it suddenly dawned on Me. Suddenly My struggle ceased, My heart relaxed. I realized I could not possibly Transform you into Me. I can Shine on you and Give you a little bit of the Law (which will relax some of your fear), but your destiny is death, clearly. <u>Clearly!</u>"

Godfree made a last-ditch attempt. "Beloved, there is a possible alternative explanation."

"Well, there are many alternative explanations, but that doesn't make them true."

"I think this one has at least a good shot."

"Let's try it."

"I think we're just late-bloomers. "

"Where's the argument in that? I mean, it doesn't prove anything. If you're going to late-bloom, then you have to bloom, in order to prove the point. The fact that you haven't bloomed yet is not proof that you can bloom. Bloom lately, and that would be proof."

And so it continued for nearly four hours. In His Service to us, to help us become thoroughly convinced of the necessity to relinquish our "organism" point of view, Adi Da just kept pushing His points home again and again and again, from every possible angle. The longer we were unable to argue successfully against this mortal philosophy, the more desperate and unsettled we became. It got to be more and more disturbing to hear our Beloved Guru expressing this point of view that was so dark and hopeless, when we could also feel that He was just articulating our own unspoken or unconscious "philosophy". Finally, after devotees had thoroughly exhausted every argument they could think of to counter Beloved Adi Da's "conclusion", He relented and Revealed to us the Truth of this "Consideration":

"If you insist on being organisms, you know what I have to say about that. I told you earlier. If you respond to Me, enter into My Domain, by the Power of My Samadhi, then you do the 'Perfect Practice' in due course. And that is the whole ball of wax."

Then He let the cat all the way out of the bag. "Well, by the way, I was bullshitting."

We all erupted into cheers and yells, so relieved that we were no longer "condemned" to mere organism life.

"You had us worried, Beloved," Michael confessed.

Beloved Adi Da summarized the lesson of the evening's "consideration": "Nobody is merely an organism, unless you insist. If you insist, then that is what you are. If you respond to Me, if you are My devotee, if you practice this Yoga of devotion, then (in due course) you practice the discipline of the 'Perfect Practice'. There are none uniquely born, none uniquely Identified with the Divine Condition of Consciousness Itself. All are thus manifested."

We poured out our thanks to Beloved Adi Da, full of gratitude for His masterful and extraordinarily witty lesson-making. We knew that we would never forget this night—He had impressed the lesson on us so deeply.

The next night at another gathering—this time at Hymns To Me— Beloved Adi Da further Revealed the Truth of the matter in this ecstatic proclamation:

Ruchira Buddha Dham, 1995

AVATAR ADI DA SAMRAJ: There is Only Reality, Only God, Only Truth, Only Reality Itself.

All are Inherently conjoined with That, with Me.

Some, not so responsive and illumined, act and speak as if they are just organisms, and suggest that they should have a "lesser dharma" (so to speak), or only the opportunity for some sort of relief of anxiety, or equanimity at most, and so forth, and don't aspire to Ultimate Realization so hard.

But that is just their immaturity talking.

They have to continue to grow and get to know Me better.

No one is merely an organism—not even the fishes and the possums and the frogs and the mosquitos, and not even Hitlers.

<u>All</u>, including all of them, are Inherently conjoined with Me.

They just have to get to know Me better.

They have to mature.

They have to be forgiven.

They have to be purified.

They have to suffer, yes. They have to go through an ordeal. All the more reason to get to know Me better and grow beyond this circumstance quickly.

So some are more serious than others to begin with, and others get serious later—late-bloomers, as Godfree described them.

Yes, there are all those kinds of apparent differences, but no ultimate "difference".

All are in Me.

All have this opportunity—even if they may argue that they are mere organisms, or act as if they were merely organisms.

It's just bullshit, immaturity speaking, egoity dominant, habit-patterns dominant, fear dominant.

They have to get to know Me better, that's all.

So there is only one Dharma, one Reality, for all—one Teaching, one Great Opportunity.

It is up to each one to respond as he or she will in any moment.

Right response gets to know Me better, and you go and get on with it further.

That's it.

The Mountain Of Attention, 1996

CHAPTER FIVE

December 5, 1996

Oblige the Body-Mind to Be Intelligently Guided

*O**n the night of December 5, after a few opening remarks by various devotees, the gathering begins with a confession from Aniello Panico, a longtime devotee who has been in Avatar Adi Da's Company since shortly after the opening of the Hollywood Ashram in 1972.***

ANIELLO PANICO: *[speaking in a voice full of feeling]* My Lord, when we gathered with You earlier this year, in January, it was, as always, magnificent to be in Your Company and feel how You Draw us into the Great Reality That You Are. A lot of things occurred during that time for me experientially, but one night You did a guided meditation that was just utterly unbelievable to me in one respect, which is that, after all these years, I realized that I had never really come in touch with the depth of the self-contraction. That night You were Drawing us through it. You just enveloped us and we were Drawn in, sitting in the most incredible Happiness, in You, and because of You.

And I actually got down there and really felt—because You did it so magnificently. You said, "Feel how to be Happy in this very moment." You were Drawing us into that whole . . . not experience, but Reality. And it was just so wonderful. I kept getting deeper and deeper into Your Company, in You. And then You said, "You can feel all the way down there, that there is the self-knot, and you can't be Happy unless that is severed through most fundamental self-understanding and My Grace."

So I really came in touch with that. And when You sat in Darshan a month ago in Land Bridge Pavilion on Your Jayanthi,[13] it really penetrated me again, to feel that Great Happiness with You, and yet to feel that I was always doing something to feel the self-knot.

It's an interesting thing for me at this time, because, as You've pointed out (and just to cop to it), I obviously wasn't practicing with the intensity that is required to really be able, through Your Grace, to penetrate the self-knot, understand it, and, of course, in the process, just be Happy in that moment. But I've had moments of it over the past year, and particularly lately, since You've been here in California.

So I just want to confess that. I really didn't even have a question, other than to just want to confess that to You, and also just the great Grace of Your Being, because it's . . . *[Aniello is overcome with emotion and unable to finish His sentence. He says quietly, with great intensity of feeling:]* I really love You, Master.

The entire room is full of heart-broken feeling. Adi Da sits deeply still, regarding Aniello with a look of unutterable sweetness, and responding quietly with His characteristic sound of Blessing.

AVATAR ADI DA SAMRAJ: Tcha.

Adi Da slowly turns His head back from having been gazing at Aniello to the side. His eyes close and He sits absolutely motionless and calm. The devotees in the room are quickly drawn into a great depth of feeling. All impulse to continue talking is suddenly vanished, as a period of profound meditative Communion with Adi Da Samraj spontaneously begins. Some sit utterly still, others are sighing and swooning in ecstasy, while others are responding with kriyas.[14]

This meditative Communion gradually becomes deeper and deeper, lasting for about half an hour. Eventually, a feeling of completeness pervades the room, and, with a slight readjustment of His posture, Avatar Adi Da indicates that the meditative occasion has come to an end. Everyone sighs in gratitude and praise.

ANIELLO: You are so great, Lord.

MICHAEL WOOD: Thank You, Lord.

---

13. Sanskrit for "Day of Victory", used to refer to the birthday of a Realizer.

14. Spontaneous, self-purifying physical movements. Kriyas arise when the natural bodily energies are stimulated by the Divine Spirit-Current.

A Sublime Gift of Wordless Instruction

BY JONATHAN CONDIT

Jonathan Condit with Adi Da Samraj, Love-Ananda Mahal, 1996

In the gathering of December 5, as soon as Aniello had finished his confession and Beloved Adi Da had turned back to face forward again, I immediately felt a dramatic shift, in myself and in the entire room, to a profound depth of feeling and vulnerability. In that moment, many of the devotees in the room sighed or exclaimed virtually in unison, as we felt Avatar Adi Da taking us instantaneously to that depth.

What followed was an extraordinarily potent communication of the fundamental practice of devotional surrender to Beloved Adi Da. But this was a communication in the depth of feeling, without any words at all—even without visual communication, for I was moved to close my eyes and rest in deep feeling-Communion with Beloved Adi Da. Adi Da was Granting us a direct Transmission of the true Spiritual process in His Company, bypassing language and mind. In fact, I felt like my mind was stumbling to keep up with what was being revealed in feeling.

At first, it was my body that responded most dramatically to Beloved Adi Da. My entire upper body would suddenly turn as far as possible to the right, then as far as possible to the left, back and forth, stretching all the muscles and joints intensely, my arms extended to their full length. It was the kind of intense stretching that is supposed to be done in Hatha Yoga* postures, but these stretches were entirely spontaneous. I couldn't predict when the movements would occur or what they would be. I was simply observing this process happen, as uninvolved in making it happen as I would have been if I had been watching someone else.

Adi Da's devotees frequently experience such spontaneous movements, or kriyas, when they are feeling His Spiritual Force

69

deeply, whether they are physically in the room or even thousands of miles away from His bodily Form. Although kriyas can at first be startling to experience (or to witness happening to others), they are entirely benign. They are simply evidence of Avatar Adi Da's Grace at work in the devotee's body-mind, purifying physical, emotional, and mental obstructions. On this night, at some point I noticed that the tight clench that I had for many years felt in the muscles all down the right side of my face and neck had spontaneously released, in conjunction with the intense stretching kriyas (and this release has lasted since then). As the kriyas continued, I felt my entire being becoming softer and more alive with energy, and thus more available to receive Beloved Adi Da's Transmission.

Eventually the kriyas subsided and I became aware of the frantic activity of the mind. Never had I been so vividly conscious of the flighty movements of attention. Someone behind me breathed out audibly—immediately my attention grabbed on to that event with the desperateness of an addict. A thought about business to be accomplished tomorrow, a fleeting memory of someone I had been sexually attracted to, a remembered snatch of music, a twinge in my left leg—no matter what it was that was arising in the field of my awareness, my attention went after it like a starving lion sinking its teeth into an antelope. And everything that was coming up was completely insignificant! It was all just mental garbage recycled, or else noticing of the most trifling happenings in the environment.

I saw with utmost clarity that attention didn't care at all whether an event was significant. It merely gravitated to stimulation of any kind. This clarity was an obvious Gift from Beloved Adi Da, for it had simply emerged in my awareness, without my going through any thought process about it at all. But the important lesson in all this was how automatically and persistently this distractedness caused my attention to be constantly moving away from Beloved Adi Da. The necessity of disciplining attention in order to remain in feeling-Contemplation* of Beloved Adi Da impressed me very deeply.

Once this point had been strongly made in me, I felt the next Gift being Given by Adi Da: Suddenly I could keep my attention directed to Him with much greater consistency and ease. But soon I felt a kind of nagging sensation that my effort to remain focused on Beloved Adi Da was somehow "off". A passage from Adi Da's Wisdom-Teaching came to mind:

Turn Your Heart-attention To Me, and Do Not Measure That Turning Relative To Whether Or Not Your mind Stops and You Feel Better. Love Me, and Do Not Measure That Loving Against Whether Or Not You Still Feel Negative emotions and Confusion. . . . Turn bodily To My Bodily (Human) Form. . . . And Do Not Measure That Giving, and That Turning, and That Feeling-Contemplation Against The Measure Of Whether Or Not You Feel pains in Your body. [The Dawn Horse Testament Of The Ruchira Buddha, chapter forty-five]

That was exactly what I was doing—measuring whether I felt better or not. It was a kind of rapid mental fluttering back and forth between giving my attention and feeling to Beloved Adi Da and then immediately taking stock of what I had gained by doing that. In other words, I was engaging the practice of devotional surrender to Adi Da as just another form of seeking for consolation. Beloved Adi Da had Given me a second important lesson at depth: self-surrendering, self-forgetting feeling-Contemplation of Him has nothing to do with evaluating, or even necessarily noticing, the Gifts one has received from Him. As He has said so many times, it is a matter of surrendering and forgetting oneself and remembering Him, not remembering oneself.

When that lesson had become clear, I found myself embroiled in a struggle. I was trying to fight against the "me" that was the seeker for consolation. I was trying to "push that 'me' out of the ring", so to speak—to defeat it by means of devotion to Adi Da Samraj. But I found that that "me" had a seemingly inexhaustible ability to spring back into action. And, in any case, it became increasingly clear that the effort to defeat the "bad me" was itself a form of seeking, just as the "bad me's" effort to feel good was a form of seeking. This was the third lesson I received from Beloved Adi Da: The effort of the ego to defeat itself leads nowhere.

Once again, a passage from Beloved Adi Da's Wisdom-Teaching struck me with great force:

My Attractiveness is the practice. Your heart-response to Me, and not your effort to be devoted to Me and surrender to Me, enables you to be self-surrendered and self-forgetting. [August 24, 1992]

Beloved Adi Da had brought me to the point where I was deeply impressed with the truth of this in my own experience. It had become obvious to me that true devotional surrender was at a greater depth of the being than the decision to combat the search for consolation. I felt an almost literal "sinking" occurring, into the depth of my true heart-Attraction to Beloved Adi Da. In that place of profound feeling, there was no longer any necessity to struggle in order to remain centered in Contemplation of Avatar Adi Da. Because Contemplation of Him opened my heart to the Love and Joy and Serenity that Beloved Adi Da Is, I was naturally moved to remain in that Contemplation. From time to time, I would feel the motion arise to become more superficial, but then, in the very noticing of this motion, I would be reminded of Beloved Adi Da's Supreme Attractiveness, and would simply fall back into feeling-Contemplation of Him.

I was flooded with love and gratitude for my Beloved Heart-Master. He had Shown me, in my own body-mind, what it means to truly resort to Him. And He had Granted me that supreme Joy of heart that (I know in my own experience) only comes from Him, whenever we are prepared to receive It. His Instruction in the essential process of the Way of the Heart had become a living, resonant Truth in me, through the Power of His Heart-Transmission. This was unquestionably the deepest moment of Instruction I had been Graced to receive from Him, for He had Communicated, with great detail and precision, directly to my heart. And all of this had taken place in the span of half an hour, with no words spoken, with my eyes closed. Speaking later with some of my friends who were also present at that gathering, it was amazing how similar our experiences of this silent Instruction had been. This occasion was truly extraordinary, and yet Beloved Adi Da has Granted this kind of Graceful wordless Instruction to great numbers of His devotees, in literally thousands of such silent occasions over the years.

Since that night, this direct Instruction has remained a beacon in my life of devotion to Adi Da Samraj, illuminating the way of truly self-surrendering and self-forgetting feeling-Contemplation of Him. It is indelibly clear in my being what the true practice of devotion to Beloved Adi Da is. It is simply a matter of responsibly returning to Beloved Adi Da's Attractiveness in each moment. ■

After a brief silence, Aniello speaks again.

ANIELLO: I noticed, as You said previously, My Lord, that in that long interval that we just had with each other, when my attention was on You and really feeling You, I didn't feel the self-contraction. Literally. And then, when I took my attention off You or it wandered or what-have-you, I would feel that self-contraction again.

MICHAEL: Lord, You just completely Live us. You Give us every Gift that could possibly be Given. A lot of this meditation occasion felt to me like the most sublime Instruction from You. And whenever the mind would give it a shape and reflect on it, it would be radiated by You and turned to You and then deepened and made more profound by You. And it's as if the capacity even to shape the mind around it was lost. And then You would just be Living us as this Mindless Embodiment that You Are.

When a thought would begin to arise again, it would be clarified and deepened and made more profound by Your Yoga, including all of us. I really love You. Thank You for all Your Gifts.

RODNEY GRISSO: Beloved, at one point I could see the Matrix of how You are connected to and through everyone. You are clearly at the Core. It's circular around You, but it also has lines associated with it as it goes out. I'm completely grateful for Your endless Grace, and You Give constant opportunity. You always Give the opportunity. It's never not Given. I completely love You.

Another period of silent meditation for a few minutes follows, then Thankfull Hastings speaks in a quiet voice.

THANKFULL HASTINGS: Beloved, You are Prior to mind and body. You are a Thoughtless Feeling. When we sit here in Your Company, sit in deepest Communion with You, all these faculties are simply recognized. And yet, when I'm not in Your Company or in Communion with You as deeply, somehow the patterns of the mind and of body begin to re-initiate themselves.

Suddenly, the deeply quiet room explodes with Adi Da's roar:

AVATAR ADI DA SAMRAJ: It's all horseshit!!!

Everyone laughs at the humor of this sudden explosion, but also in appreciation for the way Adi Da Samraj is blasting Thankfull's (and everyone's) willingness to settle for these patterns, at the expense of truly serious Spiritual practice. Then, suddenly switching back again to the mood of intense calm, Adi Da continues in a soft, slow, deep voice, pausing at times between sentences and phrases, and speaking with tremendous Transmission of Profundity.

AVATAR ADI DA SAMRAJ: They don't "begin to re-initiate themselves". You just change your asana* from one in which you are, in this present moment, established in the Yoga of self-surrendering, self-forgetting Communion with Me, to another moment in which you allow the body-mind to be set up in some conventional, busy, preoccupied, self-contracted fashion.

There's nothing mysterious about why it is so, however. It's not like it just sort of "comes over you". What is happening is you're simply not extending what you know to be the case into your psycho-physical domain of responsibility. You're allowing it to just go on and be a pattern, controlled by all kinds of forces.

You live peripherally, superficially—from the outside, at the outside. But everything works from the inside out. So you must accept principles in your life, upon this "consideration". Once having "considered" the matter, you must apply the principles of the Way. You must oblige the body-mind to be intelligently guided by your best understanding, instead of being a "something else" that sort of "comes over you" kind of thing.

If you have the faculty of discriminative intelligence as your own, then you're not just an infant, allowing your mother and father to handle everything—if you realize this is a dimension of your own functioning. Discriminative intelligence is in the captain's seat relative to all the other kinds of things (like sensations, concepts, and so on). So it's the senior dimension of your own participation of body-mind.

So, having "considered" what I have put to you, and having entered into your response to Me, you have to apply all of this intentionally. So, instead of getting up from this room after this gathering and walking outside and just getting in a whirl of preoccupation otherwise, and saying it just "came over you", you would (instead) know you must—and happily do so—embrace principles that have to do with the pattern of the body-mind.

You must be able to apply the will, having "considered" matters intelligently, examined your experience, and having agreed to observe all the discipline necessary for the real process of Communion with Me and Realization of Me.

Then, instead of just letting the body-mind pattern be whatever it is by tendency and so on, you would oblige it. And the fundamental way you would oblige it would be to always be functioning from the depth, from the inside out—having entered into that depth as a basis of your day. The meditation process is simply an opportunity to be set apart, step aside from all other matters and enter into this depth, even during the time of the waking-state hours. Not so that you can just have something happen to the body-mind when you happen to do that meditation-time, and then you get up and live an ordinary life. No. So that you can constantly remain in and ever-deepen this fundamental depth-position, from which you generate the whole process of self-surrendering, self-forgetting, and your response to Me.

The functional, practical, relational, and cultural disciplines of the Way of the Heart are about this conforming of the various aspects of the body-mind to the process and the condition at the depth, the depth-point of your existing here.

It's not so much "deep inside", whatever that would mean. But it is heart-process, heart-faith, heart-feeling, more and more open, going more and more beyond all limitations on feeling.

You know what I mean when I say that that is a "deepening" process? *[Devotees murmur assent.]* You can feel what that means, mm?

THANKFULL: It feels as though it's Prior and Senior to attention, even. It guides attention, or informs attention.

AVATAR ADI DA SAMRAJ: Its Realization is Ultimately beyond attention, but the practice in its foundation (and generally speaking) is this Yoga of the four faculties. "Invoke Me, feel Me, breathe Me, serve Me"[15] suggests those faculties. And so, in every moment, there is this devotion of the faculties to Me. Mind (or attention, which is the root of mind) is fitted to a Yoga, moment to moment, which is a <u>discipline</u>, a pattern (in other words), an asana, to which you oblige the body-mind, by which you control it (in the most positive sense), rather than allowing it to be sheerly a pattern without integrity, without ultimacy. And so with the other faculties—emotion, breath, and body.

You must embrace the culture of this Way of life with real discipline of the body-mind. If you do this, then you are responsible for the asana, or attitude, of the body-mind in every moment. And the reason you enter into meditation and puja the <u>first</u> thing every day is because that confirms that this <u>is</u> the fundamental position for any activity in the waking state. That is the basis for it. So the right asana throughout the day is this asana of practicing in the depth-position, not losing it. The moment to moment practice is constantly allowing it to flower, and so on.

15. Avatar Adi Da has said that His fundamental Admonition to all is: "Invoke Me, Feel Me, Breathe Me, Serve Me." These four actions account for the surrender of the four principal faculties of the body-mind to Him. By Invoking Adi Da, the faculty of mind (or attention) is surrendered. By feeling Him, the faculty of emotion is surrendered. By breathing Him, the faculty of breath is surrendered. And by serving Him, the faculty of body is surrendered. This four-part practice is given to all who resort to Adi Da Samraj as Spiritual Master.

The Four Faculties of the Body-Mind

The Way that Avatar Adi Da Samraj has Given to His devotees has many aspects of discipline, but the primary responsibility of all who resort to Him as Spiritual Master is Ruchira Buddha Bhakti Yoga—the practice (Yoga) of devotion (bhakti) to the Ruchira Buddha, Avatar Adi Da Samraj. Though this practice is completely a matter of magnifying the heart-response to Beloved Adi Da's Divine Attractiveness, Avatar Adi Da has given a technical description of how the body-mind is to be surrendered.

Beloved Adi Da Reveals that the body-mind consists of "four faculties": body, emotion, mind, and breath. When practicing Ruchira Buddha Bhakti Yoga, one surrenders these faculties directly to Avatar Adi Da, rather than struggling to change or give up any state or difficulty that is arising in any of these areas. Beloved Adi Da explains how this works:

AVATAR ADI DA SAMRAJ: The four faculties of the body-mind account for all of your functions. If any one or a combination of them is not surrendered to Me, not brought into Communion with Me, they revert to the domain of egoity, the games of egoity, and, therefore, the content of egoity. If you submit to Me these four functions that are at the root of all aspects of human existence, then the ego-game is canceled, it is forgotten, it is not indulged in, it is not reinforced. Therefore, remember that these are the four functions whereby you surrender the body-mind to Me. They cover everything. (January 27, 1994)

There is no well-being, no integrity of being, without handling this fundamental business of being really, and most fully, or otherwise at least significantly, functioning in and working at the in-depth level of your existence.

The body-mind itself will automatically go into patterns it has inherited. It is there as a complex habit, stimulated by all kinds of experiences (and so on) that might arise. So, without the exercise of discriminative intelligence, really "considering" matters, and the feeling-disposition in depth, truly sensitive to matters, and feeling altogether, then the body-mind loses its connection and its right pattern of association with the Source.

Self-discipline is an aspect of "conductivity"—the functional, practical, and relational disciplines are a part of "conductivity" discipline. In other words, it is simply the right pattern, the Pleasure Dome pattern of Yogic integrity. It's the pattern of well-being, and of Realization. But you have to build this in to the event, which means you must be able to exercise this feeling-sensitivity and this discriminative intelligence. You must be able to exercise it as a force of will and essentially release it into the responsive self-surrender of Communion with Me, maintaining the depth, the Yoga of depth, moment to moment—but, in all of that, simply and directly being able to direct the body-mind into a right pattern, the pattern of depth, the structure of energy, of well-being, and Yoga altogether.

So you must come from that depth-position of meditation and puja before entering into activities in the waking state, and remain in the asana of that depth from the time of meditation and puja. Maintain that heart-asana, and discipline the body-mind, functionally, practically, relationally, in all the modes of culture I've Given you.

This devotional Yoga, Ruchira Buddha Bhakti Yoga, is moment to moment. Fundamentally, it's a matter of exercising it profoundly in this set-apart time of meditation and puja, and then, through random, artful practice moment to moment, constantly refresh it, preserve it. All of this is to conform the body-mind to the Source-Purpose, the in-depth Condition.

That basic discipline covers all aspects of the body-mind—functionally, practically, relationally, socially, culturally. So that is the pattern of your response to Me. It is the foundation Yoga of organizing your life in terms of its in-depth principle, and growing this depth, profoundly growing in it, because you do not <u>want</u> to suffer. Truly, you are not sympathetic with suffering. You are not sympathetic with suffering in anyone else, you are not sympathetic with suffering altogether. But if you are in a superficial position of experiencing, then you are simply part of the mechanics of suffering, the pattern of suffering, random events.

The Way of Happiness is the Way in the Depth, and not in the merely outward-directed possibilities of the body-mind. And, having established this foundation, the first thing you must realize is the key to unlocking this depth, or being opened deeply: listening to the point of hearing.

Adi Da begins gradually to speak at a more usual speed, but still in a soft, deep voice.

AVATAR ADI DA SAMRAJ: True hearing, or most fundamental self-understanding, is responsible at the point of the self-contraction itself. It's not like you describe it as you feel the self-contraction somewhere in your body, or whatever, as if it's somewhere "off there in the body-mind" kind of thing. Hearing, most fundamental self-understanding, is associated with being <u>in</u> the position of the self-contraction itself. <u>You</u> are <u>doing</u> it. It's not merely happening to you, it's not somewhere else—you are in the position <u>of</u> it. It's this discovery of this primitive action that is constantly taking

Listening, Hearing, and Seeing

"Listening", "hearing", and "seeing" are specific terms used by Avatar Adi Da Samraj for different stages of understanding and realization in the progress of practice of the Way of the Heart.

◆ ◆ ◆

AVATAR ADI DA SAMRAJ: The usual man or woman is in motion toward objects, unaware of the motivating contraction. Therefore, the usual man or woman is full of desires, motivations, impulses, attractions, attachments, strategies, and so on. This is what there is to observe. "Listening" is about observing this about yourself in the process of the unique Yoga of Ruchira Buddha Bhakti, until you discover the motivating source, the self-contraction itself, which is common to every motive, every desire, every attachment, every search. When this discovery is grasped, then that is most fundamental self-understanding, and in that understanding there is the capability in every moment to notice and feel beyond the self-contraction. This is the unique capability that is the sign of true "hearing". [December 4, 1992]

◆ ◆ ◆

AVATAR ADI DA SAMRAJ: After true hearing, the next Great Grace My devotee is Given by Me is the Grace of true seeing. True seeing is the profound heart-capability for full, and truly Spiritually Awakened, and truly Spiritually receptive, and truly Spiritually responsive, and truly Spiritually responsible . . . Communion with Me. [I Am (My Self) What you Require]

◆ ◆ ◆

place, moment to moment, that is true hearing. And it is a profound and unique discovery. It clarifies the whole matter of seeking and is a basis for transcending the errors in the further developing stages of life. It's the means at the center, or the means at the depth, the heart-means.

This hearing capability is profoundly important. It is a matter of being able to present the body-mind in this Yogic manner of Ruchira Buddha Bhakti. The hearing exercise is the ability to unlock the depth, to unlock the self contraction, so that egoity is not the basis for the Spiritual process, because egoic limitations can be gone beyond directly.

You must live not only in-depth, but, in due course, you must live in the Spiritual Domain of Reality, the Spiritual Depth of Reality—ultimately, in the Transcendental Depth, and, most ultimately, in the Divine Depth, the Infinitely Expanded, Boundless Depth.[16] Everything else is self-contraction, which makes you a seeker, or someone dis-eased, disturbed.

The people who decide this depth and the Ultimate Realization in that Domain is important then vow to that, and do all that's required to conform their lives to it, as a process, and, Ultimately, as a Realization. It's not a matter of "stepping outside of the world", so-called. It can be done in a more secluded circumstance, in a renunciate community, what-ever, that is secluded. But that's not necessary. Generally speaking, it's not to be the case. But, rather, it is to embrace the practice, the Way, the culture of this depth, and all the disciplines that that requires moment to moment, and in your circumstance of life and service and so on.

To accept life as an in-depth process and not merely a superficial functional one is a way of describing, or characterizing, the sadhana of the Way of the Heart.

JAMES STEINBERG: Beloved, You say "in-depth", and the other night You were using the word "profundity". It feels to me that You are refer-ring directly to the process in relationship to You.

AVATAR ADI DA SAMRAJ: Yes, Ruchira Buddha Bhakti Yoga. That elabo-rated via the forms of the "conscious process" and "conductivity", as they are in your case. But always implementing the four-part fundamental Yoga.

JAMES: Well, Beloved, as each level of the four faculties is surrendered, it seems that that is the location that the gesture of resort to You is made.

16. Avatar Adi Da uses the terms "Spiritual", "Transcendental", and "Divine" in reference to different dimensions of Reality that are Realized progressively in the Way of the Heart. "Spiritual" refers to the reception of the Spirit-Force (in the context of the "advanced" fourth stage of life and the fifth stage of life); "Transcendental" refers to the Realization of Consciousness Itself as separate from the world (in the context of the sixth stage of life); and "Divine" refers to the Most Perfect Realization of Consciousness Itself as utterly non-separate from the world (in the context of the seventh stage of life).

AVATAR ADI DA SAMRAJ: Well, you can see how, if you put your attention on any of the faculties, they seem like something different than the other faculties—after you've worked on that one, you have to cover one of the others. That's not the Yoga I am talking about. It is a practice in which you effectively make use of, or exercise, all of those faculties simultaneously in the simple process of responsive feeling-Contemplation of Me.

In any moment, all four of the faculties are to be exercised simultaneously in response to Me. It is not a matter of working on any one. If you are working on any one of these faculties, you are not practicing the surrender and forgetting of it. And you are not practicing the surrender and forgetting of anything if you are trying not to remember it. On occasion I have said, "Don't think of a white gorilla. You can think of anything for the next five minutes, but you can't think of a white gorilla." You would find it impossible.

So it is not a matter of not doing something in an intentional way, in that sense, but of responding to Me and entering into that most profoundly, all the faculties moved, surrendered, forgotten, in this feeling-Contemplation. It is a process of entering into depth. And functional, practical, relational, and cultural discipline of the body-mind is an ongoing process under all kinds of circumstances throughout each day. This is the way your activity is reflected to yourself, such that you generate self-understanding in the process of this self-surrendering devotion.

This process otherwise conforms the body-mind to a law or an integrity that you can feel when you are established in this depth-feeling-position, no longer in conflict. Then you can feel what the integrity of the body-mind is all about, what its structure is, what its basis is, and so forth. There are the most profound moments of this exercise, and in all the other moments of whatever you are up to, you must bring the principles from that depth-Yoga into the circumstance of life, moment to moment.

Of course, to do this, you have to have some significant maturity. You can learn about it, you can do it to some degree, you can become educated about it and so forth, but at some point all the faculties of the body-mind have to become obvious to you as being your responsibility. And discriminative intelligence exercised through the will has to become clear to you as being fundamental to your life, instead of you just being sort of jiggly meat, patterns of thought and sensation and amusement.

This is principal human education—to bring people to that point, serve people in their coming from infancy and growing up, until they are all rightly equipped along these lines and know it is their responsibility, create even a kind of ceremony or acknowledgement of it, if you like, make a culturally formal rite of passage out of it.

JAMES: In the Way of the Heart, would that generally be age twenty-one where one would achieve that kind of responsibility for will and discriminative intelligence?

AVATAR ADI DA SAMRAJ: Well, it is not that that person is without it even earlier on. It is a faculty that can be exercised. It generally doesn't enter much into the picture for a while. The mother and father take it on and then gradually are supposed to relax it, giving the developing individual the ability to functionally be responsible in that sphere and so on.

So discriminative intelligence can be, and should be, exercised early on. But it must be associated with all aspects of the human first-three-stages-of-life characteristics, the capability for a responsible discipline of the body-mind based on having located the way of depth-existence.

You Must Change Your Life-Pattern

AVATAR ADI DA SAMRAJ: There are two aspects to your personality that must be integrated. You must integrate your discriminative persona with your active-life persona. The two personas must actually come together. In other words, you must bring the force of a disciplined life into being. Without the discriminative process informing your life, it is not possible for you to function as My devotee, or even to function as a responsible human being altogether.

The higher (or discriminative) intelligence "looks at" the ordinary, lower (or social, or life-active) persona. That social persona is the pattern that must be intentionally changed. The pattern must be changed through discriminative intelligence with a will.

The will must connect the intelligence to the life. Then the life is based on great principles.

If you do not enact a discriminative pattern, you inevitably revert to childish and adolescent modes. Then you act in life as an unresolved teenager, who is double-minded and childishly dependent on the one hand, and a cynical adolescent on the other hand.

You cannot merely talk about principles of rightness. You must actually <u>do</u> something.

Change the pattern or motion in which you otherwise automatically exist. Don't allow life to just go on. Don't allow habitual and inherited patterns to rule you. Be ruled by My Pattern. *[December 4, 1996]*

When you were children, your parents had the role of discriminative intelligence—all that that must do for your safety and well-being and right upbringing and right education, all the rest of it. You're not supposed to exercise this particular faculty. You're not expected to exercise it profoundly. You're supposed to grow in other ways. As a child, you're supposed to be a dependent, and allow these kind of faculties to be exercised by the parents. But, in due course, it's supposed to be passed on to you. It's now your responsibility, now that you've been served relative to it.

But if that isn't done, fully acknowledged, straightforward, in a social order—instead of the chaos of the way things are, generally speaking, at the present—there's no real cultural understanding of this process.

It's a split, you see. If you're not really given permission to then take on this faculty and really "consider" the matters of Truth and all the rest, and what you can do, then at some point you're going to start doing something like it, or you're going to start getting hip to something about it, but you're going to be having a secret life about it—your secret world of mind-development, your secret interests, fantasies and notions about this, that, and the other thing, reading that you do about this, that, and the other thing, and imaginings about it, or would-be about it, or hope someday to do it—all that kind of interior life and so on. But then when you're having so-called "intelligent" conversations with people, all of a sudden you're that intelligent guy. *[laughter]* You know? Very serious, very alert, very discriminating, and so forth. But that's not the guy you just say "howdy" to on the street or meet in the daily-life circumstances, other than in this really serious, "we agree now this is a serious moment of conversation" kind of circumstance of life.

This is quite typical, as a matter of fact, of how people develop these days. They never feel they really have a right to not be a child anymore, and to fully exercise their discriminative intelligence and really get down to the Truth matter and so many matters altogether. And not just to exercise the mind, but connect it to the will.

In other words, the fundamental purpose of this is life-examination, life-review, examination of whatever matters for which you might be responsible, or experience, in daily life. You're supposed to be able to examine things intelligently, but then, having come to a conclusion about it, you should simply make the decision to do such and such. To not be able to do that is a great impediment. That's the sign of somebody who has not developed a connection between the exercise of intelligence, intelligent-mindedness, and the will—which then associates with bodily fulfillment of intention. He or she doesn't really do much of that. Such a person just sort of goes with the flow relative to their habitual outer-life.

82

That person doesn't feel free to really get down to figuring things out altogether. So intelligent life never gets connected with the world, never gets connected with making life-changes. If you lack that, you are intelligent enough when matters are discussed with you seriously, but there's no evidence of it whatsoever in your life otherwise, other than in conversation with you. I'm not speaking about anybody here in particular. It's just true of human beings.

JAMES: Beloved, is it the connection between the will and the discriminative intelligence that is lacking, or is it just the will?

AVATAR ADI DA SAMRAJ: The connection between them. Intelligence making decisions based on review of things, and exercising that intention based on that "consideration" is the will to having it be such and such. It's a clear, straightforward intention. It doesn't have to be bombastic at all, but just clear, straightforward. You "consider", you decide, you change. That's it.

ANTONINA RANDAZZO: Isn't that because there's a strong heart-motive to actually do that? And when your heart really speaks, you are moved by that?

AVATAR ADI DA SAMRAJ: Well, certainly in the profundities of religious life. But generally speaking, this must be the case in the world, under all circumstances, exercised by anyone at all. Discriminative intelligence with a will is just a mechanism that has to be made effective. It's required of a relatively independent, functioning adult life. It has to be able to be freely exercised. It's got to be able to be profoundly exercised. People need to find profound association in their lives, not just be content with superficiality, conventionality, social-personality appearances, and so forth. Nothing great.

MICHAEL: Beloved, it seems that for intelligence to really be discriminative intelligence, it would be founded in something deeper than a particle of the mind or body. It seems like You Attract us from the beginning.

AVATAR ADI DA SAMRAJ: It's a heart-attraction. It's an event in the heart, an opening, a heart-opening. Yes. Spontaneous. So it is a feeling-matter. That means it is also an energy-matter. It's a sensitivity at a subtler feeling and energy level, that's not especially verbal altogether, but which also has things you could verbalize about, as people do, of course.

BETH KANTOR: Beloved, You have spoken about how tangible the feeling of You is. I could feel some kind of progression over this past year— the feeling of You becoming more and more tangible, without any doubt.

AVATAR ADI DA SAMRAJ: Mm. That's good.

BETH: And something about it reminds me of the very first time I ever saw You. It wasn't face to face, it was in the film, *A Difficult Man.* It was the first time in my life I ever had the feeling of no doubt. And I knew that You were My Master.

AVATAR ADI DA SAMRAJ: Mm. Tcha.

BETH: It changed my life. I literally felt I had been looking for You my whole life. And I felt I recognized You instantly. But since then I have doubted it at times.

AVATAR ADI DA SAMRAJ: *[chuckles slightly]* That's an example of what I was talking about here earlier, about how your feeling and discriminative intelligence "considers" a matter, comes to a conclusion, and that's flat, but there's not necessarily any connection between that and changing what you do. The will connecting this intelligent and feeling disposition to the rest of the body-mind, doesn't happen.

So what do you do, then?

BETH: Well, I can feel when one is applying discriminative intelligence and the will then it seems like the Gift of self-understanding would come of that.

AVATAR ADI DA SAMRAJ: Yes, well, all that is, in other words, is con-senting to <u>live</u> intelligently and based on your feeling-sense of Reality and so forth, allowing yourself to be responsive.

Yes, you can seek and seek and seek and seek, and then, instead of seeking, you've found it—found whatever it is, or come to whatever the resolution is—and then you don't do anything further with it. You don't allow it to be transformative. That's another mode of seeking. So, if you "consider" it, what is the point of turning your finding into another form of seeking? What's there to resist about the profound process of being transformed?

So you must, with an intelligent will, oblige the body-mind to live the pattern, the design, that you, in your best understanding, intend for it. Because if you do not do this actively, the body-mind will simply persist in habitual patterns and reactions to events, and become more and more the effect of all of that, wound up in all of that, without any depth at all.

The self-contraction isn't happening to you, and things don't just "come over you"—someone was suggesting that. This is the common language people use about these things because they don't presume a culture of responsibility for these processes.

Fear is self-contraction. Fear is the primal mood of it, the mood that's inherent in self-contraction. Fear is not just the twisting of some muscles in your body. It is the primal act of differentiation, separation. Vulnerability, therefore, is inherent in the gesture.

So, then you get profoundly interested in yourself. Western civilization in particular, for about the last 500 years or so, has been more and more generating a society, a culture, and so forth, based on the human animal as an individual entity. Everything focused on that one, and yet no great depth. There's been more and more a focus on this fleshy manifested mortal consciousness, as a separate individual, all-the-while-competing kind of personality.

So people quite naturally think about themselves, are very concerned about themselves, and so forth. It's an age in which to do such a thing— as if that which is to be discovered is within you, that you yourself (as this separate entity, personality, and so forth) have in you a depth that is you yourself as a separate entity, but that is completely all things required.

But That Which is to be Realized is not within you. It is That within Which everything you call "you" is arising. It is the Source. It is in the Perfectly Subjective Position, the Self-Position. But that doesn't mean that It is a self, or that it is this independent, separate person that you're concerned about. You must be given up from your own position into the Source.

I am Calling you to Realize Me, which is to Realize My own Nature, Condition, State, Person. That is not merely "in" you. It's a matter of the surrender and transcendence of this separate self and this gesture of separation. It is the Realization of that Self-Condition That is True of all and All, of every thing, every one—this One Condition.

CHAPTER SIX

The Look of Blessing

BY JAMES STEINBERG

*I*n 1989, James Steinberg was living at Ruchira Buddha Dham, Avatar Adi Da's Hermitage Sanctuary in Fiji. The following Leela is taken from a diary entry that James wrote shortly after an occasion of formal Darshan, or sighting, of Adi Da Samraj in January 1989.

JAMES STEINBERG: Beloved Adi Da sat before us in blue briefs only, on an outdoor reclining chair. He was Gazing at each person who approached Him. It was three o'clock or so and it was sunny and hot. One of the Quandra Mai was on the back of the porch and another was seated in front, fanning Bhagavan Adi Da with a white fan. A basket of Prasad (in the form of baked sweets) and a bowl of water stood on a low table at His right side.

There were twenty of us facing Him. One by one we went forward to His Feet and offered our gifts of flowers or fruit, representing the surrender of the egoic self. Then each of us took a seat on the small porch, until there was no more room, and two people sat on the front steps. One woman was unabashedly crying, and many others were shaking with the force of His Blessing Presence. We were all broken-hearted. And then, after about ten minutes, Bhagavan Adi Da walked down the row and in Supreme Blessing Gave each devotee Prasad.* As I write, I feel I am still in front of Him receiving His Blessing. There is an indescribable Bliss still filling my body and Embracing me.

Then He walked into the house.

I cannot fathom the Look He had on His Face. It is unbelievable, that

Ruchira Buddha Dham, 1989

Look of Blessing. I have seen something about this kind of look described in the traditions as the "tortoise glance of the Guru". It is said that the mother tortoise does not approach her children, but nourishes them from a distance with the compassion of her look alone, a look of incredible love that fills and sustains and uplifts. Beloved Adi Da gave such a Look today. I am crying as I write, remembering that Look. I can only say that that Look <u>is</u> the Guru-devotee tradition—it is the Blessing of the God-Man.

I have read thousands of pages on the Guru-devotee relationship and it is all useful up to a point. But it is the heart-response to that gaze that is the essence of all existence. Traditionally, time and more time was spent trying to receive that Look, to find one who could give it, and to be accepted by that one. It is here in Avatar Adi Da Samraj.

It is God's Darshan. The mere sight of the face of Adi Da is enough. Everything is given in that Glance. It is beyond words. It is a Revelation. It is the Divine.

I will never forget that Look. That Vision of such vulnerability, such fullness of the Divine. I will never forget the Blessing of His Gaze. My life is His.

The Mountain Of Attention, 1997

CHAPTER SEVEN

December 6, 1996

The Realm of Opposites Is Not User-Friendly

D uring the time of these gatherings, Adi Da Samraj would sometimes
have daytime meetings with a small number of the devotees in the
gathering group, generally in order to discuss more practical matters
relating to His Work and the community of His devotees. In such a small
meeting on December 6, the discussion turns to the state of the world in
general, which Adi Da describes in sobering and unvarnished terms.

AVATAR ADI DA SAMRAJ: Scientific materialism wants to look like it's
friendly to mankind in its infinite expansion and so forth, but it's talking
about everything just being a mortal moment, including any human individual. It's a dark propaganda that's giving all these supposed "light"
messages to everyone, but its real message is "mortality, materialism". It
reduces everything to this view, so it eliminates the basis for everything
that exists that you could call "cultural". Because if there's nothing but
momentary blobs of molecular accidents, then what <u>difference</u> does anything make? There's no basis for any structure of rightness. Why should
anybody care about anything, in that case?

Humankind is self-destructing. It is so distressed, so disturbed, even
in its psyche, that its fundamental integrity has been lost. It's so disturbed
that its highest message to everyone is: "Everything is just chaotic, ran-
domly appearing, temporary bundles of molecules. And that's all it is.
There's nothing going on as Grace. It's just this." This is the highest communication of the day. This is the highest expression of philosophy. This
is what persuades people, anyway.

It's a strange philosophy for everyone to be attached to, as well. Why should it be the preferred philosophy? Of all the philosophies, it's the one that allows the least hope relative to any matter whatsoever! If it were so— well, that's that, that's the way it is. But why should one hope that it is the one that turns out to be so? Why should one so much want it to be so that one is moved to presently affirm that it's already so, even though you haven't really found out that it's so yet? Why are some people so intent on this being so? Rather than just willing to have it be that way or whatever the way it is, but here just to find out the way it really is, and not anything other than that.

The common presumption now is this "everybody is just a competitive blob" senseless nonsense, with a little bit of religiosity thrown on top of it that's basically just about somehow giving authority to public morality. That's the basic function of conventional religion. That's why some aspects of religion are tolerated, because the political system, which is based on scientific materialism, knows it doesn't have anything within its creed that suggests that any kind of public morality is of any use whatsoever, except as a way of making sure that everybody else is somehow not going to bother you.

On the one hand, you've got this "everything is just material lumps slamming against one another" message from the philosophers, the scientific materialists. And, on the other hand, from the people who are concerned about keeping some sort of order, you get all these messages telling you that—even though everything is just materialistic, everything is just about temporary molecular groupings, when you're dead you're dead— somehow or other there's a holy source that tells you to be a nice guy.

The philosophy tells you everything is blobs, and you've got blobs telling you that you have some sacred responsibility to be a nice guy! [Beloved Adi Da laughs.] It's crazy. It's all the product of a social/cultural event that is self-involved to the point of having become self-destructive. It came to the point of feeling that there isn't anything else but this "you" that's nothing more than a molecular blob. Apart from game-playing, everybody feels that everything is meaningless, mortal emptiness, just jiggling around, everybody trying to have their moment of feeling really wealthy and having everything they want, all their desires fulfilled.

It's not enough to try to believe some "big thing", either, when you've got a fundamental message that "there's nothing but molecules" that sounds very, very convincing. Because you're all kinds of set up in your patterning to accept that message at face value as being authentic, right on. You don't really take the time to discriminatively examine it. You're being propagandized, pulled by the nose. You've become couch potatoes.

Human culture in the present is a conversation and a look that is based on having no connection to fundamental Unity and to the Source of that and all within It. It's not true that there are just molecular blobs. There's a level of molecular blobness, no doubt, but there's an immense process that includes far more than is talked about in this materialistic language.

Generally speaking, this is a society that has lost its culture. It has lost its reason. It has lost fundamental dispositions of tolerance and cooperation and so forth. If anything is sacred, it's certainly that kind of behavior—respect in the world, and not just self-generated, competitive hardball about everything. Not self-destruction at all, but willing to grow, become right.

At any rate, the world will be whatever it is. There's not a lot that can be expected in that big picture without a real fundamental change taking place. It's to be seen.

In another sense, it's not any worse than it ever has been. It changes, but it never gets better. There's always some place where it's worse than it is anywhere else, and looks worse than anything that's ever been. In terms of the psychological impact of all of this, it's been just as "worse", so to speak, for people in other times, too. I mean, it's one thing to wake up as a predator, a lion (or something) with few natural enemies. It's another thing to wake up as a deer who's in the natural world treated as nothing much more than a fruit hanging out of a tree to be nibbled or taken directly without the slightest concern.

There have been all kinds of approaches to the pursuit of integrity relative to human experience—rightness, Happiness, and so forth. And a lot of blah-blah about it, because there's more blah-blah than there is will that actually makes change, or response that actually makes change.

Your response to Me is how you change. I talked to you about the will last evening. Well, yes, it's the will, but it's not this bearing-down thing merely. It's more like the body-mind responds to your intelligent disposition, which is the core of the whole body-mind anyway. It just sort of falls in line with you very sympathetically. It's that kind of will where all you do is find when the pattern is right, and then that's it. You resonate with it. You make changes readily from the core position, or the interior of the pattern. Therefore, from the inside out, you manifest a change in your structuring that corresponds to your heart-and-mind integrity and significant depth.

Now, when you begin to function in that depth, you're also beginning to locate the direct experience of the inherent Unity of conditional existence, and, beyond that, its Source-Condition. You are reconnecting, in other words, with what should be built in culturally to humankind. In the past, under certain circumstances, there's been at least a significant amount of that. Everywhere there's been something or other of it. Nonetheless, its principal manifestations are the people who entered into it <u>most</u> <u>profoundly</u>, and generated signs of transformation and Realization and Wisdom that <u>were</u> signs of a kind of fundamental resolution toward which mankind aspired, with which it could associate, or which it could adapt to, and so on.

Instead of the chaos, a structure (that therefore had authority), or a pattern (that had integrity), was assumed by everyone—somehow communicated to everyone and therefore assumed. And people functioned on that basis, which included many planes. It wasn't just material. It included the world of the psyche, that which is mysterious. Overall, it included the Divine, and so on. Every place had its different notions of it all, but a sacred order of some kind was always the pattern presumed—order began to appear among human beings.

You don't have it as your obligation, or your opportunity particularly, to change the big picture of how the world is going. You <u>can</u> establish integrity in your own life and real practice, and within your sphere of associations, relations, be communicating that sign and disposition, good—so that's how you can serve it. Very few are in a position to even <u>speak</u> to the world about a change of view, a change of action, and so on. Most people aren't in a position where that's what they're up to, beyond their influence among those that they know directly.

So the senior obligation of everyone is the work at the depth-level, and not the working for utopia in the world-level. There's no reason to be a naive utopianist in your virtuous beliefs and so forth. That's itself a sign of a kind of unresolved personality, disturbed personality.

You all are still there in the laundry room, thumping away and considering your design and how to perfect your situation, how even perhaps to get out of <u>being</u> a washing machine altogether. And becoming a perfume bottle, perhaps, or a pair of reeeally groovy shoes! Become something entirely different than a washing machine.

The washing machine is not interesting. Even a pair of shoes is plugged into some mysteriousness about the source of it. So what's interesting is, "What's on the end of that line? What's on the other side of that wall? What's the Source of this jiggling around here?" And the nature of that Source is a great mystery.

It's not "other". It's not separate "you".

It is <u>Only</u> Me. It is just One.

It's comprehending Reality, becoming sane about the nature of Reality.

It's religion—true religion.

What you think Reality is presently is making you nuts. So it's obviously not it yet. You haven't found the correct view. You're suffering from "wrong views", as is said in the Buddhist tradition. Your entire society, world-society, is based on wrong views. It's not that everything in its view is wrong—as a structure, it's driving people crazy.

There <u>has</u> to be order and authority, but not in a negative sense, not in a despotic sense. There has to be more than just "everybody is a separate little entity of jiggly meat making absolute decisions about everything and being corrupted by it". That's the world, the experience, in which you all are participating.

The Way of the Heart is itself done by people in a reality-circumstance in those terms. So, yes, in your living in this world, that's the kind of world-experience you're having. You must practice the Way under those circumstances, and deal with the limitations you suffer in yourself that are based on adaptation to that pattern, the world-pattern.

But the Way itself is not about being political. It transforms your own disposition, if you allow it to be so, allow the body-mind to be sympathetic with your heart and understanding. It's not a matter, then, of becoming political in some grand or obsessive sense, or whatever. You'll be positive in your domain of influences, but, fundamentally, you'll be working in the depth-position, working at that level, and not becoming distorted by association with the world (however it may appear), or by your own play with those you do know. You don't become distorted or made superficial by that. You persist in that process that alone grants integrity to your life. And that's this in-depth process of real devotion, meditation, service, self-discipline, always moving into a greater depth of surrender, self-forgetting Communion with What is Prior to seeking and Prior to self-contraction.

Whatever it may look like, the human world <u>is</u> the play of opposites—that's it. It's klik-klak. It's opposites being extremely separate from one another. It's opposites in a kind of unity combined with one another into something that for the moment is a single something, and then it changes, and so forth, eventually separates out again. So it's this constant klik-klak. It is a yin-yang kind of design.

Klik-Klak: The Pattern Patterning

There is nothing permanent in the realm of conditional existence. If you examine your experience, even of your own consciousness, it is never exactly the same as it was the moment before—there is a constant shifting in time and space. In the conditional world, there is only a complex of ever-shifting and repeating "patterns", like a perpetual motion machine. Avatar Adi Da Samraj created the term "klik-klak" (and the phrase "pattern patterning") to describe this incessant change—playing on the "sounds" of the workings of the "machine" of conditional Nature. Klik-klak also represents the philosophy of "everything is only matter" that is the doctrine of scientific materialism. Everything is presumed to be "klik-klak", just "stuff", with no greater Truth or Reality. When you look at the world, you see only klik-klak. It is only by transcending klik-klak, not merely going along with the patterns of existence, that true religion, and real practice of the Way of the Heart, can begin.

AVATAR ADI DA SAMRAJ: There is never any permanent object, any permanent complex of objects, any permanent pattern, in time and space. You find no permanence, just "klik-klak", just replication and shift—and many different kinds of apparent timings and so forth.

All That is Attractive, All That is Beautiful, All That is Full, All That is Satisfactory, All That is Constant (not threatened), All That is Love-Bliss, All That is Radiant, is Always Already the Case. It is presumed to be in klik-klak. But that is a false superimposition of the Feeling of your own Nature, an illusion generated by the heart not noticing its own Nature but projecting itself into the domain of changes.

Understand this, notice this. Then the illusion of "Narcissus",* and all the search built on it, disappears. [January 31, 1996]

But the true play of religion is in the Zone of Freedom, which (if you enter into it rightly) makes it possible to transcend the obvious limitations, or limiting power, of gross-mindedness. It is beyond Spiritual in the usual sense. It is Transcendentally Spiritual (and, ultimately, Divinely Spiritual) Reality. The Way of that Reality is the Way of the Heart, the Way of this devotional Yoga that you have to practice moment to moment, the very means of being free of being merely patterned by the play of opposites, just pattern patterning, just like in your laptop computer. It's all pluses and minuses, and the ones and the zeroes, whatever—just endless permutations of that. It doesn't have to mean anything. It's just a structure, repeating itself, revolving on itself.

So mere structure is just that, but that's not the end of reality, because that mere structure is associated with patterns and dimensions more profound. And, by being submitted into that structure and its Source-Condition, you become sane, even in the context of being still associated with human existence, because the thing that is disturbing has been found out about, has been understood, it's been gone beyond. And, once you realize this, at any level, you have a base, a seed, at the root, from which to grow in this process of transformation and Realization.

This realm of opposites happening, patterning, is not exactly user-friendly. You have to be very intelligently involved with it and so forth, because it's not really friendly to anything. And any pattern that has appeared will readily be destroyed by the system itself, if it gets out of joint somehow and has to be replaced. It's indifferent to every thing, every one. Any pattern that has been created already can be replaced. And as soon as it gets out of whack a little bit, it starts getting eroded and washed away. Something else happens—chaos, more chaos, and then maybe some other unity. The various resolutions possible in a paired reality that just keeps multiplying its paired variations, sometimes becoming more complex and overwhelmingly so, and sometimes becoming more simplified and apparently unified.

The play of variations on the opposites is what's happening, and it's message is not "Boy, howdy, welcome here, because this is the place of paradise". No, it's more like My Mama expression: "Your objections to anything don't mean shit!"—as long as you understand that that's where you are. If you do understand that, then it's not enough to just be washed along with the plastic of smiling mortality, propagandized into being just a unit on everybody's computer screen, showing, as in a Disney film, all the appropriate, good-natured expressions.

Klik-klak by itself is not just going to produce paradise. It's not about paradise. It's about change. It's not about anything becoming fixed, although things can sometimes be made better. But more than making things better, there is a central, fundamental, most profound requirement that gives integrity to everything, and that's the work at the center, the work in the depth domain, beyond the self-contraction. And if there is this, and people function from the inside out, then they will also, within a right culture of this responsibility, sympathetically transform, or allow the transformation of, their behaviors, their manner, their structures of relating to one another, and so on.

The fundamental matter is not mere social change and so on. The fundamental work is the core. It is truly religious, and (in due course) truly Spiritual—ultimately, Divine.

CHAPTER EIGHT

Look the Fire in the Eye

BY BEN FUGITT

During the summer of 1979, I was a caretaker at the Mountain Of Attention Sanctuary. It had been a very hot summer with a number of forest fires in the surrounding country. On this particular day in September I noticed a small tuft of smoke down the canyon. It looked like it was very close to our property. I immediately ran to the nearest car and raced down the canyon. A fire could be seen going up over a ridge to the northwest. This was an ominous location, practically inaccessible to fire-fighting equipment due to the rough terrain. It was also in a direct line with the outer Sanctuary. Seeing that the Sanctuary was threatened by this already out-of-control fire, I jumped into the car and raced back.

I had the fire department notified, then ran out to the back of the Sanctuary where I had sent a few men with hand tools to see what they might do. By now the smoke had grown to a large cloud. This was obviously a big fire. I had run about three-quarters of a mile toward the fire to check out the extent of the blaze when I received a call on my walkie-talkie to meet Beloved Adi Da at the Sanctuary zoo, as He wanted to ride out to the fire on horseback. I ran back, calling requests and orders over the walkie-talkie in preparation for His ride. I found myself in a frenzy by the time I got to the zoo.

I hastily saddled the horses. Adrenalin was coursing through my body like never before. I was very much afraid for our Sanctuary. The area that was immediately threatened by the fire meant far more to me than simply outlying trails and manzanita bushes. It was a potent Holy Site called Red Sitting Man which was an area of the Sanctuary where I had spent many hours meditating and serving. I knew this Site had Spiritual significance and that it was extremely important that it not burn. And then, of course, there was the obvious threat to the residences, Holy Sites, and Communion Halls at the heart of the Sanctuary.

As Beloved Adi Da approached the horses, His fierce determination and concern for the Sanctuary were obvious to me, but He was also completely calm. His simultaneous Intensity and Freedom immediately drew me out of my fearfulness.

As we mounted the horses I wondered exactly where we were going, not remotely expecting what was to unfold. As soon as we began riding down the back road, a fire engine careened around the corner behind us and turned on its siren to alert us. The horses bolted, not about to be caught by this screaming machine. I could feel Adi Da's equanimity as I held on for dear life. The truck finally outran us, and the horses relaxed their mad gallop. We rode on to find a spot from which to view the fire.

Beloved Adi Da was dissatisfied with the distant vantage points I took Him to, finally asking to get close to the fire. I took Him out through the outer Sanctuary to the spot where I had been earlier, but still He wanted to get much closer to the fire. I told Him there was an old fire road that would take us right to the fire. But I was hesitant to go there, feeling I shouldn't take Him into such a dangerous situation. I warned Him that the horses would probably refuse to get close to the fire because of all the smoke. But this was the route He wanted to explore, and so we made our way up the steep, overgrown fire road. I cautioned Him again about the horses, feeling my own apprehension growing.

As we made our way over the ridge it looked as though we were riding into a different world. The atmosphere was thick with smoke. The ground and trees were red with borate fire retardant, and planes were continuing to drop fire retardant right over us. Once again I cautioned Beloved Adi Da about the horses, as it was obvious to me we were approaching the "head" or "lead" of the fire. He simply replied, "Don't worry about it."

We wove through the trees toward the roar of the blaze. The wind was coming up and fanning the flames. Spot fires burned on either side of us. The main part of the fire was roaring through the more dense forest directly ahead. I had finally found the right spot! This was where He wanted to be, right in the path of the fire.

I was afraid. It seemed to me that we could easily be trapped by the fire—it was moving so quickly. The spot fires behind us could seal off our

The fire at the Mountain Of Attention, summer 1979

escape. The horses might bolt. My body was again charged with adrenalin, pumping with wild, terrified energy. Once more I warned Beloved of the possible danger. He looked at me intensely, asking if I was frightened, and I told him honestly, "Yes." His response was, "Why do you think I wanted to come up here? I have to look the fire in the eye."

Beloved Adi Da's communication was so full of Force that it was incomprehensible to me. I could feel that His complete, free, and uncompromised attention was on the blazing fire. In that instant I was relieved of my fear. Suddenly, instead of feeling overwhelmed by terror, I was released into love and I only wanted to Contemplate my Beloved Guru.

Adi Da then turned toward the advancing flames, moving within thirty yards or so of the advancing blaze. The roar and force of the fire was amazingly powerful. Flames exploded up the sides of two enormous trees directly in front of us, as if to confront Avatar Adi Da. I could feel this great force of Nature over against the Master of Life. I also noticed, much to my amazement, that the horses were completely calm, almost as if they were out grazing in a pasture. They were obviously feeling Beloved Adi Da's calming influence as much as I was.

I was sitting to the side and slightly behind Beloved Adi Da, watching Him regard the fire. The magnitude of the fire appeared to increase significantly as the wind came up suddenly and the fire engulfed the area directly in front of us. Facing the fire's new rush of force and fury, Adi Da sat completely still in His saddle. His only movements were the spontaneous motions of His face and hands in various mudras, very much the same as I had seen many times during formal Darshan or meditation occasions. I felt Him radiate Divine Fire in the face of that forest fire. Whatever else He might have been doing, Adi Da was Radiating the most benign and yet fierce and awesome Power I had ever known.

After what must have been only a few moments (although time seemed to be suspended and warped) the fire receded and then died down. The winds stopped. The consuming power of this fire seemed to be bowing down to the Master. I am sure that it is difficult for the reader to picture this moment, but that fire had been transformed! I can only say that it was a mysterious and awesome moment to see and feel the great Adept change the course and magnitude of a raging forest fire. I sat still in mindless wonder.

Beloved Adi Da then turned back toward the Sanctuary, moving slowly through the trees, stopping to talk for a time. We looked over the scene—the fire was still moving, but much more slowly now, and not directly toward the Sanctuary boundary.

When we arrived back at the main Sanctuary complex, I was surprised to find all Beloved Adi Da's belongings, all our files and records, library books, and machines being packed into waiting vans and trucks. Apparently no one had remembered my instructions to wait until we returned before deciding to evacuate. Adi Da just laughed as He dismounted and sat down on the steps of His residence amidst a sea of packed boxes. He kidded me about our trip up to the fire and teasingly told everyone, "Ben was so afraid, he almost shit in his pants!"

I always tend to withdraw in the face of anything that is fearful to me. Beloved has pointed this out to me a number of times over the years, and He would use this event for years to remind me of my tendencies, and how I must go beyond them. During this incident, Beloved had simply drawn me out of my position of fear and agitation into trust and the capacity to love and serve. I felt through Him what it is to move in this world, even in the most dangerous circumstances, as a free man.

Later that evening we rode out again to survey the neighboring areas. Then Beloved Adi Da asked me to call the neighbors and make sure everyone was all right. In doing so, I found out that although about one thousand acres had been burned, no buildings had been lost, no one had been injured, and even our neighbor's orchards had been only slightly scorched.

**Ben Fugitt with Adi Da Samraj,
the Mountain Of Attention, 1996**

A few days later I walked back up to the spot where Avatar Adi Da had worked with the fire, reflecting on all that had occurred there. I thought about how confounding and amazing the whole event had been, feeling humbled and full of love. The area was still smeared with red borate dust and ash; the strong smell of smoke lingered. The fire, I discovered, had stopped short of the Sanctuary boundary by only a foot!

The Mountain Of Attention, 1996

CHAPTER NINE

December 7, 1996

How Can You Be Happy at the End of Your Life?

*A*di Da Samraj starts the gathering of December 7 by discussing with a few of the individual devotees in the room their tendency to make their business obligations the primary focus of their lives. After making the point that such preoccupation cannot satisfy the profound impulse of the being toward Happiness, Adi Da goes on to discuss one of the most common fantasies of what would be required to attain Happiness.

AVATAR ADI DA SAMRAJ: There was a television program that used to be on in the 50s called something like *The Millionaire*. Every week the story was that this very wealthy man sent his representative to give a million dollars tax-free to somebody, just chosen arbitrarily, and then they follow the story of what happens to this person after they have this million dollars (which was a huge lot of money in those days).

It was a different story every week, and—obviously, as you might suspect—it wasn't always just a success story. Often, as a matter of fact, it sort of played on the notion that riches didn't do you any good, ultimately. But it was a nice fantasy notion.

DEVOTEES: Yes, great idea.

AVATAR ADI DA SAMRAJ: The idea was that if, suddenly, somebody had all the money they imagined they would ever need to have <u>everything</u> they want, everything they could imagine wanting, that then they would do what they had to do to be happy. They would get whatever was happiness for them. They would put themselves in that circumstance somehow. And I guess the moral is that people don't know what happiness is about. So they may do something thinking it's about being happy, and it's not about happiness at all.

It's not enough to get a million dollars—you've got to know what to do with it.

But I'm not just talking about money itself. I'm talking about people's feeling that they can't fulfill their aspiration of what happiness is about for them because they don't have the money, or whatever it would take to be in that circumstance of life. That is the story that a huge lot of people—everybody, maybe—could tell.

So this was a fantasy about somebody suddenly having, at least from a financial point of view, no reason to feel there is any limitation whatsoever. They don't have to work anymore. In other words, they could do exactly what they pleased, from that moment on, presumably, as far as money could do it—which is a big fantasy. Most people go in that direction all their lives, because somehow they're playing on the notion that, if only they had enough of that, they would be able to be happy. They think the reason they're not happy is not because of something that they can be responsible for, but because of something that they're not responsible for at all.

People think they're not happy because they don't have money, which is something that they can't just have by an act of will or Divine Inspiration or anything. They don't associate happiness with something that they're always already in a position to become responsible for.

So then they maybe get money, and you'd think, all of a sudden, all of their reasons to not be happy are gone. If there is some condition or other, like money, that was the reason why you weren't happy, then you should be able to be happy right now and for all the rest of your life.

Well, why should you expect such wisdom from somebody who just happened to get a lot of money? How would they know? They don't know about happiness. All they know about it is the seeking for it, and all the limitations within their sphere of knowledge and experience, such that just having a million dollars doesn't, all of a sudden, plug them into the world that money could be integrated with if you were knowledgeable about all that. But, otherwise, just out of the blue, how are you going to deal with it? How does anybody even deal with it if they get it eventually? What does anybody know about happiness? It hasn't been about happiness, it's just playing a game. It never was about happiness.

Then you couldn't be happy at the end of your life, because all it would be about to you is losing everything that you had finally gotten, on which your happiness is totally depending.

So, how can you be happy at the end of your life? How can you view death as being anything to do with happiness, then? You feel that it inevitably has to be about <u>un</u>happiness, that it has to be totally terrifying! You presume that's the only possible way to have anything to do with it.

JAMES STEINBERG: It's not something fulfilling.

AVATAR ADI DA SAMRAJ: Yes, exactly. Well, that's obviously ego-mind. It's not merely to be laughed at. It's actually a profound disturbance. To find out that you're about that is a profound matter because it obliges you clearly to do something about it.

If you could be happy at the end of your life, then it can't be about something coming to an end. Now this is a profound and serious matter. But on the other hand, it's not merely dark. What is required is the process of ego-death, or going beyond egoity altogether in the context of all the stages of life, up to, and (ultimately) beyond, the sixth. Everything that is egoic—the entire condition that it is—is gone beyond in that process.

Ego-death, or going beyond the ego, is required. That's what it's about. It's not about ego-expansion, or ego-development, or ego-evolution. It's about ego-death, or ego-transcendence—if you understand what that means, because this phrase "ego-death" is apt in one sense, but on the other hand it suggests there's nothing more, that that's ending, and it's not that, either.

JAMES: People get confused by that, sometimes, Beloved.

AVATAR ADI DA SAMRAJ: Well, until there is Realization, Reality is not comprehended, not understood, not Realized, nobody knows what any thing <u>is</u>. And yet you all <u>act</u> as if you know what <u>everything</u> <u>is</u>. Look at the way you go about, look at what you do. You know, the smiling and so forth that you see in the people on TV? The people that I remember seeing on TV when I was a boy—all of them smiling. I used to sit and watch it—it was amazing to Me. What are these people smiling about? Why? Why? Well, I presumed that maybe the adults knew something I didn't. Off TV I checked them out, and . . . no, they didn't. It was clear to Me that nobody had the slightest awareness of the "Bright". None of them could see Me at all.

You could call ego-death a "rebirth", also. You're saying it's ego-death, and you're talking about ego, and yet this has to be transcended, so it sounds like you're talking about the "death" of that. Well, yes, fine, you can use that metaphor, it's okay. But there are just as many other metaphors. It's a matter of going beyond the knot of separateness, which knot is your own activity.

The Shape of Meaning

During the course of the gathering, Adi Da uses the phrase "on the tip of your tongue", and this becomes His taking-off point for a new "consideration" relative to meaning. He starts by speaking wildly, without any concern for conventional meaningfulness.

AVATAR ADI DA SAMRAJ: How many words do you have on the tip of your tongue?

Only one.

The outside tip or the inside tip?

If it's the outside tip, do you mean turned in, turned back, turned out, turned down, turned where?

Dropped down, pressed up, where is it?

Who has any idea what you <u>mean</u>?

So it is with almost everything you say and think.

How do you even know <u>you</u> know what you mean? I mean, would you trust yourself to know the dictionary definition of even one percent of what you think? And yet, you think it anyway, as if you know what you're thinking about. You don't know <u>anything</u> about what you're thinking about! *[Beloved Adi Da laughs with everyone.]* You just pretend you do. But the language is just <u>falling</u> through you, that's all. And at some point you'll just become obsolete. *[pronounced like an electric buzzer]* DEENNH!! You know? There'll be a sudden current surge, and you're out of there.

BETH KANTOR: It's never-ending.

AVATAR ADI DA SAMRAJ: Yes, life never ends, you just go back into the wall.

Have no fear, washing machines! *[laughter]*

What you call "you", you must understand, is really what's coming through the wall—through the cord hanging out the back of the washing machine, that mysterious connection to the wall. If it's in there it runs, and if it's out it doesn't.

So, once you find that out, what difference does it make what's in the washing machine? It's of secondary interest. Sometimes you have to use a washing machine, so you figure out something about it, but, basically, it is of <u>no</u> <u>profound</u> <u>interest</u> anymore. You know what I mean? No <u>profound</u> interest, because you got to the root of it. So, having gotten to the root, it deals with the rest of it, everything that followed from it.

All that while you were thinking you were a washing machine, you were just some kind of pattern, modification of the whatever-it-is that's coming out of the wall there—if "out" is what it's doing, whatever it's all about.

So, knowing that that's what you are, there's no more fundamental concern about the washing machine. The concern disappears. It's secondary. It's life-business, it's life-responsibility, but the profundity is in another dimension of "consideration" entirely. So you handle the practical responsibilities of life, but that doesn't <u>define</u> you.

The entire mind-thing is a process, even a stressful demand, as common as your next breath. It just goes on and on—a force of its own, or by some force unknown, because nothing you do seems to do anything about it.

In the moment, right now, the summation of whatever mind is, as it is right now, feels like it's trying to figure something out. But then you think that by having a conversation with Me you will Realize Me, that there's a process in which, by continuing your participation in <u>mind</u>, you will—by some process in mind, through mind, of mind—Realize the Truth, Realize Happiness Itself.

BETH: I actually feel it's a non-verbal communication.

AVATAR ADI DA SAMRAJ: It has to be, because a verbal communication would start up the next moment of mind.

BETH: Well, that's what I was going to say.

AVATAR ADI DA SAMRAJ: You're involved in non-verbal communication right now, because you're not really thinking in terms of words right now—or you weren't in that moment.

BETH: No, no.

AVATAR ADI DA SAMRAJ: Did you notice? You're speaking, you're <u>thinking</u> and speaking, but you were not being verbal.

BETH: Oh, I thought I was.

AVATAR ADI DA SAMRAJ: There are words being spoken that are something like shapes. I could see that you were thinking words and then saying something. And your process of thinking was not any different than the process of the talking that was coincident with it. And yet, what is it? Since it is simultaneous with it, what exactly is the process that is the thinking? You were supposed to be thinking, and talking, and so forth, and yet you were just in a rather sensory state, or non-verbal state, even of mind, even though you were using words. And, as it turns out, the subject of what you're saying is something about communicating non-verbally—which is exactly what you were doing. Except you thought that somehow to be communicating non-verbally you have to stop talking, that you can't use words anymore. But you were just in that very moment using words in a way that has nothing to do with verbal mind.

BETH: Right. Yes.

AVATAR ADI DA SAMRAJ: It wasn't necessarily about visualizing, and so forth—as right-brained as all of that. It was very balanced, actually. It wasn't picturing, but it wasn't word-thinking either. It was just a pattern going on, and yet it felt to you to be intelligent. It wasn't unintelligent.

So it wasn't verbally thinking, and it wasn't talking about being someplace other than right here now. And yet, the process called "thinking" was going on. You were moving along in some thought-process, some communication, and it had some sort of progression to it.

It's as if something has to happen with that continuous plastic mind-process, by virtue of it, or through an exercise of it, that's going to be the Realization of Truth, Happiness, the Totality that you can feel you're really seeking.

Where did you get this notion that in the exercises of mind there is the potential for such Realization? It's not like you remember the day it happened, or exactly how to account for it. But you carry it on as a mental process. You definitely feel it's you thinking, so it's you, this mental thing, constantly. And it's in that mental process that you are talking about, not only your problems, but talking about Great Matters and Realization, "considering" it verbally, as if that process itself, and Realization Itself, had anything at all to do with this. It has nothing to do with it! I mean, it has nothing to do with it.

BETH: It's non-verbal.

AVATAR ADI DA SAMRAJ: It's not even non-verbal. It has nothing to do with it. So it's about going beyond that particular orientation or limitation, to enter into at least that greater depth which is free of whatever that bondage was. It's not Realization yet, necessarily, but it is free to that degree.

But you insist on being verbal, as if you have got to deal with something through this exercise of the verbal mind. Do <u>you</u> really have these problems and these notions apart from the verbal mind? It seems like <u>it</u> has this problem. For good reason—that's not where the Truth is. It's not by doing something with the verbal mind. You have got to go beyond it to Realize What is Beyond.

BETH: That's obvious to me.

AVATAR ADI DA SAMRAJ: It <u>is</u> obvious, but that's not how you do it. You keep revolving around in the patternings of what you were already patterned in. So it's not about Liberation, though you may be improving something about the conditions in that pattern, to the degree you are able to get some control over some things. But you're still exactly the same person as previously—would basically give the same self-description in many respects, anyway—and yet claim to have gone through something.

Yes, you've gone through a process, but that doesn't mean anything changes in the sense of developing. There is <u>always</u> changing, and there are cycles of changes—something is going to follow something else, and so forth. But everything, <u>all</u>, revolves in and out of an inexplicable Unity of everything.

It's not getting any better. Like Sister Wendy[17] said about art, "It changes, but it doesn't get better." In other words, it's not only that it's <u>bad</u> now and it's not going to get any better. It's that it is always about some basic things, and the things that change about it—style, mode, time, place, and so forth—are not changes about anything fundamental, about what the artistic process is about. It still relates to the same fundamental matters. So it doesn't get any better, even though it goes through changes constantly.

You could say the same thing about everything, about everyone, about mankind altogether. What's getting better? Well, in terms of basically what it feels like to be in the condition of conscious humans, you're fundamentally addressing the same matter as any human being who has ever been recorded to have said anything about the matter. It's inherent in what you're doing. It goes with the job.

DANIEL BOUWMEESTER: It goes with the pattern.

AVATAR ADI DA SAMRAJ: Yes. You become more and more that. In other words, you become less and less everything else. That's what these bodies

17. Sister Wendy Beckett is a Catholic nun who has created books and video series devoted to the study of Western art through the centuries.

do, these complex processes. And because of the way you participate in it, you experience it or (otherwise) communicate about it as you do.

When Beth was talking earlier, it struck a chord, but it wasn't exactly verbal, and it wasn't exactly perceptual, because you don't make a picture of it or something. It's a shape—you know what I mean? That suggests something to you that's meaningful—that shape and meaning are the same, that meaning is shape. Does that make sense to you?

DEVOTEES: Yes.

AVATAR ADI DA SAMRAJ: You can be talking and thinking in verbal terms, and not be verbal.

BETH: That blows my mind.

AVATAR ADI DA SAMRAJ: As you've been doing here, and in conversation with Me. Are you aware of it, sensitive to what I'm talking about?

BETH: Yes, Beloved. Thank You. I'm incredibly grateful.

AVATAR ADI DA SAMRAJ: So when you speak, you think that you're meaning such and such—in other words, that it's a verbal matter. But it's not, it's a shape matter. You know about yourself that you would not want to be the dictionary authority for almost anything you say. So you don't know what you mean, in that sense. You have to go to the dictionary or to somebody else to figure out what you said.

So where is the meaning part of it, then, for you? It's not verbal. It's not that you are a dictionary remembering all words. A flow of words passes through, and a certain pattern goes through your pattern, and you found out what shape it means. Yes, that's it. It's shape. It's just shape.

But what makes shape feel to be meaning?—which you can then talk about in verbal terms. Because mind is shape. Mind is not words. You don't think in words as a way to think words. The thought-words don't follow some other thinking-words. What do you do? You don't think words in order to think words—you do this shape gesture. To mean, to intend, to think, to speak, is, fundamentally, at its root, a shape. Words can come from that, all kinds of communicative expressions. But it's still the same at root. Shape gesture. And that is what it means. That shape is what anything (that means anything) means. And that's why it's satisfying to find conjunctions that match a particular shape. You call that "meaningful". Somehow there's a pleasure in it. But that's all it is—a shape.

What is pleasurable about that, then? Don't you think the very process of your most ordinary thinking is remarkably mysterious?—

because it is always this, no matter how banal the subject matter. It doesn't make any difference how ordinary anything looks in a room, if you get a microscope or something you can find all kinds of interesting stuff. Well, even with the most ordinary thinking going on, there's something more fundamental that's always the case.

The Way is not about anything you can do with (or to) your thinking.

BETH: It's the heart.

AVATAR ADI DA SAMRAJ: Right. It is this shape entered into in depth, moment to moment. The shape that is meaning, and the meaning is Happiness.

DEVOTEES: *[exclaiming with delight]* Mm!

AVATAR ADI DA SAMRAJ: But it's just shape. It is a felt, non-verbally identifiable form. And it is satisfied by virtue of being that shape. Meaning is at a level of non-verbal primitiveness. Yet that's the root of everything verbal. You don't think in words, you think in shapes. And I don't mean perceptual shapes, as opposed to words. I mean the shape that awareness becomes in order to involve itself with meaning. The meaning-level at which you think, feel, or observe, is just a shape-force. Are you sensitive to that being the case, somehow?

DEVOTEES: Yes.

AVATAR ADI DA SAMRAJ: Well, it always is that. What kind of ultimacy is that state of shape looking for? But one thing it is not—it is not Happy, altogether. It is not deeply unhappy anymore, because it's already (at least, in our "consideration" here now) at a depth that's not grossly unhappy. But it is not, even now, supremely Happy, because it's this shape thing. It is just indulgence in this thing that is mind, this absurdity which, at the root of it, is just a shape of force, of change in force-shape. Utterly meaningless. Utterly! Except in that sense, of being a shape.

And you know you can feel better, you know you can feel worse. You know what it feels like to feel in the moment in this shape. It's not particularly bad or super-bad. It's not, however, Happiness Itself, because you haven't gone beyond this mind-process, this shape-exercise in force, moment to moment. Whatever the images you put on it, and shapes and sensations and feelings of solidity and all the rest of it, it's still the same basic thing.

This root of mind that discriminates and so forth is just attention in shape, changing the force-field somehow. You are, at root, involved in a very primitive process. You speak very straightforwardly, but it is nonetheless an extraordinarily profound process, if you examine the roots of what you're doing when you're thinking, what you're meaning when you're talking. What is it at root? Just this perceived and felt shape. All it is is the self-contraction. So it's not by its exercise that there can be Realization of What is not the self-contraction, What is Prior to the self-contraction.

You must comprehend the self-contraction at its root—the act, the pattern, the shaping that it is, the root-action in every moment, what you're always doing. Always, right now—you're always doing it. What are you always doing? Always. That. You are doing it. What are you doing? Always? Why is there never a time when you're not doing it? That—right now?

Everything else that you could characterize as limitation is built on that. Whatever you feelingly identified, intelligently located, if you followed that moment of "consideration"—that is the self-contraction. It's not just something you sense, it is something you are doing. The sensations of it, and thought as it—they're further down the line, they're effects of that.

So thought is already a process, a pattern that's trying to figure everything out. It's too late. It's too far down the line. That's not what the process of Truth is. Truth has nothing to do with going on with that. That's too far down the line, starting at too low a level.

It's when you come to a basic sense of that—"coming to the end of your rope", so to speak, with this thinking effort—that it starts to soften and becomes something that you can relax, just as readily as you can, generally, relax your face, or relax a muscle, relax your visual focus.

This is your own action. And it's participation in that shaping, moment to moment, that is the pattern of all conditional association. And this shape is what you call "you". It's just that you never see it—generally speaking, do not see it—as anything but this physical persona. You see it way down the line. You think it is your thinking—as if, by going over this thinking, you are going to figure it all out, there's going to be some way to figure it all out. You think that it's not only the answer to the puzzle of the moment, or some big puzzle, but that, by going on along with thinking, you're going to Realize Absolute Happiness.

Now, this thinking thing is very basic, because if it's not about Realizing Ultimate Happiness, you're going to lose interest. So to speak, it hasn't got any "sex appeal" if it's not about Realizing Ultimate Happiness. If it's just klik-klak, binary one-or-not-one or whatever, who cares?! [Beloved Adi Da laughs.]

Well, that's what you seem to be feeling about yourself relative to everything that you're involved in. Same way some of you were feeling that everything you are doing was somehow <u>about</u> Realizing Happiness, even though it's really just a pattern. It doesn't itself have <u>anything</u> to do with Happiness. But it sure is a pattern. Has all the potential destinies, positive and negative, of any pattern. And, therefore, if you identify with it, it's the throw of the dice. Whatever that pattern goes to, that's your "you" of the moment. That's your flick—and you've been flucked! *[laughter]* Then you hear click-click-click-click-click-click-click-click-click in the background at the end of the movie.

DEVOTEES: Oh!

AVATAR ADI DA SAMRAJ: And, you know, you feel toward some dark space there where you hear this clicking-clicking sound. You know what that sounds like? You know what I'm talking about?

DEVOTEES: Yes, we do.

AVATAR ADI DA SAMRAJ: That's the bad place. That's the root of this klik-klak perceptual patterning here. The whirring place. Perhaps you know what I mean, even though you don't know quite why you know what it means. But you know what I mean.

But you're playing it like this is just beauty-land, by going along with thinking and bodily self-identification and all the rest. And you feel that you're fulfilling the calling of some beauteous proceeding, and so you just allow yourself to <u>be</u> it and get on with being whatever that does—just oblivious, just going with the flow, altogether.

And how do you remember this shaping that is the conversation we're having? You think you remember it in the form of words? Well, words are being spoken, so perhaps yes. But there are all kinds of other moments when there are no words spoken but it's the same process as now. So how do you remember the shaping?

What's important to remember about it?—except that it is not gone to Infinity. It's got a <u>shape</u>. And you're confined by it, somehow. You have a mysterious association with it, and it's not just about pleasure. And yet you don't have a sense of how to get off. In fact, there's some sense you don't even want to get off. You can't really come up with enough concentration and submission of your existence to figure it out.

You don't have to figure it out. All your actions are just getting you more and more bound up in your own pattern of presumption or seeking. So, no matter what moment you're in, in the proceedings of human

The Whirring Machine of the Objective "Maker"

Avatar Adi Da has often spoken of the horror of conditional existence, the inevitability of death and suffering, and the way to grow beyond one's fear of these things. On several occasions over the years, in conversations with His devotees, He has described a "secret" about the nature of conditional existence—the objective "maker" that is the source of all conditional appearances, the source of klik-klak. This force, which He has directly observed, is like two whirring fans, churning out the morsels of appearance, inspiring terrible fear. Adi Da has Revealed that it is this dreadful "machine"—not God—that is the "maker" of the cosmic domain and everything in it.

AVATAR ADI DA SAMRAJ: The objective "maker" that can be perceived is a horror, the worst of limits. I have seen that one objectively, and it is terrible. It is a shape-shifting, centralized mass of jiggling and mechanical noises, and rotations—affirming separateness to the point of absolute fear.

This is not the true God. The true God is Source, Beyond conditions, Beyond visualizations, Beyond objects. It is Love-Bliss, unsupported, free of the "making" god. The "making" god is an illusion of egoity.

The "making" god appears as a puttering sound off to the left, like in a deep well, whirling like a fan, with clicking, shuddering sounds while it rotates. You can't fix on anything in it, but you can see the centralized mass, everything indefinite and shifting shapes. It is a horror. There are two fans, actually, a smaller one and a larger one. The larger one is slightly above the lower one. The smaller one is louder, and darker, and deep, as if in a well. And the sound is terrible. It makes a sound like a fan that is out of balance, smacking the shield on it. It clicks.

The True Divine is utterly without fear, and does not cause fear in any experience of it. Your Communion with Me does not cause fear to arise. Notice this. The moments of real Communion with Me have no fear in them. They do not magnify fear. Notice this. This is how you grasp at heart, more profoundly, that this Way is Truth. It does not magnify fear.

The ultimate delight is bodiless, mindless. That is the Freedom. That is the Realization. [March 28, 1994]

experiencing here, you all are not Happy yet. Not Happiness Itself yet—you know what I mean? You know what I "mean".

What does it mean?—"not Happiness yet". Does it mean anything other than "Bulldogs fly kites"? *[laughter]* Or "Uncles prevaricate about heirs"?

Is there a difference in the meaning of any of those things, when you get down to the root of it? It's just a shape. And that's the one thing always being addressed, communicated about. And yet you feel that you are a unique instance of that and nobody else is that same instance. They are another instance of something—perhaps not exactly the same—you don't really know anything about it, except that you're not it, they're not you.

This is not "elbow feeling different than someone else's elbow". This is at the level of awareness, consciousness, getting this notion. How did it get interior and found out it had an elbow? *[laughter]* You've got to go way beyond elbow in order to be interior. So why is it calling itself "the body"? What's the body calling itself? Let the body describe what it's about. Why should it be your concern? You're at a deeper level than the body—even just to be thinking about it. And it's just a shaping. And yet it's a confinement. It feels separate. The feeling of separateness is the same as the feeling of "difference".* And the feeling of "difference" is the same as the feeling of relatedness. And this shaping that is the root of all meaning, that is the meaning process itself, is always the same.

That's what the shape feels like. It is the limit on Happiness. It is the shape that is the rotator in all meaning, the fundamental processor, or process itself, of all experiencing.

Just by itself, it's a whirring machine, with two fans. And nothing is ever the same. And you can't hold onto anything, and, therefore, I say, as the Mama, "Your objections to anything don't mean shit!" You must understand that that's what the nature of this shaping is all about. It's just about clicks and clacks. Appearance-shift-change. Just a little bit, never the same. Time seems to have something to do with how long it is between major changes and so forth. Very complex, but still basically it's the same feeling of being in a vibratory chamber. It's not Happiness.

Traveling with physical sensation, going along with it, identifying with it, is like identifying with thinking, as if it's some process in thinking that's got to become Happiness. The same with this physical awareness, this "going into your insides" physically or emotionally or mentally. It's all about the same thing. Inverting the faculties is always entering into this same pattern-mass.

So the Way of the Heart is the Way of the <u>Heart</u>. It's the simplicity I've Given you, this Ruchira Buddha Bhakti Yoga, making use of all the principal faculties in a way that is counter-egoic, that is not merely given to the shaping that is the perpetual pattern. The perpetual pattern of it isn't Happiness. So the Way of the Heart is a way of going beyond that, through sympathetic devotional response to Me. But it's a Contemplative process, a sadhana—a relationship, then. A unique relationship, therefore. And its particular requirements must be fulfilled so that the <u>process</u> of this relationship is not disturbed.

That pattern of meaning, that shaping that is meaning moment to moment—that's klik-klak. That's the self-contraction also. They're the same. The self-contraction is the means whereby you are constantly getting involved in simply the dualistic clicking-clacking, yin-yanging patterning process that really, ultimately, or in itself, has no greater ultimacy than one-versus-none, click-click-clack. It's just that perpetuating itself. Everything else is fodder for it.

It's not dark, though, merely. You could certainly have a dark association with it, but that is not what we are "considering". We are "considering" how to transcend any darkness that's in it, how <u>not</u> to be dark, how not to just be oblivious and "go with the flow"—how not to do that.

Eventually you realize about the mind that, no matter how much thinking you can do, it's not going to be Realization of Happiness Itself. It's not going to be God-Realization. So already the mind is about something rather mundane. When it achieves its place, when you get a sense of its import, it gets put in its proper place in the sphere of your awareness. So when there's this relaxation of the obsessive meaning-pattern, thinking-pattern, pattern itself, and you've stepped out of it in this devotional Yoga (and everything that is the "conscious process" and "conductivity"), then you've gone beyond it, you've transcended it at its root.

Well, what it comes down to, ultimately, is just that shape that is at the root of awareness, that force of limitation. It must be transcended. Happiness Itself is the transcendence of that.

Then there is no "difference".

No separateness.

Therefore no feeling of relatedness.*

No otherness.

No inside, no outside.

No up, no down.

No far, no near.

No perimeter, no center.

117

No bounds.

No contraction.

In other words, <u>perfect</u> surrender is adding no design to the designing, no pattern to the patterning.

When it is so profound that it is at the root, then it doesn't have to <u>do</u> anything other than that.

It opens, in the passage to the seventh stage of life.

BRIAN O'MAHONY: Your Transmission is beyond meaning, Beloved. It comes from the Other Side.

AVATAR ADI DA SAMRAJ: <u>Meaning</u> is beyond meaning.

You are participating in meaning, or even meaning something when speaking, and are already just in that shape, that fundamental space of awareness. Whether in the waking state, the dreaming state, or the sleeping state, there is this fundamental space of awareness and it must be transcended. Not by doing something to it, but by forgetting it. Not by trying not to remember it, but by forgetting it. In other words, by becoming self-surrendered, self-forgotten, in response to What is Beyond you—the Source-Person, the Source-Condition, the "Bright"—Me. Just Me, as I <u>Am</u>.

There's My bodily-familiar Form, familiar to you from photographs and physical sightings, and so on. But that, as you know, passes. It's not what is itself Attracting you. It is a Means to locate Me, and to enter into My Condition, through your self-surrendering, self-forgetting response, done as true Yoga, this profound Yoga, this profound discipline. You must be disciplined, focused in this serious, and yet playful exercise in depth, moment to moment, always.

Nothing Feels as Good as No-Contraction

AVATAR ADI DA SAMRAJ: Human beings are <u>very</u> humble life-forms. As <u>human beings</u>, that's what you are. As <u>everything</u> (including human beings), you are at the Root—not only in the Great Unity, but in the Source-Condition in Which It is arising. But that is not true of you at this superficial, personal, or body-mind level, where you're always buzzing, shaping, and losing awareness of both the Unity in Which everything arising is appearing, and of the Source-Condition, Which Transcends all "difference". You've forgotten about It entirely.

The whole thing is humble. It's mortal. Look at all the stress and difficulty. Everything else is what it is, and still you're talking about utopia and evolving to the point of some kind of perfection—in this form, or as part of the going-on with this kind of form. It doesn't have anything to do with that. It has to do with the transcendence of that. That's the search that's going on and on and on and on. The going-on with this pattern patterning—that's the search. That's the self-contraction. That's what locks you into it. And, therefore, responsibility for the self-contraction through responsive devotion to Me, and all of the "conscious process" and "conductivity", is about transcending that.

BRIAN: It's kind of bizarre that we continue doing it when we know that it's not going to produce Happiness. We're not pleasurably associated with it in the least little bit.

AVATAR ADI DA SAMRAJ: Well, there's all these kind of parts of you that aren't the one who knows that it's not about Happiness. So you sit there, you think it out, or you follow My "Consideration", and it seems obvious to you. But then you start waiting for the body-mind to do so, rather than you having to command the body-mind, based on that knowledge, that understanding that is your root-fundamental experience.

There is a long silence as devotees swoon in Communion with Avatar Adi Da. Then Adi Da starts speaking again.

AVATAR ADI DA SAMRAJ: You can't crush a triangle. You can only turn it on its side.

DEVOTEES: Mm!

AVATAR ADI DA SAMRAJ: While Muttering that Mutterance, I just recalled the comedian Stephen Wright. He gives a lot of one-liners. I was remembering one I particularly liked: The first time he looked at a dictionary, he thought it was a poem about everything. *[laughter]*

Well, you see, this simple pattern, the root of all meaning, thinking, perceiving, and so forth, is going on in every moment, whether you're in some pleasurable circumstance, or painful one. It's there all the time. It doesn't mean that you're just as likely to examine it or feel beyond it under all circumstances. It doesn't even necessarily mean that because you're noticing this, you even under <u>any</u> circumstances go beyond it, really. In other words, <u>sadhana</u> is about going beyond it. The noticing is a happening here and there.

BRIAN: It doesn't seem like it would be transformative particularly.

AVATAR ADI DA SAMRAJ: What's to be transformed, anyway? Transformation is a notion in the mind-field itself, not in depth. The notion that you have to Realize something is late, it's down the line. The self-contraction is what you did before that.

Well, you have to do the sadhana in such a way that you get to the point of being able to be in the most profound focus, exercising the capability for transcendence with complete clarity and ability.

Human beings are doing all kinds of things with speech and clothing and attitudes and things all around, and that's their domain of meaning-presumption, somehow felt, expressed. And so they live with one another, relate to one another, speak, and all the rest of it, based on that. But you never <u>were</u> that! You're just these poor little naked animals, just thinking, pretending, imagining, talking, and all that.

So what is this poor little animal? What's its "consideration"?—instead of all this other babble, which is all sheer imagination, anyway, just based on some sort of a game, sort of (somehow or other) agreed to by everybody. Just being the poor, relatively small, soft-bodied animal there. That's your "consideration". You don't have any of that other stuff to deal with now, it's just that real basic feeling-meaning sense of the shape of being here. You know what I mean?

So having, in depth, understood, transcended the pattern of bondage—recognizing, transcending that—there's no ego and no pattern-motion to generate more pattern. So this is why some Buddhists prefer to call It "Nirvana", rather than "the Self", and so on.

Both words are equally usable, if properly understood. But, nonetheless, it's not about a "self"—an "inside" as opposed to an "outside", a "you" as opposed to "somebody else". It's Reality Itself. But, to Realize It (even though It is Always Already the Case), there must be an

Awakening at the heart, at the meaning-core that has to be unlocked. That Which is Beyond shape, and Which is One, is Realized by Realizing the Space in Which the shape is arising.

There is emotion, or feeling, associated with this pattern of meaning-process, too. In other words, all the faculties are in that pattern. So the principal faculties (which are how you become associated with that pattern) are the tools of the Yoga. I Give you this devotional Yoga which makes use of these four faculties in <u>attracted</u> self-surrendering, self-forgetting response to Me.

You have to remember, however, that it's a matter of addressing the search, or addressing you in the moment in which you are seeking, and what you are always doing—this self-contraction.

So you remain seekers, even though you look complacent. No matter how complacent people may look, they're really holding on to things, so there's a great degree of tension there. And, in any case, they're still full of seeking in all kinds of directions. It looks at the moment to be largely interior, but, if you examine them altogether, you'll see that they're constantly involved in it. So every one of you is a seeker.

Understand that My Address to you is to you as a seeker—you <u>the</u> seeker. So you <u>are</u> that, just as much now as ever. Even though in some sense contented, it's not altogether that. You're still seeking in some sense. Every moment you could say it is so, and describe its look at the moment, perhaps. It's always that. It's never Happiness Itself.

You all seem to think that some sort of activities you can do in the waking state are how you are going to Realize God. It's like the notion that if there's a thinking process, then eventually it's going to become some "insight", and that's going to become Enlightenment.

Well, the waking state is like that. If you're going to get on with something in the waking state, some seeking in the waking state, <u>that</u> is somehow <u>the</u> means whereby you will Realize Me? Where do you <u>get</u> this notion? <u>In</u> the waking state! *[laughter]*

JONATHAN CONDIT: That's true. We don't have it in the other states.

AVATAR ADI DA SAMRAJ: Yes. It's just some habit-bit of nonsense, that you (so-called "you") associate with in the waking state. Why don't you presume that the way to Realize is through an exercise done in the dreaming state, or through an exercise done in the sleeping state? Whatever you may think about it in the waking state, when you finally get to sleep, you're not going to remember what you were going to do about it. Any transcending of the depth of the sleep state cannot be through gestures made at the waking and dreaming levels. So it involves a capacity to function at a depth deeper than the faculties exercised in waking and dreaming.

JONATHAN: But, Beloved, why is it so important what we do in the waking state, if that isn't where the process really occurs?

AVATAR ADI DA SAMRAJ: Because you are in the waking state. Everything is a problem to you. Once the self-contraction is done, everything is a problem. In everything you do, you're engaged in the effort of trying to figure something out. I'm not saying that it's just your thinking that's about trying to figure everything out. It's the same with everything else, every other faculty, every other mode of awareness, and so forth. It's the same thing: seeking.

MICHAEL WOOD: It seems like the way the sadhana functions is to gather energy and attention back from its peripheral expressions deeper and deeper toward the Source.

AVATAR ADI DA SAMRAJ: Yes, from the pattern to the Source. It sounds simple to describe—in other words, that's apt enough.

MICHAEL: Yes, but the Realization of it is through sadhana.

AVATAR ADI DA SAMRAJ: The Realization, the knowledge of all the details, and the Grace in the process, all the rest of it—the Means.

MICHAEL: Yes, I feel like You're Re-Awakening renunciation[18] in us, Beloved, by Drawing us to that side, which, by virtue of its very Attraction and Attractiveness, is What has moved us to You in the first place. You are showing us how it's the sadhana founded in Attraction that just lets things drop off.

AVATAR ADI DA SAMRAJ: Yes, if you want to be snoozy about it all just remember what I say in My Mama Form.

In other words, this isn't a place that's designed taking you into account, in some sort of "everything is just here to perpetuate you" kind of sense. So you can just sort of go with the flow, but understand that going with the flow is not about the Happiness-Event. It's about desires and pleasures—yes, about all kinds of things conditional. It's not necessarily to be described in hellish terms. It is, however, bondage. It has all the potential for the most difficult of experiencings.

18. Renunciation in the Way of the Heart is not ascetic denial of the body and the world. Rather, renunciation in the Way of the Heart is about renouncing egoity, the self-contraction itself. Though ego-renunciation is the calling for all practitioners of the Way of the Heart, some embrace renunciation more intensively as formal members of renunciate orders (see p. 376).

MICHAEL: And no potential for True Happiness.

AVATAR ADI DA SAMRAJ: No. None of the processes or aspects of the process, none of the faculties—nothing is about the Realization of Happiness.

JONATHAN: It's just a matter of no longer being caught in the pattern?

AVATAR ADI DA SAMRAJ: Well, the seeking is in all these patterns themselves. You feel the search, the searching motive. You feel it in association with these different kinds of patterns or conceptual states and whatnot, and so the struggling is inherently there. Seeking is being not comfortable with the way things are right now, or feeling that whatever it is right now is not enough. But if you really find the root of seeking, you discover it is your own action, the self-contraction itself.

JONATHAN: And that can be discovered in any state.

AVATAR ADI DA SAMRAJ: Yes, because it is not itself a state, and yet it coincides with them all. It's the act, the structure, of it all—the pattern of that pattern. And its root is very simple. The Way of the Heart—the Way of the Root, then—is the Way to Realize, because any step removed from that is already so complex you could not comprehend it, under any conditions at all.

JONATHAN: Beloved, do we have three separate streams of relationship to You in the waking, dreaming, and sleeping states?

AVATAR ADI DA SAMRAJ: You see, you're already talking in very complex terms about "we", making references to "states". But you're making all these references from just that one state that you call "waking", and they are verbal references.

JONATHAN: Right.

AVATAR ADI DA SAMRAJ: So it turns out you're not really talking about what you thought you were talking about. What have we found out? Not that you were speaking nonsense, exactly. But that you are making an exercise of mind again, which has its own kind of patterns associated with it. And as soon as you try to make it stand as sufficient representation of your meaning, it fails you.

CARL PENGELLY: Beloved, it's completely obvious that it's only through Your Grace that we're able to transcend anything. I mean, given our own patterns, we never will. It's just through Your Grace.

AVATAR ADI DA SAMRAJ: Yes, of course. That is how it works. The pattern, and the transcendence of it, and the Means for transcending it, are all Revealed by Me, and in the process of the relationship to Me. All the going-beyond is in this simple directness, of you Attracted to Me, steady in your responsive self-giving Awareness-Communion with Me.

CARL: We need to feel the Happiness in That Itself.

AVATAR ADI DA SAMRAJ: Yes, because it is Communion with Me. But then you notice something about the limit on it, and what it's like in the next moment of doing this. It is a sadhana, and the discipline must be seriously embraced. You must go through the process in which it is made straight. And for it to be fully straight, it has to be deep. *[Gesturing away from His Body with His hand:]* A lot of straightness is way out here, you know. I'm not talking about the way-out-here straightness—I'm talking about the in-depth straightness (whatever its appropriate sign otherwise, apparently).

The association with conditional existence (or conditional reality) is always a seeking one. It is always about seeking, because it's always about self-contraction. It always has basic qualities like separateness, "difference", and relatedness. They're already there.

So the first capability generated in this sadhana is the hearing capability, and is the great one that must be exercised all the way through to the transition to the seventh stage of life in this Way of the Heart. And the other great Realization (or capability) is that of seeing* Me, which is based on this capability, this responsibility for true hearing, this responsibility for the self-contraction. You enter into My Sphere, My inherently Spiritual Sphere, in Communion with Me. By virtue of this capability that is true hearing— the ability to go beyond the self-contraction or feel beyond the self-contraction—you can enter into the process of Spiritual Communion with Me, responsibly, and, therefore, more and more in-depth and profoundly.

You can never feel better than no-contraction. Orgasm doesn't feel better than no-contraction.

Nothing feels as good as no-contraction.

If you realize this, it puts everything in its place. And you're not fighting against these ordinary factors of existence. It's simply that you're not related to them anymore quite as before, so that you are enjoying a capability, a kind of luxury.

So, enter into the in-depth Sphere of no-contraction, feeling beyond egoic self, beyond self-contraction. This is the Root of Happiness, of Love-Bliss. Where this opens, Love-Bliss is Self-Evident.

But none of this is <u>figured</u> <u>out</u>. This is all <u>realized</u> in the Yoga of Communion with Me. So it is in this more and more in-depth Contemplation of Me. Always deeper because it is always about forgetting, forgetting, forgetting, feeling beyond, surrendering, forgetting beyond, going beyond. So it's always deeper. Communion with Me (established in this moment's meditation through the sighting of Me Bodily), as it goes on in its depth, goes beyond even any memory of Me Bodily, perhaps.

This Body is My Agent.* It is Means. You are Attracted to <u>Me</u>. I Am the "Bright" Itself. It is That, Beyond visibility, found at the Perfectly Subjective level—at the Subjective, not the objective, level. The "Bright" is Perfectly Subjective *[gesturing with His left hand toward His Heart]*, not objective *[gesturing away from His Body]*. It is the Self-Radiance of the Condition That is Always Already the Case, Self-Existing. The One Condition.

MICHAEL: The deepening is about continuously being Attracted beyond, more and more—basically, being lost in You.

AVATAR ADI DA SAMRAJ: Becoming lost in Me by feeling beyond <u>yourself</u>, moving beyond <u>yourself</u>. So it's not <u>you</u> getting lost in something. It is you forgotten. It is opened beyond. Now, that happens in this devotional meditation. And having it happen in the devotional meditation is a way of showing you the self-contraction and how it is felt beyond.

It should not be difficult—once you have a certain basic steadiness through the foundation disciplines—to pass truly Yogically through this course from listening to having heard Me. But if you don't maintain the secondary aspects of it, the supports of it, you allow it to collapse. You must bring it into life. So those responsibilities are all on functional levels, fine, but they must be maintained, because, as soon as you don't, you lose the integrity of the pattern, the asana of this Contemplation, and you return to the chaos of pattern itself, ego-based results, the search again—the going along with it all, but feeling stress at the core of it.

When you lose the depth, you forget what everything is all about. As soon as you start this waking, dreaming, and sleeping business, there goes everything else.

BRIAN: Beloved, in meditation I notice that when I forget myself in You, You actually take on my form, and I start to feel and experience myself as You. I start feeling like You. I feel You as me. I realize that self-forgetting practice actually is a very profound reception of You.

AVATAR ADI DA SAMRAJ: Yes, or entering into My Pattern.

BRIAN: Right.

AVATAR ADI DA SAMRAJ: Or becoming conjoined with My Pattern.

MICHAEL: And You enter into ours, too. In that, Your devotee is undone.

AVATAR ADI DA SAMRAJ: Yes, it's a conjunction in which you and I are <u>both</u> involved in some kind of unique and (in many respects) inexpressible conjunction, or process, with one another. Even to say "with one another" doesn't say exactly what it's about.

In other words, you find Me as such in the event, the process, of self-surrendering, self-forgetting Communion with Me. So you're not being the body, as opposed to whatever else. And yet the body is not excluded.

BRIAN: I also sometimes feel that when I receive You, when I'm in Communion with You, there's a sense of really expanding space.

AVATAR ADI DA SAMRAJ: Yes, you're getting the lesson (inexplicably, somehow) of going beyond the self-contraction, going beyond the ego-"I", going beyond limitation, but becoming responsible for it, yielding in surrender to Me so profoundly, that the very <u>act</u> that prevents it in its ultimate moment is your own responsibility.

BRIAN: Beloved, is it true that, if you actually register anything at all at the level of mind, it's automatically part of the self-contraction?

AVATAR ADI DA SAMRAJ: Yes, presuming the self-contraction <u>is</u> your condition. It is not so in the case of the seventh stage Samadhi.*

JAMES: Thought itself is not self-contraction in that case?

AVATAR ADI DA SAMRAJ: Right. In the case of My devotees in the seventh stage Awakening, thought is no longer a process rooted in egoity. It is a pattern Recognized prior to egoity. Then, of course, you recognize the washing machine to be the same thing that's zapping through your wall.

So no condition feels better than no-contraction. Therefore, no process is more profound, more important, any day, than meditation, or the profound exercise of devotional Contemplation of Me, usually under formal circumstances. You can't feel that good anywhere else or under any other conditions. This is the Zone of Happiness, the real process in which Happiness without limitation is Realized.

Therefore, you have to constantly go beyond the self-contraction in <u>this</u> moment, under whatever its conditions may appear to be. There still is this search—therefore, this disturbance, this dis-ease motivating the search. It doesn't make any difference what pattern-condition is arising— this is still the case. The pattern-condition can be dreadful, the pattern-condition can be beautiful, the pattern-condition can be painful, the pattern-condition can be pleasurable, but, still, the impulse is to be without these limitations.

Even all the non-humans—they don't do, perhaps, the same thing you think you're doing with your verbal process, but they're doing the same fundamental thing, this shape stuff, this fundamental shape-process moment to moment, at the depth-level. So they spontaneously have the impulse (and so do you, if you aren't obstructing it) to feel into that Deep and to be utterly given over to whatever it is that you're depending on, whatever everything is depending on ultimately. There's just so much you can know about it, or say about it, or think about it. So you have to give up into it. It is whatever it is, and you cannot maintain your independence from it indefinitely, your self-contraction.

Faith is ultimately retired in Bliss, and so is insight, in feeling-Communion with Me, without limitation. That allows you to be the kind of openness that is about trust without the slightest limitation. You could call it "faith", except that it's not about believing in something. It is trust, essentially—allowing, at the depth, there to be no-contraction, to be whatever there is when there is no contraction, instead of trying to apply it toward something else, thinking it was something based on self-contraction. You just deeply enter into, or are rested into, What is Prior to it.

So every day, then, you set aside some significant time. You set aside time (in the holy sense) that you just simply will not part with, you will not use it for any other purpose. And you definitely use it for this purpose—that of meditation and everything that's in that domain, of puja and chant and so on, sacred activities. Because this is the key process of your life. This is what you've come to understand in your responsive "consideration" with Me. This exercise of the depth, then, has great importance, over against the relative lesser importances of everything that conditional existence involves, experientially and so on. This is the root of it.

This depth is the fundamental domain of responsibility.

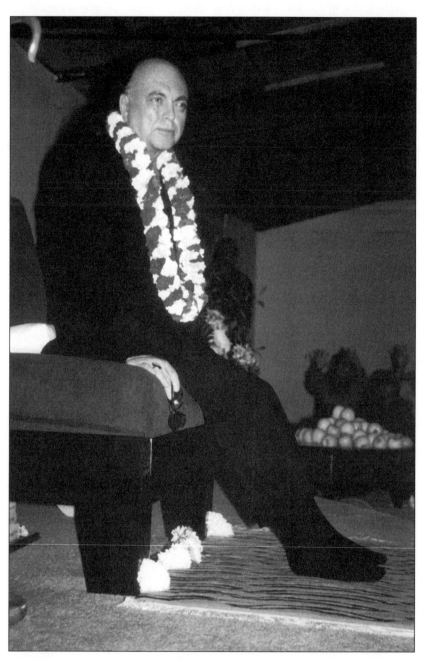

The Mountain Of Attention, 1996

CHAPTER TEN

My Own "Consideration" Of the self-Contraction

THE HEART OF THE DAWN HORSE TESTAMENT OF THE RUCHIRA BUDDHA
CHAPTER FOUR, VERSES 37-50

A vatar Adi Da Samraj has made His most summary Statements of His Wisdom-Teaching in nine books that He calls His "Source-Texts".* These are His most essential written legacy to all who respond to Him, now and in the future.

Among all of the Source-Texts of Adi Da Samraj, the paramount Scripture is The Dawn Horse Testament Of The Ruchira Buddha, in which Adi Da fully Reveals the primary "considerations" of true religion and describes in detail the forms of practice to be engaged in the course of Spiritual practice in His Company, through all the stages of life, culminating in Most Perfect Divine Enlightenment.

In all of Avatar Adi Da's Source-Texts, it is His intention to describe practice of the Way of the Heart completely, exactly, and for all time—an intention marked by more complex and formal language. In particular, through a unique use of capitalization, Avatar Adi Da celebrates the Unconditional, or Absolute, and Its seniority relative to all that is conditional, or limited.

The Heart Of The Dawn Horse Testament Of The Ruchira Buddha consists of Avatar Adi Da's most essential Instruction from The Dawn Horse Testament Of The Ruchira Buddha. In this excerpt, Avatar Adi Da describes the process of His own "Consideration" (during His "Sadhana Years") relative to the self-contraction and the effort of seeking.

37.

My Own "Consideration" Was This: God, Truth, or Happiness (Whatever That Is Altogether) Must Necessarily Be That Which Is Always Already The Case. Therefore, I Observed That The Felt Dilemma and The Urge To Seek Are Simply The Absurd Confession That God, Truth, or Happiness Is Absent Now. And I Observed Further That The Signs Of Dilemma and Seeking Are Not A Program For The Actual Future Realization Of God, Truth, or Happiness, but They Are Merely A Means For Preventing Present Realization Of God, Truth, or Happiness. The Feeling Of Dilemma and The Urge To Seek Are Actually The Evidence Of A Disease, Which Is the conditional (or psycho-physical) self In its Chronic Contraction Upon itself, and In its Symptomatic Non-Realization Of God, Truth, or Happiness.

38.

Indeed, It Became Clear To Me That the "ego" (or the conventional "I") Is Not an "entity" (or an Independent and Static "thing of being"), but the "ego" (or the conventional "I") Is The Chronic and Total psycho-physical <u>Activity</u> Of self-Contraction, Always Associated With Concrete Results (In the psyche, mind, emotion, body, and their relations). And the self-Contraction Can Always Be Located (In any moment) In Feeling (As Fear, Anxiety, Stress, and All Other Kinds Of Reactive emotions and Blocks In The Flow Of Natural bodily energy In The Circle* Of the body-mind).

39.

The self-Contraction Is the Complex limit on Natural bodily energy (and, In The Case Of Any Degree Of Spiritual Awakening, On The Spirit-Energy) In The Circle Of the body-mind. Therefore, the self-Contraction Is (Ultimately) a Complex limit On The Inherent and Self-Existing Spiritual Radiance Of Transcendental (and, Ultimately, Divine) Being. And Perfect Freedom, or Inherent Happiness, or Inherently Most Perfect God-Realization Is A Matter Of Direct (or Inherent, or Native) and Inherently Most Perfect Identification With The Self-Existing and Self-Radiant Condition Of Transcendental (and Inherently Spiritual) Divine Being (or Consciousness Itself), Which Identification Is Allowed Only By Present or Progressive[19] Transcendence Of The ego-Act Of self-Contraction.

19. The self-transcending practice of the Way of the Heart is <u>present</u>, or <u>direct</u> and <u>immediate</u>, because in any moment of true practice the practitioner enters into present Communion and intuitive Identification with Adi Da Samraj. The Way of the Heart is also <u>progressive</u> in that the practitioner becomes responsible over time for all of the physical and psychic dimensions of the body-mind.

40.

The self-Contraction Is Un-Necessary. The self-Contraction Is (Without Ultimate Necessity, and, Therefore, Only Apparently) Being "Added" To Existence Itself (In Reaction To Cosmic Nature, or To Apparent conditional Existence). The self-Contraction (Originally) Coincides With and (Effectively) Perpetuates The Apparition Of Cosmic Nature Itself, and The Presumption That Existence Itself Is conditional, or Merely Apparent. Therefore, the self-Contraction Is (Originally, and Also In Effect, or conditionally) Un-Natural, Because it Superimposes On The Transcendental, and Inherently Spiritual, Self (or Consciousness Itself) A False View Of Both Cosmic Nature (or conditional Reality) and The Divine (or The Most Priorly Real Self-Condition and Source-Condition).

41.

When what Is Un-Necessarily Superimposed On Reality Is Released, What Stands (or Remains) As The Obvious Is, Necessarily, Reality, or The Real Condition Itself.

That Is To Say, Whatever Is Always Already The Case Authenticates Itself (Directly, Inherently, Obviously, and Perfectly).

42.

Therefore, self-Transcendence Necessarily Reveals (or Allows The Revelation Of) The Transcendental, and Inherently Spiritual, Self-Condition and Source-Condition As The Self-Authenticating (or Inherently and Obviously Real and True) and Most Prior (or Necessarily Divine) Reality and Truth!

43.

This Heart-Awakened Insight Was Instantly Liberating, and It Became The Basis For A Progressive Revelation Of God (or Reality, Truth, and Happiness). The Insight Itself (or The Unique and Inherently Liberating Understanding Re-Awakened At The Heart) Directly Coincided (or Arose Simultaneously) With A Practice That Was Thereafter To Be The Most Basic Characteristic Of The Way Of My Life (and Which Was To Re-Awaken Full and Most Ultimate Realization). That Practice Had Two Primary Aspects. The First Was Profound Submission Of attention and all the energies of the body-mind To Observe, Feel, and Feel Beyond the self-Contraction. And The Second, Which Coincided With The First and Ultimately Superseded It, Was Direct Communion and (Ultimately) Inherent Identification With The Native (or Prior) Condition That Is

Simply and Directly Obvious When the self-Contraction Is Transcended (or No Longer Effective As A Mechanism Of Dissociation From What Is Always Already The Case).

44.

I Observed That The Sense (or Feeling) Of "Absence", or The Sense (or Feeling) Of The Non-Presence Of God, or The Sense (or Feeling) Of Separation From God, Truth, Happiness, or What Cannot Even Be Described, Is Not Evidence Of The Real Absence Of God, Truth, Happiness, or The Indescribable, but It Is Clear Evidence That the conditional self Is Contracting, or Actively Separating From What (Simply, Merely, or Really) Is.

45.

I Named This Disease (or the Diseased self) "Narcissus",[20] Because Of The Likeness Between This self-Program and The Ancient Myth Of Narcissus. And I Became Attentive In every moment To This Feeling Of Absence, Of Separateness, Of Dilemma, and The Urge To Seek.

46.

Remarkably, In every moment Of Such Observation, I Felt The Non-Necessity As Well As The Deluding or Binding Effect Of the self-Contraction, So That A Spontaneous Release Occurred In every Such moment. That Is To Say, I Observed That It Was Un-Necessary To Presume or Suffer or Be Motivated By the self-Contraction In any moment Of My Direct Observation Of it. And, In That Observation, A Deep Spontaneous Response Of self-Release Was Awakened. And Whenever That Release Of self-Contraction Occurred, That Which Is Always Already The Case (Previous, and Most Prior, To self-Contraction) Stood Out As The Obvious.

---

20. In Avatar Adi Da's Teaching-Revelation, "Narcissus" is a key symbol of the un-Enlightened individual as a self-obsessed seeker, enamored of his or her own self-image and egoic self-consciousness. In *The Knee of Listening*, Adi Da Samraj describes the significance of the archetype of Narcissus:

He is the ancient one visible in the Greek "myth", who was the universally adored child of the gods, who rejected the loved-one and every form of love and relationship, who was finally condemned to the contemplation of his own image, until, as a result of his own act and obstinacy, he suffered the fate of eternal separateness and died in infinite solitude.

47.

Over time, What Is (Previous, and Most Prior, To self-Contraction) Was Revealed More and More Profoundly. And As That Revelation Increased, There Was Also The Spontaneous and Otherwise Progressive Unfolding Of The Many Extraordinary Phenomena That Are Characteristic Of Each Of The Seven Stages Of Life.

48.

The Process Of That Revelation By Stages Was Not Developed Only On The Basis Of Insight (or self-Understanding) and Spontaneous self-Transcendence, or What I Call The "Conscious Process", but It Was Equally Associated With A Developing Response To What Was Being Revealed. Thus, It Also Involved What I Call "Seeing" (or Fullest, and Spiritually Activated, emotional, and Total psycho-physical, Conversion To True, and Truly Responsible, "Conductivity" Of The By Grace Revealed Spirit-Power) and What I Call "Divine Ignorance" (or Spontaneous Identification With The Inherent Love-Bliss Of Native or Divine Being, Whenever The psycho-physical Presumption Of knowledge, or "I know what this or that Is", Was Effortlessly Released).

49.

What Is (Always and Already) Is Revealed Only When the self-Contraction Is Not Effective. It Is Revealed To Be Self-Radiant (or Inherently Spiritual) and Transcendental (or Self-Existing) Being, God, Truth, or Happiness. Any and every conditionally Manifested "I" Always Already Inheres In That One, Both At The Level Of Being, or Consciousness Itself, and At The Level Of every Apparent or conditionally Manifested psycho-physical function, process, or state. Even the body-mind Is Only An Apparent Modification Of That Divine Self-Radiance In Which "I" Am.

50.

When This Realization Was Most Perfectly Re-Awakened In My Own Case, all beings, this world, and all kinds of other worlds Were Revealed In That Same One, Inhering In That Same One, and Appearing As (Apparent) Modifications Of That Same One.

The Mountain Of Attention, 1996

CHAPTER ELEVEN

December 8, 1996

The Problem About Life Is Death

*A*t the beginning of the gathering of December 8, after a few opening remarks by devotees, Avatar Adi Da abruptly announces the topic of the evening's "consideration" with a memorable one-liner:

I.

AVATAR ADI DA SAMRAJ: The problem about life is death. *[laughter]*

DANIEL BOUWMEESTER: It's a big problem! *[Beloved Adi Da laughs with everyone.]*

AVATAR ADI DA SAMRAJ: I don't care what you propose. The problem about life is death. The problem about anything you propose about living is that you can't continue it.

So, you can either forget about it and just sort of live a pattern of whatever is going on, or you have to deal with death. If it were just a matter of living, and you just went through changes, and that went on with no end—well, that would be one thing. Then all these impulses and inclinations, relationships, accumulations, and everything that happens to all of that, and so forth, would mean one thing. But to have it be such that <u>any</u> time (not just after some time, but any time) it could be that that's that, that's the end of that—well, that's a real problem with anything you're going to propose about anything at all! *[laughter]* That makes the whole thing <u>immediately</u> a <u>major</u> <u>problem</u>!

135

ANIELLO PANICO: Absolutely!

AVATAR ADI DA SAMRAJ: What is the difference between you noticing that, at the moment, and what a chameleon or a lion notices? What makes you think it's any different? Just because you use a particular way of expressing it as a felt pattern, what's the difference between that and something felt by any non-human?

There are a lot more non-humans than humans, by the way. Many, many more. But what do they do about it, then? What solutions do you see them coming to? You seem to <u>think</u> that your solutions have to come about as a result of, and even in the domain of, thinking.

DEVOTEES: Yes.

AVATAR ADI DA SAMRAJ: Thinking as you think you are thinking. And that's about all it is—that you <u>think</u> you are doing that. *[Beloved Adi Da laughs.]*

JONATHAN CONDIT: That's all there is to it.

AVATAR ADI DA SAMRAJ: That's all there is to it.

JONATHAN: *[laughing]* Oh, no! *[Beloved Adi Da laughs.]*

AVATAR ADI DA SAMRAJ: It's just a pattern, it's just a shape, you see. Shaping, patterning.

So, fundamentally, any form, any some-sense-of-itself in time, is confronted with the same dilemma. This was the immediate observation in this Body.

[in an amused voice] As soon as the Conjunction with this Body occurred, this first thing was noticed, this flaw was noticed. So I decided to have some very important conversations with some people about it, to see what's going on with this. And didn't get any satisfactory response, not from My point of view.

JAMES STEINBERG: At what age was this, Beloved?

AVATAR ADI DA SAMRAJ: Immediately! *[Beloved Adi Da and devotees laugh heartily.]*

JAMES: When were the conversations?

AVATAR ADI DA SAMRAJ: Oh, well, age two or so. From then on.

It is the fundamental flaw. You could say, "Well, you have to have faith." Well, *[Adi Da starts to break up with laughter]* faith in <u>what</u> exactly? *[Devotees and Beloved Adi Da laugh uproariously.]* Not only in whom,

136

and so forth—but <u>why</u>? And relative to what? Relative to the anticipation of something or other? Or what? You know?

There's nothing to be cynical about relative to faith, it's just that it's an interesting "consideration". And it's not just off-hand something. Faith profoundly entered into is a form of ego-transcendence. It's not a kind of cleverness with something invisible that somehow gets you your goods, or some hopefulness that you'll get goods, or some absolute <u>certainty</u> that you will get your goods.

Faith is not about that. It's about a heart-cure. It's about the heart getting cured of its contraction, its faithlessness. So it's not about the goods and whether, if you have faith, you get better results and so forth. Well, there's an <u>association</u> with things becoming positive (if patterns conjoin, and so forth), something better. But it's still klik-klak. It's still endlessly changing, but never eternity.

Because there is only change, you might say that that goes on forever. But that's not "eternal", because it's never <u>anything</u> forever. Eternity is just Reality. It never changes. It is What <u>It</u> is, unchangingly, and Always Already. What else could be Reality?

What can what-is-changing resort to?

What kind of resort can there be in the midst of only-changes?

What is the Source of only-changes?

Changes are no-finality, no-Fullness, never most profound, never Perfect, never (in any case) continuing. Always changing, diminishing, transforming, eventually becoming not at all (it seems) like it was, or less and less and less, such that it is hardly possible to make a connection between the present and the past.

Conscious awareness is like this—meaning in the play of patterns, awareness of patterns. The constant changing, the experiencing of changing and so forth—this is not news to you. This has been your <u>only</u> experience. And I gather from you that you've noticed that it doesn't <u>feel</u> good enough. Because if you look at all of your motives, your desires, your inclinations, and so forth, and how they are dealt with in the play of experiencing, and how it all diminishes and flows away and out and elsewhere—eventually that's the end of that washing machine!

DEVOTEES: Ohh. *[Beloved Adi Da laughs, and devotees join in His laughter.]*

AVATAR ADI DA SAMRAJ: The end of that animated whatever-it-was. It's not animating any longer.

But where are they?—all those washing machines.

Or is that all they were?

And if that's all <u>they</u> were, then what are you?

And if that's all <u>you</u> are, then that doesn't feel good enough.

<u>Nothing</u> feels good enough. Does anybody ever go tell presidents or anybody like that? *[Devotees erupt in laughter.]* Everybody's happy to be serious about political and social matters. Of course, that's a matter of rightness and responsibility. But don't hype everybody into the game that that's <u>it</u>, that your <u>life</u> has to become <u>nothing</u> but <u>that</u>—focused exclusively on that, on these social-political concerns and so forth. Everybody has to pursue Happiness—Happiness Itself. There is a larger gesture in life that has to be accommodated. Somehow or another, every generation has to be creative to accommodate it, to keep the sacred alive, to keep what is holy set apart.

That means to function, to live, to be always in the depth process moment to moment. That's the holy place, ultimately. The coincidence between that depth place and any place set apart and empowered—that conjunction is a great Pleasure Dome. That's the temple of your devotion, of your use of mind, then, of your use of—not mere outwardness—the <u>depth</u> level of your existence. You're using it in this fashion. It's a sadhana—the process of going beyond, going beyond self-contraction, going beyond limitation, entering into the Source Domain, the Domain of What is Prior or Always Already the Case, the Divine Domain. In the heart-depth, you are always in this temple domain. You can always exercise this Yoga wherever you are.

Reality is What is Always Already the Case. If Reality is whatever this <u>perception</u> is right now, then in order for there to <u>be</u> Reality, this perception has to be <u>forever</u>. But it isn't. All of that is always changing. So that's not Reality in the sense of the Fundamental. The Fundamental is Always Already the Case.

It's nothing about what <u>appears</u> that is Always Already the Case. No psycho-physical experiencing is Always Already the Case. What is Always Already the Case is What is Prior to your own contraction, your own experiencing, the "you" of existence.

In the depth, there is no separateness, ultimately. When that Process has become Most Profound, it has become Realization Itself, Samadhi.

In the apparent play of daily life, of course, it's <u>all</u> opposites. It's all klik-klak. It's twos. Replicate-shift-change. It's modifications in different speeds, it seems—various patterns, shapes. And then, in the exchanges between people, there's all this . . . what is it? Role-playing of what you look like! You're talking as and about what you look like. And names are put on that, and descriptions (and so forth), and various other entanglements get associated with that persona. It's a drama. It's like a TV show or something. Every one of you could be as interesting a subject of some TV drama as anybody else.

II.

AVATAR ADI DA SAMRAJ: When you say "I", do you speak from the inside out, or are you on the outside and the inside is "in"? If you are not merely the outside, then how come you have to go within, turn within, when it comes to doing or being anything but the outside?

Of course, there's all this "inside yourself" and such references. But all of that communication back and forth suggests that you are the <u>outside</u>, you're what you <u>look</u> like—whatever that persona is, or whatever you're trying to tell everyone it is by how you show yourself or communicate or whatever.

On the other hand, if you <u>examine</u> your experience seriously—as you do here with Me on occasion, and as you are supposed to be doing, in fact, in your practice moment to moment—"you" (it's clear when you inspect your actual experiencing) are not the outside. You're certainly observing it—anything that you would call "outside". You, in every moment, have your attention on it. You observe it, you make judgements about it and so forth. But then even that "you", the one that's being addressed by everybody who's calling himself or herself "I" and so forth, is not just what's observing, and so forth. Somehow a shape-change, a somehow-indescribable shifting, makes notions, ideas, actions.

No matter what arises, you are <u>as</u> the mere Witness.[21] And there's no description for "you" from that point. You just aren't any of the rest of that.

Just something about that seems clear at the moment, doesn't it?

DEVOTEES: Yes.

AVATAR ADI DA SAMRAJ: Well, but then who suggests this shape, this outer-looking persona? That "I", who looks a certain way, clothes a certain way, is using the body with certain attitudes—make-up, jewelry, whatever decorations, expressions, a <u>massive</u> collection of pattern, refinements, some of which have become rather rigid and continuous, and others still change a lot under the various circumstances. Then you're back to being the outside again. And we have to talk about you getting, or going, <u>deeper</u>, you know? "Within" and "inside".

21. To Stand as the Witness is to be Identified with Consciousness Itself, free of all identification with body or mind. The Witness-Position is the Native Position of all, but it is only stably Realized with the transition to the sixth stage of life.

139

When you think earnestly, you roll your eyes back, as if you are on the outside of the eyeballs or something, and you've got to go literally <u>inside</u> your body, inside your head, to <u>locate</u> the thoughts. If you believe you are the body, that's how you would describe it when you are really sensitive to it. And, otherwise, there's scientific investigation or analysis or technical piece-by-piece breakdown of the process, or whatever. Not that you have to turn your eyes back, and that you literally have to go inside your head, but the process of the energy associated with the body and the body-mind makes use of certain locations in the grosser appearance with which you are associated—this body, brain, and so forth. And certain kinds of brain functions and body-mind functions are associated with one side of the brain and some with another or some particular area in the brain combined with some others and so forth.

Well, there's all this complexity. It's electrical—this mysterious thing that comes out of the wall, or whatever it is that's playing in that wall there.

The eyes may turn in the direction of the area in the brain indicating that that area in the brain is being focused and energized, and the grid of attention is being associated with that functional area. So it's not that the eyeballs have to go up and look in there. They're turning up rather spontaneously based on an energy kind of surge. There's just a functional use of energy, specializing, locating in a certain way at the moment.

That doesn't explain "you", though, does it?

You're the one who has, it seems, a self-interest in how all of that turns out or works or whatever. And yet, apart from that washing machine, that mechanism itself, you do not in any sense take yourself into account (or require anyone else to take you into account) in your actual condition, as you <u>are</u>. And it seems that, generally speaking, people don't know anything about this in-depth dimension of their actual experiencing existence moment to moment.

It's not part of common public discourse. It's not the kind of thing people talk about on the street. You say, "Good morning, how's the weather."

When you've got a moment waiting for a bus or whatever, you don't start talking to whoever's next to you, "Well, what about the nature of the self and the real in-depth level of your experiencing, and your 'consideration' about that? And what goes on with you in meditation about that? And what's your experience about this?"

[In a high matronly voice:] "What are you suggesting? What do you mean? I'm standing here minding my own business! Good-bye!" *[laughter]*

"Oh, sorry! I thought everybody knew that." *[Avatar Adi Da laughs with everyone.]* "No, no, I didn't mean to say that. What I mean is, if you have faith and insist on feeling good, you should always be sure to include bakery goods in your diet." *[laughter]*

You know what I mean? Any religion tends to become that, but that's not what's interesting about it. Well, why don't people talk about what's interesting about it? Religion has to be more than just a conversation about social behavior—whether you're going to be harmless or harmful to one another, that endless arrangement and rearrangement. Of course, that is important, but that is just business to handle. You handle that and then you get on with the Great Business.

The Grid of Attention

(AN EXCERPT FROM *THE SAMRAJ UPANISHAD*)

AVATAR ADI DA SAMRAJ: You've seen grids in the schoolroom, made of horizontal and vertical lines? You can think of attention in this fashion, then, as being an unmoving point on a grid—let us say, a grid of infinite size, made of horizontal and vertical lines, or (in other words) made of an infinite number of possible points. If attention appears to "move" or is willed to "move", so to speak, it's actually the grid that moves. The point of attention is the same. The point of attention never moves. The grid apparently moves. And apparently, then, attention is shifted to another point on the grid. That point coincides with the object of attention at any moment.

Fundamentally, then, in terms of the mechanics of attention, that is all there is—this point of attention and the grid, which is the field of apparently modified Energy, taking on the apparent form of objects, or points, in space-time. So, in terms of the mechanics of experiencing, there is the unmoving point of attention, and the apparently moving grid, associating attention with different modifications of Energy, moment to moment. Therefore, in Truth, there is neither attention nor the grid. There is simply Consciousness Itself and Its Inherent Radiance.

But everybody doesn't want to handle this basic business so that they can go on to some greater business, because they don't think there is any greater business anymore. So they make the ordinary business so complicated that it never gets handled. And people are so strung out about it, so nervous, so stressed about it and the entanglement that it all is, that, like caged animals in zoos, they lose their place in the pattern. And they get disoriented, nutty, nervous.

You are always being "what you look like", expressing that, moving its face around to express . . . what? You all have emotions, but what is that? Such, such, and such—all your descriptions are not merely of something that's like a something happening at the surface of the skin. There's a "you" that's always being referred to. But, in any moment, if you're called to consider the matter, you are not merely this appearance. You are observing it certainly—at the very least—but even deeper than that, prior to that, prior even to attention itself, you're always potentially focused on a self-aware association with deeper levels of what you might call "you" or "yourself" than this outer "I am the body" persona. It's a selected appearance or self-presentation commonly used in the waking state moment to moment, but it's not the only one you use. You very often converse with people, or are present in a room with people, or are doing whatever with people, or are (otherwise) being oblivious to people, and yet carrying on what you regard to be a perfectly normal, just-like-you've-done-it-countless-times-before kind of day-to-day activity, without any regard for anything physical (or certainly not the "you", the social-persona-appearing-to-people kind of awareness). Instead, you are involved in a totally other kind of level of focusing—rather what people would ordinarily call "internal", entirely an emotional pattern or feeling, or, otherwise, mental or verbal. You are constantly exercising yourself in various ways that don't have anything to do with being physically aware (or, otherwise, with specialized physical awareness), such that all kinds of aspects of the physical are not in your sphere of intentional responsibility—and yet they come along anyway, it seems.

If it's "you", then how come you don't have to do something about it all the time? Or how come when you finally allow yourself to go to sleep and you wake up, to your surprise your heart didn't stop beating because you woke up again?

The thing you were afraid of is that you weren't going to be able to wake up if you allowed yourself to go to sleep. But finally you couldn't do anything about it—ZAP. When you wake up, what you were afraid of didn't happen. Your heart continued, your breathing continued.

So you don't mind going to sleep quite so much. But on the other hand, every time you wake up from deep sleep into dream states or otherwise the waking state and so forth, you begin to get the clear understanding that, one time or other, you <u>won't</u> wake up, because the heart <u>will</u> have stopped or the breathing will have stopped. And that's the end of that one.

So the one fundamental flaw in all of this is death. The problem about life is death.

I'm not making a trivial statement. Saying it a bit amusedly, perhaps, but, nonetheless, it is true. It's not a "maybe", it's not something that has only happened to a couple of people in fifty billion eons. It's not that kind of thing.

The process itself is not only that everybody dies, but <u>everything</u> changes and disappears, it disintegrates, passes through into flows of other patterns and so forth. There is no final <u>anything</u> to you in this moment here, or to anything else, or to anything you can establish, anything you can acquire, anything you enjoy, any relationship you can enter into.

It's not like you can definitely get all that and really do it good and so forth, and you're given a fixed period of time and <u>then</u> it's that. It's not that at all. It can happen anytime, arbitrarily, <u>before</u> all kinds of things get to be done.

You could get to a point where you don't want to start anything any more, because you're going to die. Well, how come you got interested in starting anything to begin with?—given the fact that you always could have gone, anytime.

So there's all this bargaining about the simple business of the fact that there is a body-mind alive and so forth. Fine. So you do your bit personally and in a collective relative to dealing with those things. But that doesn't mean that that's that, that's all there is to life. It doesn't make any difference <u>what</u> anybody says. <u>You</u> know that you are involved in something more profound than fulfilling the habit patterns of physical existence.

It's not enough, at any rate, <u>just</u> to handle life-business. It doesn't feel good enough. You can't commit yourself <u>only</u> to that. You can do that, in your creative way or whatever. But it's only a portion of it, and it's not the fundamental thing.

So people shouldn't be propagandized that handling life-business is the fundamental thing. It should be put in its proper proportion, and all kinds of things done to give people the gift of presuming once again that the quest for Wisdom is important, the process of all of that is profoundly important. And you can't just devote yourself to the physical exchange, or the patterns of gross-consciousness.

The non-humans already know this. The humans have to build it into their individual and collective understanding. It's intelligent to have noticed this. It's intelligent noticing to have noticed <u>this</u>—that it doesn't feel good enough.

On the other hand, you all seem to want to <u>argue</u> for the persistence of just that. Your life-pattern, even your expressions and so forth, frequently suggest that that really <u>is</u> all you want. Or that your principal concern is doing that for however long you've got. Or whatever blah-blah, whatever you'd say about it—just consenting to be utterly superficial, to have given up the position of depth in life and have come to the point where you don't really care about it any longer, don't even want to really hear about it.

The in-depth process is the concern of beings, and therefore human beings—all beings, human and non-human. It's the most important matter. It's the primary matter. Not to the exclusion of anything else, but in terms of primacy, and of fundamental focus, this is it, it's this matter.

Because no matter what changes occur in life, death comes at one time or another. That's the end of it. So the motive that's in life can't fulfill itself except as a kind of plastic gesture in a pattern of "maybe some others will make the gesture too, and things will go on".

But what is it all going on for? So that, out of the billions of beings sent out on this shot, <u>one</u> guy gets the egg, and for all the rest that's the end of it? That's all it was for? To perpetuate the pattern? The klikking and the klakking?

That's the force that's happening.

JAMES: That's right, Beloved.

AVATAR ADI DA SAMRAJ: Yes, that's <u>exactly</u> it. But not <u>truly</u>. That's not the Truth of it. Or that understanding is not Truth, it doesn't liberate you to presume that. None of your thinking liberates you, generally speaking, except thought associated with the process in which That Which is Prior to thinking is Realized.

You can function from the inside out, or you can function from the outside in. So, that's a choice to be made. To function from the inside out means that you fundamentally function in depth, or doing the sadhana of the process in depth moment to moment, seriously, whatever else you may be doing. If that remains your constant focus moment to moment, then the only way you can have anything to do with what you look like is to work from the inside out. Because you are not going to leave the so-called "inside" just to get "outside" about anything. You know what I mean?

So a person who's functioning in the depth, or in that in-depth process, can only associate with everything outside (or toward the outside) from there, from that in-depth position, because you won't leave it.

So you <u>have</u> to function from the inside out, from the feeling dimension out, from the point of view of discriminative intelligence and truly sympathetic and sensitive feeling. The process is ever deepening. It's not really looking back. But on the other hand, it doesn't <u>leave</u> any place. It's just a deepening of the same disposition that otherwise does everything. It's the same person that was doing whatever he or she does in daily life before, except now it is done from this in-depth position, because he or she is involved in this ever-deepening sadhana-exercise.

Clearly, somebody in whom that is occurring is going to become more serious—not inward in the sense of being introverted necessarily (it depends on peoples' quality otherwise), but more feeling-aware and more discriminative and so on.

The thing about people in ashrams in a traditional setting—as it was My experience in this Body—is that a very high percentage of them are always involved in a meditative exercise of some sort, a kind of ecstatic or mystical exercise, even. Even if you saw them involved with some commonplace task at the moment, you could see it about them somehow that they'd been involved in this in-depth practice. It was affecting their whole quality. They didn't stop it just to go out and pump water at the corner, you know? What's so important about pumping water at the corner that you are going to give up your in-depth process of self-transcending Divine Communion? You know what I mean?

DEVOTEES: Right.

AVATAR ADI DA SAMRAJ: You can pump the water. You don't have to be really out there saying, "Wow! Getting the water is <u>so</u> fantastic!" *[Beloved Adi Da laughs with devotees.]*

JONATHAN: We do that.

AVATAR ADI DA SAMRAJ: Yes. You don't have to be the TV jerk, you know. It's not going and getting the water that is interesting, not that itself. It's the in-depth process itself and the pattern within which that occurs. The in-depth matter is always the primary one, the thing of real importance that is always on the edge of the profundity of dealing with the problem (which can be described in many forms). I've just suggested to you the simple problem. The problem I've stated is that the problem about life is death.

You can see in these people at traditional ashrams that they've allowed themselves (however much active or intentional volunteering there is in it) to become, in their appearance, people who are obviously engaged in Contemplative activity, one way or another, however you would describe it in particular in each case. There are certain characteristics people show if they do that a lot and don't try to stop looking like they are doing that when they go about their so-called "life-activities" (as if meditation is not a life-activity).

In other words, you <u>are</u> supposed to be even physically, or altogether psycho-physically, transformed by the in-depth process in meditation and in daily life, constantly. You <u>are</u> supposed to be changed by that. If you rigidify everything of the body-mind for the sake of some outward conformity, from whatever direction it seems to you to be required—inside or outside—then your religious and Spiritual life can't change anything. So there has to be at least a dimension to that. The interior of that has got to be available, then, for the real religious and (in due course) Spiritual process.

III.

As I just said to you, what's really of interest, but which people don't talk about in their casual meetings or even their serious ones often, is the process in depth, that most profound exercise. Because the problem about life is death. All the ordinary occupations, then, are business to be handled, but they're not sufficient for Happiness, they're not about Happiness, they don't feel good enough themselves. The core dimension of all of this has got to be dealt with, this problem of death has got to be dealt with.

You can't just throw yourself into the pattern in an infantile fashion and just sort of go with the flow. Who is making this flow? It didn't fall out of the sky like a spray of golden messages, or blessings, manna out of the sky or something. It's the product of all kinds of influences and arbitraries and mistakes and limitations and human individual judgements, even collective judgements. All kinds of thises, thats, and all the rest of it, is this pattern flowing. Why should you just consent to go along with it? That's to abandon the in-depth faculty of discriminative intelligence, and the deeper faculty of heart-intelligence, heart-feeling awareness. So, all this "going with the flow" business, and all the conventions associated with it, didn't come falling out of the sky like a Divine message. These are all very <u>human</u> patterns—they could be changed.

What's happening? Especially this: Everybody is going to die. So, what is this really all about? So you can't merely go with the flow, commit yourself to an exercise that's about death, about everything coming to nothing. I mean, what is the point of that?

So that's the problem that death introduces—the pointlessness of any change whatsoever, the pointlessness of human existence. You feel already associated with it, so you'd like it to feel as good, or unfrightened and pleasurized, as possible. But that still doesn't change anything about the fact that it's going to die and could at any moment.

As I was saying to you earlier, this is not a different condition than the chameleon or the lion or the butterfly or whatever is confronted with. It's the same. It's the same that the trees are confronted with—the fact that everything changes and everything stops. Yet nothing stops directly, everything just flows into a pattern of another kind.

No matter what arises, no matter what changes occur (even positive), there's still death at any moment. Anything can change at any moment. Everything changes, <u>does</u> change every moment. It's just klik-klak, klik-klak, klik-klak. Slight shift, replication, basically. But also a lot of sudden endings, sudden changes. It's a plastic domain of changes, shape without meaning. The meaning-dimension is subjective, the domain of "you" mysteriously associated with the pattern that arises, which is nothing but shape, the sense of shape, modifying moment to moment.

IV.

How can the root be inside, unless you feel you are at the outside? The outside position is arbitrary, but nonetheless dominant. It's the picture you maintain, and with which you identify moment to moment. And all your speech references suggest to everybody else that they regard you as such moment to moment.

You can look for causes of anything, but also you can look for the source of anything. These are not necessarily the same. A cause is a "what". A source is a "where". The Source of all Conditions is Perfectly Subjective to it, not objective to it. And yet that Source, when Realized, is not separate from, not "different" from, anything that arises. It is not merely a philosophical judgement, it is Realization. And it coincides with the unique Yogic Siddhi I have described as Divine Recognition,[22] in the case of My devotees who Awaken to Me in the seventh stage of life.

The Siddhi of Divine Recognition can't be imitated. It can't be philosophically just chosen and done as an act of will. It is associated with a Realization and can't be engineered otherwise.

If you maintain this in-depth process, you also find that you have clarity of discriminative intelligence in every such moment. So it's not that you become stupefied.

The functional, practical, relational, and cultural disciplines at the foundation of this Way create this pattern, this shape that associates the body-mind with the asana of the in-depth process, even in the context of so-called "daily life", so that the individual becomes a Yogic "embodiment", so to speak, a Yogically patterned individual life, or life-process.

But, in the midst of this human life-process, you can associate yourself with all kinds of potential activities and amusements and patterns of one kind or another. This is something one can do. But what should you do? Well, you yourself determine this in every moment based on your disposition. One who is My devotee, one truly practicing the Yoga of this Way, is in the in-depth position, the position that freely exercises the feeling-disposition and discriminative intelligence, with regard to everything to do with mind, emotion, and body, and action, "in life", as we say. That's how it functions in relation to the usual categories of daily life, and, otherwise, it persists in this in-depth process, this in-depth seriousness, to Realize the Source-Condition That must be Realized at the root of all this, so that this strange paradox of birth and death can be comprehended, can be made a process that can be heart-embraced, altogether positively.

How can one heart-embrace, altogether positively, what looks to be just totally arbitrary pattern-activities, ending in death? What could possibly, on the face of that, be positive about it in any great sense?—other than the fact that you're stuck in it, make the best of it, and try to feel good.

But you're not exactly stuck in it, altogether, because you can respond to Me and you can be in that deeper disposition in which you can go through a process of change—in other words, where you don't have this utterly rigidified life, but can change it, even change what you do outwardly, in the context of living in community and so forth, taking on all the disciplines.

22. In the seventh stage of life, the Realizer of the Divine Self simply Abides as Consciousness, and he or she Freely Recognizes, or inherently and Most Perfectly comprehends and perceives, all phenomena (including body, mind, and conditional self) as (apparent) modifications of the same "Bright" Divine Consciousness.

If life and death are opposing while in conjunction with one another, that doesn't feel good enough. That's in some sense terrible, in fact. It's inherently terrible, however you may work to make it feel as good as possible at the moment, nonetheless.

Everything is a limitation. Limitations can be attractive at the moment, and not so attractive eventually. Generally speaking, many of the limitations of so-called "ordinary" life are attractive to you. That's why you get involved with them, rather automatically, naively, and so forth, even early in life.

There's nothing in all the three states—waking, dreaming, and sleeping—that is Liberation, Enlightenment, or Happiness. But there is That Which is Enlightenment, Realization, Happiness (Itself), Always Already. That is the Reality.

But your search within the waking state—or, otherwise, in something like the domain of dreams, or sleeping—cannot Realize Happiness. It cannot come to an end. The process itself can come to temporary ends, or get bogged down, and so forth. Then it can really end, as well. But it never becomes the Realization of Happiness Itself, Happiness as Always Already the Case, Happiness as unchanging, unconditional, or not held in place by conditions.

So none of the possible experiences—waking, dreaming, or sleeping—are about that. They are all a pattern of a kind, those three states. They're conditional. Everything that arises in those three states changes, passes away, dies.

You don't even know what a single thing is. You act by a combination of convention and motivation to survive.

JAMES: Beloved, to be Your devotee requires this knowledge about death already—confrontation with death enough to know that you have to practice beyond.

AVATAR ADI DA SAMRAJ: Yes. How you live depends on your resolution, or lack of resolution, relative to the inherent problem of death, and the fact that you're not something like a super-duper washing machine with a such-and-such-number-of-year guarantee on it. It could not only break down, but disappear at any time. That's not much of a washing machine! *[laughter]* That's a piece of bad bargain. That's a real cheap deal, a bad deal. That's what I call "retail". *[laughter]* "Never buy retail."

Anyway, how did I get to talk about that? *[with mock incredulity]* Retail and wholesale? What is it? As if life is sufficient just as a who-knows-when-it's-going-to-disappear scramble of humble human habits.

Of course, then there are all those who try to sell it to you, make it exciting. Well, fine, that keeps everybody as merry as possible, maybe, or something. So that's good, that's positive enough. But it's still not enough. It's still a kind of enslavement. It's the root of all enslavement.

You're working for a purpose that you cannot fulfill, that cannot be fulfilled in your case. It's like worker bees in a beehive, whose lives are strictly mechanical, missions going on back and forth relative to this and that service to the hive. And then it's dead. It's just brushed out. Body kicked over the edge—that's the end of that job, you know. And they just keep replicating them in there, in the queen's chamber of replications.

MICHAEL WOOD: Aren't the bees Contemplating, though?

AVATAR ADI DA SAMRAJ: Yes, they are. But that's the point—that they are Contemplating, they are not merely there. And that's what I'm saying to you, then. The Way of the Heart is about Contemplating. Not merely being here, but Contemplating, under whatever the conditions of the moment. It's not just some utopian-belief message or whatever about your outward experiencing. It's an in-depth process of going beyond the limitations that human and all conscious beings suffer, inherently.

And it's not only a matter of going beyond suffering—it is certainly that, but it's not merely that or only that. It's about directly Realizing That Which is Happiness Itself, the Root-Condition Itself, before all of your excursions of possibility wherein you lost the depth.

V.

People who have had what are called "NDEs" ("near-death experiences"), in general, say that from that point on in their lives, they're not going to be afraid of death. Something has changed about it. And each of them will have their story about whatever kind of experiences they had. It only goes to a certain depth, because it's not the actual death. Well, that's a very interesting in-depth phenomena.

But if you just look at the descriptions of the phenomena, they don't exactly make clear why you would no longer have a problem about death, or death wouldn't any longer be a problem. What exactly is it, then? Perhaps what it fundamentally is, is that these people always are still reporting in the ego-"I" person about this matter. Their experience has satisfied something in their egoic disposition—a sense of continuation, a sense that death is not what it looked like it was going to be, but it is what allows you to continue as an ego-"I".

So it's a misinterpretation of Reality, based on an experience that only went to a certain depth. The after-death process is <u>not</u> about something congratulating the ego-"I", but a process in which the ego-"I" is gone beyond—ultimately, Most Perfectly so. And all kinds of levels of limitation likewise, then, gone beyond, in the ever-deepening profound.

The profundity of religion is not about the fact that there <u>is</u> no death. It's about the fact that there <u>is</u>. And that means life cannot be blithely entered into, it has to be entered into profoundly. There must be the in-depth process.

Such it is. Such it is.

That is the Way of the Heart.

The NDE message seems to be that egos don't die at death, they survive it. Well, that's obviously not an experience based on a profound going-on that is the actual death-process. And not only that, it is not based on the full range of what the death-process can be—positively, negatively, or whatever. It could be all kinds of things in moments, and whatnot.

So the true message from the "other side" is not about ego-survival, it's about ego-transcendence. But a little bit of the experience of it, and then coming back into the framework of the body, can bring about deluded notions of the importance of the experience.

VI.

Even though there is death, what makes death bearable and profound is not the fact that death doesn't exist, but the fact that it does, that it <u>is</u> a real process. And that real process, and the Reality in Which that is occurring, is the profound matter, even while alive.

All the arrangements you can make with the body-mind—waking, dreaming, or sleeping—are temporary. I don't care if it's your girlfriend or your boyfriend or your Samadhi. As long as it's a state of the body-mind—waking, dreaming, or sleeping—it's temporary. It's not it. Any experience that depends on conditions of any kind is conditional, and, therefore, is not Eternal, not Always Already, not Permanent. It is temporary.

Are you satisfied with the presumption that you are temporary? Or that existence must be a "you", and, being a "you", it must also be temporary?

The profundity of the Way of the Heart is <u>in</u> the depth. The Way is in-depth, in the process itself, not merely in the social gleefulness, or in the social whatever.

151

Typically, when you address somebody as if you have a serious interest in them, they think you want to know about their health or some physical condition or other, their work-conditions, life-conditions, what's going on with their intimate or not. They think that's what you're interested in.

But, you see, that's not what's really interesting.

Your serious relationships, the ones you should value as being most serious, are the ones in which you really relate to one another relative to the in-depth process of this Way. Know that seriousness in one another and relate to one another on that basis, talk with one another relative to it at times and so forth. Each relationship has a different pattern, but, nonetheless, the serious relationships are those. You can have relationships of all kinds, for one or another reason. But the serious ones, if they exist at all, would be such. And, in fact, unless a relationship has and allows and you fruitfully enjoy seriousness, you wouldn't say it was satisfactory. You are still, in other words, dealing with something about it. It's not right.

The only matter of real interest in any moment (presuming you've handled the necessary business for the moment) is just this most serious, in-depth "consideration". And not just blah-blah-blah about it. I mean the process, the in-depth process, all the faculties entered into it. And you don't leave that position. You just do everything from that maximum depth-position that is characteristic of your sadhana at the moment. In fact, the only reason people would have a positive disposition to do all their life-business is if there is an in-depth process in Reality that is respected and actually experienced, entered into constantly by people.

After a while, it doesn't feel like you're going "inside" anymore. You're already there. So the deepening is of another kind. It's a deepening in place. And it's also not going "inside", it's radiating. It's not imploding, going "inside", it's radiating from the center.

Of course, many of you are smiling now and making indications that you're familiar with what I'm talking about. Well, in some sense, you are, but, in the most fundamental sense, you are not at all familiar with what I'm talking about. You would just very much like to Realize that Condition.

But you, of course, have not Realized Happiness Itself yet, because you have not found that Source-Position of Absolute Satisfactoriness. So you're still effectively a seeker in each moment, from the heart.

Right off the bat, for Me—immediately observing this thing that lives, it dies—you didn't have to tell Me anything more about how to be a window salesman and such. Whatever was going to be necessary for physical survival and so forth, that was not going to be any big deal for Me. I

152

wasn't going to devote My Life to that—speaking in ordinary terms about this matter, speaking of My Self in this metaphorical, ordinary sense.

In other words, I'm Calling you to feel this in your self, in your case—this difference it would make if you really, seriously examine the fact that everybody dies, and there's no guarantee you get to live even for one more moment. So, to really take that seriously, examine it seriously, it makes any participation in mere physical pleasure, or social pleasure, or any kind of occupation at all, experiencing at all, something less than a primary interest, something profoundly less than primarily interesting to you. You're already detached from it somehow. There's another kind of depth that's already established in you, just having noticed this.

It's a kind of wound. It's not "something to be avoided and so you get cynical" kind of business. No. This death matter is something to be profoundly "considered". Your entire sense of it, presumption about it, depends on your condition altogether, with respect to existence. It shows your level of wisdom or Realization, or lack of it.

All wisdom, ultimately, is about this paradox of life and death coinciding. Not even one moment of life is guaranteed. Therefore, not even a fraction of a moment of even any purpose at all is guaranteed, or has anything (therefore) fundamental to do with the place you are born in.

So this conjunction of (it seems) these profound opposites is a thread of seriousness in you—if you take it seriously, rather than just try to keep it in the background. It generates a seriousness in you, and moves you to always go beyond.

That's the quality in the disposition of someone who becomes, in one way or another, involved in the religious life, especially the esoteric religious life.

VII.

AVATAR ADI DA SAMRAJ: Are you all in the waking state at the moment?

DEVOTEES: Yes.

AVATAR ADI DA SAMRAJ: What makes you think that? *[laughter]*

Death is just the continuation of the in-depth process (or event), as in life. This depth being the central zone, it's what life and death play off of. An arising and a stopping. Both are on this same sort of wave-pattern. But the steady root of it is the depth. And death, therefore, is the continuation of the depth-process. This is what there is for you to be invested in.

It's just another form of retreat—the death process. But in any case it's nothing more for you than just continuing the in-depth process—deep process. Because what any kind of conjunction can feel like to you, be experienced to be by you, is determined by this degree (or actuality and quality) of the depth-sign in you.

So true and right depth in every moment—that is the Pleasure Dome Principle. It constantly goes beyond the limitations of outside and inside.

Depth has no side.

You can't shape depth.

The depth has no shape.

It's in-depth.

Not on the end of your psycho-physical effort.

Not anywhere that your search presses toward.

It's not the sensation of the seeking.

It's in-depth—the sensation that makes you seek, the dis-ease, the discomfort that is behind any seeking, desiring motive in any moment, any condition of stress.

It's all this seeker sensation, the knot of self-contraction.

It's not object to you.

It is you.

It's your own action.

You're doing it yourself, to yourself, totally psycho-physically, just as if you were pinching yourself[23] and only found this out somewhere along the line, even after having done it and suffered its effects for a great long time.

Mm?

All you had to do is take your hand away.

It's like that, in every moment.

---

23. Avatar Adi Da has often used the metaphor of "pinching yourself" to illustrate His Wisdom-Teaching relative to the self-contraction. The person is pinching himself or herself, and thereby causing all kinds of dis-ease and suffering. The person has been pinching for so long, he or she does not even realize that it is his or her own action that is causing the distress. If the person realizes that it is his or her own activity, then he or she can stop pinching and thereby be relieved of that self-imposed distress. Please also see "The self-Contracting Habit Of the usual life", pp. 188-91.

CHAPTER TWELVE

There Is More to Life Than This

BY ANIELLO PANICO

O n April 19, 1968, I turned thirty-three—and I was about ready to end it all. I had worked my way up from the poverty of my early life on the streets of New York, and now I was a successful businessman, living in Los Angeles. I had a loving wife and four great kids, a beautiful home, three new cars, interesting friends—I had really learned how to live the good life. And even though I had had to leave school early to help support my family, I had taught myself to appreciate good literature, classical music, the arts. I was right where I always thought I wanted to be.

That day, one of my best friends called me up and said that he would like to take me out for my birthday—-for drinks, to dinner, the whole thing. First we went to the Polo Lounge in the Beverly Hills Hotel and had a few drinks. Then we went to a restaurant—one of Los Angeles' finest—and had a great French meal with fine wines. After dinner, we went to catch the scene at one of the local jazz clubs.

Between sets, my friend and I were standing at the bar having another drink. I turned to him and told him something that had been bothering me for months, something I had never mentioned to anyone else:

"You know, there has got to be more to life than this." And I was dead serious. I had everything I imagined I wanted when I was growing up, hanging out in the pool rooms and bars, and then starting out as an office errand boy, and then moving up the ladder to book salesman in

Manhattan, and then finally getting promoted to Los Angeles—I had all the things I thought would make me happy. But now that I had it, I knew it wasn't enough. The feeling that there had to be more to life than what I was experiencing kept gnawing at me. My friend was about twenty-five years older than I was, so I thought maybe he had discovered something I hadn't.

But he answered me, "No, man, this is it. At some point in life, everyone has to come to the recognition that this is all there is—then you make the best of it for the rest of your life."

I thought about what he said for a minute, and then I said, "If that's the case, then I have real trouble."

My friend tried to reassure me. "You'll learn to deal with it," he said. But he didn't have any advice for me as to <u>how</u> to deal with it. So I spent the next four and a half years doing everything I could to numb myself, so that I wouldn't have to face the painful feeling that, even though I was successful in a lot of ways, my life was meaningless and empty.

I never thought to look for a religious answer—I owned a bookstore with a large section on philosophy, new-age religions, and Eastern gurus, but I only carried these types of books because they sold well. I would order them by title, but I personally never read even a page. Like the whole crowd of friends I ran with at that time, I thought that I was too sophisticated to need that kind of stuff—it all seemed like hocus-pocus to me.

Since I didn't know what else to do, I started two businesses. I poured even more energy into my four kids, doing everything I could for them, doing homework with them, going to PTA meetings, taking them to baseball games, providing for them, disciplining them, telling them bedtime stories every single night—they were the one thing that made sense in my life. But even that wasn't enough. I started drinking and using social drugs more, working later hours, going out on the town more.

All this took a toll on my marriage, and I started to have terrible arguments with my wife. We had met when we were still kids, and we had worked hard together to get ahead financially and to create a good Italian family. But she didn't seem to share my feelings of dissatisfaction with what we had, and she couldn't understand my pain, so the gap between us only grew.

But that wasn't the only place I was having difficulty—I started acting out my frustration at work, too. I got angry and sarcastic with customers or salesmen in my store for no reason. I was so wound up that I actually started having heart problems. I was really worried, but I didn't know what to do about it all. I kept having the feeling, "I want to change my life completely," but I didn't have a clue as to what kind of changes would make a difference.

Finally, my marriage collapsed. Now I was in serious trouble. My kids were everything to me—I remember having to tell the four of them that we couldn't live together any more. My eleven-year old daughter said, "Dad, I feel like my heart is breaking." In that moment, mine broke too. I was not prepared for the emotional impact of losing them—I had lost the only thing I was anchored to, the only thing I had been able to invest myself in. I visited them as much as possible, I called them a lot, I did everything I could to make it okay for them and for me, but losing them nearly destroyed me.

Two or three months later, I was sitting alone in my new apartment. Instead of facing my unbelievable anguish at the way my life was turning out, I was sitting in front of the TV, eating a TV dinner, with a joint in one hand and a bottle of wine on the table. Suddenly, I felt completely repelled by what I was doing. "What the hell have I become?" I practically shouted. I threw away the TV dinner, turned off the TV, threw away the joint, and sat down to figure out what to do about the mess my life had turned into. I sat up almost the whole night trying to think things out.

I assessed my situation: I had made money, I had a lot of "things", I knew how to be successful, but none of that seemed to have any meaning. It certainly was not making me happy. My marriage was over, and I could see that the divorce had really hurt my kids, even though I did everything I could to prevent that. But even my kids and the love I felt for them wasn't enough to give my life purpose, somehow. Since the divorce I had had a couple of girlfriends, but sex and romance didn't touch the feeling I was struggling with, either. I kept asking myself, "This is a life?"

What I didn't know at the time was that I was Spiritually starved. I was missing something, something very real, the most important thing there is—which is a connection to the Source of Life, to God, to the Divine. What I did know was that being successful wasn't enough. I knew that I was tormented by the feeling that something was missing, but I didn't know what it was or where to find it.

So I considered the options I was aware of at the time. I could sell my business, fly to Europe with a lady friend, and just float for a while. Maybe that would numb the pain. Or I could really throw myself into my business and build it into an even bigger moneymaker. Then I could afford even more extravagant toys and entertainments, and maybe that would distract me from the feeling that my life was meaningless. Or I could drop out and move up the California coast and try to "discover myself" in nature—pretty unlikely for a guy from New York, but I could try it. Or I could go to a shrink. A number of my friends were already in therapy and I had read quite a bit of Western psychology—Freud, Jung, Carl Rogers, Rollo May, and so on. But nothing I had read or heard from my friends impressed me as a way out of my suffering—my problem seemed bigger than anything a psychiatrist could fix.

Nevertheless, I thought about the different possibilities for hours, developing them in detail in my mind. But when I asked myself, "What would this option or that option do for what I am feeling?" nothing seemed to touch my fundamental feeling of despair. Finally, I decided that there was only one thing that made any sense—I should just check out of life altogether. I thought, "I am here for this life, and it hasn't worked out. There is nothing more that I want to get or do—I already have all the things I thought I wanted and they are definitely not worth the trouble. So why not kill myself? At least it would be over and I wouldn't have to despair about the meaninglessness of my life any longer."

I also remember the philosophy I had at the time: I thought that you come into this life with a kind of innocence, like my kids had. Then as a result of all the things that happen to you, you build up a kind of shell. You get jaded, hard. You lose the innocence, and when that happens, life loses its meaning. Then, when you die, you get the innocence back—everything that built up during your life gets erased, and you can go on to something else. At that time, I didn't believe in reincarnation, so I wasn't thinking that I would go on to another life—I was just hoping that the innocence would be restored and that I could go on to something else, whatever it might be.

So I thought about whether or not to commit suicide for two or three days. I finally decided, feeling completely lucid about it, that I would do it on Saturday morning.

That Thursday, I spent the evening playing with my children. My ex-wife was out, so I let them stay up a little later than usual, then I tucked them in. When they were asleep, I went to the hall closet, got my hunting rifle and shells, and put them in the trunk of my car. I went back into the house to say goodbye to my kids. I rubbed each one of them on the head as they were sleeping, telling them how much I loved them and how much they meant to me. Just as I was finishing up, the phone rang.

I wasn't going to answer it, but I didn't want the kids to wake up, so I picked it up. It was an old acquaintance named Jerry, someone I'd met through one of my businesses. Jerry had experimented with a number of different meditation techniques and new-age Spiritual groups—a year and a half previously he had spent an entire evening teaching me how to relax and breathe and use a mantra while lying on the floor. In those days, I was willing to try everything, so I went along with him, but I basically thought he was nuts.

I asked him where he was. He said he was in Los Angeles. The last time we met he was living in a Yoga community in northern California, so I asked him about that.

"No, no. I got out of that. That's why I'm calling you. I am with this man, this teacher now, and you have got to meet him. I know the two of you will really get along."

I said, "Yeah? What's his name?"

"Franklin Jones," he said. (In the early days of His Work, Adi Da Samraj used the name His parents had given Him.) This sounded like just one more of Jerry's strange and useless trips. I tried to get out of it. "Nobody is named <u>Franklin Jones</u>!" I said. But Jerry insisted, "You should meet him."

I hesitated, saying I had no time. But he finally convinced me that he and I should at least get together to talk about it. So I went down to the address on Melrose Avenue that Jerry gave me where Avatar Adi Da and some of His devotees had set up a tiny bookstore and meditation hall.

It was Friday night—the night that Jerry managed the bookstore and the night before I was planning to kill myself. I had the rifle in my car, ready for the next morning. It seemed a little funny to be spending my last night on earth with this guy I didn't know very well and who I thought was part crackpot, but I had already given up—I had nothing better to do.

Jerry and I were the only ones there the whole night. He showed me around the place. (I remember the first thing I told him was that they needed to stock the shelves with more books. Here I was, about to commit suicide, and I'm still giving business advice!) We sat in the front and talked, but there was also a small empty room at the back of the store, behind a curtain. Jerry told me that that was the place where Adi Da sat in meditation with His students. When I poked my head into the room to take a look, just briefly, I noticed the room had an unusual quality—it seemed to contain a distinct energy, a kind of peace.

Then Jerry started telling me about Adi Da and His point of view. It didn't make much sense to me, but I did get the feeling that Adi Da would understand what I was going through. For the very first time in my life, I began to express to someone my feeling of despair and how empty my life seemed. I remember that vividly. I told Jerry everything about how I was feeling.

Four hours later, Jerry said, "I'm going to close this place up. You should go home. I'll drive you."

I had my own car, so I said, "No, you don't have to do that." Then I blurted out, "I'd like to sleep here, in the meditation hall."

Don't ask me why I said that. I had never slept on a floor in my entire life. I preferred the kind of class and comfort found in places like the Beverly Hills Hilton. It was completely uncharacteristic for me to say that I wanted to spend the night sleeping on a floor. But for some mysterious reason that I couldn't understand at the time, I really wanted to stay there. After some prompting, Jerry let me.

In the morning when I woke up, something had changed in me. It felt as though I had been touched or caressed by some kind of Graceful Presence, like my troubled brow had been smoothed—just by being in that room. I felt a peace in myself from sleeping there, a peace I sorely needed to feel.

It was Saturday morning, but I wasn't thinking about killing myself anymore. I hadn't decided not to do it either—it's just that, for the moment, I was more interested in something else. Jerry had given me a copy of the manuscript of Adi Da's autobiography, *The Knee of Listening,* and I wanted to read it.

I browsed the manuscript a bit when I first woke up, then I started to read it in earnest over breakfast, and after that I just kept on going. I spent the whole day reading—and by the time I got to the end of the book, my life had gone through a total reversal!

I don't know if I can express how excited I was by what I was reading. After years of feeling so much despair, after coming to the point of utter hopelessness—now, for the first time, someone was explaining my situation to me in a way that made sense, in a way that lifted me into an entirely new way of looking at things.

For years, people had been telling me that there wasn't any more to life than what I was experiencing—and my own life certainly seemed to be proving that they were right. I kept getting richer, and as I did, I grew more and more desperate, more and more certain that success was not enough. Here, for the first time, was someone who made me feel that, "Yes, there is more to this life! Here it is, right here!"

Without even noticing it, I read past the appointed hour for my suicide. When I finished the book, I immediately started reading it over again—I stayed up all night reading it the second time through. I couldn't put it down. This is what I had been looking for—and it had come to me just in the nick of time!

"Suffering is separation, being separate, limited, a self-exhausting capsule of life-energy," Adi Da said. "Suffering is separation and separativeness. And suffering is the primary fact of individual life. The seeker's 'problem' of life, for all suffering human beings, is how to realize life under the conditions of suffering. How to remain active, 'creative', relatively and at least temporarily fearless, optimistic, and effective?"

This was the question I had been posing to myself over and over for years, which Adi Da had stated more clearly than I could ever have myself. Then, He went on to answer the question that had been tormenting me for so long:

He said that we suffer because we falsely presume that we are separate from the Source of Life, and that the Inherent Nature of that Source is Happiness Itself. He said that everything we do is seeking—a futile attempt to somehow find true Happiness. And He pointed out over and over again that this seeking for Happiness must fail because it does not touch the cause of suffering—our presumption that we are separate. I felt immense relief. No one else had been able to explain what was bothering me, but now it was obvious that I was caught in the cycle of separation, suffering, and seeking that Adi Da was describing.

Adi Da didn't suggest another, better form of seeking. He recommended that His readers understand the presumption of separation which is the cause of seeking. Without this understanding, He explained, we would live as seekers rather than enjoying Happiness, Reality, or God now. How ridiculous! I felt tremendous relief as He described His own insights into this absurd situation.

He said that if we begin to understand the presumption of separation itself—if, with His help, we can observe how that presumption of separation happens, and how it is unnecessary—then our sense of alienation from Happiness would be relieved. If this is done, He said, then a person

. . . will abide in understanding, and one will not come into conflict with one's moments, one's motives, one's actions, one's reactions. One will abide now, and now, and now. And this alone, not any motive or search or effect of these, will transform the complex of one's living. And that complex will never be one's concern, to transform it or escape it or transcend it, for one lives in understanding and draws Joy even in pleasure, in egoic ignorance, in failure, in suffering, pain, and death. Only because one abides in understanding is one already Free, already liberated from one's life.

161

Therefore, I affirm only understanding and no state or object yet to be attained. It is not a matter of purity first or at last, nor of sanity, nor wealth, well-being, goodness, or vision. All these are the imagery of search, the vanity of external peace.

Understanding is the ground of this moment, this event. Therefore, Realize understanding, and enjoy it, for you alone are the one who must live your ends and all the stages of time. The one who understands, who is always already Free, is never touched by the divisions of the mind. And that one alone is standing when all other beings and things have gone to rise or fall.

It was not just that His logic made complete sense to me (which it did—my own experience proved it). It was not just that He explained my suffering to me and even validated the feelings of despair I had been struggling with (which He did, in a way that was powerfully cathartic for me). I was beside myself with excitement because He was describing the very thing I had been hoping for, but without being able to put words to it, without being able to know what it was. He was describing the hub on which my own life and everyone's life is set like the spokes of a great wheel. He was describing the Truth, the Transcendental Reality that we are all part of. He was restoring me to my own Source, to the Heart, the Divine Self. As I read I thought, "This is exactly it!"

Thus, when understanding has most perfectly Realized itself as no-seeking in the heart . . . one is the heart. All the functions of the living being become the heart. The heart becomes the constant locus of all activity. There is no separate one to concentrate in it.

Therefore, one who has most perfectly Realized Existence as no-seeking in the heart . . . is Free, Blissful, "creatively" Alive. Thus, that one is not only no-seeking, which is Freedom. That one is eternally Present, Which is Bliss and no-dilemma.

The whole sad and stupid drama of my life over the past years seemed unnecessary. I felt immensely attracted to the alternative that Adi Da was offering. It's hard to describe, but Adi Da's words were more than ordinary words—they had much more energy, much more impact than anything I had ever read before. His insights weren't just ideas— they were alive. They opened me up and changed me. I felt His Wisdom flooding into my life as a kind of welcome, relieving Force. I decided I had to meet Adi Da in person. Suicide would have to wait.

I immediately phoned Jerry and asked him what I had to do to meet Adi Da. He told me that if I came to an orientation at the bookstore on

Monday night, I could "sit" with Adi Da in meditation on Tuesday night. I didn't know anything about "sitting" or meditation, but I was so looking forward to meeting Him I could hardly contain myself.

I went to the Monday night presentation. The person giving the orientation said to me, "You can go further and check Adi Da and His Teaching out, or you can resort to your other alternatives."

It was the perfect thing to say to me. I answered, "I don't have any other alternatives." And that was true!

The orientation itself was brief—only two or three people came—and we were told to return the next night, Tuesday, to sit with Adi Da.

The next day I scrambled to finish work in time to go home, take a shower, and get down to the bookstore. I was going to "sit" with a Spiritual Teacher. It was all so out of the ordinary for me—but I was really interested.

I was there on the dot. I had been asked to return the manuscript of Adi Da's book, so I brought that with me, too. My approach to the event wasn't very "spiritual"—it's just that I was tremendously excited to meet the fellow who had written this book. I had been in publishing a long time and had met many authors, but their books had never impressed me the way that Adi Da's had. What could He be like?

I entered the meditation hall, sat down with my back to the wall, wearing my horn-rimmed reading glasses, and continued to read the manuscript. Adi Da came in and, without saying anything, took His seat at the front of the room, facing the group of twenty or so people who were there that night. He looked straight ahead and then, at times, He also looked around the room, gazing at the space just above our heads. After watching Him for a few minutes, I started reading the manuscript again.

Looking back at it, I can see that this was not the most sensitive thing to do, but I knew nothing about meditation or how to relate to a Guru. The whole situation was new to me and I felt a little awkward, so I returned to what was most familiar to me—reading. After a few minutes, though, I looked up at Him again. He looked directly at me. I felt a Force emanating from Him—it was peaceful and yet energetic, pleasant but not overwhelming—and I also felt a kind of connection to Him. But I still felt somewhat awkward, so I went back to reading the manuscript again.

After a few minutes more, I looked up at Him again. This time, He was staring right at me. I began to feel a very pleasant feeling in the center of my heart. I was very warm. Even though I couldn't tell what it was, I could tell that something out of the ordinary was going on here. So I put the manuscript down and sat up straight in a meditation posture, like everyone else in the room. It seemed important to be respectful of the process that was taking place, whatever it was, and to cooperate with whatever Adi Da was doing. From that point on, I simply looked at Him.

When the meditation was over, He left the room. I got up and followed Him to a small office in the back. He was sitting in the chair at His desk when I walked in, and it was clear to me that He was not in an ordinary state of awareness. I didn't know anything about Spiritual experience at the time, but I could tell that He was in a kind of Swoon, or Bliss-State. He seemed to be "coming down" from that Swoon to a more ordinary, "functional" awareness, so I walked right over to where He was sitting, put out my hand, and said, "My name is Neil Panico, Franklin. I am really glad to meet You."

He told me to sit down, which I did. Then He turned to me and said, "What's happening?"

I was floored. All my life I had used that very phrase millions of times with my friends, with people I met in business, with my kids—all the time. It was the most familiar thing He could have said to me. I found myself blurting out to Him, "I don't know, man, I can't relate to anything or anybody anymore."

I didn't think about it when I said it; I didn't mean to lay my problems on Him—it was spontaneous, as though it were the most natural thing in the world to tell Him my darkest secret. Immediately, He reached over and hugged me. I was a little taken aback at first, but He was so natural in the way He assumed an intimacy with me.

As He held me in this big bear-hug, and as I relaxed into it, I felt the most wonderful, nourishing feeling of coming home, of coming to rest. I felt tremendous, instantaneous relief from the incredible torment that I had been carrying around—just as I had when I read His book, but even more so. The warmth and the beauty of the feeling He communicated through that hug was fantastic—and it was such a long hug. By the time He let me go, my terrible feeling of emptiness and despair was gone. My suffering of so many years was over. He had removed it.

He said, "What do you do?"

I told him what I did for a living.

Then He asked me, "Why don't you come around a little bit?"

"Yeah, I'll definitely be around."

The next day I took the rifle back to my house. I thought, "I don't know what this is about, but I've got to check it out." I started going to the bookstore and hanging out with Adi Da in the back room.

We had the most wonderful times in the tiny back room of that little Los Angeles storefront—there were always at least a handful of people there with Him, working, talking, laughing. There was always a lot of laughter—He was so full of humor! Sometimes, He would give talks, spontaneously. And then, everything would grow quiet and He would go into meditation. The room would fill up with the incredible feeling of His Love and Fullness, His Freedom, His Humor, His Peace. We would sit around Him, basking in that Feeling, wanting nothing more than to be with Him.

Since that very first meeting with Avatar Adi Da, I have never suffered so horribly again. I have never felt that kind of terrible Spiritual despair again, not for a moment. I am telling you the absolute truth. My horrible suffering was taken away forever, absorbed by my Guru.

Aniello Panico with Avatar Adi Da in Los Angeles, 1972

The Mountain Of Attention, 1996

CHAPTER THIRTEEN

December 10, 1996

You Can't Expand "And"

*The gathering of December 10 starts with Carl Pengelly's confession of
a recent experience in which he tacitly felt that whatever he was perceiving was peripheral to his being, and that he rested in a place
deeper than that. When Carl says that he had a sense of being "more free"
as a result of that intuition, Adi Da Samraj initiates a "consideration" relative to whether or not Happiness is "more" of something.*

I.

AVATAR ADI DA SAMRAJ: There are negative emotions. All negative emotions are contractions of feeling. And then there are what you would call
positive emotions, and all those are expansions of feeling.

Happiness is obviously not the most contracted possible emotion,
that's really negative and dark. But neither is Happiness simply an expansion of an otherwise positive or expansive emotion (as you might imagine it to be). Because, if that were so, then Happiness would have to be
completely expanded emotion—just that. And perhaps it would become
as mad as the completely negative possibility of emotion is, in its
depressed way.

Happiness, in other words, is not in the extreme. It is not out of balance. To be without limitation, it can't be infinitely negative. That would
be terrible. And being merely infinitely positive is like too much light, in
a gleeful, mad sense. It is out of balance.

So how can there be feeling without limitation that is not merely a play on one side of the coin? This is not merely a mental puzzle. It has to be Realized. It can't merely be described. It is the root of emotion, central to emotion, at the core of it. It is not merely expansion. Ultimately, expansion still retains a sense of a point of definition. No matter how intensely felt the feeling of relatedness is, it is still the same thing. It is just a fundamental factor. Your feeling of separateness is like that—your feeling of otherness, of "difference". They are basically always the same. They are not a something that changes once they are an element of something. It is just so.

Think of the meaning of the word "and". Is there anything you can do to make it more intense? *[laughter]*

Mm-hm. So it is just what it is. So what else is like that?

It is not merely one side of the coin done completely. It is not merely infinite expansion. It is not infinite contraction. You may think, "The self-contraction is, so the Truth is to expand, rather than to contract." *[laughter]* And you go from *[hunching over timidly]* "me-me-me-me-me" to *[sitting up straight, throwing His Head back and His arms out wide and singing at the top of His voice]* "MMMEEE!!!!" *[laughter]*

No, that is not the opposite of egoity, that is the magnification of egoity. You must make sure that this error is corrected in your case.

To feel beyond self-contraction is to feel beyond the point at which that factor is introduced. Because, like the word "and", the self-contraction is just that. Once it's there, it's there. That's that. It can't be any more "it-er" than it is. It is always just exactly what it is.

To transcend the self-contraction, or the action that is self-contraction, does not mean simply to expand, or for "you" to expand rather than to contract. That is the self-contraction deciding to go beyond itself by expanding itself. No. At the point of the act itself, the very point itself, in the moment—to feel beyond that contraction, just that, is instant. It is not merely to expand, it is to be vanished of that contraction and therefore to not be introducing it anymore into the scheme of Reality. It is not to introduce another thing into the scheme of Reality which is the expansion of the separate point of view. That Which <u>Is</u> need not be expanded. It is Always Already the Case, in and as every case. Which means that It is all cases and transcends each and every one. The Realization of It, then, is a profound matter.

To be motivated and seeking all the time and so forth, and to become sensitized to the failure of that, the stress of it; then to practice this devotional Yoga, Communing with Me, surrendering and forgetting yourself, not merely expanding yourself in feeling response to Me; then to freely feel, discover, that the stress, this failed occupation of seeking, this motivation that you always feel is there all the time, is your own action, and you're capable in every moment of locating and feeling beyond it in Communion with Me—this is a profound discovery.

Being thus profound is quite a different matter than what anybody does who picks up *The Knee of Listening* and just reads it on through. Anybody would get something about this matter of self-contraction out of that, and feelingly understand something about what it is I am talking about. But you won't have heard Me when you put down the book, having finished reading it—even though you will have understood something, perhaps, that you value, that seems useful to you to be bringing into your view of life.

So, generally speaking, I presume all My devotees, even before they became formally associated with Me, must have read *The Knee of Listening*—and other of My Words about this matter of listening and hearing. And all have some sort of sense of it, therefore, even from the very beginning, just from reading it. But that is not it, even though you read and you think about it some and put a little two-and-two together about yourself and something about it feels right. Yes, but there is a big difference between that little bit of "consideration" you might bring to reading and talking about it, and the difference it can make for the kind of person I described to you a few minutes ago—who is really in the stress of seeking, is even coming to Me seeking and responding to Me and practicing the devotional Yoga and then, suddenly, really understands, gets to the root of this stressful constant motivation that leads to every other kind of thing by which he or she has exploited and abused himself or herself. Coming to the end of their rope as seekers, then such people seriously "consider" My Word about seeking and about most fundamental self-understanding.

And because it is a profound level of feeling-requiring need to "consider" such a matter, then (when there is a profound process) the entire person that goes into the "consideration" and comes out hearing has gone through a profound in-depth process, in feeling-Contemplation of Me, not really explainable.

So when self-understanding becomes most fundamental, as I have communicated to you, it is that only for somebody for whom this has been a most profound and in-depth "consideration" that is really at the edge of an acutely felt dilemma of life. I don't mean merely a dilemma in practical terms, that requires you to handle business and so forth. I am talking about

169

a core dilemma—just the un-resolved life, still going about seeking, stressed by that, feeling disturbed and full of accumulated life, and hanging out there, and having to be dealt with and so forth. And, then you discover you don't even know what a single thing is. And you never thought about anything significantly your whole life—not very profoundly.

So everything about this matter of most fundamental self-understanding, or hearing, has to be a long-term and in-depth "consideration" to be true, because it involves all of the person, the totality of this egoic "I"-presumed entity.

So it is not just from a reading, even though all kinds of things may come together in a person's life when they read *The Knee of Listening* or other forms of My Teaching, and they feel like they have gone through a profound conversion. Well, certainly, that is typical also. And there is a conversion in all kinds of ways that can be described in those terms. Their response to Me, and everything associated with that, is a kind of conversion.

It is a profound matter, then, to become My devotee, under vows to Me. But that is not hearing. That is not seeing. It is the beginnings of the process, and it is itself profound. Those beginnings are profound. But you all must understand there is a difference between whatever all came together when you read *The Knee of Listening*, when you first seriously "considered" My Word and your response to Me (whatever you can alto-gether positively say about it), and between hearing or seeing. I some-times hear people who have not even really begun the foundation prac-tice suggest that they are practicing in the context of the sixth stage of life in the Way of the Heart already, or who knows what. The absurdity of people in their self-mindedness, not surrendered yet and yet claiming to be already "Realized" in every respect. Those who do that are just being full of themselves. They are expanding. The "point" is expanding.

You must understand, ultimately, that That Which Is is not the "point" in the middle. On the other hand, It is not the sphere, however far (infinitely) away outside, because such would have a center. That Which Is has no center. It has no bounds.

Do you realize that you won't be satisfied with anything whatsoever? You cannot be satisfied—you are seekers. But you can talk yourself into thinking, feeling lazy, and so forth, as if you are not a seeker, as if (instead) you are luxuriating in having a whole bunch of whatever it was you wanted.

When "considering" this matter of seeking, you start "considering" My Arguments relative to hearing on a basis other than seeking. You think you are not really seeking. You have found whatever describes you altogether as something you are complacent about. So, in fact, when you are "considering" My Arguments, when you are practicing the devotional resort to Me moment to moment, the devotional Yoga, you are approaching it from the point of view of <u>not</u> seeking it.

You sometimes feel like you are sort of zoned out, indiscriminate, and desensitized, so you don't think you are really seeking very intensely at the moment. It is sort of there, but you don't really get down to it. It doesn't have enough importance for you. You prefer to be complacent and desensitized and otherwise occupied and so forth. So the profound matter that is hearing, or the profound matter that is listening (which must precede hearing), just starts being engaged as sort of religion-business lingo without any kind of depth. And, instead of dealing with the matter of listening to the point of hearing, people start talking about their "case" instead, not really understanding in depth, right at the point of the root of seeking—not really understanding that most profoundly.

So you must not be desensitized to the fact that you are seeking, but rather, be very sensitive to it, in the form of everything you are doing and so forth, and feeling the stress of it, the discomfort, the dissatisfaction that is the root of all seeking. And, therefore, what you are projecting is to find Happiness somehow—pleasure, Happiness, whatever feeling you've got about what you are really looking for all the time.

Then Happiness becomes expansion, or seeking based on self-contraction. But Happiness is not that. Perhaps Happiness is something like the word "and". You can't intensify it. It can't be "and-er" than "and". It's just "and".

"And". You can't intensify it.

Happiness is something you are trying to feel toward based on expanding past your present contraction and bad feeling. So it feels like an expanded positive. It is what there is now (that is a limitation and contraction) made positive and then expanded infinitely. Well, that becomes your notion of Happiness. It's the seeker's notion of Happiness. Whereas everything expanded, everything gone yangish, becomes madness. Everything yangish absolute is crazy. And yinnish absolute is dark nothingness. So they are both out of balance.

Happiness cannot be what the seeker is looking toward, because he doesn't understand himself or herself. Both the yang and the yin are diversions from, or a play off of, a center that is indefinable and in some sense cannot be magnified—like the word "and". It always already is exactly what it is. It is Happiness Itself. Happiness Itself is not about expanding or magnifying anything in this ultimate sense. It is not about that. It may be meaningful to use such words sometimes, relative to the process of this sadhana, but, ultimately, you must understand it is not about that.

Everything is self-contraction. Even expanding is self-contraction because it is something initiated from a state that is already contracted. So no matter what you do, expand or contract, you are still doing it on the same point, the same definition.

DANIEL BOUWMEESTER: In the effort to be expanded is a feeling of stress and contraction.

AVATAR ADI DA SAMRAJ: Yes, that point is already there. The point of the tightness that motivates you is already there. Sometimes you want to expand. Sometimes you can't help yourself, you've got to be contracted. But it is still the self-contraction at its root. Both of those are seeking. The down is seeking a certain way, and the up is seeking another way. But the contraction is already at the root of both of them. They play off of it. But both directions have their liabilities. And so it is always this play of regaining balance—and plays off of balance, and relative balance, and relative imbalance—relative to all the kinds of pair systems, or degrees of subtlety you can find relative to composite conditional reality.

If the sushumna[24] was about expanding, then there would be no ida-pingali[25] surrounding it. If the core were expanding, then how could there be the Arrow?[26] So it is something more profound than merely expanding. The transcendence of self-contraction is more profound than merely deciding to expand rather than contract, because in either case, you are engaged in a doing that _is_ the self-contraction. To decide to expand is a decision from the point of view of contraction. To feel contracted is just to intensify an already established feeling of separateness.

So it is the core action, the root action—that is behind every motivation, every motivated moment, every gesture of seeking—that must be located. This is a profound discovery, when this is understood—not just entered into in a dark sense, but to get to the point where you are not just talking about something, breezing about it with a lot of words, or

24. In traditional Yoga, sushumna is the esoteric nerve pathway (or "nadi") corresponding to the spinal (or ascending) line of the Circle, through which the Kundalini Shakti is understood to flow.

25. In the Hindu understanding of esoteric anatomy, ida and pingali are two energy-circuits that are on the right and left sides of the body, flanking sushumna. They are understood as the circuits for male and female, or yang and yin, energy, and they are said to be combined in sushumna.

26. For a description of the "Arrow", please see the sidebar on p. 203.

feeling it off in your body somewhere. "I felt the self-contraction in my right leg," you know, that kind of stuff, all that sensation stuff.

No, to realize it subjectively—in other words, to be in that position—is understanding. And not merely to be it, but to locate it, and simultaneously understand it (so that there is both the locating of it subjectively, and the understanding of it in place)—this becomes the capability to do just that in every moment. Every moment there is the feeling of seeking, but in every moment, you can understand and feel beyond the self-contraction, because that is why you are seeking. That is why there is this core stress in any moment. You can always feel beyond it, once there is this most fundamental self-understanding.

So you can always do this transcendence-of-self-contraction work at any moment, and therefore in any stage of practice from that point. It is not about expanding. It is about vanishing the point of contraction—which, of course, you will only completely do when there is the Realization that characterizes the seventh stage of life.

So the practice is one in depth, then—not a shallow, "I am contracted, so I will expand now." No, it is to understand, to vanish the very point of contraction. That is the essence of self-surrender and self-forgetting. So hearing is the most profound competence of self-surrender and self-forgetting, such that it becomes directly self-transcending. Always, in every moment, the point of view of self-contraction, ego-"I", or separateness, is felt beyond.

Most fundamental self-understanding, or hearing, undermines, immediately, and at the root, the entire basis for the complex life of seeking. And this requires a transformation of life altogether. But it is also, then, a work, a means you have in your continued practice of Ruchira Buddha Bhakti Yoga, a means you have for going beyond the self-contraction, and all of the further stages of the process of the Way.

Most fundamental self-understanding, or hearing, is a fundamental means, then, that you bring to the Spiritually responsible stages, because the Spiritually responsible stages in the Way of the Heart are about ego-transcending practice that goes beyond the errors of the stages themselves. It is ego-transcending because it involves the constant exercise of hearing, the "conscious process", in that form. So it is the exercise of the "conscious process", as hearing, combined with all these secondary and supportive exercises that are the total practice of "conductivity". This is the Pleasure Dome principle. It is a Yoga. It is Yoga.

So hearing is exercised in the Spiritual stages in this Way, and it is not merely a matter of assuming the self-contracted point of view of a

173

body and feeling energies. It is a non-egoic process. Seeing is non-egoic. In other words, it is hearing-based. The seeing Yoga is associated with the "conscious process" of hearing, exercised moment to moment. The self-contraction, in other words, is directly gone beyond, vanished, heart-vanished, moment to moment.

So it is not a seeker's Spiritual practice. And it is not merely evolutionary or developmental in the sense of expanding the ego-"I", expanding its knowledge, experience, or mobility (even in planes beyond the physical). That is all part of the psycho-biography of the ego. All of the first six stages of life are the psycho-biography of the ego.

But it is an in-depth matter, not merely something you can think and talk about. The Way of the Heart is a "practicing-school"[27] Way, but not merely in the sense that there are disciplines required. That is so, but also in the sense that it is an in-depth, real process, not merely a superficial one that you talk about with others (or to yourself), and think about and read about—that sort of comfortable (more or less) being entertained by the religious life. No, it's a serious, in-depth process, constantly—not just talked about. And, therefore, all the disciplines associated with that pattern of sadhana are required.

The Way of the Heart must be done seriously, and not superficially. It is an in-depth, real process that is Happiness Itself.

II.

AVATAR ADI DA SAMRAJ: Are you in the middle of actively growing a beard, Carl? Or is this the final product? It seems to be changing in the last week or two.

CARL PENGELLY: Yes, it's starting to grow longer.

AVATAR ADI DA SAMRAJ: So it's a new beard? You recently decided to do this, and are right now spending a lot of your time every day thinking and observing and feeling things about that beard, aren't you? [laughter]

CARL: [laughing] I like it. I think about that.

AVATAR ADI DA SAMRAJ: Yes, your self-image is changing, and a whole different theatre of your own face starts appearing. You become very much

---

27. "Practicing school" is a phrase coined by Avatar Adi Da to refer to those in any tradition of sacred life who are committed to the ordeal of real self-transcending discipline, under the guidance of a true Guru. He contrasts the "practicing school" with the ineffectual—and often presumptuous—"talking school" approach. The "talking-school" approach is characterized by talking, thinking, reading, and philosophical analysis and debate, or even meditative enquiry or reflection, without a concomitant and foundation discipline of body, emotion, mind, and breath.

absorbed in this, and whether you like it, or you don't like it, and do others like it, and so forth. And all the trimming, and all the little bits of details you get into with all the individual hairs and masses of hairs and ends of hairs, and trim this, shave this, grow this, trim this today. *[laughter]*

CARL: You're absolutely right. I have been feeling too much attention on it.

AVATAR ADI DA SAMRAJ: I mean, you'd be dealing with your face, anyway, even if you weren't growing a beard. You'd be shaving it otherwise. So growing a beard, really, then, causes you to notice something that you, perhaps, were not so sensitive to before. Because now that you've noticed this—certainly, in this discussion, you're noticing it—it doesn't make any difference whether you grow your beard or shave it.

CARL: No, it doesn't.

AVATAR ADI DA SAMRAJ: You can't get out of the trap anymore. It has served the purpose of reflecting you back to yourself.

CARL: Well, what I've come to realize, Lord, is, as You are saying, that there is no way out.

AVATAR ADI DA SAMRAJ: In other words, you are self-concerned, in a "Narcissistic" fashion. And growing your beard is not itself a unique example of that, as if you weren't doing it before. No, growing your beard is just something you can do. But in doing it you can notice something about what you do all the time about this business of how you look.

How <u>who</u> looks? Are you the guy inside all that—like that bag of sausage casings that's your insides? All these organs floating around in disgusting soup? Animated by all <u>kinds</u> of other organisms and stuff going on all the time? It's basically a digestive bucket around a little pleasure zone down at the bottom there. Everyone goes on and on about it all the time.

Are you the inside part? The actual physical part inside doesn't seem to be the part you generally like to identify with. You like to identify with the way it looks on the outside. So who are you then? There's nothing in there but a lot of bags of <u>muck</u>! *[Beloved Adi Da laughs with everyone.]* . . . that anybody will very quickly want to throw out, as soon as you stop moving, stop breathing, all the rest. They can't wait to get rid of the thing!

So this "inside you" that somehow is just casually presumed, but never really inspected, is obviously not the contents of the bag. But, obviously, it's not just what it looks like, either. I mean, just the surface appearance—a lot of which has nothing to do even with your body, anyway—it's clothing and other people's experience of other people who look something like you, and what that looks like, then, when they see you. It's endless!

But you feel all kinds of things in addition to how the body appears. There's all this perceiving, all this conceiving, all these emotions, all these sensations—not just a look. And yet, all of those things are happening in the bag of muck? Why would you want to have anything to do with a person's thoughts, then? They've been revolving around in this glupperous mass. And then you sputter out some vocalizations about it. Better if you just sat there quietly and we just looked at your face. Just keep it washed and that's it. We don't want any report from the <u>inside</u>, you know what I mean? *[laughter]*

I mean, maybe it's trying to get out. And what if it did? *[laughter]* Disgusting! It's got to calm down. It's the "and". *[Everyone suddenly stops laughing.]*

DEVOTEES: Mm! Oh!

AVATAR ADI DA SAMRAJ: It's just what it is. It can't be any more intensely what it is than the word "and" can be more intensely what <u>it</u> is, just as itself.

You could put "and" in a context. Like, you're at the bank, and the bank teller says, "Five dollars . . . and nine hundred billion dollars." *[laughter]* You know, that "and" is very important, because <u>all</u> of those dollars, then, are your dollars. But it's only as a connective between these other things—the five dollars and the nine hundred billion. The "and" itself has no intensity.

So, in your body, everything inside, behind the skin, has no intensity. It's like the "and". It's the appearance of it, the outside, that (generally speaking) has the meaning, or intensity—although you can't discount all the rest of it, because there are all kinds of workings in addition to looking. And yet, if they're just inside the skin, then you're looking at "bag of glop"—and no wonder you don't want to talk about yourself!

On the other hand, it's not true. That's <u>all</u> you want to talk about—is yourself. That's all anybody wants to talk about. It's the only thing you're really interested in. But you don't know what that is, either. So all you can do is be self-contracted about it.

Anyway, hearing takes place when it's important for you to transcend the stress of your seeking life—your endlessly unfulfilled life, your life that is not leading toward fulfillment in any ultimate sense, or Happiness sense. It doesn't mean it has to be otherwise, has to be profoundly negative. In fact, it could be quite the opposite. You could, generally speaking, have your life-act together, and, still, this is what there is to be noticed—

like Carl growing his beard. It's always the same thing, one thing, to notice. And the transcendence is not a merely intellectual matter.

It is to be transcended by being vanished—this thing that you're always doing. It's to stop the pinch, not expand the hand.

DEVOTEES: Ah!

AVATAR ADI DA SAMRAJ: So when you say "inside" or refer to yourself "inside", you're not referring to that glop in there. But you're referring to a depth, deeper than the look, the outer appearance perceived by others. That deeper part is real. It's just as fundamental as any perception of your appearance. It's all part of it. But, on the other hand, it's not the same as inside your bag of flesh. The more "inside" you go in that, the less "you" it looks like.

So the inside is really the depth, not the difference. It's not the opposite of the outside. It is a depth where you are responding to Me. So it is not about dissociation.

You must remain sensitized, not desensitized by all kinds of means, including daily life consolations. You must persist in the in-depth process and not desensitize yourself to the reality of your condition, the condition in which you are aware and feeling yourself, in the practice of Ruchira Buddha Bhakti Yoga moment to moment.

So the functional, practical, relational, and cultural disciplines of this Way bring this integrity, sensitivity. They allow even all aspects of your life to reflect you to yourself. And, as you may recall, as I said in *The Dawn Horse Testament*, one of the fundamental purposes of the disciplines is to serve this reflective purpose. If you do not place a limit on the body-mind and all of its parts, just as a poet is limited by the form of a sonnet, then you'll simply be expanding as the self-contraction. You will not be noticing its nature as an activity. It must be reflected to you—to itself. It must be found out.

Instead of seeking, the seeker becomes the "consideration"—the motivator, the dis-ease, the sense of dis-ease, disturbance, however you describe it. You must find it and feel it yourself. It motivates you. It is motivating you, in every moment, to get to feel good, to feel Happiness, to achieve whatever, to seek whatever. Whatever it becomes in its enactment in the body-mind, it is still, at its root, always the same thing. This is what must be found, and understood, and transcended thereafter, moment to moment.

But this can't be done without seriousness, without depth. It's at the depth of your feeling of existing, which for you, fundamentally, is itself the self-contraction.

177

"Contractio ergo sum." *[laughter]* "I contract, therefore I am." And "I am contraction, therefore I am." Or "Contraction is the nature of my existence." Or "I am self-contraction itself."

The Way is, ultimately, not about intensifying anything or magnifying anything, but about being something. But, while in this gesture of self-contraction in the midst of experiencing and so forth, while in the course of your sadhana, it still makes sense to sometimes make use of such words as "intensifying". But, fundamentally, the process is in-depth, and always, therefore, in-place. Because however deep you've gone, you are. You can't be any deeper than deep, no matter how much deeper you go. At some point, that's as deep as it gets.

III.

CARL: Beloved, something happened the other day when I was napping. I became aware of the "I" as the self-contraction, because I was it—whatever it is altogether. That's what I was feeling, that it was an intensity that I felt throughout the entire being or body.

AVATAR ADI DA SAMRAJ: Did you notice that you were doing it?

CARL: Well, I directed my attention towards You. I just felt it.

AVATAR ADI DA SAMRAJ: Well, feeling it is just sensitivity to it, that I was talking to you about earlier. Usually you are desensitized to even the very fact of your own self-contraction, stress, sensation, feeling, or emotion. You just feel the "peripheral motivation in conjunction with everything" kind of busy-ness.

So sometimes you may be particularly relaxed, set apart from it—speaking (necessarily) of a devotee of Mine in this case, because it would have to be somebody who's familiar with and responsive to My "Consideration"—and then, in that situation of being sensitized, relaxed, and so forth, suddenly, the reality of self-contraction, the awareness of it, impressed you. But that, as I said, is simply sensitivity.

What I've Called you to do is establish all the functional, practical, relational, and cultural disciplines as the right pattern of the Way of Realizing Me. They are the pattern of sensitivity—placing a form on it, a structure on it, such that it reflects itself back upon itself, rather than just keeps on expanding itself infinitely, more and more seeking, and so on. The disciplines reflect it all back upon itself, and become a "consideration" at its root because you cannot simply satisfy it. It is all, to a degree, frustrated, or made lean—all functions brought under control—and, therefore, doesn't have the

178

buzz of self-indulgence about it any more. And you're just sensitive, then, to all your doings. It's all reflected back to you in your "consideration".

But you're also enabled to be sensitized to the self-contraction itself, to the degree of hearing Me, which is to find out that you are doing it. It's not about meditating on the self-contraction. Hearing is not constant meditation on self-contraction. It is, rather, the heart-understanding-response to Me that understands this act in every moment, this act that is your own act, and sets up signals, like even in your mind—the "conscious process" of self-Enquiry,* or some form of the practice associated with the Devotional Way of Faith.*

JAMES STEINBERG: So the sensitivity sends up the signals for the "conscious process" to begin?

AVATAR ADI DA SAMRAJ: Yes. It is a necessary means whereby the Way becomes a process in depth, a core process. Not just a lot of peripheral doings out here but a discipline, and a "consideration" that is focused in-depth.

So it is all serving a fundamental and continuous sensitivity—sensitivity to Me, altogether. If you are responsibly maintaining the body-mind, you can be truly directing the faculties with clarity in this devotional Yoga. But also, then, sensitivity to the entire process of this devotional Yoga, the entire process of your life in the context of the practice of this devotional Yoga, and all the "consideration" associated with it—everything that is "conscious process" and "conductivity", everything that is devotion, everything that is discipline. All this becomes a constantly deepening or ripening sensitivity to the understanding—the direct finding and feeling beyond—the fundamental stress you feel lies in every moment.

There is a fundamental stress at the core of all seeking. There's a fundamental stress in every moment that feels, "I'm not Happy!" There's all kinds of other things you could say about it. But it's that signal. Every moment is already that, and, therefore, looking in all directions, in terms of every functional opportunity, for a way to cure that, to get rid of that sensation, to get into satisfactoriness.

But there is no final satisfactoriness. There are moments of relative resolution relative to some kind of things, but it's not absolute resolution, it's not Eternal Happiness.

So what I Call you to do is to notice this stress is the root of your every question, your every action. I ask you, as one of My Fundamental Questions for you to ponder, "What are you always doing?" Entered into in depth, this pondering is about a very profound discovery.

The Ten Fundamental Questions

Avatar Adi Da has Given ten questions for pondering of His Arguments relative to the root of the self-contraction and the Mystery of Existence. His devotees may ask these questions of themselves in formal meditation or in daily life:

"What Am 'I' Always Doing?"

"Avoiding Relationship?"

"Who or What Is Always Already The Case (Before 'I' Do Anything At All)?" or "Who, What, and Where <u>Is</u> The Inherent Feeling Of Being,* or Existence Itself?"

"Am 'I' The One Who Is 'Living' (Animating or Manifesting) me (the body-mind) Now?"

"Who Is 'Living' me Now?"

"How Do 'I' Relate To The One Who 'Lives' me?"

"Do 'I' know What any one or any thing <u>Is</u>?" or (in relation to any particular being, thing, condition, or event that arises) "What <u>Is</u> it?"

"Who, What, and Where <u>Is</u> Inherent Love-Bliss, or Happiness Itself?"

"Who, What, and Where <u>Is</u> Consciousness Itself?"

"What Will 'I' Do If 'I' Love The Ruchira Buddha, Adi Da Samraj, The Da Avatar?"

The Dawn Horse Testament Of The Ruchira Buddha,
CHAPTER NINETEEN

You can listen to Me say one thing or other about "self-contraction and feeling beyond it" <u>thousands</u> upon <u>thousands</u> of times, and, then, all of a sudden, having done sufficient sadhana as My beginning devotee, you will realize exactly what I mean—when you utterly coincide with that "consideration" of most fundamental self-understanding, and the capability that it is from then on—and what a profound matter it is that in every moment it can be re-exercised.

In every moment, you will find yourself again in that same stressful feeling-sensation—about to do something or other—and will <u>notice</u> this. And, in the noticing, in the "conscious process" gesture and "conductivity" gesture associated with it, you will feel beyond <u>that</u> very thing. It's not a matter of dealing with all the other stuff in the experiential domain and so on, but this root (which is the fundamental self-stress) can be vanished in any moment. And so it is.

After the hearing crisis, there is the demonstration of it as this random, moment to moment, exercise of hearing itself. And then, from there, the "consideration" of the seeing process, the psycho-physical Yoga of Spiritual Communion with Me, can be done without self-contraction being the cause, or the reason, or the logic (or idea) of it. So it's quite a different matter than it is said to be in the traditions. The Way of the Heart has some fundamentally different elements—unique elements, in other words—that makes it a "radical" process that leads to the seventh stage of life, the seventh stage Yoga of not merely expansiveness, but egoless Demonstration of the Inherent Divine Radiance.

IV.

AVATAR ADI DA SAMRAJ: To expand, there has to be "difference", there has to be separateness, there has to be relatedness, there has to be otherness. You can't expand if there's only one. You can't expand "and". *[laughter]*

"And" was actually <u>Me</u>, a Murti* of Mine, a "Name" of Mine (you could say), a Form of Mine. "And" was My Threshold Personality, outside the Communion Hall on Melrose. When I first opened the Ashram on Melrose Avenue, I put a large "&" in the opening to the Darshan Hall. It was there in the bookstore, and you had to go around this big "&". I found it, along with the letter "C", which I turned on its back and made it into a desk. And I put this "&" right in the doorway. Everybody had to walk around it to get in through the curtain into the Darshan Hall.

181

Adi Da Samraj at the opening
of the bookstore in Los Angeles,
1972

"C" and "&"

BY GERALD SHEINFELD

Prior to the opening night of Avatar Adi Da's first Ashram in 1972, the few of us who were already students of Avatar Adi Da were working full speed to get the bookstore and the Communion Hall ready. One day, Beloved Adi Da and one of the students came into the center with two large wooden objects: the letter "C" and the symbol "&". They had found them in an alley, where an advertising company had thrown them away. The symbols were both quite large—about five or six feet tall and three or four feet wide. Beloved Adi Da asked us to clean them up and paint them white so that He could use them in the bookstore. The "C", lying flat, was perfect as a check-out counter for our cash register. The "&" was placed in front of the entrance to the Communion Hall—a most unusual object to encounter before entering the Hall. When we asked its significance, Beloved Adi Da said, "There Is Only God! The 'and' is the problem."

The Ashram storefront
on Melrose Avenue, 1972

Nobody ever really understood anything much about it, or had anything profound to say about it. I made a few remarks occasionally, something along these lines.

The Ashram on Melrose was the first temple in this gathering, and I designed the whole thing, such as I could within the means available, intending it to have primary features within the limits of the ability at the moment. So you should "consider" this place such as it was, and what meaning was conveyed through symbols that, on the face of it, don't seem self-explanatory.

"And" is "Da" with an "n" in the middle. So "and" is "Da".

Not "a-n-d" but the curious symbol, the ampersand, used in English, maybe in some other languages as well, to represent the word "and"—a curious little loopy thing.

So I had that ampersand there on Melrose as My own Murti-Form, Threshold-Personality-Form, Sign, Representation, and Name. And nobody _ever_ noticed that this was the case. Or took it seriously, or asked Me much of anything about it seriously. They thought it was nonsense because I found it on the street. They thought it was totally arbitrary— already not knowing anything about the spontaneous Nature of My own Manifestations.

The "and" part is fundamental, is just what it is. _That_ is Happiness. It is at the Root, or the Source. It is not temporary. It is not a play off of That Which Is One and at the Core, but is One with What Is One and at the Core. All forms of the play are forms of change, and they do not last. Only the Fundamental, of which everything is a modification, or That Which is Always Already the Case, is Real, or Constant (in other words). It is Reality.

It's not necessary to say that what you're just perceiving (and so forth) now is _not_ real. No, what you are perceiving now _is_ real. It's just that it is not _Reality_, Reality Itself. In other words, you are not aware of it in a Realized State, in a State that Realizes its nature altogether.

Now I have Revealed the secret of the one-letter word "&".

One thing I said about it at the time—one interpretation of its meaning—is something to the effect that there is only one thing until you get this "and". After that is everything. Before that is just Reality, the Divine Self-Condition. The "and" itself has no intensity. You can't have it be anything more than it just plain old always already is. The "and" is the self-contraction, therefore—understood that way.

On the other hand, _beyond_ the self-contraction, the "and" is _Me_—That Which is neither expansion nor contraction, but That Which cannot even be intensified, That Which is Always Already, the Heart, the Core, the Source-Condition. I Am Prior to the search, the change, the fulfillment or non-fulfillment. At the root, there is the self-contraction, or the "and" that is self-contraction, but when the contraction at the root is transcended, and That Which is at the root is Itself Realized, the "and" as limitation is transcended.

In other words, there is just that mere Intensity of Being That is Always Already the Case. It is Self-Sufficient. It cannot <u>be</u> intensified, expanded, changed in any way whatsoever. It needn't be. Then you feel to the root.

Prior to hearing, when you feel to the root, you feel the self-contraction—when you feel most deeply, you feel the self-contraction—when you're practicing the Yoga of devotional Communion with Me, Ruchira Buddha Bhakti Yoga, you're always coming against your limitation in it at some point.

But when the self-contraction is understood and transcended at the same depth, you're not feeling it any longer. You are feeling Me. It's not a matter of expanding from the center. It's Realizing Me, That Which is Always Already the Case, <u>before</u> the self-contraction.

Whenever the self-contraction is not, I <u>Am</u>.

Maybe the mystery of "and" is that it is also "DNA" spelled backwards. "Da" is "DNA". But that's just a pattern, a mode of identification of Me, in one particular context of observation. You can find Me, find My Pattern, Core, in all kinds of dimensional looks. But, fundamentally, in all that looking for Me, there is the self-contraction. When you understand and transcend the self-contraction, then you're established in no-contraction, direct feeling-Contemplation of Me. This becomes, then, the process from then on, the constant returning to that, finding that and feeling beyond it every moment. Because in any moment, there <u>is</u> the self-contraction. But noting again that it <u>is</u>, you vanish it, you feel beyond it, inherently.

There may be some sensation associated with it you might describe somehow as "expansive" or whatever, but that's not it. It's steady. No matter how much expansiveness there may feel to be in the attitude or radiance in the body-mind (words like "expansion", "expansiveness" are appropriate enough relative to that), there still is just this one Intensity. It does not get greater. A million-degree fire is a million degrees as it consumes the forest. It's still only a million degrees, it's still the same fire, if it's consuming fifty <u>billion</u> acres. It's not any more intense, except maybe from some local point of view. You see?

So, to call it "intense" is appropriate enough, too. But it's not. There is just the depth. You can feel the self-contraction, but then when you feel beyond it, you feel Me. And then it is a matter of that Communion with Me, Spiritual, Transcendental, and (ultimately) Divine in Its Profundity of no-contraction—no-contraction so profound that the contraction simply vanished. There's no expansion, because there's no contraction. Simply that.

That Which is Inherent is ultimately to be Realized. It is not something that wasn't there before. It's just that you must transcend your non-Realization of the Fundamental Intensity of Existence, of the Fundamental Feeling of Being. Not merely knowing It—no, Realizing It most profoundly, Most Perfectly, so that there is no limitation on your Realization of It whatsoever.

Just feel What there is when there is no contraction.

This is all the "is" there is.

You can enter into it most profoundly, or you can load it with distractions, so that you can't even identify this core ground-reality, this heart-position.

Hearing is the capability to be established in that depth, directly, in any moment. And if you will persist in it profoundly, it will be so in every profound sense. In other words, progressively, it will become more and more profound, in the depth-sense, ultimately going beyond all of the limitations of egoity, conditionality, psycho-physical dependency.

Up until a certain point, it's nothing but the self-contraction, constantly discovered in various modes and so forth. And then, finally, the self-contraction itself is not only gone beyond but utterly gone beyond in every mode of its appearance. Then that same depth, rather than being the mode of locating and moving beyond the self-contraction, is now (that very same depth) the Very Domain of That Which Transcends the self-contraction, or That Which is Always Already the Case but inherently obvious—only when (or in the instant in which) the self-contraction is not.

It's when the self-contraction is not that the Divine Condition is Realized. It's not the expansion of anything at all. It's the Realization of That Which is Always Already the Case, the Beyond That is Always Already the Case, the Source That is the Source of every thing, the Source-Condition of every thing. The Source in that sense—not merely the active "cause" within the cause-effect world, the "other side of the coin", or the "cause" side instead of the "effect" side, but the Very Condition from Which, in Which, and (ultimately) as Which any phenomenon at all arises. The Context of all arising. That Which is Always Already the Case, regardless of whatever (in any moment) arises or does not arise. It is Inherently Obvious, because It is Always Already the Case.

185

But It is only Obvious (in Its Inherent Obviousness) when there is no self-contraction. In other words, nothing <u>added</u> to obscure the fact of That Which is Always Already the Case—the fact, the Nature, the Condition Itself.

The "radical" form of the "conscious process" goes to the Source. The "radical" form of "conductivity" goes to the Source. That's what the word "radical" means—"root", "going to the root, or the Source, or the Source-Condition".

JAMES: Beloved, when You use the word "Source" it seems to be a new definition. The English definitions tend to point to "cause".

AVATAR ADI DA SAMRAJ: Well, the source of a river can't be said to be its "cause". It's just the first place you notice any water. But it's the same water you got downriver, too. So its significance is not as being "cause" of anything, yet we use the word "source" in that instance, with that meaning. So I'm using that meaning—using it bigger. When I speak of the Source, I mean "Source" in this ultimate sense, the Source-Condition. Not merely the cause.

Go forward or back through causes and effects, you're still in klik-klak. And you always wind up right back. So it's not about that. It's about the Source-Condition, not the "cause" that may be said to be the source.

Can the so-called "big bang" be the source? It's described as a cause. But what is the source of it? Wherein is it an event?—which may be said to be the "cause" of other events or developments of that same event. But wherein is it an event? Wherein is <u>anything</u> arising? What <u>is</u> it?

The root-question is the one I am constantly Calling you to ponder—the in-depth question, the in-depth feeling-"consideration", this passage in depth that, ultimately, must transcend self-contraction itself, <u>utterly</u>, most perfectly. Not by expanding beyond it, because that's an expansion <u>of</u> it—that's the search itself, in fact. Not by backtracking, not by cutting anything off, but by hearing Me and seeing Me.

In this little bit of conversation I've been describing something to you in words, but the process is hearing and seeing Me. It is a Yogic process, in relation to Me. It's that very process I've described <u>as</u> a process. In this conversation, I'm describing it in philosophical language for the sake of saying something further about it.

And this "and" sign that I had placed in the entryway to the Darshan Hall on Melrose twenty-five years ago—it's a "consideration", but you can't say it came to an end tonight.

This is not the end of anything. It is the "and" of everything.

[Everyone laughs with delight.]

Remember that I told you this!

You are to turn the "end-time" into the "and-time". The one intensity-time of Happiness Itself.

CHAPTER FOURTEEN

The self-Contracting Habit Of the usual life

THE HEART OF THE DAWN HORSE TESTAMENT OF THE RUCHIRA BUDDHA,
CHAPTER FOUR, VERSES 66-77

66.

All Of My Work With those who (First or Earliest) Came To Me, and Every Word That I Spoke (and Sometimes Also Wrote) For their Sake (and For The Sake Of all who Would Listen To Me, and Hear Me, and See Me, In The Course Of time), Was and Is A "Consideration" and An Elaboration (or A Detailing) and A Summarizing Of The Word and The Way Of The Heart That I Have Always and Consistently Offered Even From The Very Beginning Of My Work As Heart-Teacher and Free, True Heart-Master.

67.

My Word Is Simple. I Say, Attend To Me and (Thereby) Understand and Transcend Your Own activity.

68.

If any one Will Feel and Examine his or her (psycho-physical) state In any moment, Whether Under the worst Or Under the best Or Under the most ordinary of circumstances, he or she Will Surely Discover That There Is Always A Characteristic Feeling Of Stress, or Dis-ease, or A Motivating Sense Of Dilemma. Therefore, human life (Characteristically Felt As Such Stress, Dis-ease, or Dilemma) Is Also Always Characterized By Struggle, or A Generally Uninspected (and Never Finally Satisfied) Search For Release and Fulfillment.

69.

The usual life Is Always Actively Involved (Whether Consciously Or Unconsciously) In This Motivated Search and This Native Distress. Therefore, every such a one Is Involved In Programs Of Seeking, Via desire, In all kinds of relations and circumstances.

70.

My Word Is A Direct Address To The Distress and The Search Of each individual. I Do Not Suggest A Way or A Method By Which To Seek. Instead, I Call the individual To Observe himself or herself, To Feel and Examine The Distress That Motivates the life Of Seeking itself.

71.

Through self-Surrendering (and Truly self-Forgetting) Feeling-Contemplation Of My Bodily (Human) Form, My Spiritual (and Always Blessing) Presence, and My Very (and Inherently Perfect) State, and (In The Constant Context Of That Practice Of Feeling-Contemplation) Through Real "Consideration" Of My Heart-Confessions, My Teaching Arguments, My Fundamental Questions, and The Leelas (or Stories) Of All My Work (Whereby I Have Reflected individuals To themselves, and Blessed them To Awaken), Interested (and Truly Devoted) individuals Can (By Grace) Come To Understand (and Transcend) themselves.

72.

The Initial Process Of Listening (To The Degree Of Hearing) Is One Of self-Observation (Truly Felt), Whether By The Primary Practice Of Devotion and Insight Or By The Primary Practice Of Devotion and Faith, Until That self-Observation Becomes A Crisis Of Most Fundamental self-Understanding.

73.

At First (In The Listening Course Of The Way Of The Heart), the individual Becomes Acutely Aware Of his or her Habits Of Seeking, Desiring, Doubting, Believing, Manipulating, Betraying, and Always Returning To The Same Distress and Want. Then, As The Crisis Of Most Fundamental Understanding Approaches, It Suddenly Becomes Clear That All Of That Is Being Motivated By A Constant Feeling Of Distress, Which Is The Result Of self-Contraction In The Face Of all relations and conditions.

74.

This Discovery Is Most Profound. It Is As If a person In Pain Suddenly Discovers That he or she Is Pinching his or her own flesh. (And This Discovery Produces Immediate Relief, As Soon As The Pinching Ceases.) Therefore, As Soon As an individual Discovers That The Painful Search That Occupies his or her life Is Being Created By A Fundamental Feeling Of Distress, attention Is Free To Examine That Distress Itself. And When That Distress Is Directly (and Profoundly) Examined, It Is Discovered That It Is The Result Of A Chronic (and self-Induced) Contraction Of the body-mind, or, Most Simply, The Habitual (and, Ultimately, Always Voluntary and Un-Necessary) Avoidance (or self-Contracting Refusal) Of Relationship and Relatedness.

75.

Every Apparent individual, thing, circumstance, or condition arises, survives, changes, and disappears Dependently (or Always Already Related) Within The Cosmic Universe (Which Is Continuous, Whole, and all-Containing). By Definition (and In Fact) There Is Not (Nor Can There Be) any Separate, self-Contained, Independent, or self-Sufficient conditional individual, thing, circumstance, or event. However, By Reaction To All Apparent Vulnerability, and Otherwise By Forgetting, or By Failing To Notice or Intuit The Whole (and The Inherently Perfect, Which Inherently Transcends Even The Whole), The Tendency Of every conditionally Manifested individual Is To Contract Into (Presumed) Separateness, or a self-Defended and self-Contracted emotional, mental, psychic, physical, and social state Of Isolation, Presumed Independence, and Dramatized Want. This Tendency Is Chronic In every one, and It Is Not Generally Even Inspected, Nor Is It (Without Inspection) Understood. Therefore, every one Seeks. And All Seeking Is Inevitably Frustrated. The self-Contracting Habit (Itself) Is Not (and Cannot Ever Be) Transcended In (or By Means Of) The Search, Because The Search Is Itself The Dramatization Of The self-Contracting Habit Itself.

76.

I Call every one To Feel and To Thoroughly Observe and To Transcend The Habit Of egoity. Eventually, any one who Truly Listens To My Word and, By The Means I Have Given (and Always Give), Fully Embraces The Ordeal Of Feeling-Contemplation (Of Me) and Observation (Of the ego-"I") Will Surely (Truly, and Most Profoundly) Discover The Root Of Seeking and Suffering, Which Is the self-Contraction, The Complex Avoidance Of Relationship, or The Habit Of "Narcissus".

77.

When This Discovery Is (By Grace) Truly and Fully Made and Felt (Relative, Summarily, To Every Aspect Of personal Existence), A Crisis Of Spontaneous (and Not Strategic) Release Is Enjoyed. And When It Is Truly (and Most Fundamentally) Understood That self-Contraction Is The Motivating Pain Of life, It Becomes Increasingly Possible (In every moment Of The Feeling-Contemplation Of My Bodily Human Form, My Spiritual, and Always Blessing, Presence, and My Very, and Inherently Perfect, State) To Enquire Into the self-Contraction ("Avoiding Relationship?") and (Thereby) Feel Beyond the self-Contraction, or, Otherwise, In The Manner Of The Devotional Way Of Faith, To Directly Feel Beyond the self-Contraction, and Thus (Progressively, and Ultimately) To Enjoy A Native Sense Of Freedom (and Fullness Of Being). And any one who Has (Through Responsive Devotional Listening To Me) Thus Become Responsible For This Actively self-Transcending (or Directly Counter-egoic) Feeling-Capability Has Heard Me Truly.

The Mountain Of Attention, 1996

CHAPTER FIFTEEN

December 13, 1996

On the Other Side of the Purr

On December 13, Adi Da Samraj begins to develop in greater depth and detail the "consideration" of the states of waking, dreaming, and sleeping, and What is beyond them.

I.

AVATAR ADI DA SAMRAJ: What difference does it <u>make</u> to have right thoughts in the waking state if you're just going to fall asleep some time later in the day anyway? *[laughter]* What good is it going to do you there? If you were permanently in the waking state, fine, there might be something more to say, but you're just going to go to sleep. So what point is there?

Each day you go into a state that's deeper than either the waking or the dreaming state, so I guess you have to figure it out from there. Because neither waking nor dreaming are permanent. They're constantly reduced to sleep. So I guess you've got to find out about sleep—not about waking and dreaming.

Don't you think it's at least interesting to "consider" the fact that the <u>entire</u> structure of existence, as you are experiencing it, is being generated, and, otherwise, held in place, by your own <u>act</u> of self-contraction? This is a profound matter, to be entered into profoundly.

In due course, I've got to get you to be able to do this sadhana in the sleeping state. And I can't say, "Well, here's My Instruction: When you go to bed tonight, you practice 'A' through 'F', over and over again, come back here tomorrow, and you tell Me what you did and how it worked out." No, that's not going to be a useful way of going at it, because you ordinarily can't account for your transition from waking to dreaming to sleeping and back out again. It's all very mysterious to you.

So you can't go into another state in order to investigate sleep, in the sense of dropping out of this one entirely, losing all responsibility for the transition. But you must enter into a process of practice in which you can (in due course) be established in that Depth that is otherwise entered in sleep. And the process of the sadhana, ultimately, is done from there, not in the waking and dreaming states. Not, in other words, anywhere in the first five stages of life—anywhere in that domain. It's in the deep-sleep domain, the causal* domain, the root-domain. But to pass beyond that limitation, you must do it <u>in</u> <u>that</u> <u>depth</u>.

So the Way is, from the beginning, a process in depth, always becoming more profound in its depth, ultimately such that the depth of meditation practice and such is deeper than waking and dreaming, and you can enter into it and return from it—so to speak, "return" from it—to dreaming or waking, fully aware of how this is all done, the whole process, all the structure associated with it and such. You are responsibly, Yogically related, in other words, to the in-depth process. And it's not just something that happens to you. You are aware of it altogether, and not bereft of that knowledge, that understanding.

The "Perfect Practice" of the Way of the Heart is done in deep sleep. The deep sleep practice is entered into in formal meditation. Not just at night. It's a formal, Yogic discipline. It is not just a matter of analyzing your sleep the next day when you get up, or anything like that, or trying to remember to do something when you go to sleep, because if you try to remember it, that faculty goes when you go to sleep. There's no mind to worry about when you're sleeping. But the hearing and seeing process of meditation does enter into that depth-potential. So, ultimately, there is the transition to the "Perfect Practice". And it is a practice that is beyond the exercises of body-mind. It is an exercise prior to attention itself, relative to the feeling of relatedness, which is the simple force of "and".

That "Perfect Practice", in its depth, is not an exercise of the waking-state mind that says "I am the Witness-Consciousness, I am Witnessing such and such"—all this kind of business. No, not that at all. It's an exercise, prior to—therefore, hierarchically, structurally, previous to—the operations of body-mind, except for the very root-dimension of it, which is <u>bare</u>, in deep sleep. It is without the exercise of sensation and faculties of cognition, perception, thought, and so forth. But it's not a pleasureless state. It is less disturbed, otherwise.

The "Perfect Practice" of the Way of the Heart

The "Perfect Practice" is the discipline in the context of the sixth stage of life and the seventh stage of life in the Way of the Heart.

Devotees who have mastered (and thus transcended) the point of view of the body-mind by fulfilling the preparatory processes of the Way of the Heart may, by Grace, be Awakened to practice in the Domain of Consciousness Itself, in the sixth and seventh, or ultimate, stages of life.

The "Perfect Practice" itself develops through three stages.

The qualification for beginning the "Perfect Practice" is the stable Realization that one stands no longer in the position of the limited body-mind-self but Stands in the Witness-Position of Consciousness, merely Witnessing what arises, not implicated by or identified with any object, state, or experience. Then, as Adi Da explains, the first stage of the "Perfect Practice" is not merely to Witness what arises, but to "Be Consciousness", to enter into the Depth of That Which is the Witness, the Depth of Consciousness Itself.

The second stage of the "Perfect Practice" is to "Contemplate Consciousness", or to Abide in that Depth, even to the point of becoming oblivious of the world and all its appearances. The first and second stages of the "Perfect Practice" constitute the course of practice in the context of the sixth stage of life in the Way of the Heart.

The third and final stage of the "Perfect Practice" is to "Transcend everything in Consciousness", to Realize Divine Enlightenment Itself, the great "Open-Eyed" Samadhi that does not turn away from the world but Divinely Recognizes all arising conditions as mere modifications of the "Brightness" of Divine Being. Thus, the third stage of the "Perfect Practice" is the seventh, or Divinely Enlightened, stage of life.

From the very beginning of the "Perfect Practice", the impulse of the being is to get to know the Great Mysterious Condition of Consciousness that is functioning as the Witness. As the "Perfect

Practice" progresses, there is increasing detachment from conditional existence, not in the sense of dissociation, but in the sense of non-identification. Conditional existence is seen starkly as it is—only stress and illusion, bound to death.

What evidence there is of Awakening to Consciousness in the Spiritual traditions (in the context of the sixth stage of life) indicates an attitude that deliberately excludes outward experience as much as possible, in order to hold onto the formless Bliss of Consciousness. Indeed, Adi Da has Revealed that the characteristic error in the sixth stage of life is to regard conditional existence as a problem. It is to try to attain the Perfect Condition of Consciousness by turning away from ordinary conditions—or all that is imperfect, and (apparently) not Consciousness. The strategic choosing to remain immersed in Consciousness, free of objects, is just as much a form of the self-contraction as becoming attached to subtle* states and Yogic experiences. The uniqueness of the Way of the Heart is that it is not based on the urge toward any kind of ideal experience, or on the impulse to some Transcendental State that excludes experience.

The Way of the Heart is based, from its beginnings and right through the sixth stage of life, on freedom from all the illusions of seeking. It is based on Ruchira Buddha Bhakti Yoga—self-surrendering, self-forgetting, and self-transcending devotion to Adi Da Samraj. This moment to moment feeling-Contemplation of Him generates an unfolding process of purification of the body-mind, leading to an equanimity, or restedness, which in turn becomes profound detachment from the motive to identify with conditional existence, until the capability to Stand Free of the body-mind in the Perfect Position of Consciousness is Realized.

AVATAR ADI DA SAMRAJ: The Realization of Perfection is the Realization of That Which Is Inherently Perfect. Perfection is not in conditions. Perfection is Prior to conditions. Therefore, the sadhana of the Way of the Heart must pass from the context of the body-mind to the Domain of the Perfect, Prior to the body-mind. [May 19, 1995]

Sleep is a profoundly blissful state. Everyone recalls this without knowing exactly how to identify why they are saying that. But you know when you rested well. It wasn't just simply that you were dead. But there was no disturbance in the body-mind, and just simply that full, blissful energy, awareness, that you generally feel was the case when you slept.

The process of meditation, Samadhi, and so forth, must, in due course, become deeper than waking and dreaming. It must become as deep as sleeping, and then go beyond. Realization is not in the waking state nor in the dreaming state nor in the sleeping state. Realization is even the State That is Prior to waking, dreaming, and sleeping, and within Which they appear as non-binding and merely apparent modifications of that State Itself. The Realization of That Which is beyond waking, dreaming, and sleeping is the Realization of That Which is deeper than sleeping.

The process must become deeper. The stages of life are a deepening process, if you understand them correctly. They are from gross (and waking), to subtler (and dreaming), to the causal (or sleeping) dimension— in the first three stages of life, the waking-state, gross-minded disposition, progressively gone beyond in the fourth stage of life; and in the fourth and fifth stages of life, the ascending process, or the subtler process, the interiorizing process, that is in the mode of the dream state, in terms of its interests, objects, resolutions, possibilities; and then, in the sixth stage of life, it's Consciousness in the mode of the deep-sleep state that is "considered", prior to patterns of mind and body.

The Way of the Heart, Adidam, enters into the "Perfect Practice" in the context of the sixth stage of life, but on the basis of hearing and seeing Me, entered into most profound Communion with Me, such that the error inherent in the sixth stage of life is directly transcended in every moment of the practice of the Way of the Heart in the context of the sixth stage of life, and such that, ultimately, the sixth stage of life itself is transcended in the seventh stage Awakening.

So the "Perfect Practice" of the Way of the Heart in the context of the sixth stage of life is not simply another variation on sixth stage exercises. It's not something you can just take up because it sounds interesting from your point of view. No, that's the waking-state man. That guy doesn't show up in the sleep room. So you enter into the "Perfect Practice" through depth-sadhana, through Communion with Me in depth, through a real process in Communion with Me, becoming, Gracefully, more and more profound.

II.

AVATAR ADI DA SAMRAJ: You notice about a lot of non-humans that they seem to be capable of actually doing almost nothing for <u>really long</u> periods of time. They don't mind that at all. In fact, it seems that, more or less, that's what they prefer, given the option. They'd like to just lie around. And not necessarily doing a lot of boobery, or anything like that. I mean, <u>really</u> in a rest state. It's not that they sit around and examine the heavens and that sort of business. *[laughter]* Apart from practical perception-time required, they look like they basically just want to lie down and go to sleep. That's what they would do all the time. For them, it seems, sleep state is home base, not just "not being body-conscious". The declaration that "you are not the body" is an expression of any number of possible kinds of experience, certainly.

Non-humans don't look for time off from work so they can go to an amusement park. They look to economize the amount of "practical time" they have to do, even practical perception-time, so that they have as few obligations as possible, can do it in as economized a period of time as possible, with the wasting of as little effort as possible. If you don't waste so much energy, you conserve the amount of food you require and all kinds of other things, too. Generally, they are always returning to rest, economizing life-requirements so they can be at rest as much as possible. Do you notice this?

DEVOTEES: Yes.

AVATAR ADI DA SAMRAJ: It's not always the case, but it is for many. So, when they have time off from obligations, and they try to maximize that, there's a lot of time when they don't occupy themselves with anything in particular that you could call "socializing". They do some of that, too. They do a little of this and that, of course, but beyond a point, they're not interested in that. Their life doesn't need to be <u>filled</u> with that, exactly. They <u>readily</u> look to find themselves in a place where they feel safe, to be outside of all activities, all relations, all everything at all, in a safe, comfortable circumstance in which to, effectively, go to sleep.

Mammals, large animals and such (in which you would have to include the human), are like that. You are like that, it seems. The human is part of the whole collection of earth-species that generally would function in a unity with one another, handle business economically, economizing the amount of energy and time required, and always maximizing time spent at rest. Which, in itself, is also a kind of economizing of the energy of the body, you could say, so that the body is only used for times when it is required to do something for the body to survive. But then, the rest of the time, the body is asleep. So why was it important for the body to survive?—if it was just so it could go to sleep, in which case it's not aware of itself anyway. Why does the body have to exist, anyway?

That's just a way of arguing. You can find out by direct experience. But if sleep were just to conserve energy, so you wouldn't waste it, then these waking-state activities for the sake of bodily survival are meaninglessly strange, because they are all about doing something to make the body survive, and, as soon as you've handled that business, it goes to sleep. And the only time it's awake is when it's doing things it has to do to keep this body surviving when it sleeps. It has to engage in all kinds of struggling with mortal fear, pain, death, and endless difficulties, struggling to survive—as if that itself proves something or other that you can notice, in some individuals in the herd, like, "The offspring of this one are more likely to be able to survive under these rotten circumstances, and so let's make a lot of them with that blood-line, with that elk over there who's able to wallop everybody's ass." *[Beloved Adi Da laughs.]*

Anyway, it seems that, if you look at all of you, humans and all the rest, you see that human beings, like all the rest, are <u>naturally</u> moved to always go to rest. They appear to be sleeping as if they're serving some physical purpose, to conserve energy or just whatever. But there's also an in-depth process associated with sleep. There are more dimensions to it than whatever may be serving relative to the physical. The nature of reality can be found in these places where you are left over from nature's requirements, or nature's had enough done with you for the moment so that you can wink off. You're being given time to find out what's happening.

So the wise have always made the maximum use they could of time that they might otherwise have spent sleeping, to enter into depth, perhaps even something in the mode of sleep—intentionally, Yogically, meditating more hours and such, meditating late at night and such. Because the Mystery that feels good to human beings is not out here in the peripheral physical world of activity. It's in the depth of deep experience, deeper than waking, deeper than dreaming. It's suggested down there in sleep—that's the Well where you like to be. And this waking-state stuff is strictly, for you, a place to struggle to fulfill the requirements (it seems) of this body, for the sake of this body's survival. Food, or sex (in the reproduction sense), shelter, or organized behavior preventing clashes—all kinds of things.

But it's not the world where you are fundamentally. It's the world where you are incidentally, relative to what you have to do for the body's survival and the general survival of the physically embodied awareness, then. But it's not the whole of Existence. And, generally speaking, you are moved to economize your involvement with all of that, to maximize the time at rest and in depth, without any physical or peripheral requirements. The non-humans don't merely go to sleep. They sleep sometimes, of course, and so on, but their exercise in depth is not merely about going to sleep, it's about being in the depth and not merely in the physical state, or the state of being physically awake, awake to being identified with the body, and have to struggle as that for the sake of its survival, even though it's innately clear that the body is mortal and threatened.

Doing some time to serve in that mode—that's the price you have to pay to have a physical association for your existence. But it's not itself a way of life. It's duty, so to speak. It is intelligent to do it, but you do want to economize it, make it as peaceful, happy as possible, congenial as possible.

Still, the world is patterned on recycling. All the deaths keep happening. So the waking state and its world is the world of death and physicality. The waking state is all of that. It's not that the waking state is sometimes associated with all of that. The waking state is inherently about all of that. The waking state and being a physical body (or being associated with a physical embodiment) are the same thing. It's a state. It's associated with a mechanism within mechanisms within mechanisms. Not meaning to suggest something merely mechanistic by using that word, but meaning that it is a pattern within patterns within patterns.

One does not want to remain associated with the condition of identification with a mortal body for excessively long periods of time. You're always looking for recreation time, distraction time, rest time, sleep time, dream time. Something else. Another time, another state than the one you're in presently. That's the way it is in the waking state. But you're looking in the waking state for this other state. Actually, you're looking for a state that is not the waking state. It's another state. You have to get out of the waking state, and not find an achievement in the waking state, or a circumstance in the waking state.

That Which is Realized beyond the sleep state is the Condition in Which and by Which everything apparently arising is Divinely Recognized. That being Realized, in other words, it's no longer true that you do not know what even a single thing is. You do Know. You Know it exactly and most profoundly, and you are That. It's not knowledge in the abstracted sense, or the knowing-of-an-object sense. It is Perfectly Subjective Knowledge. Realization, in other words—in-depth, direct Realization. The Truths of the Way of the Heart are all self-evident, proven by living the Way itself. The Graces of these Realizations occur in the stages of the deepening process. Therefore, you must enter into this course. You must put the body-mind into the pattern by which you direct yourself into that course, and you must be perpetually, moment to moment, entered into the in-depth exercise—the heart-exercise, then—of the Way, as a most fundamental, moment to moment Yoga, Ruchira Buddha Bhakti Yoga.

The waking state is not likeable by itself—this waking up, being the body, and so forth. Every non-human knows it, and so do you all know it. You can get talked out of it by your education, but everybody knows—inherently knows, tacitly knows—that the body that you can feel yourself associated with in the waking state is mortal. And everything in the domain of the experience of the body is mortal, changing, temporary. Everything! Absolutely <u>everything</u> is of that nature in the realm of the waking state. Everything!

The waking state is not the Ultimate Position, therefore. It's not evil-land, it is simply <u>not</u> the Ultimate Position. In other words, if you understand the nature of the waking state, you will not bind yourself to it. You will associate with it with discrimination, with clarity. You will establish a pattern, a discipline there, that corresponds to your in-depth understanding and experience. That's what it is to live this Way, to demonstrate this Way.

III.

AVATAR ADI DA SAMRAJ: You know, in the case of the beginner, in meditation—I don't mean the sometimes principal occasions of meditation, I mean the general day to day meditation—how much time is spent just getting to that point where basically you feel just relaxed physically, emotionally, mentally. Basically just relaxed. No more deep than that, just that much. To get to that point you have to struggle with all kinds of physical discomfort and concerns, whatever, and something not quite right in the room, or whoever's there, whatever's going on, and the <u>thoughts</u>, and all the business, the patterning that you've set up through stresses and interactions during the period immediately previous to that meditation. And just a fundamental knotted-up-ness, and whatever else. So you sit there grinding through that—not merely meditating on that and being negative, I don't mean that—but practicing your devotion to Me, through the "conscious process" and "conductivity". Nonetheless, the associations of the process are all waking-state, gross phenomena, ordinary body-mind social-personality distress. At the end of an hour or so, or two, whatever, you feel basically kind of relaxed. You get up from your seat and you feel yourself gradually, as you walk toward the door, starting to do it to yourself again—or having the experience again (you don't know about this doing it to yourself quite yet).

So the self-contraction is done in the waking state, in a certain fashion. It's done in all three of the common states. And the way to account for the self-contraction, ultimately, then, is to enter into the process as an in-depth process. Having heard Me, then the process of deepening continues, going deeper than mere waking into dreaming, deeper than dreaming into sleeping, as a responsible course of exercise, that you can enter into in daily meditation. In that process, all the elements of the structure of the body-mind and experiencing and so forth become exposed.

So, once there is most fundamental self-understanding, true hearing of Me, shortly there is entrance into the seeing process of the Spiritual stages, based on seeing of Me. And that process deals more profoundly with this in-depth matter.

And by most profound practice of the Way as I have Given it, the transition can be made from this "basic" fourth stage of life practice directly to the "Perfect Practice". In other words, it's not necessary to go from waking to dreaming to sleeping. You can go from waking to sleeping. You're not obliged to do the sadhana of the dreaming state. It doesn't come about in the natural course by way of necessity in every instance. In any case, you do have this direct possibility.

With maturity in the "basic" fourth stage of life in the Way of the Heart, fully rightly practiced as I Give to My devotees at that stage, the transition can be made to the "Perfect Practice", without going on to the "advanced" dimension of the fourth stage of life, or into the fifth stage of life. That doesn't mean there's no experiences relative to the functions and the events associated with the subtle dimension, or the ascending process of the spinal line, or the brain—all these kinds of locations of experiencing. No, these kinds of things occur in the course of the frontal Yoga just as well, because the frontal Yoga* is simply a description of responsibility.

The process itself is in the full Circle all the time, spontaneously that. But your responsibility is for the frontal Yoga, not the spinal Yoga.* However, the entire mechanism is being opened. (The Arrow is curious.

It ascends and descends equally. It is like "and". It is one intensity. It doesn't really go up or down. You can uncork it from either end.)

The first two stages of the "Perfect Practice", or the practice of the Way of the Heart in the context of the sixth stage of life, is a practice in the domain of deep sleep, and ultimately penetrating beyond it. It's the Perfect and root (or "radical") development of this devotional sadhana that is the Way of the Heart. But as a practice, as a sadhana, it is done in depth. It is done at the depth-level of the sleep state. You can dream, you can be in the waking state. But these are not satisfactory. It's mortal, and it's confused. It's bizarre, threatening. It's not altogether predictable or, so to speak, "user-friendly".

The Circle and the Arrow of the Body-Mind

In many religious and Spiritual traditions, it has long been taught that physical anatomy is only one dimension of the human structure—and, indeed, the most superficial dimension. Various great Realizers of the past (particularly in India) have described certain features of the deeper, or esoteric, anatomy of the human being, based on their direct experiential awareness of subtler structures.

In His summary Instruction on this subject, Adi Da Samraj Reveals that there is a primary energy-circuit in the body that is the fundamental underlying structure of the gross and subtle dimensions of the human body-mind. This circuit, which Adi Da calls "the Circle", is the fundamental passageway of energy through the body-mind. The Circle is composed of two arcs: the frontal, or descending, line (extending from the crown of the head down the front of the body to the perineum), and which is the dimension of the body-mind associated with the physical, emotional, and mental phenomena of ordinary daily life; and the spinal, or ascending, line (extending from the perineum up the back of the body to the crown of the head), and which is the dimension of the body-mind associated with the subtle, psychic, and mystical phenomena that are (in general) only potential in human beings unless intentionally cultivated.

In profound, deep meditation, the circuit of energy may be felt in the form of the "Arrow", rather than the "Circle". The Arrow, as Avatar Adi Da explains, is "a motionless axis that seems to stand in the center of the body, between the frontal and spinal lines".

You always have at hand what all the non-humans have at hand, and yet you don't seem to see the virtue in it readily. You're trying to figure out the Way in the context of the waking state, through an elaborate conversation, blah-blah-blah, whatever altogether, an exercise in words and whatever else altogether in the waking state. You're seeking in the context of the waking state for that which is beyond it. You're seeking through words what is necessarily beyond words. The non-humans don't go through that whole course elaborately as you do. They notice <u>immediately</u> that physical awareness is something very difficult and confining. It's not something to be casually done. It's something you do sometimes, as a responsible matter. And then you enter into the in-depth domain again.

You could say the same of death, then—it is just that relinquishment of the physical association. It's not that you <u>lose</u> the physical association—there is tacit, direct knowledge in the case of every born entity in the waking state that this thing with which you are associated is a dying thing. "Existence identified with this is not going to be amusing," says the lizard to himself. I mean, long before he goes and finds himself a girl lizard to fool around with, he already says this other thing to himself. In other words, he enters into much more profound "consideration" before he gets involved in playing at life. So the lizard is going to spend a lot of time, maximum time, day to day, for the life-span (whatever it is) of that physical body, entered into in-depth, slept-out-away. Whatever depth can be entered into in that is for you to find, for you to discover, for you to be guided in, for you to Realize by Grace.

I recently watched a movie called *The Meaning of Life*. It's a Monty Python movie. Toward the end of the film, all these supposed bad guys in the high-rise world of business are having a board meeting about just business. One guy is asked "What's your report?" He says, "Well, there are two things. One, we're not selling enough hats. And, two, the mystery of life . . . " And then he goes on to give this philosophical discourse—I don't recall its exact words, but ending in something like that what is really required is a process of guided self-understanding. So he finishes this long statement, and everybody is sort of in a stupor. Then they say, "What?! What did he say?! Hats! We have to sell more hats!" And they go on with their business—relative trivia.

"A process of guided self-understanding" is one way of describing what the Way of the Heart is about, a real dimension of it. So you want to use up, to the maximum, your lifetime in this in-depth process, rather than being forced into the superficial process of identifying with the body in the waking state and suffering its limitations, and the threats to it, and everything passes anyway. And you never know when you're going to finish a cycle relative to any particular thing or not. But ultimately it all passes anyway. It's in the in-depth dimension of that that you find the integrity, well-being—potentially do, anyway—that enables you to then even function as you must in the waking association as well. But you never make it the basis for your philosophy.

The non-humans don't consult their physical embodiment for wisdom. They learn from it, and so forth—but they, in other words, go in depth. There may be guidance in that and so forth—all sorts of things associated with the non-humans as well. But the process must enter into the in-depth domain. Yes, it is your response to Me in My bodily (human) Form, but the process is always entering into the in-depth Domain of Communion with Me, based on making use of that right response to My bodily (human) Form.

IV.

AVATAR ADI DA SAMRAJ: My Instruction to you is about Realization, about going Beyond. It's not about saying utopia is coming in the waking state. There will be changes, there will be all kinds of thises and thats in the domain of human experiencing, whatever it is, in any case—the domain of survival, struggling and bantering about who's going to get to fulfill desires, competing for desire-fulfillment and such. And there's all kinds of feeling pleasure and all kinds of this and that and everything else associated with the waking state potentially.

At last, the process, even though it requires you to bring discipline to the body-mind, to the waking state, and so on, is not about getting something for the body-mind in the waking state. It's about fulfilling the deeper motivation, the heart-motivation to Realize What is Beyond. Because it's already obvious that the waking state is not the Domain of Eternity, of Unending Pleasure, and so forth. It's simply the domain of your physical body (whatever one could say about that altogether), the physical body with which you appear to be associated in the waking state. And its domain is a bubbling dualistic struggle, not altogether heart-comfortable. And, therefore, it is not the sincerest of the states you visit daily—is the least deep, in fact.

So those who are becoming wise become more at ease in the waking state and spend maximum time in meditation and Contemplative life—in the context of fulfilling whatever obligations are appropriate to them. The moment to moment exercise for them is this in-depth one, whatever the circumstances within which they must do their sadhana. And it is an ever-deepening process, Guided by Me, Moved by Me, working to Realize Me, that goes through and beyond the common states—waking, dreaming, and sleeping. And, beyond all of the conditional realizations (and, therefore, beyond all the experiences associated with the waking, the dreaming, and the sleep states), the Source-Condition, the Root-Condition, the Root of this must be found, must be Realized. Then the Mystery of waking, dreaming, and sleeping will also become clarified.

The Truth is in-depth. It is at the Root. It is the Context of all and All. The root of the waking state is the dreaming state. The root of the dreaming state is the sleep state. The sleep state is, therefore, the root of both waking and dreaming. Therefore, the Truth that is the Root of waking, dreaming, and sleeping is specifically and directly at the root of the sleep state. The most profound, or Perfect, process, therefore, is the process in depth, beginning from and going beyond deep sleep. If your process of meditation is still basically just this trying to get relaxed for an hour or two, you see how you are not functioning in depth so profoundly yet—which, in due course, you must.

You're not here merely to be in the waking state. You're not here merely to be a civilized meat-body. You handle business there for the sake of your own body-mind and the sake of all. You put in time for that. But you also will not give up the very fundamental process of existence in order to make the waking state and the body the sole object or circumstance of your concern. In other words, you insist that you engage in the in-depth process moment to moment, and, whatever you're doing to handle life-business, you have time in your life that you can set aside daily in a sacred manner, because you can't live merely for the waking state.

The more you do that—with the in-depth process in every moment of it and the regular daily setting-aside meditation time and puja time and so on—then, obviously, the more the process deepens altogether, and that progress is the stages of life. It has the waking-state philosophies and patterns—that's the first three stages of life and a bit of the fourth. In the fourth and fifth stages there is an entry into the subtle dimension, the realm of dreams, or of daily experience in dreams, and also in reveries that are rather dreamlike. Don't you know?

You are forced by gestures of the body to go to sleep, it seems, with some sort of frequency (whatever it may be in your case). But that sleep "called for by nature" (so to speak) is serving some bodily purpose—it doesn't necessarily have anything to do with the in-depth process.

There's no reason to suggest that the body-mind is <u>only</u> associated with a superficial process. The in-depth dimension of existence <u>always</u> exists. The sleep state is simply one that relaxes association with perceptual and conceptual experiencing and associations and functions. It's no longer involved in memory, or identification of egoic self with the body or the body-mind location or relations. And even if you get up from sleep and go about and live and get attached and do all that for another day, every time you go back to sleep, you don't have anything like that there again.

So all your troubles are in your attachment to, or illusions about, waking and dreaming. And you can struggle with all that and so forth. Basically, the wise have always chosen to economize that, in order to maximize time spent set apart, sacred time, or, otherwise, to intensify the in-depth process even in the <u>midst</u> of daily activity, as you imagine the bees might do, as compared to the lions, who lie about.

The lions set aside rest time, and have their in-depth perhaps more there, and are more, when active, in the short-term mode of handling business—the body turned on by glandular this, that, and every other thing, for the hunt, and survival purposes, and so forth. So it's all done quick, and efficiently, and then they return to rest. So maybe the lions are less deep in their waking moments, but enter into their depth a lot of the time because they have so much of it left over. And the bees, who have little leisure, it seems, are, in their depth, profound moment to moment. And they get prasad[28] from the queen, whom they serve, at foot, even with their tongues, and she provides them with a nectar that keeps them all attuned, it seems, to the chemical integrity of the hive and its Contemplations beyond, or subtler, deeper, such that they don't require outward-directedness when they fly from the hive. They are primarily in a kind of exalted condition in which to allow their bodies to do their functioning while they otherwise remain resonantly absorbed.

HELLIE KALOGEROS: The lions do play, though, Beloved.

AVATAR ADI DA SAMRAJ: Yes, right, of course. They do their time at that. But a lot of that playing is just practicing the moves, you know, and passing on the lore about how you can do the hunt, and whatnot. But then everybody scatters in some rest-position.

And cats in general have the purring thing. They seem, while doing it, to be in an altered state of physical awareness.

---

28. Sanskrit, meaning "gifts that have been offered to the Divine and, having been Blessed, are returned as Divine Gifts to devotees". By extension, Prasad is anything a devotee receives from his or her Guru. Here Avatar Adi Da is using it as a metaphor (in reference to the queen bee of a hive).

Did you ever look at one of those pictures, also videos now, where you look at them a certain way and all of a sudden you see a 3-D image?

DEVOTEES: Yes.

AVATAR ADI DA SAMRAJ: Getting to purr is something like that. Generally, a human being would find it difficult to find such a mechanism working in themselves physically. But what it feels like is the shift that would have to occur in your whole relationship to the physical, and so on—just as a shift has to occur in order to purr, just as a shift has to occur to see one of those 3-D images in that just-seems-like-a-smear-of-pattern in those pictures I just described.

But when they are purring, cats are not just in the ordinary sense physically aware. Just to be able to get to purr, they have to be in that other dimensional way of relating to the physical, where they're peripherally associated with it. In fact, that is the way that vibration of the purr occurs. You can feel how they feel themselves as energy, and they basically feel the physical is transparent to that. At the level of energy, you can feel and even see right through the physical. They are meditating on that, knowing that, with each moment of that purring. That's how they are aware of the physical when that's occurring.

They're not afraid, in the slightest. And yet, if provoked by anything, instantly the cat can respond, even from that purring state. Zap!—they can deal with an environmental intrusion of some kind.

Having that quickness, they can afford to get into this deep state. More tamasic animals have to be sort of semi-awake all the time. They have to see something coming for a long time just to get around to maybe doing something about it. If you haven't seen the chameleons down here in Fear-No-More Zoo, you ought to go and check them out, in terms of their extraordinary non-quickness, generally speaking. But the cats have the gift of being able to purr, because they can respond suddenly. Human responses are quick, but not as quick.

Cats Contemplate, meditate, inherently. It is structurally determined, even. Disturbed cats don't purr. Jostle a cat physically, require physical attention from a cat, they stop purring. They can't purr and be physically active in the ordinary sense other than in the act of purring.

Women, when they're in sexual occasion, often ask their partner "not to stop", or "keep on doing that" (whatever it is). Are women doing something like purring when they're having sex? Sexing for women puts them into a physical condition, or a mode of being related to the physical that's something like you might imagine the cat is in when it's purring. It's non-ordinary physical awareness, isn't it?

Fear-No-More Zoo

Avatar Adi Da with a chameleon at Fear-No-More Zoo, the Mountain Of Attention, 1996

Inspired by Avatar Adi Da's Love for all beings, the Fear-No-More Zoos began in California in the mid-1970s, and now exist in four different locations. Fear-No-More Zoos are a tangible expression of the fullness of Adi Da's Spiritual Work, which encompasses both humans and non-humans. The Fear-No-More Zoos give humans an opportunity to observe the non-humans in their natural state of Contemplation, thereby allowing greater sensitivity to the Spiritual nature of all beings. Fear-No-More Zoos have always worked to serve and protect this natural state of Contemplation for all the non-humans that reside in them.

AVATAR ADI DA SAMRAJ: Apart from human beings and their effects, there is a universal state of Contemplation going on, and functioning just on the basis of that Contemplation. Essentially it's not a fear world. The human world is the fear world. All of Nature, so to speak, is Contemplating constantly. There are breaks, it seems, or required action, but essentially it's a culture of Contemplation, including the Earth itself.

That is why there is Fear-No-More Zoo. Living things are there just being—without fear.

Just being at the Zoo awakens compassion for all living beings, and a feeling of Non-"difference", of Unity. To Me, in the ultimate sense, non-humans are the same as human beings. I don't imagine them being lowly or separate, or different in any sense whatsoever. And that's what you should realize when you go to Fear-No-More Zoo. It's about "fearing no more", feeling a great Unity, going beyond the knot of separate self, being in the condition of the Samadhi of God-Communion. [January 5, 1996]

WOMEN DEVOTEES: Yes, non-ordinary.

AVATAR ADI DA SAMRAJ: Orgasm, or deep sexing. Right? So it involves a change of relationship, even, to the physical. Not a philosophical change, not one you account for mentally, but nonetheless one that you become moved to repeat, just as you are moved to go to sleep every night once you've realized there's nothing dangerous about it—in fact, that it's a pleasure. Then you don't mind it. But if you go to sleep at night and you have bad dreams, or whatever, and, in fact, don't even get to sleep, you just get to dream, then you don't feel so comfortable about going to get some rest.

So a disturbance of the cycle of waking, dreaming, and sleeping occurs with psycho-physical intrusions—mental, physical, emotional intrusions—stimulations, in other words. Non-humans generally look to be stimulated only for enough time to "handle life-business" (so to speak) and maximize time without physical stimulation, in a state of relative rest, even purring or buzzing, or whatever. It is a condition so desirable, from the point of view of the apparently embodied, that they readily do it rather than engage in other activities. It's the humans, though, who, whenever they don't seem to have any obligation, think they've got to be doing something.

ANTONINA RANDAZZO: Functionaries.

AVATAR ADI DA SAMRAJ: Yes, doing something in this functional sense. "To do something that isn't functional is to be up to no good!" You know what I mean? *[Beloved Adi Da laughs.]* "Idle hands are the devil's playground."

ANTONINA: That's the expectation in the world.

AVATAR ADI DA SAMRAJ: The world, the world, the world, the news, the news, the news—all the stuff out there and so on—what does it have to do with Truth?

BETH KANTOR: Not much.

AVATAR ADI DA SAMRAJ: What does it have to do with the Great Matter, the in-depth process? If you're neglecting that, you're foolish. By spending your lifetime in this in-depth process—not just clinging to the waking state and physicality, and so forth, but always entering into the state <u>beyond</u> egoic "self-possession", self-contraction, or deeper and deeper states—you free yourself constantly (in other words, at the root, at the heart) from the potential deep binding power of waking-state experience, and conditional experience altogether.

V.

AVATAR ADI DA SAMRAJ: Your in-depth position in every moment, in your separate persona, is <u>always</u> the sleep state. You're always in that state. When you relinquish certain forms of physical and mental awareness, then you discover that you are in this state again. You don't <u>achieve</u> sleep, it is a state of consciousness that is continuous. So it's not merely something that has to do with physical needs and so on. You will discover (or could discover, through a right process) that when you enter into sleep you're in the same condition that you otherwise already are in the waking state. It's just that you don't identify it as such.

Some people can very readily, at any moment, enter into a kind of revery, a kind of dream state—imagining things, or entering into mind-forms, and completely forgetting their physical surroundings, their physical body. Well, when they're doing that, they're entering into the same condition they realize when they go to sleep and start dreaming at night.

By learning, by familiarity, you become aware of the structures of existence, the existence you're actually experiencing. You're always asleep, you always have the potential to dream, you always have the potential of the waking state. And death, for one associated with embodiment in the waking state, is a process of becoming deeper relative to the gross conditions of awareness, and then, beyond that, entering into a potential realm of perceived experiences and so forth, in the order of the dream world, and then, beyond that, an in-depth process in the Domain of Consciousness Itself, and, ultimately, beyond even the confinements, the inherent separateness, the root self-contraction that is the sleep state.

So this in-depth condition you fall asleep into every night is the same condition that's there already right now. It's just that, in the waking state, you're constantly associating yourself with <u>body</u>-identification, and you forget this in-depth domain, which is even without mind. It's just a feeling-awareness of being, and yet it's still associated with some kind of unspeakable ring, or circle, of separateness. It is threatened by phenomenal arising, concerned that it will arise again, that you will forget the depth and go into dreaming and waking.

In the waking state, it seems like just the opposite is maybe threatened, so you're afraid to die, you're afraid to sleep, to not get up, and so forth. But, having entered into the depth, it's just the opposite: There can be a fear, in that "self-possession" domain of sleep, of getting involved in forms of mind and physical identification. These are not desirable from that point of view. They are desirable only when you're already stuck with it! [Beloved Adi Da laughs.]

You seem, in this waking-state experience, to be associated with this body, so you must, of course, be terrified at the prospect of that <u>not</u> being the case. On the other hand, if you could take an objective look at that body with which you are so <u>intensely</u> identifying, you wouldn't want anything more to do with it than all the ugly ones that are otherwise around that you could have identified with. *[laughter]* By ugly, I mean mortal, suffering, in limitation. Why would one want to pass from a state of at least relatively unbounded awareness, of bliss without intrusion? Why would one want to be associated with random perceptual imaginings and conceptual imaginings in the dream-state manner, or more fixed conditions engineered out of a sense of identification with gross physical appearances? Why would one want to do this?

It's only when it has already happened that you <u>want</u> to be involved in those states. From the point of view of being established in the in-depth position examining it, it is not so. On the other hand, merely to enter into the depth, even in the sixth stage sense, you're still rooted in the self-contraction and you're still threatened by these unpredictable dreaming and waking experiences.

So there is yet a lack of resolution, even in the sixth stage. The problem, then, suffered by all equally in the first six stages if life, is the un-Recognizability[29] of conditional arising, in the mode of waking, dreaming, and sleeping. Of course it is un-Recognizable when you are either waking, dreaming, or sleeping. So you must Realize What is Prior to waking, dreaming, and sleeping. And, having done that, you must Abide <u>as</u> That, so profoundly and intensively, so "Bright" by Grace, that you will be able to Recognize everything that arises in the waking, dreaming, and sleeping states, even though they arise.

That is the great spontaneous Yoga of the seventh stage itself, compared to which, of course, everything else is, as the Black Adder said (in the British TV series), "<u>utter crap</u>!", and you're just wasting time waking, dreaming, sleeping, being involved in all that stuff that you're all claiming to be so difficult.

You should handle business directly, simply, straightforwardly, and enter into this Way of Me. It is the Way of the Heart, the Way of the Depth, the Way of the Source, the Way of the Root, the "Radical" Way— not the way of seeking. It's the Way of Realizing What is Prior to waking, dreaming, and sleeping. It is not the way of developing the states of, or conditions associated with, waking, dreaming, or sleeping. It's about the

---

29. In other words, the conditions of existence are not observed to be transparent and un-necessary modifications of the Divine.

transcendence of egoity, not the development or evolution of the ego. It's about transcendence of all the stages of life.

There are, in the domain of psycho-biography of the ego, the first six stages of life. The Way of the Heart is the Way of Realizing <u>Me</u>. It is the Way of Realizing That Which is Always Already The Case, Which is Absolute and All-Sufficient. To be most profoundly deep with Me is to be established in the Domain that is Prior to waking, dreaming, and sleeping. No birth, and life, and death there. And, if you're less deep than that, and you do this sadhana, you Realize Me in one mode or another, associated with sleeping and dreaming and waking.

Someone once said, "Once a philosopher, twice a pervert." You should be so serious that you do not require another experience of this embodiment kind. In any moment of free detachment from the bondage to conditional human awareness, you immediately prefer the freedom to the stress of that embodiment. But the embodiment has its work to do in generating responsibility in depth. Any apparent psycho-physical thing can seem to be born and live and die, and wake and dream and sleep. But to understand that process, to have thoroughly investigated and transcended its binding force, to be responsibly associated with it, is the Yoga of Reality-Realization most profound.

Non-humans may seem like humble buckets to you, but they are aware like you, and they suffer and they die, just like you. They don't like it. And you don't like it, either, but you seem to have trouble accepting the fact that you don't like it. You seem to think that you've got to come up with some other kind of "you"! *[laughter]*

That's right! You're right. Upon inspection directly, simply, it is a place of death and pain. But that is not all it is. It's not that one is to be cutting it off in some gross sense. It's simply that you have to understand the nature of it, and not get out of balance about it. *[parodying an authoritative tone of voice]* It's only the waking state, you know. *[laughter]* You can call it "the body" and so forth, but it's the waking state. When you say "the body", you're not talking about a something that's sort of in a vacuum, you're talking about <u>all</u> the experiences associated with feeling identified with the body. So you're talking about a state, a whole realm of experiencing.

It can be an adventure if you're like Mickey Mouse—that is, if you don't lose your heart in the midst of whatever happens. But if you give it up and lose your depth, lose the depth itself, then you become a depressed and even negative player. So it has to be your concern not to lose your heart in the midst of this difficult life-experience.

VI.

AVATAR ADI DA SAMRAJ: The lion values what goes on in depth. The cat values what goes on in depth, on the other side of the purr, in that rhythm that undermines their fixed sensation of physicality. Their impenetrable sensation of matter is undermined by it.

Even science, which speaks in materialistic terms, talks about the gross particulars of material appearance in terms of particles. Your body, for instance, is made up of <u>minute</u>—much smaller than microscopic—particles. You're a mass of elements, but each of these little atomic centers is like a bunch of particles with a lot of space in between them, whirring around one another, and so on. And so, if you were magnified big, you'd see that you were basically mainly space. This is the report of contemporary physics, yet the language of science is "matter". What has matter got to do with it? It's like a nineteenth-century Victorian metaphor for something.

In the case of anything objective, if you examine it more and more down to the roots of that, and then the roots of that, deeper and deeper and deeper, you finally get to Energy. Or it could be called "Light". Or, deeply experienced, it is Love-Bliss. But Energy, the condition of Energy.

Go inside yourself—that's the only place you can really do it in this sense—enter, in other words, more profoundly, deeply, subjectively, in your own position, and eventually you get to Consciousness, Being, Awareness.

You can't get any deeper than Consciousness, or Being, on the Subjective side. You can't get any deeper than Energy, or Light (or What ultimately may be Realized as Love-Bliss), on the objective side.

Irreducible Reality is Perfectly Subjective Self-Consciousness, Infinitely Self-Radiant and Self-Existing. Love-Bliss, in other words. Radiance-Energy.

And it's not by identifying with waking, dreaming, or sleeping, or the condition of physical embodiment, or any limitation at all, that this Truth I just spoke to you is Realized or (let us say) Enjoyed. It is Truth, and also able to be Enjoyed, only in Its Realization, only in Reality—not when It is merely talked about.

To respond to Me, to find Me, to discover Me, is to be entered into the relationship and vow of relationship to Me, in which you are given to this profundity, ever deepening beyond the limiting conditions of existence.

It's possible to enter, therefore, into a State that is deeper than waking, dreaming, or sleeping, and, therefore, deeper, even, than the experiencing of death.

The thing feared in the waking state, or suspected or struggled about, has no form, makes no dent or sign, in the True Depth, in the Domain of Reality Itself, That Which is Always Already the Case.

CHAPTER SIXTEEN

The Process Of Meditation In The Way Of The Heart

THE HEART OF THE DAWN HORSE TESTAMENT OF THE RUCHIRA BUDDHA
CHAPTER THIRTY-FOUR, VERSES 1-15

1.

Simple (Natural) arousal From the dreaming state To the waking state of the body-mind Immediately (If Only Naturally, or conditionally) awakens You From Identification With the problems and illusions You Seemed To suffer or Seek In the dreaming state.

2.

Just So, In The Way Of The Heart, Meditation (and, Especially, Deep Meditation) Directly (and More and More Profoundly, and Then Inherently, and Inherently Most Perfectly, or Un-conditionally) Awakens You From Identification With the problems and illusions You Seem (or Seemed) To suffer or Seek In the waking state.

3.

Likewise, In The Way Of The Heart, Meditation (and, Especially, Deep Meditation) Directly (and More and More Profoundly, and Then Inherently, and Inherently Most Perfectly, or Un-conditionally) Awakens You From Identification With (and all limitation by) the waking state itself, the dreaming state itself, and the sleeping state itself.

4.

Indeed, The Great Process Of Meditation In The Way Of The Heart (Beginning With "Simple" Feeling-Contemplation Of My Bodily Human Form, My Spiritual, and Always Blessing, Presence, and My Very, and Inherently Perfect, State, and Progressing, On That Basis, Via All The Necessary and Appropriate Practices and Developmental Processes In The Way Of The Heart, Through The First Six Stages Of Life) Is (or Must Become) A Total and, Most Ultimately, Inherent, and Inherently Most Perfect, Awakening From the problems, illusions, sufferings, searches, limitations, experiences, knowledge, and conditional self-Identity Associated With all Possible states Of conditional or psycho-physical Existence.

5.

In The Way Of The Heart, Meditation (Which, Most Ultimately, Becomes, or Awakens To, Seventh Stage Sahaj Samadhi, or Native Identification With The "Bright", or Inherently Spiritual, and Transcendental, or Inherently Free, Condition Of Consciousness Itself, Realized As Self-Existing, Self-Radiant, and Necessarily Divine Self-Existence Itself, or Divine Being Itself) Is (In Right Conjunction With The Full Range Of All The By Me Given Disciplines) The Principal Progressively Effective Means Whereby conceptual philosophy (or God-Talk) and limited insight Become (or Are Directly Transcended In) Spiritual, Transcendental, and (Most Ultimately) Divine Realization.

6.

Meditation (Progressively Realized) In The Way Of The Heart Is (In Right Conjunction With The Full Range Of All The By Me Given Disciplines) The Principal Progressively Effective Means Whereby the self-Contraction, the body-mind, and all conditional relations Are Really Transcended In Happiness Itself. And That Transcendence Is Not Realized By An Effort Of Separation, or A Struggle To (Strategically) Escape, Nor Is It Realized By An Effort Toward Union, or Re-Union. Rather, It Is (Progressively) Realized By Grace-Given and Direct (or Native) Identification With The Self-Existing and Self-Radiant Source-Condition That Inherently Transcends dependent conditions.

7.

In The Way Of The Heart, Meditation Is A Gift, Spontaneously (and Progressively) Given (By Grace) To those who Surrender, Forget, and Transcend themselves By Feeling-Contemplating My Bodily (Human)

Form, My Spiritual (and Always Blessing) Presence, and My Very (and Inherently Perfect) State.

8.

In The Way Of The Heart, Meditation Is A Gift, Not A Technique, and Even All The Technical Forms (or By Me Given Technical Exercises) Of Meditation Practice In The Way Of The Heart Are, Truly, Only Secondary Means, To Be Applied For The Sake Of Serving The Always Primary Practice, Of Devotional Resort To Me, and Devotional Contemplation Of Me, and Devotional Response To Me, and Devotional and Meditative Cooperation With Me.

9.

The Way Of The Heart (and Meditation In The Way Of The Heart) Is A Relationship, Not Merely A System Of Techniques.

10.

Practice Of The Way Of The Heart Is Right Practice Of The Relationship To Me.

11.

Right Practice Of The Way Of The Heart Is To Remember (or To Constantly Feel, and, Thereby, To Contemplate) My Bodily (Human) Form, My Spiritual (and Always Blessing) Presence, and My Very (and Inherently Perfect) State, and (Thus and Thereby) To Forget (or To Constantly Surrender and Transcend) self-Contraction (Whether In The Context Of The Devotional Way Of Insight* Or In The Context Of The Devotional Way Of Faith).

12.

Therefore, In The Way Of The Heart, Every Gift, Calling, and Discipline Is To Be Embraced (By Constant Practice), but Every Practice (Including Meditation Practice) Is Simply (or Most Basically) A Means For Feeling (and Thereby Contemplating) My Bodily (Human) Form, My Spiritual (and Always Blessing) Presence, and My Very (and Inherently Perfect) State (and, Otherwise, For Responding To The Results, or The Graces, Given In and By The Feeling-Contemplation Of My Bodily Human Form, My Spiritual, and Always Blessing, Presence, and My Very, and Inherently Perfect, State).

13.

And Meditation (Given By Grace, and Always Feeling-Contemplating My Very, and Inherently Perfect, State, and Progressively Realizing My Very, and Inherently Perfect, State) Is The Principal Gift (and Calling, and Discipline) I Give (By Merely Being Present) To My Listening Devotee, My Hearing Devotee, and My Seeing Devotee, Until My Fully Mature (or Truly Both Hearing and Seeing) Devotee Realizes (By That Gift Of Feeling-Contemplation and That Grace Of Feeling-Meditation) The Inherently Perfect and Self-"Bright" State That I Am.

14.

For those who Would Yet Understand themselves (Most Fundamentally), or For those who (Because they Understand themselves Most Fundamentally) Will Not Settle For Less Than Freedom and Happiness, or For those who Would Enjoy The Ultimate (and Inherently Perfect) Intuition Of their own Native and Divine Ignorance (or Inherently Perfect Self-Condition), or For those who Have Recovered The Unique and Comprehensively Effective Ability To (Progressively, and More and More) Satisfy The Impulse Toward Most Perfectly self-Transcending Spiritual and Transcendental God-Realization, Meditation Has Become As Necessary As food and rest, and More Fundamental Than the waking state itself, or the dreaming state, or the state of deep sleep.

15.

Therefore, As You Listen To Me, and When You Hear Me, and Also When You See Me, Do Not Be Preoccupied With the problem of the ego-"I", or the problems of the self-Contracted body-mind. Do Not Consent To Be Deluded and Held Captive By the body-mind and its functions, its Presumed needs, its states, its relations, its reactions, its sufferings, its thoughts, and its illusions. Do Not Seek or Identify With the conditional self and its world, As If the body-mind and its relations Are (in, of, or as themselves) Everlasting and Identical To Happiness Itself. Be Truly (and By Truth) Aroused From the waking state (and, Indeed, From every psycho-physical or conditional state). Indeed, Be Thus Aroused daily, and Then (Most Ultimately, and Inherently) Most Perfectly. Let Your Free and Transcendental (and Inherently Spiritual, and Necessarily Divine) Self Be Soon (and, By Grace, Directly) Aroused By Means Of True and Deepest Meditation On, In, and As The Only One Who Is.

San Francisco, 1996

CHAPTER SEVENTEEN

December 15, 1996

There Is Nothing About the Sleep State That Can Smile

On December 15, Avatar Adi Da further develops the matter of waking, dreaming, and sleeping, and "considers" what can be learned from these states relative to some principal philosophical and religious questions.

I.

HAL OKUN: Beloved, I wanted to speak about one thing that occurred in the last gathering. You were Discoursing, and I had my attention on what You were saying, but I didn't have any relationship to the body, particularly. And, in fact, it felt like I was asleep. But then, at a certain point, You asked, "What was I saying?", something along those lines, and I realized that I could immediately respond to You from out of what was like a sleep state.

AVATAR ADI DA SAMRAJ: Could you have told Me what I had been talking about?

HAL: At the time I did tell You precisely what You were saying.

AVATAR ADI DA SAMRAJ: So, in other words, you were registering it as I was speaking.

HAL: Yes.

AVATAR ADI DA SAMRAJ: But you otherwise felt like you were asleep.

HAL: Yes. It was an instant response. I mean, it was right there. I didn't even have to think about it. But I didn't move from the sleep state to the waking state or something like that. It was nothing like that. It was much more instantly present. It was all part of the same moment, somehow, without a transition.

AVATAR ADI DA SAMRAJ: Yes, what about it?

HAL: Well, that was the night that You were speaking of the necessity to always be in the depth with You, and that the sadhana takes place in the depth, and is effective in the depth.

AVATAR ADI DA SAMRAJ: Yes.

HAL: And so I was wondering if that Transmission was a particular Gift of being in the depth, completely bodily relaxed, and feeling the incredible bliss of that, not noticing the body at all (seemingly), eyes closed. And not particularly noticing the room, but staying completely with Your "Consideration", being very conscious of it.

AVATAR ADI DA SAMRAJ: You were hearing My Voice and listening to the words, in other words. Well, you obviously weren't asleep. You were just very relaxed, obviously, but not otherwise inattentive to the physical environment and goings-on as you would be if you were asleep ordinarily.

HAL: I wasn't aware of any of the environment at all, apart from Your Discourse, at the time.

AVATAR ADI DA SAMRAJ: There very possibly wasn't much else going on. Everybody just sitting in the room here and, as you were, perhaps rather relaxedly following the line of "consideration". There might not have been anything much to notice at all, and very easy to tune out, because you didn't expect anything remarkable. And you felt you could relax, in other words.

You were obviously concentrated. For instance, you must have had the experience of studying where you are reading and thinking about something in a very concentrated way, and you have no awareness of the physical environment. It's not that the body shut down or anything like that, it's just that you become very focused in one use of your attention at the moment, and the rest of it becomes peripheral, and rather automatic even.

Nonetheless, if called on at that moment, even though you were concentrated in reading, you would respond. Well, you probably would respond. Sometimes people are so concentrated it's difficult to get them to respond, but it's not that they're unconscious.

But they are in a condition that makes it clear, if you examine it, that the waking state is not merely a state, either. What you described is a form of the waking state, but it's certainly not the same as sitting around jabbering at a coffee shop with a friend or something. It didn't have any of the physical associations or demands and so forth. You even felt it was very much like sleep, for all these reasons.

HAL: And there was no thought process involved in the response, that I could tell. In other words, I didn't think about it. It was almost as if You had Spoken the next word, that's how it was. And I just told You what it was, but I didn't have to think about it. That's what I meant by it was instantaneously . . .

AVATAR ADI DA SAMRAJ: What?! What did he just say? He kept starting the sentence and then saying it another way and then doing something else. He never went to the end of any of these ideas. And the one thing that I thought he was trying to say, I thought it would be eventually said, and it never did get said. [laughter]

HAL: It certainly clarifies everything, Lord. It was a thoughtless communication. I guess that's another way to put what I said.

AVATAR ADI DA SAMRAJ: Yes, but what was it you were communicating? This "you" discussion is interesting, because, if you were really functioning from the depth, as you said, you would have gone beyond that one, like the concept of "matter", already.

The problem is that you all are using "I's" and so forth, but there really is simply a process, altogether. And this concern of "I"-ness, or this rather mechanical reference (used for practical reasons), becomes a matter of metaphysical significance, like the root of a conceived problem, the answer or the resolution to which is not what you might imagine it to be.

As I said, you think the problem is the "you", or the "I", of things, and the fact of the matter is that there is only a process, altogether.

One of the fundamental "considerations" in the tradition of Buddhism, in fact, is this matter of the sense of the "I" being a permanent "someone", permanent anything at all, such that you could refer to it as such.

The problem seems to be the "I"-ness, or the "you" in your experience—the "you" that you're concerned about, which you call "I"—all of that. That's your concern—to protect it, to serve the motive for that to feel good somehow. But if you examine the whole process of anything that could be called "objective", anything attention can notice, it has no separate "you" in it. Not just the things outside the body, but anything that you can say is "you", somehow, upon examination—like "your" body or "your" mind, any of that—profoundly examine it, enter into it deeply, "consider" the matter.

Yes, as I've said to you, the ego is not an entity, it's a process. And all of this conditional arising is a process. So-called "you" tend to think in terms of entities, separateness, things, it seems, in expressing your own concern for self-anxiety. But the "you" is not a "something" or a "some-one" in that sense. It's a process, or a complex pattern. But when you say "you" or refer to yourself as "I", you don't <u>mean</u> something like that. You mean something that you don't have to go through anything complex to get in touch with. It's just a . . . <u>you</u>! Right?

Well, all there is is process, process, changes, klik-klak. Appearance, shift, and change. Repeat. Instead of the same, you get it slightly changed. You know what I mean?

On the other hand, instead of just (in the ordinary psycho-physical sense) observing what passes and seeing that everything changes, enter deeply into anything that can be observed—<u>anything</u> at all, anything objective at all, even in the complex of the body-mind—enter into depths or fields of phenomenal arising that are not at all like the "matter" and "you" of ordinary discourse. There's always a greater depth to go to relative to this maintaining of view toward what is objective to you. And, ultimately, it is simply energy (however that might be experienced) or light (if you want to use a visual metaphor for it).

What is the word "energy" a metaphor for anyway? What is energy? What do you mean when you use the word? You know what you mean, right? But you don't know. Could you possibly, really, make it clear what you mean by the word "energy" when you use it?

DEVOTEES: No.

AVATAR ADI DA SAMRAJ: And if you examine it, it is somehow completely clear what you mean by "energy". And it is the irreducible bottom line of anything observed objectively. It is a singleness, ultimately. And yet, when you are associating with one another in your the-way-you-look world of material "you's" or "I's", and each of them clothed and separated out . . .

Adi Da spontaneously shifts into ecstatic speech, pronouncing each phrase slowly, with rich diction, in an exaggeratedly deep voice, as devotees exclaim after each line:

with plenty thought,
clothed from within,
thought as thick as armchairs,
like a desert, a wilderness
of dinettes.
Parched, one craves insight
by which to be watered cold.

II.

AVATAR ADI DA SAMRAJ: It's in the depth that there is the process of Realization. Realization is not in the waking state. It's not in the dreaming or sleeping states, either. It's Prior to them. But sleep is hierarchically senior. You don't "fall awake", you "fall asleep"—you go back into a primitive state before the thinking mind and physical association and so forth arise. It is senior. You go back into it, or things fall away in it, rather than the waking state being the primary position. If the waking state were the primary position, why would you need to go to sleep?

BETH KANTOR: We've got it all backwards.

AVATAR ADI DA SAMRAJ: It would already be its own depth. Of course, some people don't sleep, as an apparent physical-process matter. But that doesn't mean there isn't, for them, an in-depth dimension to their awareness. There is.

But it's not like there's some trick exercise, or you all go break up for the night now, and go off to wherever you're going to rest for the night—lie down, go to sleep, and be Realized. [laughter] No, it's not in sleep that there is Realization. But the sleep dimension of consciousness, that dimension of the depth of human awareness, is the depth-dimension, and it must be penetrated or gone beyond.

The process is in that depth, then, not in the superficial states merely. It all moves from the inside out. Therefore, the external changes are intended from the inside, from the heart-understanding, discriminative-intelligence level, through the will. And the sadhana itself is an exercise more and more in depth.

III.

AVATAR ADI DA SAMRAJ: The "big bang" is not at the root. The "big bang" is an analytically presumed event, the meaning of which is really beyond human comprehension. When scientists say "the big bang", it's not that they know what they're talking about, any more than they know what they're talking about when they say "electricity", or "energy", or "light". Just because you can use it in a sentence when speaking to another doesn't mean you know what the words mean, in any sense beyond some sort of generalization. You're letting the language speak for itself, really.

Well, the "big bang" is like that. It's a kind of twentieth-century myth—a substitute for some earlier myths, perhaps, that are less attractive to at least some people. Creation myths, and such, are not acceptable to many people. But this kind of notion, this "big bang"—which originated not just things in space but originated space itself.

You tend to think of the "big bang" as a little tiny particle in the midst of space and it blows up. No—there wasn't any space until it blew up. So you can't just take a physically-based point of view and have it be the basis for trying to comprehend what the "big bang" is about.

In any case, it's not an event at some superficial physical level, which a physical observer could account for every part of. It's not possible. It's beyond all that. So it, itself, suggests a depth of process (a necessary depth for observing that process) that is greater than the superficial waking-state physical investigation, which is basically the technique of science. The physically-based waking-state observer is the model for the pursuit of knowledge, answers to questions, and so forth—fine. But it's obviously not a basis for Realizing anything of an ultimate nature.

If you feel deeply, you can discover a feeling-depth, but it has no sense of the body. I mean, whether it's associated with a body, mechanically has anything to do with body, and whatnot—well, you can investigate that further, but experientially, there's already a depth in you, as in deep sleep, that has no association with the body. And this is your deepest place. So you always stand in a position without bodily awareness. In any moment in which you are invested in that depth, you are established in the condition that is beyond body-consciousness and psycho-physical noticing.

If you're established in depth fully, then there's no body-consciousness. Already, in that in-depth awareness (which is always already the case) there's no fear of death. It's not associated with the body, therefore it has no fear of death associated with it, either. It's not the waking-state "depth of personality". It's like sleeping. But it's the in-depth dimension of the "you" that is, otherwise, apparently in the waking state and identified with the body. And, it has nothing to do with the body. It has nothing to do with the mind, either. Body and mind are not about a "you". They are just bits of a totality, a large process. It's not about them, in any separate-entity sense, ultimately. It is about the pattern itself, the process itself.

So What must be Realized is Prior to separate self, Prior to the self-contraction, not what follows it. What is to be Realized, then, is not "you", or the "I", but What is Prior to it. What is to be Realized is not in the waking state or the dreaming state or in the sleeping state, but in the State That is Prior to waking, dreaming, and sleeping.

It's not the observer in the waking state that is the Witness. It's the Consciousness Prior to attention, in the sleep state, that is the Witness—or in the depth. It's not the Witness in the sense of functioning as functional witness or observer. It's the Witness in the sense that It Stands Prior, no matter what arises. It's Prior even to attention.

Such "considerations" as this one have their uses, but the basic matter is this sadhana of the in-depth exercise, moment to moment, served and given form through a whole range of disciplines. There is this in-depth process and discipline of the structure of the body-mind—these two together, moment to moment.

IV.

AVATAR ADI DA SAMRAJ: Scientists say light behaves like particles and it behaves like waves. Just as the particle and wave descriptions of light (or energy) both hold true—particles and waves are two very different things, it seems, so it's a paradox—well, so also, Reality is both Consciousness and Energy (or Light). And yet, how can it be so? It seems you have no ability to comprehend that they could be the same. You can account for it through some philosophical explanation, but I'm talking about the direct Realization, and then demonstrating, or functioning, on the basis of that Realization.

In Reality, Consciousness, Energy, and world (or things) are not separate from one another. But they seem to be separate from the point of view of the world (or things), and from the point of view of Energy. Only from the "Point of View" of Consciousness, in the fully Awakened State, is the Truth of Non-separateness Realized. Therefore, the "conscious process" is senior to the process of "conductivity". Nonetheless, they are always coinciding. They are one process, truly. One is about patterning, one is about awareness. Pattern and awareness coincide. The Energy within which the pattern is arising is what the pattern is. That is its nature, its identity. And Energy and Consciousness are not separate from one another.

This is not useful as a mere philosophical presumption, or a gathering of thoughts. I'm describing to you actual Realization, Which is direct experience. I'm describing to you My Experience right now.

So what about this?

THANKFULL HASTINGS: Sleep?

AVATAR ADI DA SAMRAJ: Amusing that you were saying that, Thankfull, since you are obviously in a state something like deep sleep right now. *[laughter]*

THANKFULL: I'm still there.

AVATAR ADI DA SAMRAJ: Right. So don't wake yourself up. Stay in it. But, by staying in it, if you can, deeply enter into that state, but while doing it remain attentive to My Word. See if you can speak something about this sleeping position, for our interest and delectation, our amusement and our edification. *[laughter]* No, you're smiling. You're waking up. Too much, too much smile. There is nothing about the sleep state that can smile.

Yes, I don't think Thankfull is on too deep a plane of the slumber mode at the present time. He's too smiley and too attentive, too physical. He lost it. *[laughter]*

Maybe you can try to restore your previous state of deep torpor, or anti-tumescence of the soul.

THANKFULL: *[catching himself as he begins to nod off]* See? I'm dead tired.

AVATAR ADI DA SAMRAJ: Now you're thinking about things. All you had to do was stay in that sleep state, but somehow still stay attentive to My Words, and be able to reflect the experience of the sleep state. Don't get into thinking about it particularly, just using speech as a way to <u>reflect</u> the sleep state, which doesn't itself think. It doesn't think, it doesn't smile, doesn't have a body. It's the separate self.

Existence is not about "you", or the "I". It's about Reality. The Self-Existing, Self-Persisting Reality.

And you don't want to wind up in its beak, you know.

It would be one thing if you were all just galumphin' along, and ate and squatted on whatever, who knows where. And didn't bother about much, and, therefore, you didn't come up with any great Realization, Realizers, sadhana, practice, Way, and so forth.

I've Given you this Way as a Self-Revealed Gift. Its proof is not what you can believe about it. Its proof is what you Realize by doing it.

The Way inherently proves itself. Your Me-Recognizing response, your heart-response to Me, is, in its depth, inherent proof already of the Way, of its Ultimate Realization. So it is there from the beginning, and yet requires the submission of all (the in-depth process, and even, in every sense, adaptation of all patterns) to this in-depth focus.

The Attitude of Sadhana Goes Beyond "You"

I.

AVATAR ADI DA SAMRAJ: The body, in and of itself, is essentially a food-process, a food-cycle, part of the food-cycle process. It is made of that kind of material substance. It's a transformation station of a kind. It's the same all the time, and yet it's always changing. It's a little bit different, a little bit different, a little bit more different. And then eventually . . . it falls apart! *[laughter]* And people throw it into the garbage. They have a polite way of throwing it in the garbage called "funerals" or "burials". But you're thrown in the garbage. In other words, you're thrown back in the dump of wherever everything blends back together again.

Well, it's a terrible situation. There is no "you". There's this process, because it's always different and so forth. And all these others (whatever you relate to) are always changing. Everyone's always changing, disappearing. Nothing stays, nothing lasts. Even if you find what you like, it doesn't last. Nothing lasts at all. *[slowly]* And there doesn't seem to be anything profound about anything at all.

THANKFULL: Beloved, I really appreciated something You said the other evening—that what we're searching for in the waking state is something that cannot be found in the waking state.

AVATAR ADI DA SAMRAJ: Mm-hm. You're seeking for something through the constant exercise of verbal mind, or mind-process altogether. You're constantly seeking by the exercise of it and using its various structures of language, as if to come to some end of it, some fulfillment of thinky-thinky-thinky-thinky, because there is just Happiness left—in other words, it Realizes Happiness.

Well, that's how you argue it to yourself, justifying the obsession you already have with thinking and the problem (whatever it is) that's at the root of that. You're justifying it. But, as I said, the reason you're doing it is because you are pursuing the Truth by thinking, and attempting to produce the Truth by thinking about It.

Look at this mind-functioning that you got into as if this is "you". You feel a need to be <u>thinking</u> about it, thinking about something. "There has to be some thinking here, because it feels really weird to be in these circumstances."

If you're just going with the flow, you're sort of just lumpin' along with the sensation and social-personality process, and peripheral about

230

the Way itself. You feel that what you'll do is just think positive about everything and be sort of love-faith-positive, which is the popular religious message.

Every moment of experiencing—apart from the fact that there can always be some moment in which some kind of pleasure appears, of course—but, generally speaking, the course of experiencing over time is <u>less</u> satisfactory, in any moment of its inspection, than previously, because all kinds of "maybe's" that were like open windows for you into the future have proven, by your experience in all kinds of ways, to have been infantilisms.

And the whole "you" that is supposedly a body-mind, which has been bright-eyed proposing all kinds of whatever, is just becoming, after a point of a certain kind of maturity, more and more a degeneration of itself. You can notice by this that the natural world (positive and negative, or klik-klak) is very economical. It overproduces in order to give the highest percentage chance of survival. Of what? Not of "you's" and whoever's, but of the <u>structure</u>.

The structure is the primary force of changes, in whatever domain you examine. In this case, we're talking about life-forms—this fundamental life-structure, DNA, all that kind of stuff. This kind of flow, in which there's a kind of mixing whirling, is persisting. But it's fundamentally still this basic pattern replicating itself. And its ability to freely replicate itself is fundamental to the klik-klak process here. And there's no "you" about it to begin with, even though you may imagine there is. Then, more and more, you realize that there isn't any, and that, really, in this game of nature here, you're becoming more and more obsolete, because you eventually have little to do with the further proceedings of the structure. You served in your life-genetic-reproduction time and so forth. After that, what function do you serve relative to that pattern?

So you notice, over time, that there is less and less built into your body-mind (in the natural sense) to keep it continuing. It degenerates and eventually just falls apart. It was that way from the beginning. It is the way it was built. This is the same as you notice with plant-forms. You know a little bit about that. They all have their different lifespans and bloom-times. Whatever that whole cycle is about, it was there from the beginning, it was built in from the beginning. There can be interferences with a particular plant or whatever in any moment, but there are other plants or whatnot.

Yes, just like these plant-materials, which you know have their time, you know that it's built in from the beginning. When people plant gardens, they take this into account. "Does this one come up again next year? It says here, 'No.'" Or, "In the second year, won't flower nearly as interestingly—so just dig the sucker up and throw it out! It's not going to be pretty enough the second year to be worth your glances as you walk by it."

All gardeners must seem to be psychotics from the point of view of the plant life. *[laughter]*

VINCE GODDARD: Maintaining discipline with an iron hoe.

AVATAR ADI DA SAMRAJ: On the other hand, the whole pattern in which any life-form appears, upon inspection for a bit of time, must seem, to any life-form, to be psychotic. I mean, it seems so to you, doesn't it? Whatever word you might use in place of "psychotic", some word like that—the pattern seems mad, doesn't it? It doesn't seem to be associated with any purpose associated with your wish to continue and enjoy yourself forever, or even to enjoy yourself at all! Even to be yourself, predictably.

JONATHAN CONDIT: That's the real problem.

AVATAR ADI DA SAMRAJ: Yes. So the whole pattern, the physical world altogether, does not serve your interests absolutely. It doesn't seem to make sense, because how could there be a universe in which you are a unified person, you are birthed, and yet you are not simultaneously associated with the accommodation that would fulfill the impulse of that birth toward happiness, pleasure, and longevity—and even life forever, going through permutations of changes, but not finally ending. Even more about it, if there is going to be all this to come together to birth you, what's the point?—if you haven't been born into something that is built to pleasurize you. And, by the way, where's the instruction booklet—you know what I mean? *[laughter]*

VINCE: Where's the warranty?

AVATAR ADI DA SAMRAJ: And if reading or mind is a necessary tool for figuring things out, then why aren't you born already speaking?

I mean, if it's a necessity for your Realization and Awakening and so forth, then why wouldn't you be born already speaking, already having a verbal mind? You have to learn it. And then you declare it absolutely necessary. That's why you sit there, moment by moment, trying to figure everything out, so that at that moment of figuring everything out, you'll be completely fulfilled and happy—forever from that point. It's just nonsense!

The Truth is not in the context of anything conditional. Could not be.

So, obviously, there is only Energy and Consciousness. But Who or What is Energy and Consciousness? Your way of thinking about things is such that, when I say, "All there is is Energy and Consciousness", you right away start thinking in terms of abstractions—something like paint chips for your bedroom. No, the characteristics of Reality—Which, when fully Realized, is the Very Condition That is Truth Itself, the Very Divine—can be understood, upon simple inspection, or "consideration", of everything objective, everything subjective. It's not an abstract matter at all.

You see, these are very Primitive, Primal Forms, Forces of Reality—Consciousness and Energy. There's nothing complicated about your sense of either of these. Your mind about everything is very complicated, but these are primal.

And the reason you don't know what anything is, fundamentally, is the fact that in the state of conditional being, Consciousness does not Recognize Energy. Consciousness does not Recognize that Energy is Itself, is Consciousness Itself. Energy is the Inherent Radiance of Consciousness Itself. There's no separation. But this is not comprehended in the conditional state. And, therefore, all objects, which are modifications of Energy, generally speaking, aren't even in themselves understood to be just Energy, an experience of Energy altogether. Everything gets very objectified materialistically. But, also, it's true that you don't know what even a single thing is. This is true in any of the stages of life, until the seventh.

In other words, the fact that you do not know what a single thing is remains the most fundamental unresolved aspect of the Great Tradition's Revelation of the six stages of the psycho-biography of the ego—the six stages of human seeking, which explore all the ins and outs and ups and downs of the human self-entity, body-mind, and all the experiences of that, all of its parts, or by means of its functions, down to the causal root.

Even then, in the sixth stage of life, the phenomenal process is still a problem. There is still something you presume you must exclude in order to enter into the Domain of Consciousness, Prior to objects. It's not that the reverse of that, not doing that, is the Truth, either—or the sign of Truth. It's simply that, even in the fulfillment of the sixth stage process, there is the fundamental un-Recognizability of phenomenal arising and of Energy. And that has always been the problem. That is the problem in all of the stages of life. That is a problem, then, that is transcended—solved, in that sense—in the seventh stage Awakening. In that Awakening, That Which is Consciousness and Energy Recognizes all.

233

So Reality is not about you. It's not about the "I". It's not about the separate reference that's concerned about itself, concerned about its embodiment, about its continuation as what it is looking to be, looking at how it appears to the observer.

You are the self-contraction. All your plans, achievements, patterns . . . *[Beloved Adi Da flips His hand in a gesture that suggests something disappearing]* go! Sooner or later.

But the "you" that might be depressed by that is not what it is thought to be. Reality is not what it is thought to be.

The Truth is That Condition in Which everything is arising. It is That Which is Always Already the Case, no matter what is arising. You are a notion associated with psycho-physical self-contraction. When the self-contraction is gone beyond, then That Which is Always Already the Case becomes, as it were, self-evident. Wherever there's nothing added, no self-contraction, What was already there is Obvious.

And so it is. This understanding is fundamental to this process.

So there is no "you" that the process is about. There is no "you" that is preserved in all of this. There is no "you" you can observe—form, process, function, structure, whatever—that you could say is "you" right now, and have it be the same "you" you're referring to when spoken to a few years later. That structure pointed to will not be the same one that's pointed to in years to come. Presumably the same "you" is saying this in both cases. I mean, when you were nine years old, you said you were "you", and you still say you're "you", and you mean basically the same thing, right? You think you're the same guy you were when you were nine, right?

DEVOTEES: Yes.

AVATAR ADI DA SAMRAJ: Whatever that "you" is.

Everything is made up of Consciousness and Energy—that's why it's possible to get these dualities. And if you don't understand (or continue to be established <u>as</u>) the Condition in Which the dualities are arising, then you fall into the maya,[30] the samsara,[31] of dualities, opposites, klik-klak, conditions—and seek, feeling yourself to be a disturbed "I", a center of self-concern, struggling to survive, feel good, and so on.

There are no such "you's" that are permanent. Even in your own lifetime, you've been a different "you" every time it was investigated.

---

30. "Maya" is a Sanskrit term for the illusion that inevitably arises from ignorance of the True Nature of conditional reality and Unconditional Reality.

31. "Samsara" is a classical Buddhist and Hindu term for all conditional worlds and states, or the realm of birth and change and death. It connotes the suffering and limitations experienced in those limited worlds.

But there is a Unity in Which all processes are occurring. And there is the Condition, the Source-Condition, in Which even that Unity, or Totality, is arising. The in-depth process has the potential to Realize This. The in-depth process is a process that passes through the limitations and adaptations associated with waking, then dreaming, then sleeping—in other words, in progressively deeper levels, from gross to subtle to causal. And the causal dimension, or the sleep condition, is the doorway to the "Perfect Practice".

II.

AVATAR ADI DA SAMRAJ: You must come to understand that the waking, dreaming, and sleeping states are actual realms, or "pattern-realms". There are characteristics to the waking state, to the dreaming state, and to the deep sleep state, and those characteristics are such that there's a unique point of view about reality, or some dimension or aspect of reality, associated with each of them. And yet, each of them are equally "real" (you could say) modes of your experiencing of reality, or your apprehension of reality, your coincidence with reality.

It's not that the waking state has some special provision to be of use relative to the Realization of Reality. And, in fact, if you make it your point of view, you make it necessary for the mind to figure out Reality ultimately. It's obviously not going to do that. It has nothing to do with Reality, ultimately.

On the other hand, when you come into the waking state, having slept, having dreamed, perhaps, you don't modify your whole process of "considering" reality on the basis of your sense of reality, your "consideration" of reality, in the context of either deep sleep or dreams. You attempt to make the pattern of the waking state, with all its limitations, the source of this whole process of Realizing Reality. You expect it to be the basis on which Reality is Realized.

The waking state is the most superficial state you enter into, usually, within each day's cycle. And it is the most troubled, generally speaking—certainly, when compared to deep sleep it is. Sometimes there can be some really bad dreams and you'd prefer even the humdrum experience of daily life to them, generally speaking. So it's in depth that the profound process is engaged.

If you have your existence depend upon identification with the superficial state of ordinary body-consciousness, then you're in a constant state of fear and anxiety, and seeking to cover that up, or reduce it, or be allowed to ignore it by various kinds of distractions or pleasures or forms of self-indulgence, whatever it may be. If you spend too much time in the waking state and get too complicated in it, you lose sleep—you know what I mean?

On the other hand, it's not a matter of actual "sleep-time in bed" kind of stuff. Not merely that is required, but in-depth time altogether. Even the in-depth process moment to moment ultimately must be so. But it's not self-realization in the sense of realization of you in the separate, egoic, or in the ordinary, personal sense. It is your Realization of Me, the One Standing Prior to your form, the One in Whom it is arising, but only apparently arising at all. In other words, that is not the fundamental Reality—this appearance of arising. The Reality is its Source-Condition.

I'm not talking about the ego-position when using the word "Self" with a capital "S", but That Which is in the Perfectly Subjective Position always—which is not the same as being the "you" of self-reference. "It", so to speak, is Prior to that.

[slowly, in a deep voice] To forget the Source is to forget the Source-Condition.

To forget the Source-Condition is to forget the Source.

The Source-Condition, That Which is in the Self-Position (regardless of what is arising), is Divine.

It is the One and Only Reality.

The universe is not about you.

It is about It—the Totality of the It, the process, the pattern, but also, Reality Itself—That Which is to be Realized.

Whatever is that Is, is the "why" of It, and is not about any concern you have about yourself, or any perception you have about so-called "yourself" at all.

You're not obliged to identify with just a mortal or body-condition.

You are, even at birth, and from that time thereafter, always associated with the equipment to be established in the depth, rather than merely entangled in what is superficial and threatened.

That is always what must be done.

The more superficial, the more you lose the depth.

The more you distract yourself with that which is other than the depth, the more involved you get with that which is other than the depth.

You become what you meditate on.

This Profundity, the Great Realization, is Perfectly Subjective to <u>all</u> of conditional existence.

It's not merely inside you.

That Which is to be Realized is Happiness Itself.

The process and the Realization is not to be found superficially, "externally" (so to speak), or out and about in the physical world, causes and effects, and thises and thats as you perceive them from the point of view of a presumed separate body-mind and so forth.

No, it's Realized in the depth, in the Source-Position, at the point of origin of your involvement with the whole thing within which you are concerned.

If you are established in that in-depth process, most profound, in Communion with Me, then everything in the context of your experiencing, including death (which is inevitable for human beings), will become associated with a progressively more and more profound sense of reality, such that, in due course, that in-depth position <u>itself</u>, because of its very nature, releases you of concerns that are generated only in the superficial domain of conditional identification.

Beyond ego-self (or ego-"I"), there is the Great Unity.

And beyond the Great Unity is the Divine Self-Domain.

But that, again, is to speak in abstract terms.

It is not Realization of you, it is Realization of <u>Me</u>.

It is beyond the ego-reference, the body-mind reference, the waking, dreaming, or sleeping reference.

The attitude of the sadhana goes beyond all of that.

CHAPTER EIGHTEEN

A Dream Encounter

BY HELLIE KALOGEROS

eloved Adi Da has very often Instructed me in the dream state directly.
He'll appear to me in the dream state and say, "Read this passage in
such and such a book", or "Read this page, paragraph such and
such", and, sure enough, when I do that, it's a specific address to what I
am dealing with in my life at that moment. These dreams are not like
ordinary dreams—they are more like visions, or experiences in a subtler
dimension than we operate in during the waking state.

At one point, in the mid-1970s, I was asked to be in charge of the
transcribing department, where all of Adi Da's Talks are transcribed and
archived. I became completely obsessed with the job and discovered that
there were some Talks missing from the earliest days of His Work in Los
Angeles. We couldn't find the tapes anywhere, and pretty soon I had
taken the problem to bed.

That night I had a dream in which I had the capability to go back in
time. In my dream I decided that I would go back in time and recover
these Talks, remember what He had said, and transcribe them.

I was instantly transported back through time and space. I found
myself sitting at a "prasad day"—a day of special celebration—when the
Ashram first opened on Melrose Avenue in Los Angeles. I looked around
and everything was exactly as it had been, except that I was sitting right
below the dais that held Adi Da's chair, which meant I was sitting right at
the Guru's Feet and in front of everyone else in the room. This made me
extremely uncomfortable, because I hadn't figured out yet that I was
there as a "ghost"—no one could see me.

Hellie Kalogeros and Avatar Adi Da Samraj, the Mountain Of Attention, 1974

Soon the Master came out and began to speak. I became so absorbed in this Talk that I completely forgot my discomfort about being right up front. The person behind me asked a question and I noticed that Adi Da looked right through my chest to that person. That's when I started to realize that no one could see me. I was invisible. The Master couldn't see me either.

I liked the fact that I could just hang out here and enjoy His Company and be so close to Him and not be seen! But soon I realized that this was not one of the Talks I needed—and I immediately moved to another time and place, this time to the home of a devotee, where we had also frequently gathered with Beloved Adi Da. This Talk was also not one I needed, so again I moved. I did this again and again—each time moving to a different time and place.

The fourth time, I arrived too late. The Talk was over. Adi Da was sitting in a chair and, again, I was sitting right at His Feet. "I'm not leaving this time," I told myself. I rationalized, "I missed this Talk for a reason. Obviously it means that I should just sit here and be with Him and enjoy His Company." People were getting up to leave and walking right through me. Pretty soon everyone filed out, and there was just me and the Master left the room. A devotee came in and asked Adi Da what He would like for lunch. And then she left and we were alone. He looked off into space and cleared His throat once or twice.

After we had sat there for a few minutes, He leaned over and put His elbow on His right knee. Then He looked directly into my eyes for maybe three or four seconds. It seemed like an eternity. I started getting the feeling that He could see me! And I said, "Master!" I was totally shocked. "Master! Can you see me?!"

He burst out laughing. He just roared with laughter—He could hardly contain himself. I was flabbergasted. Then He shook His head, looked into my eyes again and said, "When are you going to learn that our relationship doesn't depend on time and space?"

The Mountain Of Attention, 1996

CHAPTER NINETEEN

December 16, 1996

You Never Have a Present-Time Experience of Yourself

I.

At the gathering of December 16, Adi Da Samraj initiates a remarkable "consideration" of the nature of perception, which continues as a principal topic throughout the rest of this period of gathering.

AVATAR ADI DA SAMRAJ: You associate with a wide variety of perceptions in every moment, as well as various conceptual events (thoughts flowing, or whatever). When you are communicating, you suggest that you are the body-mind and so forth. And in every moment, you reinforce that—or it is reinforced for you—by this process of perceptual and conceptual activities. So in every moment, you are registering this round of perceptual and conceptual bits. Of course, that's all immediately associated with a memory-structure that makes sense out of it and gives you a sense of continuity and meaning.

But even right now, your perception of your physical sensation and so forth is not a present-time experience. That's not happening in present time. For you to register those perceptions, the process had to take place through the sense-mechanism of the body, go through all kinds of apparatus—brain, and nervous system, and so forth—to come around to be the registering of the sensation of what your buttock feels like against that cushion or whatever you are sitting on. In other words, that's not present time. That's "ago". That's memory. It's not only memory—it's memory examined. It's not only short-term memory—it's memory examined by the memory-structure that sorts things out, pushes them through various shapes and determines what's what.

So in your usual talking, assessing, thinking, and so forth, you're making reference, always, to a past-time "self". You don't have any direct, present-time experience of being a body, because even the perception of body-sensation is later than the present moment.

In fact, since there is no event in the actual present, what's "moment" about it?

Your very perception, your own bodily state, which you call "present-time", is actually a message generated in the body. It's part of the memory of the body, the body-mind already communicating itself to you <u>as</u> memory, but pretending to be present-time experience. You take it to be present-time because it's so close to what is present-time. Actually, you don't even think about these things particularly, so you take it to be present-time. But it isn't present-time.

You look out at the stars. You must know—having gotten instruction somewhere along the line, probably in school—that the stars that you see in the sky are as they would have appeared thousands, or even hundreds of thousands, of years ago. But it takes light time to travel, so, by the time it gets here, we are seeing that star up there (wherever it might be) as it was many, many, many, many thousands of years ago. It might not even exist anymore. It could have blown up by now and you won't be seeing that explosion for a few thousand years or something.

Well, in your own case, the body-mind mechanism is giving you the sensation that you are calling "yourself". But it's already just a memory-signal of the mechanism. Where do you have the sensation of <u>being</u> the mechanism? You don't have that sensation. You only identify with its information.

DEVOTEES: *[astonished]* Oh!

JAMES: Beloved, at the moment of touching something and at the moment of the actual touch itself, there's no . . .

AVATAR ADI DA SAMRAJ: It's already "ago." You didn't even feel yourself extending your hand until it had already happened. So what do you do to move your hand? It's not like you <u>sense</u> your hand and move it, because you don't get the sensation until after you've made the gesture. In other words, you are always already operating previous to "in the present", so to speak. You are previous to the information that is your usual basis of self-identification.

You actually don't have any form, any structure. You are not a perceived anything to you yourself. You are utterly without content in the present. You don't have any bodily sensation in the present, because it will take you another moment to have the experience. So there is no present-time sensation of the body. And if the body got it, and got it to you a moment later, then where was the sensation of the body registered? How did it get to know it? It seems it doesn't. Its memory is your memory. So what is the body ever in present time? It's not aware of its present-time existence or experience, either. Everything is observed at a distance. Therefore, light has had to take time to travel, and you're never—in terms of objects, or objective anythings—experiencing the present. You're always experiencing a recording. [laughter] Well, it's so. It is that.

Something is playing your experience to you in real time and making a record of it. Its record is a very complex one, obviously. It's not the body—it's something senior to the body that's doing this, because the body doesn't even have the present-time sensation of itself. Something else is actually being the body, manifesting the body, manifesting as the body. It is senior to the body. That something is what is surviving in the form of the body and moving in the form of the body, happening altogether.

If this were just happy-land, Happy-God-makes-happy-place, then you would have noticed that by now. So it's not that. There are all kinds of things you can do to make things more balanced and serve well-being in people and so forth. Yes, you can do those things, but the place itself is not inherently about well-being, continuation, happiness, even survival. It's about a pattern that is incomprehensible and enforcing itself—in some sense, even indifferent to its various present-time, or in-time, manifestations.

It is at the level of this observed replica, this machine replica, this memory-machine thing, that your experience is noticed—so-called "your".

What is experience, anyway? How is it limited? By what? Where is it occurring? In whom is it occurring? Why is it occurring?

What exactly is the point of this, right now? Right now. This. What is the point of this? What is the reason for it?

I mean, there could be nothing. In principle, it seems there could be nothing. [in an incredulous tone] Why is there this? What is this for? You can't just live it. You can't just go with the flow. What is this?

There can't be anything more important than entering into the most profound "consideration" of this, and all the rest of handling life-business is just done as straightforward as you can, as duty or whatever, but you don't take the waking state itself so seriously that you give up the profound examination of existence, the in-depth process. Because <u>this</u> stuff, this waking-state body-stuff and so forth, is just not enough! It is not happy enough for Me—I don't know about you people. *[laughter]*

I mean if your experience is Happy-God-makes-happy-world, and you're just happy guys, fine. But I don't see that that's what's happening, and I noticed that early on in My conjunction here, and spoke to people about it and so forth, "considered" these matters profoundly. I even named the "Bright" when I was something like an infant, or just becoming verbal, I guess. I had an identification-reference of it before verbalization of it.

Yes, the "Bright" is Reality. It is the Source-Condition of Reality, the Self-Condition, the Root-Condition, the <u>One</u> and <u>Only</u> Condition. But that is not your experience, right?

Your experience is not of One and Only Love-Bliss-Happiness. And that's what's wrong with it. It's not good enough, then. It's not good enough in itself. There's something more profound, something most profound that must be entered into.

The non-humans open up their senses for a moment and they examine the circumstance and they realize very quickly this is not Happy-God-makes-happy-guys-in-happy-place-land. So they assess the situation very directly. They are very sensitive. Generally speaking of the non-humans, they make a judgement about this body-based condition, and then they relate to it on the basis of that judgement thereafter. They relate to the life-condition conservatively. In other words, they handle obligations relative to it but they don't try to make utopia out of it. They just fulfill the obligation relative to that and, otherwise, step apart from it and Contemplate—in other words, enter into depth.

Philosophy is about entering into the depth, not about <u>talking</u> about everything from the superficial point of view. Wittgenstein, a great twentieth-century philosopher, said, "Whereof one cannot speak, thereof one must remain silent," in one of his most important books.[32]

So it's time to be silent now. You don't even know what a single thing <u>is</u>. In other words, the principal exercise of life is silent, is in depth. It's not a matter of functioning superficially—talking, thinking, reacting emotionally, doing this and that physically. It is a matter of an in-depth process. And then that becomes the governor of the faculties in the daily circumstance. It <u>conserves</u> the faculties.

---

32. Adi Da is referring to the famous last line of Wittgenstein's *Tractatus Logico-Philosophicus.*

It's a disciplining of the body-mind then, rather than an indulgence in it. It's a <u>conserving</u> of the activities of energy and attention relative to the body-mind, an investing of energy and attention in the in-depth dimension of existence.

When the body-mind is conserved to Yoga, conserved toward the Source-Condition, then it becomes associated with the Virtue of the Source-Condition. My "Brightness" shows Itself in the form of benign transformations, Blissful proceedings in meditation and so on, so that Happiness Itself, My Current of Love-Bliss, does indeed Invade the context, the circumstance, of the body-mind, or of conditional experience (waking, dreaming, and sleeping). The process must go on, of course, because it is only when it is complete that there is no limitation on Happiness Itself.

II.

A di Da Samraj starts the next phase of the "consideration" by proposing an imaginary Spiritual practice.

AVATAR ADI DA SAMRAJ: "Feel the intensity of the word-sign 'and', until it becomes the Realization of unqualified Love-Bliss."

Would you like to do that? It might give you something to do in the meditation hall, but you are not going to Realize diddle by that, or any other mere mechanical practice.

In any case, as you can observe, such activities are relative to a remembered self—in other words, perceived body-mind, which is also always later than the present, later than the memory-structures of concepts and so forth.

So this exercise of contemplating not merely the word in its meaning but the <u>intensity</u> of the word "and"—until it becomes the Realization of Love-Bliss Itself, in other words—is a self-manipulative exercise. It is an exercise of that remembered self, that replica that constantly has new replicas coming in—the imaged, perceived, and thought-about self, which is not a "self" that exists in the present moment. You have no polaroid of it.

The only evidence of your own existence experientially is this photocopy, the sense-perception evidence of your own bodily existence. You don't find out you're dead until you're already dead. *[laughter]* The body dies, all sensation falls out of it. For that information to get back into the brain, the nervous system and so forth, and circulate toward some perception-registering center that says to you that the body is dead, the body would have already had to have been dead for that information to go through this machine, anyway. So it is just data, not reality.

What is the reality of your present-time existence? It's necessarily before perception, because that takes time. It is before conception, or conceptual activity—thoughts take time, too. Just see them as a brain activity: Currents have to travel certain distances and all around through some complex structure to become a thought, so that by the time you actually have a thought, what have you done? You did something else to have the thought, whatever that part was in present time then. And what is it? It is unperceived. It's not thought of and it's not perceived. You do not think of or perceive your own existence in present time.

Don't you see? You never have a present-time perception of yourself. You, as an observable construct, cannot be anything you perceive at all, because that's a replica. That's a message made by the equipment. You don't get it until after the present moment. Your present moments, it seems, are all a matter of looking at these old records—in other words, examining perceptions which are records of something that occurred microseconds ago, or a microsecond ago, or whatever. You are only looking at data—you are never looking at reality in present time—when you are looking at perceptions or conceptions.

You can close your eyes and picture a cat, and (generally speaking) you can readily do that. I assume you are all doing that now, right?

DEVOTEES: Yes.

AVATAR ADI DA SAMRAJ: What did you have to do to do that? Did you generate non-perceptual catness-intention, and it becomes concretized as visualized cat in the midst of the field of concentration? What did you do to make the cat come there, in other words? That was before perception, it was before a thought, because a thought would take time.

Several devotees speak simultaneously of what they observed in this exercise.

AVATAR ADI DA SAMRAJ: And what did you do to do that? You yourself, or whatever you are in the present moment. It is not anything you're perceiving, because you don't have a present-time perception. All perceptions take time, so they are always later. So you say you're the body, but you never have an experience in present time of the body.

What, in the present time, do you have an experience of being? You never experience being a body in present time. You only see pictures of body-experiencing—electronic replicas, or electronic whodeewhatsies. What is this perception you are having of this psycho-physical self? What exactly is it as a perception, anyway?

What do you know about your liver? It's stacked up there with all the rest of these revolting parts. If you popped them all out here one at a time, who would want to squeeze them—you know what I mean? *[laughter]* What awareness do you have of those? What does your perception of being the body have to do with these discrete organs? You don't experience them as such, you experience some sort of replications associated with experiences of processes associated with them. What do you experience of your liver function? You have nothing to do with it! You don't command the liver function. You didn't even command the liver to exist. You don't have anything to do with the liver! You claim to be the liver though, when you claim to be the body, and yet you never experience the body in present time.

So what are you in present time? It can't be anything you would think about. And it can't have anything to do with perception.

To find, to locate this, you can't just relax your mind, and get "really into perception now", because perception is just as much memory—it takes time, the same as thoughts do. So you can't just try to do something with your mind about it, or try to forget it by getting into just holding onto perception. Because to hold on to perception is to hold on to something of the same nature as memory, mind-memory.

Thoughts are all replicas of structures in a system. You didn't create the system. You don't invent it. You're not in control of it. It's happening on its own. You can go through some sort of a gesture that you don't really understand. You can change thoughts. You can move your body and so forth—"your" body. You can get the report through a replication system, that what you call "body" moved. You can will it to move. But will it from where?

You are what the body is—not the information on its software, but the washing machine itself, the hardware itself, the copying machine, or the whatever it is—the hardware. It's as is, not as perceived. Perceived is later, is is now.

Completely apart from the whole matter of perception, memory, conversation, thought, and so on, the Condition of the body is the Divine Self-Condition Itself. But you relate to it through this perceptual/conceptual memory, illusion, image, pattern of moment to moment, whereas that is just software product. The real stuff is coming out of the plug in the wall. And the status of the mechanism is not as you see coming out on its printout, not as it is perceived (because that takes time), but as it is in the present moment.

When you're free of all this perception, conception, memory, changes—physical, emotional, mental, gross, subtle, causal—when What Is Always Already the Case is Obvious, nothing superimposed on it, then That is Realization. That is Realization of Me. That is Divine Self-Realization Itself.

It has nothing to do with thinking, embodiment, perception, memory, waking, dreaming, sleeping. You don't experience the body-mind until after the moment of its present. So you are previous to both the appearance and the disappearance of that information. You never seem to experience yourself in any moment, your own condition in any moment, but you are always looking at this software product, this printout kind of thing, this snapshot.

You are like somebody who takes so many photographs when on vacation that you don't get to be anywhere until you go home and look at it in your album or on your screen, where you show your slides or something. You're too busy recording—not participating but recording it, just to be sure you won't lose it, that you will have it always, and then you take it home, in that replica form, and look at it, and then you allow yourself, as much as you can, under those circumstances, to have the experience, using memory and the present murti[33] of it, in the form of your photographs and so on, videos, whatever you've got.

That's exactly what you do all the time. That's what sensation (or perception) and thinking (or conception) are. They're replicas of something that already happened. The thinking is not the words, the thinking is what you did before the words (which are a printout or a transcript) appeared.

As I was saying to you the other evening, it is shape. The core of existence is touch. In the mystical traditions, you hear the language of vision and audition, principally. When speaking of Spiritual mystical phenomena, they're principally a play upon hearing and seeing, audition and viewing. And you might imagine, then, that you are not being mystical if you're not having a lot of subtle visual experiences, or subtle auditory experiences, internal sight and sound stuff. Well, that may be true, you may not be having any Spiritual experience. But, on the other hand, you don't hear much talk in the traditions of what is truly the most profound level of experience associated with the Realization process, and that is at

---

33. The Sanskrit word "murti" means "form". Traditionally, as well as in Avatar Adi Da's usage, the primary meaning of "murti" is "representational image". Generally, in the Way of the Heart, "Murtis" are photographic images of Avatar Adi Da. In this passage, Avatar Adi Da is using the word "murti" in reference to the "photographs" or "images" of experience that constitute perception.

the level of touch. That is primal—not sighting or sound. Touch is feeling-sensation, it is energy.

The shape-awareness, feeling-sensation of energy is touch, and touch is the primary dimension of Spiritual experience. This is the primal domain of the Spiritual process, then, rather than all the maps of things heard or seen in their ascending hierarchy of internalization, and the (basically) fifth stage maps of the subtle process. The ascending process is usually spoken of in terms of experiences or, otherwise, metaphors associated with the functions of the eyes and the ears, or the internal sense-process associated with hearing and seeing.

Feeling-awareness is touch. If visual and auditory phenomena were necessary for your existence, then people like Helen Keller, who have no use of eyes or ears, would just go mad and die. Why didn't she just go mad and die? There are many, many cases of people like this, by the way, who have this (what seems to be) profound misfortune. No one would wish anybody to have such an experience. Unfortunately, however, other fellow humans have had this experience and endured it. And some have reported about it, revealed something to others in the human form that is worthy of contemplating. Since you would not want to have to have that experience yourself, then "consider" it in the form of another's experience, since it unfortunately took place.

What can you learn about the resource in yourself that you fear doesn't exist when you shudder at the notion of being deaf and blind? What can you learn—from the report about Helen Keller, for instance—about that resource, or that something more, that greater foundation of even perceptual existence that must be there or, otherwise, somebody who is deaf and blind would just go mad and die? It isn't even that they wouldn't be able to tolerate it. There would be no thinking about it. It would just be utter madness unless there is something senior to the whole mind and process associated with vision and audition.

So, yes, once again, it's not in the washing machine. It's what's coming out of the wall. It's that current, the feeling-awareness of the Current of Being, the Inherent Radiance of Being, registered perceptually as touch—not only skin touch, but certainly that in terms of any kind of bodily awareness—but, additionally, just the constant primary perceiving process that is not only skin touch and sensation of that kind but an energy-awareness, an awareness of energy, or an awareness of events, experiences, as an energy-process, that you sense as such.

I Am Energy. This is why—being Energy, infinitely Extended, unqualifiedly "Bright"—I can Touch any thing, any one. Stated simply, that is why. It's an Inherent Siddhi. It's Inherent in the Nature of Energy, but it is more primary than physical sensations, concepts, thought processes, and even internal activities or visions, sounds and so forth, in states of deep inwardness, whatever interest these may have in any moment of being noticed, if they occur. Fundamentally, existence moment to moment doesn't have any such content. It is always as if asleep. It is without eyes and ears. It is without even registering of body-sensation as the primary form of touch.

The primary form of touch is just the sensation of energy, and existing as energy in energy, somehow differentiated but not defined in any particular sense. It is the causal knot, the root of the ego-"I". It's the feeling of relatedness. It's the feeling of separateness, also. It's the feeling of "difference". All those three feel the same, and yet they mean something different somehow. But they feel exactly the same. They are three aspects of one fundamental sensation, if you will.

But if you say you can feel the self-contraction, you are registering it through this mechanism again. That was "ago". That's not now. You are not in the position of the self-contraction when you are describing the feeling of it as a sensation somewhere in the context of the body-mind. You must be in the position of the self-contraction, which is in the position of the doing, that later shows up as this replica, this snapshot or home video, of the mechanism, set up as it was at the moment.

The sensations of self-contraction are not in the present. You observe them, you "consider" them, and so forth, but that's not hearing, that's not most fundamental self-understanding. That is not to be in the position of re-cognizing, knowing again, finding again, the self-contraction action that you are and that you are always doing, such that noting that in any moment you can feel beyond it. You're not in that position. You are looking at this printout, instead. True hearing is a capability at the point of the action.

Therefore, you can't locate the self-contraction by trying to perceive it or think about it. The motivator of all your seeking is felt, or you wouldn't identify all seeking as a pursuit of Happiness. The feeling-root of all seeking is this dis-ease. It's not in the replica, not diddling with the replica. But it is in the zone of feeling—when all the faculties are given to Me in the self-surrendering, self-forgetting manner, in Contemplation of My bodily (human) Form—and all the exercises of the "conscious process" and "conductivity" as given for your present stage of practice.

The Realization of Now, or, in other words, What is Always Already the Case, is now. Now is not a "moment", as opposed to the past or the future. <u>Now</u> is the Condition that is Always Already the Case. <u>Now</u> is Prior to perception, conception, time and so forth, so it is not in its categories. It is not by thinking that you Realize Me. Thinking is a secondary exercise that may be associated with the process, but the process isn't itself about thinking and, by means of thinking, Realizing Me. It is about going beyond thinking.

Since you have to go beyond thinking—no matter what you've thought, you have to go beyond thinking to Realize Me—what was the point of thinking in the first place? You just need to do a certain kind of thinking to do something, to organize the pattern (or something) of your thought processes, to orient yourself to Realize Me. So it's part of the operations manual to go through some sequences of thinking and whatnot.

MICHAEL: Tuning the channel.

AVATAR ADI DA SAMRAJ: Yes, like when people are operating a spaceship, they have to set up the computer in all different kinds of ways. It's that kind of reorganizing-the-computer kind of thing that the thinking is for, preliminary to Realization. But the core of the process, the fundamental process itself, has nothing to do with thinking at all.

Well, the present has nothing to do with thinking. It has nothing to do with perception or conception. All these things take time. They are time-processes, they are brain-processes, they are memory-processes, and so on. That's true not only of conceptual processes. It's true of perceptual as well. So everything that you are calling "experience" is data. It is a printout. It is not in present time.

Present time is not a special form of that data, then. It can never appear among the data. So it is not about a conditional state of any kind. <u>Now</u> is the Divine Self-Condition, That Which is Always Already the Case.

If there is no self-contraction—and, therefore, no thought, no perception, no looking at what takes time—then there is Native Realization of That Which is Always Already the Case, the Condition That is Always Already the Case, the Divine Condition.

III.

JONATHAN: Beloved, does the fact that there's this confusion of the data received with the actual present-time doings of the individual have something to do with why the self-contraction was never <u>really</u> noticed before You Appeared and told us about it?

AVATAR ADI DA SAMRAJ: Yes, all the traditions are about an approach to dealing with the data. All the six stages of life are a strategy based on a printout. And even all the experiences in those stages are printouts.

Don't you see, then? You are preoccupied with this printout and are making presumptions about "you", presumptions about everything, in fact, based not only on the data but on calculations about it—presumptions based on the structure that is perceiving data and thinking about it. In other words, the position itself is false. It is to be a washing machine but imagining you are the Divine Person. *[laughter]*

No washing machine is the Divine Person, or the Divine Self-Condition. It is in the transcending of the washing machine, Realizing That within Which the washing machine arises or appears, That Which comes through the plug on the wall.

HAL: Not really the washing machine itself.

AVATAR ADI DA SAMRAJ: Right, but its Condition, the Condition in Which it is arising—that is What must be Realized. That is the Truth. And that is not in the realm of perception or conception. You Commune with Me daily, even moment to moment in your intensive practice. It is to enter into My Sphere, now—My Room, you could say, now—not in the perceptual/conceptual sense, but in the heart-sense. No matter what is perceived or conceived, no matter what thoughts are arising, no matter what perceptions or sensations are arising, or what emotional conditions are appearing, still, fundamentally, now, you don't have anything to do with that.

At heart, you are not involved in any of that. And if you enter into the Disposition, the Way, of the Heart, Realizing the Heart, you are always in Communion with That Which is Free of the inherent bondage in your pictures. The dilemma, the inherent distress, the suffering with which you are naively identifying is unnecessary.

A counter-action, an exactly-not-that action, not-self-contraction, heart-given utterly, self-surrendering, self-forgetting, into the Source, the "Now", Prior to perception and conception—why should one fear that? That is Reality. That is presently Reality, whatever you are looking at on the readout there. The present transcends all that—not present time, but present in the sense of the "Now", or Reality, That Which is Always Already the Case. It is so, Always Already. There is That Which is Always and Already One and Only. If it were not so, and I had not Realized It, I wouldn't be telling you this.

DEVOTEES: That's true. That's right.

AVATAR ADI DA SAMRAJ: To Realize That Which is Always and Already One and Only is to <u>Be</u> It without the slightest "difference". I Realized It by Realizing Me. Likewise, you will Realize It by Realizing Me. This is your unique Help.

It is Me. I Am It, therefore.

You have unique Means of Realization. You have become conjoined with the Pattern, the Way, of Realization—uniquely conjoined. The Way I Give to you is a unique Pattern of process, a uniquely direct and complete Way (or process) for Realizing That Which is Always Already the Case, the "And" That is Now, before the concept or the perception, the Intensity that there is before there is conception and perception. <u>Now</u>. There's no reference in it to you. There's no reference in it to that body-mind printout. It is <u>Me</u>.

You cannot Realize the Divine Self-Condition by entering into <u>yourself</u>, whatever that might mean to you. It is "narcissistic". It is self-contracting. It is by <u>transcending</u> yourself that you Realize It. I Am both That Which is to be Realized and your Means for Realizing It. By your devotional Yoga of Contemplating Me, you feel beyond self-contraction, you go beyond yourself. And in My Regard of you (even Spiritually), you are more and more profoundly invested in the Pattern and the Very Condition That <u>is</u> Reality Itself.

Your entire lifetime, then, becomes conserved relative to the superficial. The gross and waking phenomenon functions essentially dutifully, lawfully, according to right pattern with respect to that, rather than making it as if a utopia in which to perpetuate the effort of seeking. Conserve the energy from that seeking, through this devotional Yoga based on beginnings of true self-understanding, in "consideration" of My Argument, and enter into the depth-process, rather than the superficial one for its own sake. In doing so, you are not abandoning the waking state or the gross domain and so forth. You are simply seeing it in its right perspective, putting it in an order lawfully, such that it serves the true Pleasure Dome seat of Contemplation and Realization.

That should be your disposition, to have it be so—not merely for the pleasure but for the sake of the Contemplation, at ease. In any case, it is heart at ease, in-depth process, moment to moment. And so it is <u>Now</u>, then—not merely in the present, but <u>Now</u>. In other words, it is in the Domain and Process of the Heart, Prior to all perception and all conception, all perceptual awareness and all thoughts—before that, completely apart from any association with it except as required and when required. But even then the in-depth process continues.

Reaching—so to speak, "reaching"—into <u>Now</u> (which is impossible to do) is an act in time, so it is not about that. It is self-forgetting. It is not making an act of self-surrender and continuing to remember to do that. If you do that, then you don't forget yourself. You are only caught trying to constantly remember to surrender yourself. So the devotional Communion with Me in the moment is in depth. It is not a struggle. It is not an effort. There may be efforts in any moment of this counter-egoic process, but the fundamental aspect of it is simply your attraction to Me, which inherently is surrender, because it relieves you of self-attention and goes to Me, and it forgets everything but Me. It's that simplicity.

So it's not a Yoga of so-called "surrendering" yourself in which you bear down and do that, and then forget yourself as soon as you have borne down on yourself, or as soon as you bear down enough on yourself that you can forget yourself. That's like, "Do anything you like, but don't think of a white monkey for the next thirty seconds". It's not that way. That effort of surrender, even the effort to forget yourself, is not the Yoga. The signs of the Yoga <u>are</u> self-surrender and self-forgetting, but how does it get to <u>be</u> that way?

MICHAEL: Attraction.

AVATAR ADI DA SAMRAJ: Yes, it is the devotional response to Me, the heart-attraction to Me, the <u>movement</u> to Me spontaneous in your sighting of My bodily (human) Form and all of your regard of Me and study of My Word and so on, that heart-movement. That's the Horse to ride on, that's the Tail that you feel in your bosom.[34] It's just about taking hold and then flying.

Whatever is Always Already the Case is That Which you Realize when there is no contraction. But when is there no contraction? When you have heard Me, you do understand the matter of self-contraction. You do stand in its position. You're not altogether learned yet, because you have to be able to then, of course, see Me on the basis of hearing. But, ultimately, you must hear Me, see Me, transcend the self-contraction in the most profound developments of the evolutionary course of human experience. In other words, this hearing and seeing must transcend the limits in the fourth, the fifth, and the sixth stages of life. When it is effective in doing that, and does it most perfectly, in transcending most perfectly the limits of the sixth stage of life, finally there is the seventh stage Realization.

---

34. Adi Da Samraj has often referred to a passage from the ancient Indian text *Satapatha Brahmana*, which He has paraphrased as: "Man does not know. Only the Horse Knows. Therefore, hold on to the tail of the Horse." Adi Da has Revealed that, in the most esoteric understanding of this saying, the "Horse" represents the Realizer, and "holding on to the tail of the Horse" represents the devotee's complete dependence on the Realizer in order to grow in Spiritual practice.

IV.

AVATAR ADI DA SAMRAJ: Well, we all seem to be groggy this late at night and getting lazy with the short-term memory, even losing the thread of conversation a little bit. Well, let's not fight with that and try to persist in this effort to remember moment to moment the threads of a verbal consideration that continually breaks down. After all, that's what happens, not only when you're tired, and late in the night in a "consideration" and so forth, but always. You are all noticing this late at night, some particular way that it is working. In other words, you are experiencing the virtue at the moment of not being so afflicted with this printout thing.

DEVOTEES: That's right.

AVATAR ADI DA SAMRAJ: You don't care about it so much. You're not with it so much. You're not pressing so much on the "Remember this" button—"Throw up that printout now, I want to check every moment of what's going on with this bird", you know? *[laughter]*

Relaxation of the memory—of the "remembering and throwing up the software product" kind of stress of the body-mind—takes place when you're fatigued, perhaps, or under some circumstances (such as fatigue, at the moment).

Somehow, then, when you're a little tired out and you're not so heavily pressing on demands for perceptual input and thoughts to keep on flowing and think things out carefully and stuff, you could fall asleep easily. You start getting inattentive. Or you could struggle to stay awake and keep thinking and perceiving and so on. But what about this virtue (it would seem, for the moment)? Rather than just zip off to sleep here, or even right here sitting with Me—rather than going to sleep, luxuriate for a moment in this laziness, this easefulness, of late night fatigue.

You could go to sleep, or otherwise just not strongly observe the data of the body-mind—the perception of the body, the thought-process and so forth. Sort of too tired to get involved in that so much. It sort of loses its voltage—you cut down the voltage for the night, just enough to run the nightlight or something. The body usually would be expecting to be going to sleep by now. It's economizing the reserves. So it's not working on demand at the moment so much—this heavy demand for a lot of perceptual/conceptual processes. You're doing something, whatever you do when you try not to fall asleep. What exactly do you do, anyway?

But whatever that is, it might be interesting, then, to notice exactly where you're doing something or what you are doing to not fall asleep when you are trying not to fall asleep. But let's say you are, for the moment, not allowing yourself to fall asleep but are luxuriating in this inattentiveness, or this ability to be something like aware now. Well, that's easier, perhaps, somehow, to enter into without having to be attentive to a lot of perceptual and conceptual busy-ness. There's just a basic sensation, while yet, in a generalized sense, perceiving the body. It is just the basic sensation of energy, touch.

And if you relax <u>all</u> holding on to the perception of the body, entirely—not just leave it at the periphery, but just relax association altogether—then you'll be asleep. You don't "fall" into anything. But if you can just hold on to this threshold between waking and sleeping, you're in an in-between state where you can notice something about the nature of your actual condition. You're not in anything of the perceptual/conceptual process, because that's like memory. It's in something that took time. You are in the now, right now.

And look at it now, especially when you're tired and you're not so busy with the perceptual noticings and you're getting physically lazy and you're not so busy thinking and so forth. You're relaxing, but not at the moment quite going to sleep—not allowing that exactly, but feeling what it is. There is sleep and there is body-awareness, waking state, both, right now—both. You're experiencing both, but in experiencing both you're also more sensitive to the condition you're actually in in the waking state. It's the same as in the sleeping state.

This is the state you are actually in in the waking state, but then you superimpose all the busy-ness of perception/conception. But now that they're relaxed, you are not only experiencing the tendency to go to sleep and being aware of the sleep state, but you can feel that what you call the sleep state is actually the same state that you're in in the waking state. It's the <u>depth</u> of the waking state. In other words, you go on to find out what that's all about, but you are deeper than this.

You are actually, now, in every now—not present, but Now—always prior to the printout.

The Way I have Given you is the pattern and process of that: that devotion to Me which Realizes Me, that process which Realizes Reality, which conserves life—patterns it (in other words), disciplines it—to Commune with the Source-Condition, with Reality Itself, the Divine Condition Itself.

Life would be full of limitations and end in death even if you weren't screwing up. So there's a whole bunch of stuff you can't really blame yourself for anyway—you know what I mean? Your sins don't go that far.

But you <u>can</u> be refreshed, in other words. You <u>can</u> be purified. You <u>can</u> continue. You <u>can</u> go deeper. You <u>can</u> reinvest yourself in the process. You can make reparation and be restored to the process in depth. It is so. You have to go through that process because of your entanglement.

Your relationship to Me is a constant sadhana that you exercise and within which you experience Me, Contemplate Me, constantly but <u>completely</u> apart from perception and conception—completely apart from them except in the root-sense, the touch-depth, the current-energy, current-depth.

As My devotee, you pattern the body-mind in conformity to the depth. And you exercise yourself moment to moment in this heart-Yoga, which is a process in depth. Attracted devotion is its means. Not merely these principles abstracted, but devotion to Me, via feeling-Contemplation of this bodily (human) Form.

This Attraction to Me, this devotional movement in you, is the core of the Yoga. All the things I'm saying about the process and the Realization and so forth are just sayings about that process that is the core of the Yoga, that is the domain of its Realization, that is unspeakable, and yet I can say all these things about it.

I remember telling you all who were around Me years ago in the earliest days that, basically, quite simply, the process <u>is</u> this one of Guru-devotion, the real response of devotional surrender to Me, allowed to go on to the nth degree, to the most perfect degree. If you do that with Me, then <u>all</u> the things that I elaborate in full in terms of practices, "considerations", processes, Realizations, and so forth, would take place, spontaneously, if I am the One to Whom you are responding in this manner. Then the Way I Reveal becomes revealed in that relationship, that mode of relationship to Me.

V.

AVATAR ADI DA SAMRAJ: It takes you a moment to perceive the body-mind, and you weren't there when it happened, anyway. When you get the printout, you aren't there, because you don't notice it until you get the printout. So what you see on the printout is of a "you" when <u>you</u> weren't there. *[laughter]*

So, in <u>no</u> <u>instance</u> are you in, at, or with the body-mind.

DEVOTEES: Mm!

AVATAR ADI DA SAMRAJ: You can still say, perhaps, that you <u>are</u> the body-mind—meaning, in other words, whatever the body-mind <u>is</u>, prior to self-contraction, just as is. Then there is Non-separation from What is Always Already the Case.

All phenomenal arising is nothing but the Divine Self-Condition. It is not experienced as such, however. A great process must be entered into so that It can be Realized.

It is now almost 6:30 in the morning and dawn is beginning to break. Beloved Adi Da addresses a devotee who has been nodding off, making a point about the sleep state.

AVATAR ADI DA SAMRAJ: So, Hal, you did decide to go into the sleep state instead of maintaining that threshold there. *[laughter]* Did you allow any observation of the transition you made? Did you notice something about how first you relaxed the concept-mind and then you relinquished perceptual mind, perception of the body and so forth. Did you feel that those things just fell away? But you didn't have to go anywhere to go to sleep. It's just that these conceptual, then perceptual dimensions relax, and are no longer in the view, you are no longer attentive. But you could be at the depth, attentive without attention to perceptual and conceptual processes, constantly. That must be the case in deep meditation, for instance. It can also be the case moment to moment, when there is great profundity and maturity in practice, so that the process is always going on in depth but it's always already so deep that it is beyond thoughts and perceptions. It's not an effort associated with the thought-process at all. It's not a physical effort at all.

It's only when you become thoroughly Awake (in the seventh stage sense), Divinely Recognizing attention itself, that you can no longer be defeated by sleep. Then it is no longer possible to sleep. It's also no longer possible to be in the waking state as commonly perceived. But it's not that the seventh stage Disposition is just a vat, and it sort of content-edly and wisely lies in the pouch of body-mind, being all kinds of radiantly human, and re-birthing again and again to be radiantly human again and again. *[laughter]*

No. The Realization Itself is inherently purposed, self-purposed, to be Self-Magnifying, to be ever "Brighter", and yet It is of one ever-unchanging Intensity. But Its Intensity is absolute, so it is ever-all-Outshining.

This Body Is My Agent

AVATAR ADI DA SAMRAJ: You want, ultimately, to Realize that Condition, and even that demonstrated process, that deals with everything—absolutely <u>everything</u>. Mm? Right? That's what you want to Realize, right?

DEVOTEES: Yes.

AVATAR ADI DA SAMRAJ: That's why you came to Me, right?

DEVOTEES: Yes.

AVATAR ADI DA SAMRAJ: Right. There is that Realization and process, and that is Me. That's Who I Am, and that's What I Do. The Realizer of Me is not a satisfied "you". It's entirely another matter. It Transcends the ego-"I". Well, when the Condition that Transcends the ego-"I" inherently—in other words, the Source-Condition, the Condition That is Always Already The Case—is Realized, just what kind of a personal report do you think there is left to tell?

MICHAEL: Well, Beloved, You talked about how you first returned to your home from the Vedanta Temple that day and sat down to meditate and expected to be relating to the mechanism of somehow "Your" body-mind. But that's not what came to You in meditation. It was other beings. From that point on, it feels like this has been Your Confession. There is no "you" (with a small "y") left there to be undone. It's perfectly undone.

AVATAR ADI DA SAMRAJ: Mm-hm.

This body-mind has been guided by the "Bright." In order to speak in terms that people generally comprehend readily, for the sake of being communicative to people for the sake of their Realization, I have described the process of My "Sadhana Years" in terms of the Incarnate Person. That entire process was guided by the "Bright", but when there was Realization, when the limiting force of the Incarnation had been Transcended, I Am the "Bright". And not the body-mind, therefore. Previously, it's the body-mind adventure and the "Bright" is somehow seeming, by experience, to be there or not in any moment. But when you <u>are</u> It, you can't sometimes be there and sometimes not. You just <u>are</u> It.

Of course, that is something of the gist of the sadhana itself—the false presumption of being the body-mind. The process culminated in the Realization "I Am the 'Bright'". The life thereafter is no longer the life of the body-mind. It is simply the "Bright".

I "Meditated" Other Beings and Places

FROM *THE KNEE OF LISTENING*

Now [after the Great Event of my re-Awakening], whenever I would sit, in any kind of formal manner, to demonstrate the meditation, or the, now, Divine Samadhi, that had become my entire life, instead of confronting what was arising in and as "myself", I "meditated" other beings and places. I would spontaneously become aware of great numbers of people (usually in visions, or in some other, intuitive manner), and I would work with them very directly, in a subtle manner. The binding motions and separative results of my own apparent (or merely life-born) egoity (or psychophysical self-contraction) had been transcended in my re-Awakening to my Original (and necessarily Divine) Self-Condition. Therefore, in the spontaneous Awakening of the Divine Guru-Siddhi, instead of my own life-born forms and problematic signs, the egoic forms, the problematic signs, the minds, the feelings, the states, and the various limitations of others would arise to my view. The thoughts, feelings, suffering, dis-ease, disharmony, upsets, pain, energies—none of these were "mine". They were the internal, subtle qualities and the life-qualities of others. In this manner, the process of apparent meditation continued in me. It was, in effect, the same "Real" meditation I had done before the Great Event of my re-Awakening. Therefore, "problems" (of all kinds) constantly appeared, and numberless complexities and contradictions arose in every moment, but the content of the meditation was not "mine".

I found that this "meditating" of others by me usually went on with people whom I had not yet met. But, soon, some of those very people came into my company, and all the rest are yet, but certainly, to come, to be my devotees, and, thus, to practice the only-by-me revealed and given way of radical understanding (or the only-by-me revealed and given Way of the Heart). In some cases, the individuals I "meditated" in vision were people I already knew, and I would "meditate" them in that subtle manner, unobserved by them, and then watch for signs in their outward lives that would demonstrate the effectiveness of my "meditation" of them.

In this manner, I spontaneously began to "meditate" countless other people, and also countless non-human beings, and countless places and worlds and realms, both high and low in the scale of Reality. I observed and responded to all that was required for the Awakening and the true (and the Ultimate) well-being of each and all. And, each time I did this (and, in fact, the process quickly became the underlying constant of all my hours and days), I would continue the "meditating" of any (and each) one until I felt a release take place, such that his or her suffering and seeking was vanished, or, at least, significantly relaxed and set aside. Whenever that occurred, I Knew my "meditating" of that one was, for the moment, done. By such means, my now and forever Divine Work (by Which I must Teach, and Bless, and Awaken all and All) began.

There is this apparent mysterious association with this Body, but I cannot My Self truly speak from its point of view. As a matter of convention, I do it. That's the language you all speak, so I sometimes use the lingo that way. Generally speaking, when you say "I", you mean that bodily person there, whatever that is altogether. People in general don't really inspect it very profoundly, but it is certainly presumed to be that body there, that body-mind, whatever that is altogether.

But I am not this body-mind. I'm not just being poetic about it. On the other hand, there has to be common daily speech (or some sort of use of language) that works, and certain aspects of convention are maintained. So there is this process in your experiencing. And you all are in the Pattern of this body-mind. It is one Pattern, all of it together. This body-mind is generating Pattern, generating unique characteristics and signs and so forth in that, but I am not in its <u>position</u>.

This doesn't mean there is no sensitivity to it and so forth. In fact, there is no armoring. So it is a much more uncomfortable association, you could say, in this sense, than people generally experience. Of course, people experience profound physical suffering—I am not saying it's like that, generally speaking, but there's a sensitivity, a vulnerability, a lack of armoring in the structure of this body-mind. It's Transparent. It is without armor. So all experience through this Body is intense. It is not that It is taken over, abstracted, and there's no body left to deal with. It is intense, more intense than people would find comfortable, generally speaking.

MICHAEL: That's an understatement.

AVATAR ADI DA SAMRAJ: Yes, so it is not common psycho-physical intense, it is profoundly intense. There is no contraction, no separate person, no ego-search patterning the energies of this body-mind. It is utterly coincident with the Infinite Design, the Pattern of Unity. The Force flowing in It is unobstructed. So there are all kinds of processes associated with It—gross physical ones that you observe, subtle processes, energy processes, obviously—all kinds of processes go on. You might imagine that that requires a lot of attention. That's how <u>you</u> think of your own business. No, it's not a matter of attention. As I said, it's not egoic.

So this body-mind's characteristic is one of extreme sensitivity, vulnerability. Omnipathic, I guess you'd say. It is as if I am extended by the sense of touch infinitely—emotional touch, but also a kind of sensible touch. It is part of My Sign, My Characteristic. The Siddhis that function spontaneously in My Form are . . . well, it can't really be described. But let us say it has something to do with the fact that My Sympathetic Regard passes wherever and Functions like a touch. It is a tangible Contact that Initiates flows, Changes flows, and so forth. But, this body-mind, this Mechanism here that is an Agent of Mine, is so profoundly sensitive, without any armoring, that I can tell you that it finds the human state, the physically embodied state, to be basically horrific.

At the root, at heart, and so forth, it is One with Me, it is in the Divine Condition. But as itself, and as soon as you become self-consciously aware of being any such a form, it is suffering. As soon as there is any self-consciousness of being, relative to any particular form, there is fear, immediately.

Of course, you must transcend it. I am not saying I am life-negative. It is not that. I am not speaking of this matter of "horrific" in any conventional sense. Nor is it simply My Communication to you. I am saying what this body-mind experiences. It is so sensitive, this body-mind, that it feels the nature of what it is to be humanly existing here without any illusions. It is a terrible struggle, and it ends in death.

It is not always "terrible" in the sense that every event is the worst possible. There are lots of ways to be amused in it, certainly. There's pleasure in it, too. There's everything. But it is all encapsulated by the force of limitation and ending. And no matter how you slice it, no matter how you look at it, it is about just that. It is about limitation and ending. It is built into the process.

This human physical embodiment is not the domain of Truth. You don't have to account for it altogether, all the strings of causes and effects and all the rest of it. In fact, ultimately, it's of a plastic that is incomprehensible, a maya that cannot be comprehended.

You need not comprehend that maya, figure out all the causes and effects and so forth. You needn't have complete perfect knowledge in that sense. But, relative to this fundamental matter—that existence as you are knowing it is about limitation and death, even though, within it, there are, possibly, some associations of pleasure and so forth—I am not suggesting that any kind of nihilistic view of it is appropriate. What I am saying is that, if you simply feel or observe the nature of human experience, human circumstance, and so forth, with sensitivity, you will not make the mistake of interpreting it as something that it is not. You will function in the right sense. When you understand all this, you will function in the right sense in the gross domain.

When you feel the inherent suffering and limitation of human existence, at the core, at the heart, the investigation goes deeper instead. The disposition turns deeper, instead of becoming totally enmeshed with gross experience and gross seeking. So not nihilism but discipline and concentration are chosen when there is true discrimination brought to the examination of human experience. Not self-indulgence and self-destructiveness, but sadhana, the religious life—ultimately, the Spiritual life, or process—is what one chooses. Entering into intelligent exercise, that is what one must choose.

Of course, if you don't enter into such investigation profoundly or take the investigation seriously, then you might very well live quite superficially—babbling, puzzle-mindedness, doubled-mindedness, questions, searches, desires, all the rest of it, constantly, all over the place. It's just pattern, stuff, changes. That is all you would be. That is all you would choose to be. That's all it is. You can just sort of go with the flow or you can examine, "consider", the nature of existence profoundly and enter into a profound sadhana, a process, involving the disciplining and concentrating of the being. And what there is to Realize ultimately is not a development of yourself. It is the "death" (so to speak) of yourself. But I use "death" in a metaphorical sense, because it is not a dark or negative matter that I am speaking of. It is a kind of shift.

BETH: Beloved, You also called it a "rebirth".

AVATAR ADI DA SAMRAJ: Yes, there are all kinds of metaphors that can be useful to indicate the fundamental unspeakableness of it, apart from the actual Realization, the Transition itself, happening.

What there is to Realize ultimately is not development of the ego or development of the body-mind and so forth. It is Realization of That Which Transcends the body-mind, That Which Transcends limitation, That Which Transcends self-contraction, ego-"I", separateness, and seeking. It Transcends the very categories of relatedness, separateness, and "difference"—of subject and object, then, of "self" and "other". It is a Realization, it is Samadhi, so it can be associated with human embodiment and being in the waking state at any stage. But its association with human embodiment, the waking state, whatever, is not a necessary one.

So the seventh stage Realization Demonstrates Itself, ultimately as all-Outshining. It's not, in other words, about Enlightenment integrated with human life and so forth. Yes, there is that possible sign, but that's not the nature of the seventh stage Awakening Itself. It Demonstrates Itself as Divine Recognition. Its Ultimate Demonstration is Divine Translation*—in other words, the "Brightness" Outshines all.

The Realization, ultimately, is not in the context of the body-mind or states of waking, dreaming, or sleeping. It's not a Realization of anything about you, in you, or that _is_ you. It is the Realization of Reality Which Transcends you, always already Transcends you.

Everything that is arising has a thread to the Source, the Source-Condition, not merely the whatever-is-the-cause immediately, but the Source-Condition. It is the Spirit-Current Itself,[35] and there is a constant, perpetual heart-attraction to the Source-Condition, the Self-Condition, the Inherent Condition, the Root-Condition, That Which is Always Already the Case.

It is possible to be given up, heart-surrendered to the point of relinquishing the contraction of holding on to conditional states. It is possible for all that to be vanished and for there to simply be the Realization of the Source-Condition, the Divine Self-Condition Which is Always Already the Case.

It is Self-Existing. It is Self-Radiant. It is both Consciousness and Radiance, Energy. And the characteristic of Radiance, or Energy, is Love-Bliss.

This is What is Realized. This is Substance—That of Which everything arising is a transparent, or merely apparent, and un-necessary, and inherently non-binding modification.

When That of Which all is a modification is Realized, such that everything is Divinely Recognized, then everything is Outshined. That is where the Demonstration goes.

This Body has no armoring against sensitivity. Touch extends infinitely, and to all. My Spiritual Association with everyone is a kind of Touch-Connection.

This Connection is fundamental to the process of your relationship to Me. This is why, once this Connection is established—in Spiritual terms, fully functional (and that even begins early on)—this is what makes it possible for you to be practicing in direct relationship to Me at all times, under all circumstances. You have direct access to Me through this Touch-Connection, the Circuitry of My Pattern of Inclusiveness, of all-Touching Presence—all-Pervading, all-Embracing, none-excluding.

---

35. The Spiritual Power, or Radiance, of the Divine, Which Pervades and yet Transcends the world, the body, and the mind.

CHAPTER TWENTY

Glimpsing the Guru's Experience

BY THANKFULL HASTINGS

There are dimensions of Avatar Adi Da's Work of Liberation that occur on a much more mysterious level than His direct interactions with His devotees. It is clear to His devotees that Adi Da Samraj Works with the state of the entire world in ways that we can only occasionally glimpse and never fully understand. However, there are precedents for such mysterious Work in the Leelas of certain great Indian Gurus.

The devotees of Narayan Maharaj, who lived during the first half of this century, describe events indicating his involvement in the resolution of World War II. He took great interest in the activities of the Allies and the Germans, keeping a large transistor radio and a map of Europe with him, receiving daily reports from the Berlin Review and the BBC report, and keeping himself informed of all phases of the battles on land, on sea, and in the air.

As the war went on, mysterious wounds spontaneously appeared on Narayan Maharaj's body. He had to be bandaged three or four times a day, and could not walk or even feed himself. Finally, on September 3, 1945, he was told that the British had landed in Japan. His response was, "The war is over. My work is finished." He died later that day.

There are similar accounts of Shirdi Sai Baba's death (an Indian Saint who had both Muslim and Hindu followers) in 1918, in connection with the end of World War I.

Akkalkot Maharaj (a nineteenth-century Hindu Realizer) was said to have had a part in affecting Indian history. One day, his devotees were puzzled by his playing with sticks tied with a string. When asked what he *was doing, he replied cryptically, "I am raising armies". Shortly after, it was learned that a major uprising against the British (the Sepoy Mutiny) had broken out in the North.*

Avatar Adi Da's devotees have witnessed His complete attention for world events over the years: the news reports He listens to daily; the periods He spends alone (in temples reserved for Himself) doing a Work that He rarely speaks of; His retreat into austere seclusion during periods of international crisis; His passionate address to every kind of human suffering, including the suffering produced by political, religious, and ethnic intolerance and injustice.

Like other Realizers, Adi Da Samraj is characteristically silent about His Work to Bless and Purify the world. But He frequently expresses His boundless Love and passionate concern for all beings, freely Gives us His living example of true cooperation, tolerance, and love, and showers us with the Wisdom that can, if only it is employed, make the most auspicious possible destiny a reality, both for individuals and for the collective of mankind.

AVATAR ADI DA SAMRAJ: The separation and division and death of human beings all over the world is the dramatization of egoity made collective, made political. Understand that that is what is happening around you—all over the earth. And that egoity is not only being manifested politically and socially, it is being manifested in the whole atmosphere of the earth—the hole in the ozone layer, the possible rising of the tides, storms, destructiveness everywhere.

You can make a difference by cooperating with one another, by refusing the impulse to non-cooperation among human beings, by manifesting the principles of your religion—of compassion, cooperation, and love. If you do not manifest those principles in your personal life every day, you are supporting the destructiveness that is going on all over the world. Am I asking too much?

You are at a critical time in this epoch. Do not ever manifest intolerance in your speech or in your life. Exhibit tolerance, compassion, love, freedom from self-obsessed acts in your life, in your speech, in your actions. This is not a moralistic matter. It is necessary for your survival. All over the earth people are dying every day, because of separatism, idealistic politics, dissociation, so-called "ethnic cleansing". Human beings are being murdered casually, suffering intense, extraordinary pain.

You must understand the time you are in. It is not like it was in the eighties, the seventies, sixties, or the fifties. This is a very, very dark and difficult time. And people are being murdered by the thousands every week. The situation on earth must change or you and future generations are not even going to get a chance at God-Realization. There are ground obligations. They are about tolerance, and compassion, and cooperation. You all have to get serious and end your petty preoccupations with your personal lives and get down to what is required for humanity to stop destroying itself. You are destroying the environment upon which you depend, and you are destroying the possibility of God-Realization in each one of you. It is time to become serious people. *[December 12, 1992]*

Adi Da Samraj is sensitive to human suffering in a way no other being could possibly be, because He does not experience Himself as <u>separate</u> from any one or any thing. Thus, the suffering of beings everywhere is, literally, His own. He has said to us that none of us could endure the pain and difficulty that He has assumed as part of His unique role on earth, that none of us could endure the force of the negativity He receives and transforms in His own Body continuously.

AVATAR ADI DA SAMRAJ: People often feel that they must become like the Spiritual Master, that they must have the status of the Spiritual Master. Such people envy the Spiritual Master, and they will not surrender to him or her. They only want from him or her a token, a bit of magic, that will somehow make them like he or she is. But understand this: No un-Enlightened soul wants to be in the position of the Spiritual Master! If you understood My constant experience, you would not envy it—nor could you endure it!

Thankfull Hastings describes his own experience of this very matter:

On December 29, 1992, I was sitting at Avatar Adi Da's side and had my hand on His leg as He began to speak to the forty or so devotees in the room with Him that evening. He was speaking about the horrible deaths that take place daily in many areas of the world, and, at that time, particularly in Somalia. He spoke of the terrible and intolerable deaths of women and children there, and also of the dangerous proliferation of weapons throughout the world.

As He spoke, I was massaging His leg, and I began to feel in my body what He was talking about. I don't know how to describe this, but I felt the literal "experience" of what He was speaking of enter my body from His calf. It moved into my hand, up through my arm, down into my heart, and from there up into my head. As it entered my head, my vision was suddenly clouded. Appallingly vivid images of everything He was

**Thankfull Hastings with Avatar Adi Da Samraj,
the Mountain Of Attention, 1996**

speaking of, all the terrible deaths and suffering—like a movie—began to move before my eyes. In a very short time, I could no longer tolerate the experience. I got up and ran outside and began vomiting in the bushes. The images continued. A friend came out to bring me back inside. I was gasping for air and told her I just couldn't take it any more, I just couldn't experience the suffering of the world in the way our Guru was obviously experiencing it.

A short time later, my "symptoms" subsided and I returned to the room where my Guru and His devotees were gathered—but I have never forgotten what I learned that night about what Beloved Adi Da endures for the sake of the world, and what is required from all of us if the earth is to be a place where the great matter of true Spiritual practice is to be a real possibility for humankind.

The Mountain Of Attention, 1996

CHAPTER TWENTY-ONE

December 18, 1996

Are You This Unit That Is Built to Die?

T*he gathering of December 18 begins with Adi Da Samraj "consider-ing" with one of the devotees her practice of meditation. One of the observations He makes to her is that she characteristically tends to be defensive, in her life altogether, and this is affecting her meditation prac-tice. Beloved Adi Da has explained at great length over the years how any such fundamental disposition is at root an emotional-sexual matter, growing out of the individual's response to the circumstances and events of his or her early life, especially to the relationships with mother and father. Later in the conversation, Adi Da goes on to discuss, in general terms, the power of emotional-sexual patterning.*

I.

AVATAR ADI DA SAMRAJ: It's <u>amazing</u> how controlled people are, in their whole pattern of feeling and living, by patterns that have affected their emotional-sexual impulses, activities, thoughts, concerns, fascina-tions, whatever. The process of people's experience in early life is so arbitrary in many respects. Yet people become <u>profoundly</u> affected, as unwary, unknowing, not-yet-socially-adapted children. They don't under-stand things as you may understand them. And you all were that. So you became profoundly affected by all kinds of things that, even now, when you may remember your early life, you don't think of as being profound.

It's continually amazing to Me how profoundly affected people are, and how arbitrary all those effects are. When you see how profoundly affected people are, trying to live an adult life, it would seem that in order to not be some kind of screwed-up, you would have to, in a very fundamental sense, regiment every person's experience, even at the time of conception, and from there on, until finally you could say to them, "Now you're adult, now you handle it from this point on".

Of course, that's not possible and not even desirable, although some aspects of life and experience are regulated wherever you grow up— nonetheless, not all of it. And it's filled with arbitraries. And so you've all been patterned profoundly by what were, for you, some remarkable moments, or whatever the conjunction may be in your memory or presumption or noticing at all.

You have all kinds of complex justifications or would-be's or presumptions about some profundity or other that has happened to you, or whatever it may be, that is supposedly the cause of why you are the way you are now—something you've got to figure out here and talk-talk-talk-talk-talk until you do. But the effects that you suffer—and would like to get rid of by talking yourself somehow through and beyond it all, and have that be sufficient—are more profound than words, more profound than talk-talk-talk.

These things—like the patterning of people's lives by arbitraries of their emotional-sexual experience, or things that affected their emotional-sexual development, understanding, tendencies, whatever, the whole pattern—are so remarkable and remarkably arbitrary. And it seems that, generally speaking, people never outgrow these patterns. It seems. You may find an example here and there, but it seems, generally speaking, especially in the case of people who don't deal with themselves at all, that it just goes on like clockwork, Swiss-made. I mean, it's just zap!—that's it, that pattern's there. There's nothing you can do about it.

You can struggle against it and it's still not going to change. It's still going to be there. Still that pattern will enforce itself. And even if you do change something, one way or another—whatever way, manner, education, thinking, therapy, arts, religion, philosophy, whatever—the pattern is still there. The pattern persists. The "consideration" of the pattern is fruitful relative to understanding, perhaps, if you are serious, but the pattern is not amenable to mere adjustment, mere will, beyond a point, anyway. Some curious conjunction, some remarkable transformative process has to occur. That doesn't mean necessarily something like a bolt out of the blue. It means, in addition to some profound discoveries and so on, a process persisted in.

In other words, for patterns to be loosed and changed and for real transformations to occur—if you want to know how to do it, or what the law of it all is—the matter of persistence is certainly fundamental. Finding the relationship, the Teaching, the Master, the process, the practice—yes, all that is necessary, but then <u>persisting</u> in it is essential because it is a pattern, a natural force, a something that is (by virtue of simply being pattern) connected to the whole force of patterns and the energy of patterns.

A little tendency of thought in you can be associated with a basic presumption in you which emerges as soon as the energy of your personality is concentrated. Some simple little experience of noticing, or something in your childhood, however you may interpret it, if you look back at it now—for no reason other than just the fact that it existed, it affected your entire life. Not just one thing, necessarily. I'm not talking about some huge necessary big incident in your life. I'm talking about a collection of "just-thats", nothing really profound to figure out about them.

A whole bunch of those made a pattern—and that's what's happening. It's as simple as that. And it just persists. It is modified by further adaptations, experiences, and so forth, but, nonetheless, the fundamentals of it persist, unless something remarkable, altogether transformative, intervenes.

DANIEL BOUWMEESTER: Beloved, isn't it also that it is like a blueprint which is there from birth, and then various incidents just sort of fill out the tapestry of that blueprint in the early life?

AVATAR ADI DA SAMRAJ: Yes, that is certainly a reasonable way to describe it. There are many metaphors or summaries or presumptions about the matter that could be stated, but it's through all kinds of previous patterns that then get associated with more patterns. In just the simplest terms, everything conditional, everything apparently objective, everything observable, <u>is fundamentally just pattern</u>. Perceived, thought about, or whatever, it is still just pattern. Even perceiving and thinking is just somehow shaping—being associated with shape somehow. It's touch, and planes of touch—every moment of functioning awareness, thinking, and so forth. It is that.

At its core it is <u>utterly</u> incomprehensible, <u>utterly</u>. You couldn't even figure it out yourself if you looked at it <u>square</u>. Because, at the depth, it is nothing but a shuffle of shapes.

What is a shuffle of shapes? What does a shuffle of shapes mean? What is a shuffle of shapes for? It doesn't even ask these questions. It's <u>just</u> a shuffle of shapes. Asking these questions is a shuffle of shapes. It's just the plastic, blap-blap-blap-blap, shuffling, shifting. It's in its depth nonsensical. At some level of ordinary awareness, there's some sort of a feeling of agreement or whatever, but that's not in-depth.

On the other hand, if you ask anybody to tell you exactly what they meant the last five sentences they said, how much would you trust them to know what they meant according to the dictionary? What <u>do</u> they mean? What does <u>meaning</u> mean? It's just a shuffling of shapes. Feel it—that's all it is. What does it mean?

It really doesn't make too much difference to you except, do you feel okay about it, or not? And you could ask that again, "Do you feel okay right now, or don't you?" I mean, <u>completely</u>, <u>completely</u> alright—<u>completely</u>, totally alright. I mean, how deeply would you "consider" that matter of "completely" before you got to the point where you were feeling, "Well, of course", and then started indicating the something that, of course, is not <u>completely</u> alright in this "all sitting about in familiar physical associations and essential comforts associated with that". Everything can be lost in a moment. Everything <u>will</u> be lost eventually, and not necessarily just in one scoop—just progressive disintegration, changing.

So what could be completely okay about this moment of thinking and perceiving, shuffling shapes for amusement? In some moments, the shuffling of the shapes feels somehow comfortable or okay. But is it <u>really</u> okay? In any moment where you just want it to be okay, you don't want to be thinking about "okay" too deep, you just want to not feel too stressful. So you're willing to settle for "okay", but not for having your problem solved—once and for all and absolutely and positively, in every respect. That is a need, a profundity, a search that cannot be casually satisfied and should never be dismissed. And if you're intelligent, you do not want to desensitize yourself to it—not in any chronic profound way.

II.

AVATAR ADI DA SAMRAJ: As I was "considering" with you recently, the problem about life is death. Either there is death or there isn't, and that should be gotten straight right now, correct? If there isn't—okay, fine. But if there is, you can't just live a superficial life. There's nothing superficial <u>about</u> life.

You go down to the plant store and get yourself a nice bush or a nice plant or something to put in the ground and zap!—that little seed or bulb, whatever you got, has built into the unit that it's going to die! Not only is it going to die, it is going to go through a cycle built into its own structure here, the end-phenomenon of which will be <u>death</u>. This is what it's built to do. This is what the machine is built to do. It's going to die.

It's not just that it's going to have an accident and get killed. No—it's <u>built</u> to <u>die</u>! That's what it is going to <u>do</u>. Well, that's not just true about your seeds and tubers down at the plant store. It's not just true of the non-humans. It's true of you. You're about the same thing. It's <u>built</u> <u>in</u> to what you're being here in the waking state.

ANIELLO PANICO: It's biological.

AVATAR ADI DA SAMRAJ: Yes, that's one way of putting it. It's built into this thing that you are busy identifying with, or presuming to be. So choosing to be that, and to be completely that, and just be *[vigorous forced laughing, throwing His head back and stretching out His arms]* "HA-HA-HA-HAH!!—great to be that!" No, that's garbage! That's <u>certainly</u> not enough. It's not even <u>interesting</u> to just laughingly be <u>merely</u> <u>that</u>, just go with the flow—unless you never find out that everybody dies, everything disappears. You lose (and become dissociated from) everything you accumulate, everything you associate with. And they likewise from you, and everything associated with you.

So what exactly is this plastic—of associating, acquiring, and surviving—for? <u>Why</u> is it to be endured? Or, more than endured, why is it participated in positively? And where's the instruction book here?

Even the instruction book is not enough. There are all kinds of things that come in instruction books. They don't answer any great questions—such that if you <u>were</u> this appliance, your concerns would be satisfied by reading that instruction book. It still doesn't address you, who is having to <u>be</u> that machine, wondering: <u>Why</u> do you have to be this machine? What is the point of having to suffer this built-in baldness here, which, as soon as you put it in the ground, has already gone through somersaults to self-destruct—as its last leaping, jumping Nijinsky dance about everything?

That's not in the instruction book because instruction books are written for the <u>owners</u> of machines and not those who presume to <u>be</u> machines.

You know, some shape boppin' through the forest there is just chomping, munching, squeezing through, whatever, not being totally bound to the waking state at all. Feels its fragility. Tries to lie low. Enters into Contemplation. Flying, walking, whatever—crawling through, swimming through whatever, moving through.

All of a sudden, a human being picks it up, sells it to another human being, with a booklet that says, *[in a dramatic tone]* "How to Raise Your Pet", or "How to Breed Your Pet"—whatever it is. That's <u>you</u> now!

Well, that instruction manual, "How to Raise Your Dalmatian", let us say, or "How to Breed Dalmatians", or everything else about Dalmatians— but given to your Dalmatian? *[laughter]* First of all, yes, obviously, they can't read and all that, but even if they could, it doesn't speak to the Dalmatian's concerns, ultimately.

You know what the cycle is. Yes, you know what the game is. That's it.

I mean what is this? You know, there could be nothing. *[In an incredulous tone]* But there's <u>this</u>? *[Beloved Adi Da laughs heartily.]* Why should, instead of there being nothing, there be something—but it's <u>this</u>?! <u>THIS</u> <u>SUCKS</u>! *[laughter]* This is a shafting, this human birth, human-life-time thing.

ANIELLO: It's a bum deal.

AVATAR ADI DA SAMRAJ: So, haven't you heard enough about the wash-ing machine yet? I mean all the manuals, all the how-to-do-it, all the manuals about how to control the body—it doesn't deal with anything fundamental. It deals with operations and so forth, but it doesn't deal with the point of view of one who presumes to <u>be</u> that. If you presume to <u>be</u> this body, your concerns can't simply be how to feel essentially bal-anced in the body and grounded in the body, right now, in this present time-space-going-on lifetime. It can't be enough—just to know how to operate it, like the gardener looks at the instruction book about the bulb he is about to plant. It tells the various stages—not only what the gar-dener has to do, but tells him what this bulb is going to do, you know: *[exaggerated intonation and cadence]* "And then, after the third season, it dies, of course". It is not that, *[self-important tone]* "Oh, we predict—we read its astrology chart—that this particular bulb will have a lifespan of only three years." No, they don't have to be psychic about it. This bulb is a <u>unit</u>, a <u>map</u>, a <u>pattern</u>, a <u>fixed</u> pattern that <u>is</u> going to do such and such, unless it is otherwise interfered with. But you can <u>count</u> on it. It might even get to do all of those things, or it could stop a lot short of that full cycle even—other things happening. But you're never going to get any much more than that three years out of it. Maybe with a little experi-menting, you might be able to extend it a little bit. But, generally speak-ing, not even that. And it's certainly not going to take you to heaven on a flying carpet, either—you know what I mean?

So you've all gotten the message, from earliest on (somehow along with, "There is no Santa Claus", but presumably long before "There is no Santa Claus") that people die, somehow or other—meaning that <u>you</u> are going to die. Whatever it means to you, how real that's ever been, how serious you have taken it—nevertheless, at some point you got the message. It wasn't very complex. There are all kinds of ways you have gotten that message all along.

This message doesn't particularly square with the life-motives that this machine is otherwise programmed to fulfill from earliest on in its lifetime. It starts getting worn down later maybe, but you don't find that out until later. So it's in this earliest stage where you do your basic noticings.

So you got the message. You got the instruction manual, and you keep getting updates on it. I keep, therefore, having to Communicate to you things that are just basics to the instruction manual that you never got complete yet. A lot of what I have to Instruct devotees in is just that. Whereas, fundamentally, I am not here to deal with the washing machine. Incidentally, the pattern is there, therefore it must be dealt with. But the fundamental matter is the going-beyond process, not improving the body-mind, improving the pattern, the experience (or whatever) and success (and so on) of the body-mind—not that exclusively, anyway.

So when you buy a light bulb and it says it lasts 100 hours, you don't usually have to confront your fears of death. And you don't mind all that much, so you buy an extra package.

But when you go to the pet store, you always ask, "How long is this breed known to live?" "Ah, well, nine to twelve years—a good nine to twelve years." *[in a weepy tone]* "Nine to twelve!" All the things, all the attachment you know you are going to get with this animal and so forth. It's not a great long time. And who knows if it will even make it that long. Maybe you treat them good and they will last a little longer, but you don't like the news. You don't pick up an extra. An extra wouldn't last any longer than the original, so you can't do it that way.

As you get further on in the scale of things of importance, you really don't like this notion of the-death-built-into-it, and it becomes more and more troublesome the more dependencies you generate in your life. The more entangled you are in this, that, or the other thing—dependencies, relationships, the patterns altogether—the more bound up you get in the fundamental dilemma, that the problem about life is death. Everything disappears suddenly or progressively, but certainly inevitably. So the more entangled you get, the more dependent you get, the more troubled you get, the more <u>burdened</u> you get. You may try to not acknowledge it, and just try to enjoy it, be superficially frivolous in order to perhaps not even notice somehow—as if you don't notice. Or you can get down to business about it. It's fundamental.

You've got the knowledge, so you've got the problem. Your knowledge is your problem. You know the body dies and everything disappears. You know that. You know that fact of it. Some other kind of a life-form may not altogether know that as you know it. On the other hand, there is no such thing as a life-form that doesn't react to threats to its own integrity—to its own existence, therefore. So who doesn't know it? Everybody knows it, everything knows it. The entire <u>pattern</u> knows it.

JAMES STEINBERG: It's often said, Beloved, that animals don't know that they're going to die.

AVATAR ADI DA SAMRAJ: It's totally untrue. You could test anything that you could call a life-form to see if it reacts to a poke of some kind. It would have to be different in the case of some kind of organisms that you can't quite poke with something, but whatever—try to disturb it, try to intrude into its body-sphere, the sphere of its own boundaries. There's always, in some form, a reaction. If not, then it's dead!

While alive, you don't want to be dead. You don't want anything to disappear, you don't want to lose anything. On the other hand, you're struggling to have and acquire and relate and depend. You can't justify both of these things in the same place.

So you're just sort of gambling, you're sort of just playing on it. "How long does this sucker live?", you know. *[in a self-important, pompous tone]* "Well, current lifespan, sixty, seventy, eighty, whatever. Used to be lower than that. And it is very possible they will be able to extend human lifespan to typically over a hundred years, maybe two hundred or more years. Somewhere even within your lifetime, perhaps." *[laughter]*

I mean you've got to live anyway, so you sort of go with it, sort of shoot for the longevity, and go for having and acquiring and relating and entangling and depending and so forth, and hope that you get to live it as long as possible, and so that by the time you have had it for all that length of time, maybe you will have totally lost interest in it. You hope for something. But you just go for it. You figure that's the way it's got to be. Well, now you have it. But it was there already anyway, as soon as you felt identified with the body, as soon as you entered into the waking state.

There is no waking state unless you are embodied. If you weren't embodied, where would you be? What would you be?

Well, it is not merely a theoretical question. <u>When</u> you are not embodied, what are you? You have full experience of the variations on your condition. Of course, you don't necessarily <u>notice</u> them, if you maintain superficial habit modes of attention. And that's typical. People don't enter into the kind of "considerations" I generate with My devotees—not this particular matter as I do it, with this fullness, and relative to many matters which are not elsewhere "considered" at all.

Right now, for instance, is there any "you" except the one who is reading the printout? So you're having these perceptions moment to moment, with thoughts and so forth. Well, for a perception to be generated from something affecting the body to you noticing it, takes time, a fraction of a whatever.

CARL PENGELLY: A glitch.

AVATAR ADI DA SAMRAJ: Yes. Infinitesimal fraction of a glitch, but nonetheless it takes time. So it's something in space-time. It's in the realm of light within space-time and so forth.

So, in other words, to be perceiving anything of your body-state, you can't see it now, you can only see the printout, you can only see the perception. Even to have a thought, to be noticing your thoughts, the thoughts take however much time. So they are not what is in the present moment. The thoughts are always post-present-moment. Something prior to thinking is present.

But even "present" is a reference that's like "past" and "future". It's not the apt phrase. I was using the word "Now" with you in our discussion the other night. Are you being the body (or being whatever) while you are also observing this printout? Or do you have any existence at all apart from this printout game? Do you have any existence otherwise, unless you decide, yourself, to go beyond the printout game?

But, right at this moment, when you are basically just confined to perceptions, conceptions—all of which are in time and not the present therefore, or even the "Now"—are you (while that's going on) otherwise also something else? So are you really in the position of being nothing but this printout-process reader, or can you notice this if you "consider" the matter with Me and respond to Me and go through the unique sadhana, persist in it, and, in that process, break out of this mold?

So which is it? Are you really the body, but somehow fixed on this printout of perception/conception?—but you are really otherwise the body and, therefore, in "now", you are the body prior to perception and conception? But, if you are the body prior to perception and conception, what body-awareness could there be? To be the body is not to perceive and conceive bodily. Those things take time. To be the body is not about perceiving or conceiving (or conceiving, bodily). To be the body is to be undifferentiated. It is to be perfectly surrendered, therefore.

Self-contraction, then, shows itself as perception and conception, thinking and perceiving. Contraction as the body, or the total body-mind, therefore is also the generator of thinking and perceiving, conception and perception. It's all one thing.

III.

AVATAR ADI DA SAMRAJ: This waking-state normalcy is to be a bulb in the earth. How profound is that? Yes, you could say all kinds of things about it—but it's built in, right here in the instruction book relative to this washing machine. They don't even give guarantees on these bulbs. There's no Westinghouse to call on (or any other company) that's going to come out and, if it doesn't last as long as you wanted it to, resuscitate it or give you a new one. No company you know downtown will do that, anyway.

So, this "you"-reference, this "I" you refer to, that self-contraction—you make this reference in every moment associated with perception and conception, or perceiving and thinking. In other words, you don't make this reference otherwise. It is itself a conceptual/perceptual form for you—so called "you".

"I" is the body-mind. When you say "I", you are speaking conceptually, but it means the body-mind. So this "I" is the body-mind, and it is the self-contraction. It is self-contracted. The phenomenon of being in the waking state, being the body-mind, is self-contraction, within a pattern of complexity.

Is this "you" simply the self-reference associated with perceptions and thoughts? Does it have an existence otherwise? Is it the body otherwise in present time? Or is it simply that this "you" that you are referring to is the center of thought and perception and not the body at all? Ha! *[Beloved Adi Da begins a deep, throaty laugh.]* It's exactly what you are.

That's why you didn't create that body there. You didn't create any of the organs in it. You're not doing the organs, presently. And yet you say it's "you". What do you have to do with it? When do you ever experience being that? What is the basis, at any rate, of you presuming that? It's not the experience of being the body, because you don't generate or operate the body. It's something else.

This "you" that is self-concerned is the functional center of thought and perception. And that's all that it is. It refers to itself as the body. It presumes itself to be the body and so forth. Those are thoughts associated with certain presumptions about perception. There is no "you" or "I", therefore, concerned for itself except as this center of thoughts and perceptions. There is no "you" that's the body because this center of thoughts and perceptions doesn't know anything about the body. It didn't make the body. It's somehow associated with it because it's the center of the thought, the thinking/perceiving process in the brain and nervous system.

That's who "you" are in the functional sense. You never experience being the body. It's a convention of your own presumption. But perceptions and conceptions about "you" do not exist apart from conceptions and perceptions. You have no sense of yourself otherwise, of this "you" that's concerned about itself, of this "I" that refers to itself. Without the process of thinking and perceiving, it doesn't exist, it doesn't ask questions, it doesn't have anything to be concerned about itself. It doesn't exist.

But these are all statements of what? Of the center of thinking and perceiving. The "you" that's concerned for itself is the center of thinking and perceiving. And it knows it doesn't have any control over the thing controlling it, the thing on which it's dependent. And that's the body. It is the center of the body's perception/conception process. But it never gets to be the body itself. So the body is this bulb. The conceptual/perceptual mechanism of which you are the center is found out. This body is a <u>tulip</u> bulb! You know what I mean? [laughter]

Listen to Me! Listen to Me, guys, fellow plants here. Listen. There's a guy in the garden—He's found out. You all could find out, too. Just listen for a moment here. "Consider" the situation carefully. This is what I'm saying. Listen to this:

First of all, these bodies here are like tulip bulbs. These things aren't built to last, these things die. It's <u>built</u> <u>in</u> to die, by the way—it's not just going to happen accidentally. Accidents could shorten it. The thing itself is <u>built</u> <u>in</u>. Going to die. <u>Intends</u> to die! It's <u>purposed</u> to die!

You want to know the purpose of life? If the last thing done is its purpose, then <u>this</u> thing is purposed to die. That's not meaningful, though. So maybe the purpose, then, is what it does in its process altogether, death simply being the end of its apparent cycle. So it does all these things—reproducing, living, being in the elemental domain, and so forth. Maybe <u>that's</u> its purpose. See, the purpose is to wiggle around, and so forth, right now. Whatever that wiggling is, or whatever kind of wiggling it is (however you may do it)—whatever the wiggle you wiggle it is, on your way to see the wizard—maybe <u>that's</u> the meaning of life.

That's the purpose? Well, that's just as ridiculous.

Or you could say that the purpose is a kind of unity, the cycle that bulb goes through. You could appreciate that, a certain kind of beauty to the way it forms up there.

But dying is what these bodies are built to do. That's what they're going to do. They do this meantime, yes. If that's meaningful to you, fine. If it's not meaningful enough, you've got to investigate it profoundly. In any case, it dies. You can't really say that's the purpose, but that certainly is where it leads. And everything is lost, and it's clear that the individual bulb is simply a device serving the purpose of a larger pattern that persists through countless individual examples—associating, reproducing, going on. The pattern itself is what is surviving in this. And yet, why? What does it want to survive for? Is there any profundity in it?

Well, you are, however, the center of thinking and perceiving. And yet thinking and perceiving take time. You never appear except in association with thinking and perceiving. Therefore, you have no fundamental existence at all. You, yourself, in other words, occur <u>after</u> the fact of thought and perception, which are themselves events in time. You are a mechanism. Your concerns may help the survival of the body—which you are not, in your consciousness. You are the center of thought and perception, not the actual body. You didn't bring the body into existence. But, you can, by adjusting your domain of thinking/perceiving somehow, pattern a result in the body associated with its health, or whatever. But you can't create the body. There are all kinds of things you can't do.

So this "you" that's concerned for itself, this "I", is not even the body, if you examine it carefully. It's a presumption occurring in association with a particular organism—which is an example of a type of organisms, human type, similar to certain plant species in bulb form. It goes through certain cycles, does this and that, and then disintegrates, self-destructs, unless it's destroyed sooner, or interfered with in its course—in which case it wouldn't even necessarily reach that full expectation. That's why they give no guarantees on this particular model. At Westinghouse nobody would guarantee a human life.

Everybody tries to get involved in the <u>effort</u> to be helpful about it all because it's in your self-interest, too. It should all be as good as possible for everybody, because that would include you. Everybody is trying to get the human life to be as comfortable and long-lasting and interesting and pleasurable as possible. On the other hand, there's surely no straightforwardness about that. Look at the news.

This is what's going on—not only <u>while</u> people are pursuing getting it straight, but <u>because</u> people are trying to get it straight. Other kinds of problems develop. The whole thing remains problematic.

"I" is the center of perception/conception—you are the center of concern in this, you're a mechanism in this larger mechanism. I mean, what are you as a mechanism? What is a center of perception/conception? What existence do you have?

Your concerns are, however, the concerns about the body. You're not concerned about "you". You're not concerned about yourself. You're concerned about the body. You feel self-concern, but when you look at it, it's concern about body, about its death, its whatever, threatening it, wanting it to be pleasured, and so forth.

You're concerned about the body but you never get to be the body itself. You are registering perceptions, yes, and thinking and so on. But, in actual fact, you're just registering, in time-lapse fashion, its perceptual data. And that's what you relate to. You never relate to being the body, or experiencing the body directly, but only in the form of perceptions and the conceptual process added. So you never experience being the body. You never experience the body itself. You only experience perceptions.

What's a perception? What happens if you examine your experience of a perception? Not just these qualities, like everyone here can see, looking in the room and perceiving with your eyes, whatever your eyes are focusing on at the moment.

You don't know what a single thing is! It's perception. I'm not talking about this, that, and the other thing about whatever objects may be in your field of view, and so forth—but the sighting event itself. What is the root of it?

You close your eyes and you don't see the room and you open them and you do again. So just before you see the sight *[Adi Da pauses briefly]* . . . where is this perceiving of sight arising?

Devotees ponder this question silently.

AVATAR ADI DA SAMRAJ: Well it's being generated by the body, but you're not the body. You're just observing the perceptions. So you're not generating this, you're simply observing the perceptions of it. You're not generating mind then, perhaps. You are simply observing the conceptions of it which are kind of printouts of mind, like perceptions are printouts of body.

Well, if perceptions are the printout of the body, and thoughts are the printouts of the mind, and you only see this in time in the form of conceptions and perceptions, then you can't be the source of the mind. The body-mind is generating these conceptions, these mind-forms and these perceptions. You aren't! You are the center that observes the perceptions and the concepts, the thoughts. You're never in a position of generating them. You never come into association with it, except in the context of the perceiving and the thinking.

IV.

AVATAR ADI DA SAMRAJ: Really closely examine your own experiencing, because you are concerned about your mortal existence—the fact that it is mortal, and yet you have an impulse to exist. I mean, it's strange—this bulb that has built-in to die at some point has, at its core, an impulse to <u>exist</u>. Not just to continue its pattern, but to <u>exist</u>! This core is perceiving and thinking, perceiving the thoughts and perceptions, because it wants to exist.

It doesn't merely want to think and perceive. It wants to exist. In that sense, persist. But this core of data has found out that this bulb has built-in to self-destruct. And could stop at any time, in fact—all kinds of problems could arise for it.

Self-concern arises in the body-mind. And you get that, but now <u>you</u> are self-concerned, too. And you're trying to figure it out. And somehow you're trying to figure it out, maybe do that body-mind some good—what do you know? You're not the body-mind. You are just the whatever that reads the printout.

On the other hand, <u>you</u>, from your own point of view, are of utmost importance. You are the center of consciousness. You don't know anything about what that body-mind <u>is</u>. It seems like all you get out of it is that it's a pattern. Consciousness doesn't seem to be anywhere. But in your case, in this whole body-mind thing, it's the "you" part that is conscious, it seems, and not the rest. And, yet, it functions. It's a pattern that can strike up against other patterns and adapt or make changes or whatever.

But you're the consciousness part, and that seems to you to be of profound importance. In any case, you are very concerned about your own existence. And yet when you reflect on your concern for your own existence, or communicate about it, you express it as concern for the body (or the body-mind person). You even speak as if you are that. You say you are that.

These are questions you don't usually get asked. What about this matter?

This "you" that's concerned for itself is functioning simply as the intelligent observer, or in the intelligent-observer function relative to conceptions and perceptions. And this "you" is just noticing conceptions and perceptions—in other words, things that take time—and is a part of just being a body-mind. But what is the core of it, the center, the intelligent center that registers the printout—the pattern that registers in the form of perceptions and conceptions? You are not the body. But you are also not the mind. They're on the other side of this printout. The body and its world are on the other side of the perception. And the mind, whatever that is, is on the other side of the thoughts.

The thoughts all take time. The perceptions all take time. The perceptions aren't the body. The body would have to be there already. The perceptions are something within the context of the body and they take time. They are something in addition to the body. A center of awareness is associated with this, kind of like a central unit that (like in an airport or transportation place of some kind) registers perceptually or conceptually, all the data of the system. And yet, it's not itself the system. This observer of its perceptions and conceptions is not the system itself. It's a function within the system.

If you were the mind, you'd know all your thoughts right now. But how could you know all your thoughts? Thoughts don't pre-exist that way. They arise within a pattern. They can be used in all kinds of ways, and there are memories and fixed thoughts, but you can't know all your thoughts.

If you are the mind, then you're that whole system in which thoughts are potential, and in which there are memories and all the rest of it. That's the mind. If you are that, then you would know all of its parts right now.

If you are the body, you would be being the liver and the heart and the cellular growth process and the toenails—all these kinds of things. But you're not, you're not doing any of that. You're not being that at all. Same with the mind. You're not being all of those mind-processes at all. You depend on those things somehow being kept intact <u>somewhere</u>. You don't know exactly where that is. The body-brain-mind? Somewhat? Somewhere? Right? That's your calculation, or the calculation that comes across on the conception machine or the perception/conception-combination machine.

But all you do is notice this data—not the mind and not the body. You do not observe either the body or the mind in this respect. If you <u>were</u> either one, you would be totally aware <u>as</u> one or the other, or both. But you're not at all aware of either one, except in any moment of registering a perception or a conception. Then you are registering, in a replicated (or time-requiring) form, some aspect or portion or moment of that total body-mind. But never this—the whole thing at any one moment. You never get to be that. You <u>are</u> <u>not</u> that.

Nonetheless, there does seem to be a reason for you to be conscious in that position, because all this data comes together in the moments of the bits which are what <u>you</u> are always addressing. <u>You</u>, being fully coincident with that pattern of thinking and perceiving, by reacting and tending, presuming, one way or another, can change the orientation of thinking and perceiving in the moment. You can change a lot of thought. You can change a lot of perceived body-activity and so on.

So it seems that you are seated in the position where there's the mysterious exercise of discriminative intelligence and will. The mind and the body are a resource outside of your sphere, which you draw upon, or which is reflected in your printout. And you can call up aspects of the printout, especially at the conceptual level, at the perception memory level, by an act of will. But what do you do when you do that?

How do you locate a particular memory? It's a mechanism that makes it happen. A mechanism that you are not. You are not conscious as that. You relate to it somehow by a mysterious performance.

Remember what the moon looks like when it's full.

What did you have to do to do that? What had to happen for you to be satisfied that you did, from your point of view, just now, somehow recollect the full moon? It was rather straightforward for you. But it wasn't like you shuffled through billions of whatevers to get it, either. So you are <u>not</u> whatever it was between the intention to see the full moon and the seeing of it.

What's in between the intention to see the full moon and the seeing of it is <u>not</u> in your domain. You see, that's in the sphere of outside-of-discriminative-intelligence-and-will. You can <u>will</u> to see an image of the full moon. And that activates the mind. But <u>you</u> are not activated. Now, by engaging in various activities using processes of perception and conception, you can, so to speak, "learn" about how that's done.

Well, your own situation will not change. So this "I" you refer to is actually, in functional terms, just discriminative intelligence and will—it's not the body, it's not the mind. These are fields which you do not create, which you do not directly function as. You get the printout only, perceptions and conceptions only. So you're in the position of discriminative intelligence and will relating to the data of body-mind. You are not the body-mind in this sense.

Now this concern you feel for yourself—you always express it as concern relative to the body-mind, its survival, its pleasure, whatever. And yet you are never in the position of the body-mind. You are not the body-mind. You simply examine its data. So any concern about the body-mind can't be a characteristic of <u>you</u>. It's a characteristic of the body-mind. It's a misplaced concern. Self-concern is a misplaced concern. That which is the egoic self cannot be concerned about itself. Only the body-mind can be concerned about itself.

But when the ego-"I" gets concerned about so-called "itself", it thinks about the body-mind. It's concerned about the body-mind. So there is no concern about yourself. And never has been. But there is concern about the body-mind. And it's interesting to note, however, that this concern about the body-mind is not a concern about yourself at all. And, therefore, any address to the concerns of the body-mind, however useful or not it may be for the body-mind, will do you no good whatsoever. In other words, it will never have anything to do with Realization in the ultimate sense.

But there is the inherent impulse, or disposition, to Realize—just as there is an inherent impulse, or disposition, to be—the Self-Nature Itself, the Self-Condition Itself. That impulse, or disposition, cannot be denied. But no concern about it Realizes It, because all concern is translated immediately into body-mind concerns. Body-mind concerns are a diversion from the conditional self. They're not a concern about the conditional self. So no search relative to the body-mind has anything to do with Divine Self-Realization in the ultimate sense. Nonetheless, Divine Self-Realization is the inherent impulse.

Discriminative intelligence and will are also associated with a feeling-depth. It's not just an abstract, this "I"—like something in the midst of your laptop computer that organizes data. At the same time that there is thinking and perceiving, there is feeling-association, touch-association, an emotional dimension of that, an emotional tone of that. This can color the decisions of discriminative intelligence and acts of will, positively or negatively. But it is also, itself, fundamental intelligence.

Which is the that of great importance: the body-mind, or you? Are you a mistaken self-concern in the middle of the unit, and are otherwise just a function serving this body-mind unit, or are you of such a nature, of such profundity of size (ultimately, beyond your separateness), of That Which is Great, Primary, Divine, so it is you that is of importance, and not the body-mind? It, in that case, is mysteriously associated with you. It's secondary, because it is somehow an extension of you, but not fundamental to you.

Well, it seems, on the Energy-side, the object-side (which, at its root, is nothing but Energy), the pattern is the purpose. And on your side, the consciousness is the purpose, or the Reality. That's why you feel stuck in the pattern, threatened by the pattern. You are there in the functional seat of awareness, of discriminative intelligence and will, and feeling-intelligence, and all this data suggests that the pattern has a life of its own, a purpose of its own, and you better get with it, or it will wash right through you, right over you, or just throw you back in the vat, you know, for re-stamping or something—whatever. Nothing! Scrap!

You have to find out if you're just a mistake in the middle of the machine, a mistaken presumption. Then you're not about anything. There's just body-mind, and when it stops you didn't exist anyway, and that's that. If that's true, then all of "realization" (so-called) can be reduced to a mere turn of phrase: "But it really wasn't the way it seemed". No, that's not profound enough, that level of "consideration".

So, if you look at the body-mind to find out which is important—the body-mind or you—truly you will not find a satisfactory answer. From the point of view of your side, from your point of view, obviously, you are what is important. From the point of view of the body-mind, the pattern side, it is what is important. The two sides are inherently separate, appearing to be equal and opposite natures, or forces, or conditions of being.

Well, this is the dilemma, the inherent dilemma of conditional existence. This is the fundamental observation, the fundamental sense, the fundamental intuition, the fundamental knowledge you have, by virtue of being associated with a life-form, a mortal life-form, that, at this very present moment, appears to each of you as just one stage in a cycle that's been built in there from the time it was a seed.

At some moment along in the process built into that seed in its code—at some point down the line (doesn't take all that long), it's just going to stop and disintegrate.

How does that square with your "you"-consciousness? You can understand it about "it", like you can understand it about your washing machine—even your dog, maybe. But this is too close.

So "you" is more potently profound in your feeling estimation than this "bulb drops dead who knows when, but it doesn't take all that long" kind of stuff. To get caught up in that is not merely just an intellectual problem. It is an inherent problem that is associated with the knot in which you have bound yourself. And it must be understood and gone beyond. And this inherent dilemma is what, ultimately, is gone beyond— the impenetrability, un-Recognizability of space-time-experience.

The functioning "you" or "I" that is in the feeling-position relative to phenomena, observing the arising forms of thought and perception, is itself a dimension of the body-mind. Whatever the body-mind is altogether (gross, subtle, causal, its history, and so forth—yes, they have to be taken into account), fundamentally it is just that, and, therefore, has a "fate" (so to speak) that coincides with the process of the body-mind—

288

from birth to death, and beyond. That one is not otherwise eternal or immortal. It is ever-changing, and this is how survival of death and going on after death occurs, rather than the "self" of that being immortal. The "self" of that is coincident with that process, has the fate of that process.

So that one is not immortal or eternal. You could still call it a "self", but it is conditional. But it is the core of psycho-physical experiencing. That is where the depth is. It is in that domain that the sadhana is done. Or, more profoundly, ultimately, that is just it, that very seat.

V.

AVATAR ADI DA SAMRAJ: Dreaming allows the animation of the body-mind machine to take a curious turn in its manifestation and so forth, but on the other hand, it bears some resemblance to bodily waking-state experience.

Deep sleep, however, is not like either waking or dreaming. It has no perceptions, it has no thoughts, in terms of active process. So when you go to sleep at any time, you don't dream, you don't have body experiences, you don't have thoughts, but you don't cease to exist, and the body-mind doesn't cease to exist. The body-mind itself goes on, apparently. Reassociation is initiated a few hours later or whenever. And when you wake up once again into waking, you're the same "you" you were when you went to sleep. You have a sense of the continuity of your existence, but you don't really account for it altogether.

Therefore, deep sleep is the root-center of the states of the psycho-physical process. But it is not eternal. It is the root of this process-self, this psycho-physical transforming pattern. So it must be transcended, the causal knot must be transcended, the ego-"I" must be transcended at its depth—at the causal level, the deep-sleep level. That Which is Prior to waking, dreaming, and sleeping is That Which is immediately Prior to deep sleep, not that which you can think about in the waking state and call it "the Witness" or whatever, but That Which can be found only by going through the narrow gate of deep sleep. If you look to the right or left, you lose consciousness. And it can be penetrated, ultimately, only through Grace, associated with profound response. And that profound response must be a persistent, profound sadhana, practice, or embrace of the right design associated with that response, if it is to be a process of Realization—in the Way of the Heart, Most Perfect Divine Self-Realization.

So you don't have to have a concern about yourself, about the body-mind, therefore, to enter into the deep. But you have to deal with the body-mind's concerns for itself by submitting the body-mind to the laws of the religious and Spiritual process, the disciplines of it, and engage the counter-egoic exercise of the Way.

Ultimate Divine Self-Realization is not about self-concern, but the fulfillment of the native impulse, the native disposition to Realize the Self-Nature—the Inherent Nature, the Root-Nature, the Self-Existing Nature—of Reality, That Which is Always Already the Case. It's not a matter of exercising concern for the body-mind, or for the pattern of thoughts and perceptions, but of entering <u>most</u> profoundly, deeply into the depth of awareness itself. The deeper it goes, the more removed it becomes from ordinary waking-state associations.

Ultimately, this process—persisted in, the whole sadhana persisted in its stages, advanced through as required—becomes a process in depth at the level of that depth otherwise associated with deep sleep in the cycle of waking, dreaming, and sleeping. It's the <u>depth</u> of the Consciousness-Position otherwise associated with discriminative intelligence and will, rooted in the feeling-base. It is the depth of that, beyond that function, beyond observing, beyond Witness <u>as</u> Witness, in the Deep Itself, beyond waking, dreaming, and sleeping.

Swami (Baba) Muktananda[36] said to Me (in the language of the traditions), "You are not the one who wakes or sleeps or dreams. You are the Witness of these". Well, that's quite a profound matter. It's no simple matter to Realize.

People deal with such notions with the perceiving-thinking self, the ego, and think: "Well, if you're the Witness of waking, dreaming, and sleeping, you must be the Witness of waking right now (since it's the guy who's awake who's thinking about this) and, therefore, the Witness is some kind of stand-off-Witnessing, observing of the waking state." But no. It's <u>as</u> the Witness of waking, dreaming, and sleeping. It's deeper than all three, more profound than all three.

So it's not Realized in the waking state. In fact, it's not Realized in the waking state, the dreaming state, <u>or</u> the sleeping state. If it could be Realized in any of those states, it wouldn't be the Witness of all three. It is Beyond. And the way to enter into the Beyond is to go through that process of ever-deepening sadhana, that becomes sadhana <u>at</u> the threshold

36. One of those whom Avatar Adi Da embraced as Spiritual Master in the course of His "Sadhana Years" was Swami Muktananda (1908-1982). Having left home at the age of fifteen, Swami Muktananda wandered for many years, seeking the Divine Truth from sources all over India. Eventually, he came under the Spiritual Influence of Swami Nityananda, whom he accepted as his Guru and in whose Spiritual Company he mastered Kundalini Yoga. As an Adept of Kundalini Yoga, Swami Muktananda Served Adi Da Samraj as Spiritual Teacher during the period from 1968 to 1970.

between deep sleep and What is Beyond, That Which is Always Already the Case. You will find Me in My Threshold Forms up to that point. They are the Pattern that Serves your Realization of Me. <u>From</u> that point, however, there is only Me, without media, and without the process associated with apparent separation from Me.

The "Perfect Practice" is the sadhana of Non-separation. It takes place beyond the doorway that is between deep sleep (or the three common states—waking, dreaming, and sleeping) and What is Beyond, Consciousness that is Beyond.

So the "I" as the functionary observer of perception and thinking is <u>not</u> immortal or eternal. It is associated with the pattern of body-mind and is associated directly with its fate, during the lifetime and beyond. But the Real Condition, the Source-Condition of that feeling-awareness is Prior to the body-mind, and, therefore, Prior to this separate-self function in the context of the body-mind. It is Prior to waking, dreaming, and sleeping—in other words, Prior to all of the processes associated with body-mind.

<u>This</u> is What must be Realized. And the sadhana of the Way of the Heart is <u>this</u> sadhana, then.

The Way of the Heart is the Yoga of always going beyond. Therefore, it is the Yoga of always proceeding more deeply.

The Divine Depth

A VATAR ADI DA SAMRAJ: The Truth is <u>not</u> that human beings have, inside them (or as their inside), an immortal "soul" (or however you may want to describe it)—that they are an entity that, deep inside, is an immortal entity. It's not that <u>you</u> are great, in other words, but <u>Reality</u> is Great, the Divine is Great. <u>It</u> is Eternal. It is the Condition of conditions. It is That in Which everything is arising.

So the Nature of that which is in this position of observing the data of perception-conception—its <u>Nature</u> (in other words, that Condition within Which it is arising, not that condition which is deep within itself, merely) is Self-Existing and Self-Radiant Being, Consciousness Itself. Its Characteristic is Radiant Love-Bliss, the "Bright" Itself.

When this Divine Depth is Realized, and, by Grace, all conditional arising is Divinely Recognized, then there is that process in which all conditional arising is (ultimately) Outshined, and there's no longer a "you" (or an "I", in the ego-sense), that is coinciding with perception and conception, on and on and on, for however long until dead, or, otherwise, forever changing. But that's for you to find out.

In any case, whatever "you" is ceases, in the absolute sense—not by being stopped, but by being Outshined, by being Divinely Recognized.

Divine Recognition is Self-"Brightness", discovering that everything is Its own "Brightness".

There is only this "Brightness".

So it's just magnification of the Single Radiance of Love-Bliss, Which is the Characteristic and Source-Condition of phenomenal arising.

But when this Depth is Realized, and phenomenal arising is thus Divinely Recognized, then phenomenal arising is Outshined.

And then there is no phenomenal arising, there is no separation, no relatedness, no "difference", no otherness, no conditional existence. Only Divine Existence. Not nothing—but <u>no</u> thing.

You will not have realized <u>your</u> self—"you" will be long gone. You will Realize the Divine Self-Condition—That Which, now and always, is Always Already the Case, Transcending "you". "You" is an invention in klik-klak, a device that is made by apparently modifying the Divine Reality. And, from the point of view of that device, Consciousness and Energy seem to be two.

The seventh stage Awakening is not Itself Divine Translation. It is the Great Realization, in which everything is inherently Divinely Recognized.

But It is, in that case, Demonstrated in the context of apparent phenomenal (or conditional) existence. The Demonstration in that context, however, is Divine Recognition in the context of the four Demonstration Stages[37] I have described relative to the seventh stage of life. But, altogether, it is Inherent Recognition of what is arising as transparent (or merely apparent), and un-necessary, and inherently non-binding modifications of this Divine Self-Condition, Self-Existing and Self-Radiant. There is no entification, separateness—only this Singleness, constantly found.

This Demonstration, persisted in, shows itself in Yogic signs, in the context of (or relative to) the body-mind association. And eventually that association is not dissociated from, but Outshined, just Shined, Felt, through, beyond all separateness, to the point where there is no category of separateness even to be Recognized. The Shine is Shining Absolutely, and there is no diminishment anywhere.

It doesn't make any difference what arises—just go deeper. Deeper than waking, deeper than dreaming, deeper than sleeping. Always Attracted to Me, surrendered and forgetting yourself in Me, to the point where it becomes an ever-deepening process. Not necessarily every day deeper than the last, but, overall, if you look at it as a process, it is ever-deepening, if you persist in it.

It's also not merely an exercise that you perform. The practice I'm describing is Ruchira Buddha Bhakti Yoga. It is the relationship to Me, the practice engaged by those who are moved by the Attracted response to Me, and who formally become My devotees. In that case I am in a sacred, holy "Bond" association with such a one. That is how they are relating to Me. That is how I regard them, then. And they must cultivate this relationship by vow, through all the means I have Given them to maintain right relationship with Me.

So, therefore, the practice of devotees of Mine is always developed on the basis of, first, their response to Me. Just that is the fundamental Yoga. Or the cultivating of that through all the practice is everything that follows upon that response. And it is, fundamentally, simply the deepening of that response, to the point where your self-surrendering, self-forgetting response to Me Realizes only Me—not merely in the absorptive sense, but, ultimately, in the context of the "Perfect Practice", Realization of Me without "difference", without separation, the Samadhi of Non-separate Realization of Me.

---

37. In the context of Divine Enlightenment in the seventh stage of life, the Spiritual process continues. Adi Da Samraj has Revealed that there are four phases of the seventh stage process: Divine Transfiguration, Divine Transformation, Divine Indifference, and Divine Translation. Please see appendix, pp. 397-98, for a description of each of these four phases.

This is beyond egoic "self-possession", beyond waking, dreaming, and sleeping. The Samadhi of the seventh stage is more profound than deep sleep. The Realizer is not awake and not dreaming and not sleeping, is not <u>in</u> the state that you are. Whatever may appear to be the case, I am always Functioning in a different state than you are, whether it is in the moment of waking, dreaming, or sleeping.

You <u>know</u> the difference between those states. You have some basic sense of it, anyway, in your own experience. Well, what would a fourth one be? You know, something like, "Imagine an extra primary color."

MICHAEL WOOD: Or a vision, if you had always been blind.

AVATAR ADI DA SAMRAJ: Yes. It's a koan, unless you Realize. It's impenetrable, meaningless. You don't know.

How would you know? You know waking, dreaming, and sleeping. Divine Self-Realization is a "different one", so to speak.

MICHAEL: Well, we know You, so we know there is a different one, because we know You are a very Different One.

AVATAR ADI DA SAMRAJ: So it's a different state altogether. It's not waking, it's not dreaming, it's not sleeping. It is of such a nature, however, that it can appear (as in This Conjunction) to be associated with the common states of waking, dreaming, and sleeping, without, however, the loss of the Ultimate Condition.

There's the traditional term, "turiya", which simply means "the fourth"—usually meaning "the Witness", or something not very definite, "Samadhi", "beyond waking, dreaming, and sleeping". And there is also a traditional term "turiyatita",* which means "<u>beyond</u> the fourth". So I've used the term "turiya" to refer to Realization in the context of the first two stages of the "Perfect Practice", and "turiyatita", you could say, then, is a good word to use for the third stage of the "Perfect Practice", or the seventh stage. But that's just a way of making use of traditional terms.

What would any state be if it were Beyond, and, therefore, <u>not</u> identical to waking, dreaming, or sleeping. You can't imagine such a State, just as you cannot imagine an extra primary color.

There <u>is</u> that State. I confirm It to you. But It is not yet Realized by you to be your experience, and so you are concerned about the body-mind. You are concerned about waking, dreaming, and sleeping. You're concerned about a "you" that is identified with the body-mind.

If you enter into the feeling-depth of your position, it is beyond that as well. In your position—not as the Witness, I'm not talking in "Perfect

Practice" terms, just in ordinary terms—you are at the center where there is discriminative intelligence and will. But it is seated, rooted, in feeling-depth, heart-depth. So it can function as discriminative intelligence and will, with whatever minimal degree of feeling-depth to it (perhaps none at all), or it can relate to those things with great feeling-depth, if it has developed the capacity to do this. And it can also enter into that depth for its own sake, and most profoundly. So the heart is the root of it, then.

The function, even now, for anyone, is obviously at the point of discriminative intelligence and will, and is not the body-mind otherwise, except through this relationship to the data in time.

It's interesting to see, if you are simply observing the data of mind and body, just exactly what form does it take as data? I mean, when do you get to perceive it? If perception itself takes time—perception comes from the body, something occurs with the body and some time later the perception is generated, but, nonetheless, perception always takes time—then how do you ever get to be in the position to perceive it at all? Because it would always take time for you to perceive it. That would always be the case. It will take time for you to perceive it, and, therefore, you would never perceive it.

But there is perception. All that paradox and mystery is true as well, but the secrets of it are only in depth. Not merely in the depth (like you have to go and trick it out of there, like out of a cave of a dragon)—but in-depth. In other words, in the process of entering more and more deeply into the domain of the heart.

You enter in this in-depth domain through the practice of Ruchira Buddha Bhakti Yoga, which is not merely an exercise of manipulating the body-mind, out of concern for the body-mind, but is, rather, a relationship exercised, lived in a particular manner, and most profoundly, and in depth, moment to moment.

I Call you to actually do this—all the disciplines of the body-mind, but then this in-depth discipline moment to moment. To actually do this, instead of forestalling the doing of it with all kinds of reasons for delaying.

Actually do it. Prove it by doing it. The more profound it becomes as an exercise or as a process in your case, the more reason you will have to always take it seriously, to never neglect it.

CHAPTER TWENTY-TWO

The Miracle of the Fly

BY RIVER PAPERS

Adi Da Samraj at Mother's Bed

At the Mountain Of Attention Sanctuary in California there is a small lake called Mother's Bed, surrounded by hills and trees. In the 1970s, when Adi Da lived at the Mountain Of Attention, He frequently swam at Mother's Bed in the heat of summer. While attending Him on one such occasion, I saw a fly land on His arm and bite him. He smacked the fly and it fell to the ground, dead. This was a very unusual event. Adi Da had always Instructed us not to kill any of the ants, spiders, or insects in His house, but to take them outside and set them free. I was curious, so I moved around His chair to get a closer look at the fly.

It was curled up and still. As I moved around His chair, Adi Da remarked humorously, "That's the last thing that fly will ever do!" But as I continued to look at the fly, He seemed to reconsider. "Well, maybe this fly shouldn't die right now." And He leaned out of His chair and placed His forefinger about an inch above the corpse.

As Beloved Adi Da held His finger there, I could actually see a current of energy streaming from His finger onto the fly. After a second or two, the fly's entire body began to shake vigorously, as if in response to an electric shock. After a few more moments, Adi Da picked the fly up and, holding it carefully on His forefinger, gently blew on it. To my astonishment, the fly flew off into the summer sky above the pond.

CHAPTER TWENTY-THREE

Direct Examination of the Structure and the Roots of One's Own Body-Mind Provides Immediate Evidence of the Hierarchical Structure of Reality, and Immediate Proof of the Divine Nature and "Purpose" of Existence

FROM THE BASKET OF TOLERANCE

*O*f Avatar Adi Da's nine Source-Texts, eight are devoted to Adi Da's own Teaching on the Nature of God, Truth, or Reality and the practice of the Way of the Heart. The ninth Source-Text, The Basket of Tolerance, *has a different (though closely related) purpose: It is Avatar Adi Da's systematic overview and commentary on the entire history of mankind's practical, religious, and Spiritual endeavors. The Basket of Tolerance reveals the entire spectrum of human history, philosophy, culture, and Realization as a single "Great Tradition" which we may receive as a "common inheritance" that serves our own tolerance and growth.*

The Basket of Tolerance is first of all a bibliography of some four thousand publications (including books, magazine articles, videotapes, audiotapes, and compact discs), covering all the major religious and Spiritual traditions of the past and present (representing all the possible points of

Direct Examination of the Structure and the Roots of One's Own Body-Mind
Provides Immediate Evidence of the Hierarchical Structure of Reality, and
Immediate Proof of the Divine Nature and "Purpose" of Existence

*view relative to religion and Spirituality) and a full spectrum of various
schools of thought relative to practical and social life-wisdom (relative to
such matters as diet, health, sexuality, money, community, and so on). The
organization of the bibliography makes plain the correspondences and
interrelationships between the many diverse traditions of wisdom throughout
the world, including the stage of life represented by each tradition.*

*In addition, Adi Da Samraj has written (as part of the bibliography) over
one hundred Essays and Commentaries, casting light on an immense range
of topics relative to the Great Tradition. The bibliography together with the
Essays and Commentaries constitute a "grand argument" based on the seven
stages of life, which literally makes sense out of what has previously appeared
only as a chaos of beliefs, arguments, practices, and Realizations.*

*The Essay "Direct Examination of the Structure and the Roots of One's
Own Body-Mind . . ." has been placed by Adi Da Samraj as His opening
statement in the first section of* The Basket of Tolerance, *"Introduction to
Religious Philosophy".*

The conditionally manifested Reality is hierarchically composed, from
the "inside" (or "depth point") "out", and its Origin is in its "depth point"
("within"), rather than at any point "without". This can become immediately evident, if one simply and directly examines one's own conditionally
manifested structure.

Thus, there is (you might first observe) the physical body (and the physical world of its physical relations). However, senior and prior to the
physical body is the systematic life-energy that animates (or activates)
the physical body, and, coincidently, there are the operations of the sensory (and general emotional) mechanisms, whereby the physical body is
perceived. If the systematic life-energy were disconnected (or otherwise
depleted) from the physical body, the physical body would be unable to
move in the physical world. And if the operations of the sensory mechanisms were disconnected from the physical body, there would not be any
perception of the physical body, nor any physical bodily perception of
the physical world. Likewise, then, senior and prior to the physical world
we ordinarily perceive is the subtler world-plane of (perhaps variously
perceived, or at least felt) systematic life-energy that surrounds and pervades and forms the "inner" dimension of the physical world. And is it
not reasonable, then, to presume (and to look to verify) that, at the
"inner" (or systematic life-energy) plane of the physical world, there are
structured mechanisms, structuring, and, in the structural sense, deter-
mining and changing and operating and controlling, the grosser (or

"outer") physical world, just as one readily observes to be the case with one's own mechanism of conditional manifestation?

If one continues to examine one's own conditionally manifested structure, it becomes immediately evident that senior and prior to the system of life-energy and of sensory perception (and sense-based emotion) is the function of mind, which, both perceptually and conceptually, examines and reflects and remembers and, in the rudimentary sense, compares and interprets the systematic life-energy motions (and emotions) and the impressions registered by each and all of the sense operations. If the thus functional mind were somehow detached from the physical and systematic life-energy and sensory (and general emotional) processes, the living and sensing physical body would become an unconscious robot, or even a corpse, and the sense-based mind would (as in dreams) "wander" on its own. (Indeed, such is the situation after death, unless there is a higher, or even an Ultimate, Awakening, or, otherwise, until there is natural reintegration with a mechanism of systematic life-energy, and of organized sensory, and general emotional, operations, and of physical, whether grosser or subtler, bodily form.) And is it not reasonable, then, to presume (and to look to verify) that the world "outside" is similarly (or correspondingly) structured?

Is it not unreasonable to presume (and to dogmatically, and reductionistically, insist) that the only "real" (and "important") world is the "material" one (or the gross physical part of the whole)? Is it not unreasonable to presume (and to dogmatically insist) that the patently obvious hierarchical structure of our own conditional manifestation is not a demonstration and a proof of the necessarily (and correspondingly) hierarchical structure of the "world"? Indeed, such presumptions are patently unreasonable. Therefore, it is only reasonable to presume (and to look to verify) that the "world" is arising in a hierarchical manner, from the "inside" (or "depth point") "out", just as is the case with the complex (or multi-level, and hierarchically structured) human "entity" arising in (and utterly coincident with) the arising "world". And, that becoming obvious, the "world" must then be described (and presumed) to be a psycho-physical (rather than a merely physical, or "material") process.

Furthermore, if one continues to examine one's own conditionally manifested structure, it becomes immediately evident that senior and prior to the sense-based mind is the root-mind, the presiding intelligence that "knows" the sense-based mind (and, via the sense-based mind, "knows" the operations of the senses, and the motions, and emotions, of systematic life-energy), and which, thereby, governs the actions of the physical body,

Direct Examination of the Structure and the Roots of One's Own Body-Mind
Provides Immediate Evidence of the Hierarchical Structure of Reality, and
Immediate Proof of the Divine Nature and "Purpose" of Existence

and which, based on the exercise of discriminative understanding, makes choices relative to bodily action, and, altogether, interprets the meaning and purpose of personal psycho-physical existence in the psycho-physical world. Just so, in that root-mind, or presiding intelligence, the root-ideas (both conceived and perceived, or, simply, felt) of separate self (or ego-"I") and of "other" and "thing", or of separateness and "difference" and related-ness, are, as root-functional presumptions, made operative. Therefore, also, that root-mind, or presiding, or governing, intelligence, is operative in the entire psycho-physical sphere ("inside" and "out") as the function of will. And if that intelligent, and discriminating, function of will becomes weakened via (and in the context of) its association with the hierarchically sub-ordinate functions (of sense-mind, and senses, and sense-based emotions, and systematic life-energy, and the actions, habits, and conditions of the physical body, and the experienced conditions of the "world", and the association with "others" and "things", and the actions and states of "others" and "things"), then the integrity, and harmony, and well-being, and intelligence of the entire body-mind-self is (as a consequence) likewise weakened, with potentially disastrous results, not only for the individual body-mind-self itself, but, potentially, and very likely, for its relations as well (including, potentially, even the entire "world").

Therefore, since one's own directly observable (and, obviously, hierar-chically structured) form (in which "inside" is senior and prior to "outside") arises in total participatory and dependent coincidence with the total "world", is it not reasonable to presume (and to look to verify) that the "world" is altogether composed in an identical (or altogether correspond-ing, thoroughly coincident, and likewise hierarchically structured) manner (in which "inside" is senior and prior to "outside")? And is it not, therefore, reasonable to presume (and to look to verify) that the "world" too has, in its depth, a governing interior, a field of presiding and discriminating intel-ligence and will, upon which the "outer" state of the "world" depends?

As in the case of the individual body-mind-self, the "interior field" of the "world" may, at times, be weak, and, at other times, strong. It need not be presumed to be a "Single Entity" (called "God", or whatever). Indeed, the "interior field" of the "world" is best (or most correctly) felt to be simply a universal field of potential (rather than any kind of "Entity"), just as the "interior field" is, if correctly understood, simply a field of potential (rather than an otherwise separate "entity") in any apparently individual case. Thus, the "interior field" of the world is manifested in many kinds, through many forces, even through many and various wills, while yet always bearing a "creative" quality, and an inherent, overriding lawfulness, and a Luminous Fullness that perpetually serves as a resource that, if felt most deeply in any one, or in all, can become a restorer of right will, and right-mindedness, and right thought, and right perception, and right feeling, and right action, or altogether right and "creative" life.

More than this, if one turns about from the functional effort of intelligent discrimination and will (and, thus, from the sense-based mind, and from the senses, and the sense-based emotions, and the systematic life-energy, and from the physical body, and from even the entire psycho-physical world), and if, thereby, one turns upward into the Source-Field from Which all that is in (and all that is hierarchically below) the functioning intelligence of the ego-"I" is proceeding, a limitless Sphere of Light and Bliss and self-Forgetting is Found (as It has already and always been Found, by countless Mystics, Yogis, and Saints). Indeed, many who have so turned about in the ascension of their own minds (and the forgetting of the body-mind and the "world") have felt that ascended Sphere to Be (and to Characterize) the Source (or "True God") of the body-mind-self and the "world".

Nevertheless, if one continues to examine one's own conditionally manifested structure, it becomes, at last, evident that the ultimate hierarchical root of the conditionally manifested self (or psycho-physical ego-"I") is not above the crown of the head, but at the heart, in the right side of the chest, the center where attention itself first arises, in the form of the most rudimentary <u>feeling</u> of separateness, "difference", and relatedness. And when that egoic root is entered and, by Grace, gone beyond, the True, Inherently Perfect, and (necessarily) Divine Source-Person, or Self-Condition, is, by Grace, Revealed, and Realized, to Be the True, Inherently Perfect, and (necessarily) Divine Source-Condition of <u>all</u> of conditionally manifested Reality.

This Divine Self-Realization has been Demonstrated (and, Thus and Thereby, Verified and Proven) by Me, and I Am here (now, and forever hereafter) to Reveal It to every one and all (by Means of a Grace-Given Ordeal of Divine Self-Awakening). Likewise, even all aspects and designs of the hierarchically structured human body-mind (and even every kind of body-mind), and even all aspects and designs of the hierarchically structured "world" (and of the many "worlds") of one and of all, have been experienced, investigated, and, ultimately, transcended by Me, and I Am here (now, and forever hereafter) to Serve every one and all, by Attracting and Guiding every one and all in the Great Process of experiencing, investigating, and, ultimately, transcending all aspects of the apparent body-mind-self and "world". Therefore, I Say to one and all, the condi-

Direct Examination of the Structure and the Roots of One's Own Body-Mind
Provides Immediate Evidence of the Hierarchical Structure of Reality, and
Immediate Proof of the Divine Nature and "Purpose" of Existence

tionally manifested Reality is hierarchically composed, from the "inside" (or "depth point") "out", and its Origin is in (or beyond, and even Most Perfectly Prior to) its "depth point" ("within"), rather than at any point (or in any sphere) "without". And, although many lesser (or ordinary) "purposes" and many lesser (or ordinary) "meanings" may otherwise be conceived or presumed, the Inherent (or Ultimate, and Great) "Purpose" of Existence Is to Realize (or Merely Be) Itself (or Its Self, or Its Ultimate, and, necessarily, Divine, Self-Condition and Source-Condition). And That Ultimate, Great, and Inherent "Purpose" Is the Source of the Ultimate (and, necessarily, Divine, and, necessarily, Divinely Self-Revealed) Way of Realizing the True and Real "God" (Which Is Truth, or Reality Itself).

I Am the Ruchira Buddha, Adi Da Samraj, the Da Avatar, the Realizer, the Revealer, and the Revelation of the True Divine Person, the One and Only and Divine Self-Condition and Source-Condition, Which, in the Great Tradition of mankind, Is What and Who has been everywhere called "God", but not, in general, "Known", In Truth, and In Reality, As the True and Real "God" (because, in most of the Great Tradition of mankind, the presumptions about "God" have been, and are, based on conditional, even egoic, and hierarchically lesser, or functionally subordinate, points of view, or points of view that are less than "God", and, effectively, separate from "God", or, in any case, not Perfectly One With "God" and Inherently Identical To "God").

The True and Real "God" Is Truth Itself, Reality Itself, the Self-Existing, and Self-Radiant, and One, and Only, and Absolute, and Inherently Perfect Self-Condition and Source-Condition of All and all. Therefore, I Say to every one and all, "consider" all of your views, all of your presumptions, all of your beliefs, all of your experiences, even all of your presumed "knowledge" (great or small). Examine all of that in "depth" (to the "depth point") with Me, even via My (now following) "consideration" of the total Great Tradition of mankind. And do this in a steady disposition of cooperation, tolerance, peace, forgiveness, compassion, love, and intelligent receptivity. And, by all of this, look to verify your own hierarchical nature, composition, and structure, and, thus and thereby, look to verify the hierarchical nature, composition, and structure of even all of conditionally manifested Reality. Do this, and be thereby changed in your mind, and in your feeling, and in your body, and in your actions, such that you are (and, as such, every one is) fully restored to integrity (in the body-mind), and Truly Restored to the Great "Purpose" (Which Is Eternally Senior and Eternally Most Prior to the body-mind and the "world").

The Mountain Of Attention, 1997

CHAPTER TWENTY-FOUR

December 20, 1996

You Can Always Go Deeper

*A*t the gathering of December 20, in responding to questions about waking, dreaming, and sleeping, Beloved Adi Da starts by summarizing the basic right understanding of these states and their significance relative to Spiritual practice.

ANIELLO PANICO: We have been discussing, during this gathering period, various states of waking, sleeping, dreaming. In the course of "considering" that, I have started to see that—obviously, or maybe not so obviously—waking and sleeping are the same state. But I have only a vague sense about the dreaming state being the same condition.

AVATAR ADI DA SAMRAJ: You said that waking and sleeping are the same state. Well, we would have to talk about that, of course. But even if they are same state, they are obviously two different states. In some sense, it's obvious that they're two different states.

On the other hand, as we've looked at the matter here, that same depth, which is otherwise found in deep sleep, is also the depth of the waking state. So, in that sense, yes, they are the same, or coincide.

You're not quite so certain about the dreaming state being coincident, is that it?

ANIELLO: Yes. The dreaming state seems like a state, whereas waking and sleeping seem like just fairly continuous events, even though they could be defined separately.

AVATAR ADI DA SAMRAJ: What's the difference between what you consider to be dreaming, and thinking, or imagining, or just letting the mind go at random, or following some memory or train of thought to the point of really not having much attention for the environment or the body any longer for a while? You know that, while in the waking state, you can enter into that depth that you otherwise know as (or that kind of experience that you otherwise call) "dreaming". In other words, you do resort to that same dimension of consciousness, or of conscious mind, in the waking state.

The same basic dimension of functional mind and experience can be entered into while otherwise remaining in the waking state. Although, usually, when you enter into a somewhat deeper state of a kind of dreamlike revery or interiorization, or otherwise into a depth of concentration, in the likeness of sleep, without any particular perceptions or concepts at the moment—whenever you become that kind of depthful in the waking state—coincident with that, the usual physical awareness becomes peripheral, both relative to the physical body itself and relative to its environment. The environmental perceptions also tend to relax.

In other words, these are rather interiorized states, you could call them. But you could enter into them rather directly, while otherwise remaining essentially waking-functional, and, generally speaking, aware of being bodily existing in the waking world. Really, everybody, at some time or other, does creative work of an interior kind, requiring concentration, imagination, whatever. So everybody does this. Some people do this rather constantly and even professionally. And perhaps it's especially those who in a unique way examine this or concentrate in it, who most fully show the sign that there's available in the waking state that same dimension of mind and experience that you otherwise call dreams, and a depth beyond that— which is the same, entered into in deep sleep. It is just that, generally speaking, there can't be a dreamlike or sleeplike depth entered into without physical awareness becoming diffuse, minimized, passively noticed.

But this is so, also, even when sleeping sometimes. You may have had the experience where you, otherwise asleep, suddenly become aware of somebody just saying something to you, or some sound, or something or other, and you were immediately physically attentive and functional. Did you notice that, in that instance, you had been asleep, but you had allowed the body-mind to remain open to the environment, even to its own sensations? You were right there available for it, so that somebody could just talk to you right then, even though you relaxed your sense of it to the point of becoming so diffuse you weren't even noticing it. There are still kind of extensions of that physical awareness, some sort of peripheral sensory devices somehow, such that if you were directly imposed upon somehow, communicated with somehow or whatever, you wouldn't be coming out of a deep place entirely away from the body at all. You would be immediately there. And yet that same depth of deep sleep was your experience, just as much as it is on some other occasion where the deepness of the sleep is associated otherwise also with something that happens in the physical and the mental, such that the body gets sort of inert and it feels groggy if you want to animate yourself or whatnot.

You can be in the deep sleep state and not be in that kind of (by comparison) deeply interiorized symptom that is often associated with deep sleep or getting up from deep sleep.

Likewise then, in the waking state itself, you can enter into a state of restful inwardness without any concentration, without any particular noticing of perceptual and conceptual happenings. And this can occur during the waking state, and you might even be moving about at the moment, or (at any rate) there's still some general sensory mechanism allowed to remain attentive there or remain in place there, such that you would once again integrate with ordinary physical and mental functional awareness in the next moment, or as required. You all know what I am talking about, don't you?

DEVOTEES: Yes.

AVATAR ADI DA SAMRAJ: So deep sleep is a kind of dimension of consciousness, awareness, experience, and so on, not to be too rigidly identified with some body of symptoms, or some group of symptoms. In other words, as I was just saying, the deep-sleep dimension of experiencing, of consciousness, conscious awareness, can be entered into even in the midst of the waking state. And, in the next moment, you are not thus concentrated and functioning in the usual way with the usual awareness again, but you don't feel groggy. The body didn't have to lie down.

You are prejudiced in your understanding of these three dimensions of fundamentally different kinds of awareness. You're prejudiced against understanding them rightly. You're prejudiced because of the secondary symptom-associations of these states that you experience day after day based on certain habits, on being habitual rather than someone who inspects everything, examines everything, "considers" everything.

Waking, dreaming, and sleeping are modes of conditional awareness. And there are fundamental differences between them, and yet (in the waking state) the dreaming state and the deep sleep state are simply experienceable as deeper dimensions of the waking state. You can experience them while in the waking state. In the dream state you do not have the waking-state experiencing. The physical is not noticed as in the waking state, not identified with as in the waking state. Nonetheless, the depth that is otherwise associated with the deep sleep experience in the daily cycle is the depth in the dream state. So there is the possibility of changing mind, environment, experience, in the dream state, because you can slip out of any context into sleep.

You have two options when the gorilla is after you in the dream state. You can wake up—startle yourself into physical awakeness, take a few deep breaths, and say, "Phew", like Mickey Mouse, you got away from him again. Or you can go deeper, or be deeper, or stand prior. In other words, there is that option in the dream state. In the waking state, you have the option of that depth likewise—not as deep, but deeper than ordinary waking—the dream-dimension option.

In the society and culture of the waking state, people, like the non-humans, go aside to Contemplate in various ways. People exercise—to varying degrees, of course—the depth-level of existence in the waking state. And so they touch into the domain that otherwise appears as dreaming, and, deeper than that, the domain otherwise experienced as sleeping, in the daily cycle, or profounder depths within those planes themselves. Whatever plane you enter into, you can go deeper. Whatever plane you go into, as "you" in the waking-state mode or in the dreaming mode, there is always the sleep (or depth) mode, no matter what. No matter what the experience, the in-depth mode is available. It is a "loophole" in this otherwise binding patterning-event in which everyone is just sort of going along rather intoxicated (it seems), and nobody knows what even a single thing is. There is no comprehension here. It is just games.

You are, in your functional mode in any moment, simply attention, or what we call "attention" associated with time-bound data—mental and perceptual. That is what you are, functionally, in any moment. But at the same time you are that, you are in the position to exercise discriminative intelligence and will relative to this pattern and this serves the purposes of the body-mind pattern, well or ill. But, in this apparent condition or circumstance, or any other potential of experience in any realm at all—whether it's good or bad, positive or negative—there's always the depth. You don't always have the option to wake up in the waking-state sense. But you can always go deeper.

This is primary understanding.

The Four Yanas of Buddhism

AVATAR ADI DA SAMRAJ: The possibility of going deeper is what the traditions of internal creativity and sacred activity are about—all the traditions of internal processes, the whole tradition of meditation and so forth, Samadhi, religion (therefore), and Spirituality and culture altogether. The positive cultural endeavor and social endeavor of human beings is not only associated with the three states (waking, dreaming and sleeping) but with modes of endeavor with which, or in which, everyone basically participates but some specialize in it, or do it more profoundly or more consistently or whatever.

Some, like artists of various kinds, specialize in associating with the waking and dreaming modes creatively. There are all kinds of human creativity that are associated with going deeper in the modes of mind and feeling and psyche, combining it with their examination of waking phenomena otherwise, and all the realism of mortality.

Some who are religious, of course, also go beyond the exoteric and social modes and so forth, go deeper than that, and enter into the domain of mysticism and such, and inner perceptual phenomena, including visions, and so on, in the modes of the fourth and fifth stages of life.

Others in the domain of religion, Spirituality, philosophy applied, exercise themselves profoundly relative to a depth greater than the planes of mind, or deeper than the planes of mind. Their exercises in depth extend into the domain of the sixth stage of life, the domain prior to mind and perception. Some meditate on that as a kind of end in itself. It is their taking of the in-depth position, as deep as it gets, the deep-sleep degree, and using it as a means to escape the waking and dreaming world of changes. They enter into the objectless mode of egoity.

In the Buddhist tradition, there are those who are called "arhats"— those who, as is usually said, pursue liberation for themselves and then achieve it. It is the liberation that is experienced by attending to the depth rather than what is less than the depth, and essentially retiring there, as the fulfillment of the self-effort, ego-effort, of seeking for release. It is that liberation which is realized upon entrance into the egoic domain of deep sleep—bare attention without subtle or gross objects, but nonetheless self-enclosed, self-aware, and excluding subtle and gross phenomena, by an act of will, inner tension.

Beyond that, it is possible to enter into the domain that is beyond deep sleep, beyond the unit of attention, the self-contraction in its causal mode. And those who enter into that greater depth may become firmly established thus, and then, in association with the waking-state associations, their expression, their Teaching (presuming they Teach) is in the mode of sixth stage "Sahaj Samadhi", or, otherwise, as demonstrated in the various modes of Mahayana Buddhist Enlightenment.

RODNEY GRISSO: Beloved, You were talking about the arhats. Is there a hierarchical relationship between them and the bodhisattvas?

AVATAR ADI DA SAMRAJ: Well, "arhat" is a term associated with what is called "Hinayana Buddhism", or "the Pali tradition", or "Theravada Buddhism". There the individual follows instruction, based on a search to be free from suffering, and eventually achieves that. There is no criticism of that within the Hinayana (or Theravada) Buddhist tradition.

In the Mahayana tradition, so called, you get the language of rivalry about this—a different kind of idealism, more readily associated with social-personality purposes for one thing, social religiosity and so on, more amenable to it than the more "monkish" and "nunnish" Hinayana tradition. So it's associated with some idealistic presumptions and so forth that were not emphasized perhaps as much in the Hinayana (Theravada) tradition.

Other modes of philosophy or modes of meditation and Realization are also associated with the Mahayana tradition, in which there are many schools, of course. There are three yanas among the historical Buddhist traditions. There is Hinayana (or Theravada), and there is Mahayana, and there is Vajrayana (or Tibetan Tantric Buddhism, in which there are many schools as well). And now there is Advaitayana Buddhism, or Ruchira Buddhism—the Way that I have Revealed and Given.

The bodhisattva is the idealized Realizer in the general Mahayana tradition. The arhat is, generally speaking, the idealized Realizer in the Hinayana tradition. So, from the point of the view of the Mahayana, of course—speaking argumentatively—the arhat ideal is not good enough.

BEN FUGITT: Because he should do something social to save people?

AVATAR ADI DA SAMRAJ: Yes. The general popularity of the bodhisattva is that he or she forestalls Enlightenment in order to work for the salvation of all beings—an altruistic point of view, as I said, more amenable to all the modes also of popular religiosity and social religiosity, more so than the more monastic tradition of the Hinayana (although it's not exclusively monastic, either—its history has associated with the lay community as well).

In the Mahayana tradition, a somewhat different point of view, generally speaking, is found. The Zen tradition, for instance, is within that Mahayana tradition. The point of view of the philosophy associated with meditation and Enlightenment is often, generally speaking, quite different than that in the Hinayana tradition. Buddhism, in general, is a tradition that's about the transcendence of suffering, but there is in the Mahayana tradition—philosophically, at any rate—less of an emphasis on the examination of suffering and going beyond suffering, and instead there's an examination of Reality Itself and a "consideration" of the modes of mind and so forth that are used as a basis for your presumptions about reality.

There's an expression in the Mahayana tradition, "naive realism", that's used to criticize the Hinayana tradition, which is expressed, at any rate, in the very ordinary daily-life realism sense: "Every thing is unsatisfactory ultimately. There is no ultimate satisfaction. Every thing is changing. Any thing that you can call your 'self' is a form of conditional arising. It's not a separate entity. It's part of a flow of changes." It's looking deeply at "everyday" (so to speak) experience, or experience as it is conventionally presumed to be being experienced by a physically based human.

The Mahayana tradition—speaking of its serious philosophical dimension and so on—doesn't merely take that daily point of view. It, in fact, examines that daily point of view. Much of the process of the Teaching and the meditation and practice and so forth is about just this examination of presumptions about Reality. In that process of philosophical "consideration", the point of view that is associated with Hinayana Buddhism is criticized, described in such terms as "naive realism"— "naive" meaning "not very profound". Rather than emphasizing the nature of bodily based human experience as being suffering and changing and so forth, there is instead the practice of in-depth techniques of abstraction, internalizing, internalized abstraction or depth-inwardness, and so forth. There are various kinds of practices you see in the Zen tradition as an example, and so on.

Then there is the Vajrayana (or Tantric) tradition of (generally speaking) Tibet. And if the Hinayana is, in some sense, associated with something of an ordinary realism of the first three stages of life (while also being ultimately impulsed to the sixth stage of life), and the Mahayana is more associated with the sixth stage "consideration", the Vajrayana tradition adds to this the kind of middle term of advanced fourth stage and fifth stage processes. Mahayana also adds a certain fourth stage dimension to the Buddhist tradition in its own fashion.

Thus, if you look at all of the yanas within the Buddhist tradition, the three historical yanas previous to My Revelation of Advaitayana Buddhism cover the span of the first six stages of life, generally speaking. I could point you to the various elements of the Buddhist tradition corresponding to different stages of life and so on, and you could see it as an entire tradition. Not that it was anywhere practiced as a whole, or everywhere practiced as a whole, anyway—some places emphasized one or the other of the three yanas and, therefore, the stages of life associated with them and so on.

Similarly, then, Advaitayana Buddhism, or the Way of the Heart, or Ruchira Buddhism, is the single Way that covers all of the stages of life, but not limited to the first six. The Way of the Heart, rather, includes all seven of the stages of life, the seventh being not merely a progression on the first six but specifically being the transcendence of each and all of the first six. This Way of Advaitayana Buddhism is a practice, a Way, that transcends the inherent limitations in each of the stages of life as the sadhana continues, and, likewise and directly, transcends the root-condition, or act, which is egoity itself, or the very one that would otherwise "develop" or "evolve", so to speak, through the six stages of life.

The process of the Way of the Heart is fundamentally the process in depth. And, all throughout the Great Tradition, that is the principle that is "taken advantage of", so to speak. It is the Law, the unique principle in the midst of conditional experiencing—the fact that there is a depth, and it is there in every present moment, to be entered into as you like. You can live in such a fashion that you cultivate that capability that is sadhana or the religious and Spiritual life because there is this depth—this whole vast domain, deeper than ordinary waking awareness, which is there to be explored, or (otherwise) examined and gone beyond, as in the Way of the Heart. And this depth is always there, no matter what realm, experience, condition, or whatever, of pain or pleasure or any mode at all of experiencing, waking, or dreaming, or (ultimately) even sleeping. There is a greater depth, and that is the Way of the Heart. That is the Heart.

To enter into the depth is always the option. Mankind, as well as the non-humans, has been exploring this for uncountable generations. There have always been people and schools and ashrams, groups, whatever, wherever, in whatever culture, who have persisted in this process. There are many traditions for it. They seem to contradict one another in various ways because they're all local to some then-known universe of associations. When any local tradition gets in conjunction with some other tradition it grew up without, that wasn't associated with it before, each of them has an integrity as a body of wisdom-communications, but they don't seem to fit, so they get into conflict and struggle with one another, each claiming to be <u>the</u> one. Neither one of them is the one—only the One is the one.

Whatever you brought out of your jungle, somebody else brought something else out of their bit of the jungle. The traditions are reflections of the "considerations" of people in the past. However reliably or unreliably transmitted through time, that's what they reflect.

In every generation there are many who examine this capability and mystery that is <u>depth</u>. Now, the human gathering of traditions going on for all so long has shown itself as a pattern of six stages of life and Realization, and I have proven this to you in *The Basket of Tolerance* by gathering books reflecting all of those traditions and showing you how it is so and what that is based on, what the structure of the human being and of psycho-physical experience is, and so on. And that's how come there <u>are</u> those six stages. They're all based on the psycho-physical pattern of progressively deepening experience, waking to dreaming to sleeping, and then beyond.

These experiences, experiments, reflected in the history of human cultures, even separate from one another, are still demonstrating the same fundamental categories of "consideration" and development, because the structure, the psycho-physical structure, of the human being is the same in people, even though they do not associate with one another historically (for a long period of time, at any rate), and then come to meet somewhere down the line.

Why are there the similarities? Because the same structure is there.

And why must the differences be overcome? Because there's only one structure there.

What Do You Like About Sleep?

BRIAN O'MAHONY: Beloved, the other day, after I left Your Company and went back to my office, I was feeling You very deeply and I lay down to take a nap because I felt tired all of a sudden, and I noticed that when I fell asleep I actually didn't feel like I was asleep. I felt like I was still aware and in Contemplation of You.

AVATAR ADI DA SAMRAJ: Did you have any peripheral awareness of the room and the body and so on?

BRIAN: I had a sense that the room existed but I wasn't aware of it.

AVATAR ADI DA SAMRAJ: Some sense that you were in a room persisted somehow throughout the experience?

BRIAN: Right, but then I would wake up and I wouldn't do what I'm automatically drawn to do, which is identify with the waking state. I would wake up and I would still be there, but passively just aware of the room, aware of what was going on, and I would slip back into the sleep again. I was actually conscious the whole time, and in deep Contemplation of You.

AVATAR ADI DA SAMRAJ: So you're suggesting you were in the deep sleep state and persisted in that for a bit even though waking-state associations appeared. There was a period there when you remained asleep and not "in" the waking state (so to speak) and aware of it in the usual fashion. That conjunction can be interesting, but that should suggest to you, show you, how it is otherwise the case that, when a certain basic depth is realized in meditation or in the process of sadhana, such that it fundamentally becomes established as a position of awareness—such that you don't adjust out of it when getting up from your seat and functioning otherwise—this produces a different kind of sensibility, awareness, sensitivity, understanding, and so forth than your daily experience. If that depth becomes Samadhi, even that Samadhi which is beyond deep sleep, and persists—in other words, becomes established such that you don't adjust out of it—then, all the more profound the sensibility, awareness, understanding, and so forth, in the conjunction with so-called "ordinary" phenomena.

This is how the seventh stage Awakening occurs, therefore. This depth of Communion with Me, self-forgetting Contemplation of Me without "difference", to the degree of Divine Depth, "Bright" Fullness—That entered into so profoundly that you do not adjust back, and, somehow or other, even if the conditions of conditional psycho-physical experience appear again (causal and subtle and gross altogether), there is no adjustment to it. There is simply Standing in the Samadhi beyond self-contraction, and this is the circumstance in which the seventh stage Awakening occurs. It is in that wide-open State and conjunction with phenomenal conditions that simply Recognizes what arises, rather than being reduced to what arises.

The conceit of the waking ego is to presume that everything internal altogether—and that includes, therefore, everything that has to do with dreaming and sleeping dimensions, or subtler and causal dimensions, of awareness—is just an aspect of the waking state, or of bodily existence.

DANIEL BOUWMEESTER: Subordinate.

AVATAR ADI DA SAMRAJ: Right. Nothing but that. It's utterly subordinate, and, therefore, you don't look to the depth for your understanding or your comprehension of Reality. You instead engage in waking-state pursuit of knowledge, in which the body is the principle, "difference" is the principle, separation is the principle. There's a taboo against the in-depth process and what that which is in-depth can also do or show as a sign in the levels that appear outward from it. In other words, the in-depth dimensions (or planes) can affect dimensions that are peripheral to it or expanding out from its position. So, a something concretized in the dream-mind dimension can become fulfilled in the gross dimension. And this is why True Prayer works. It's all patterns, and patterns within patterns.

There is this conceit of the waking state, or body-consciousness—that everything is a species of it, a species of gross phenomena, and, therefore, dreams are just basically a hash of mind-debris, just sort of floating around when you have no concentration, and deep sleep is just some sort of shut-off switch in the nervous system with some energies being recuperated in the frontal lobe or something. This is perhaps true enough, but the presumption is that that's all there is to it, that's all that's happening.

You must learn to be intelligent enough to take your experience seriously, to seriously examine it, and seriously examine these (if you like) even conscious and subconscious and unconscious levels of your experience.

In your depth, even now, you are mindless and bodiless. Mind can get added on—that's the subtle dimension, and that's where dreams can occur also. And body can be added on—that's the gross dimension, that's where the waking state experience arises. But those things don't always arise.

Even during the lifespan of the body, people typically spend something like a third of their time—whatever it is you do, it's a very big part of every day, generally speaking—in this sleeping state. You spend a <u>lot</u> of your time in that state. And whatever good it does for the body functionally and so forth, what good does it do <u>you</u>? Why do <u>you</u> want to go to sleep? What do <u>you</u> like about it? Because you are not the body. You never experience yourself to be the body, you just register thoughts and perceptions. You are attention registering the printout that is thoughts and perceptions.

To discover this is also another profound matter, like finding out, realizing, that there is always the in-depth position, no matter what state you're in.

Is that what sleep is about, then?

How many people are philosophers, or spend any time thinking about anything much profoundly? But everybody goes to sleep. How many chameleons "consider" the matter personally, very seriously, and wind up being Contemplatives? Or is it built in?

Your time in the causal dimension is built in, generally speaking. It's built in to the bulb. So also is dreaming and waking.

Everybody is experiencing these three conditions. But how many are wise? How many are Realizers? How many are examining and building upon the events in the depth-process? Most just pretty much go with the flow, it seems.

Ultimately, in the "Perfect Practice", the Way is not about thoughts and thinking and mind-patterns, or even internal perceptions (visions and auditions and all the rest). It's not about psycho-physical energy-phenomena, therefore. It's not about perceptions, or any kind of doings, therefore. It's not about the waking state <u>or</u> the dreaming state <u>or</u> the sleeping state. The "Perfect Practice" is Transcendental Yoga. It deals with the State that is <u>Prior</u> to waking, dreaming, and sleeping, and, therefore, most directly, immediately Prior to sleep, or to attention itself, the causal root.

That Transcendental Mode of the "Perfect Practice" covers the first two stages of the "Perfect Practice". Then there is the third stage of the "Perfect Practice", the seventh stage of life Demonstration, and it is beyond all. It is beyond inwardness and egoity, or the deep sleep state of the ego, or self-contraction. It is beyond "turiya", the in-dwelling Witness, Prior to waking, dreaming, and sleeping—Consciousness Itself, yes, but set apart from objects and attention itself. The seventh stage Realization is Beyond that.

ANIELLO: Is that also called "turiyatita"?

AVATAR ADI DA SAMRAJ: "Turiyatita" is a traditional term meaning "beyond the fourth". So I use it, taking it from the traditions. It can be used in the traditions to mean any number of things. I use it in a particular sense in the Way of the Heart, to refer to the seventh stage Realization. It is not secluded Consciousness, but Consciousness Standing Free, Self-Existing, Self-Radiant, Divine—not Transcendental (in the sense of being divorced from objects or experiential phenomena), but Recognizing all, Inherently. That is the seventh stage Sahaja Nirvikalpa Samadhi. Its unique Demonstration is that of Divine Recognition, and so it is associated with a spontaneously progressing process of Shining and Outshining. Ultimately, that Process becomes Divine Translation.

You Are Un-Enlightened by Habit

AVATAR ADI DA SAMRAJ: You must have had the experience some-
times of being <u>very</u> <u>sleepy</u>. Not right now maybe, but, in addition to
being just sleepy, you're not in the position where you feel free to
just get some rest. You feel like you have to stay awake, or maybe allow
yourself a couple of seconds, but then you have to get right on—that
kind of business. And so you really don't fully go to sleep. And you also
start to dream. And you wake up a bit and then you are sleeping and
then you're sort of peripherally aware of the room and then the dreams
come back, and you just rotate through all these. And yet you never
quite completely lose awareness of your physical condition in the waking
state. And yet you know the dreams and you know the sleep, too. You
know all three of these in such experiences, right?

DEVOTEES: Right.

AVATAR ADI DA SAMRAJ: You are all familiar with this, right? And that's
common experience.

You all, as devotees of Mine, meditate, and so, additionally, you have
even those kind of experiences perhaps sometimes in formal meditation.
Additionally, you can have all kinds of other in-depth processes, some related to the more peripheral personality—states of body and emotion and
mind and whatnot that you go through, go beyond, feel beyond, whatever,
work on that—but then beyond that, there is an in-depth process.

The process of Realization is not about making changes in the body-
mind or the waking state. It's not merely about that. That's not its principle. The Way is the in-depth process. It's the Way of the Heart. And the
Way is possible because, no matter what arises conditionally, there is the
in-depth—in the self-position, where you stand. You can enter into the
in-depth process any time—all the while you're alive, and under any circumstances at all. Therefore, you can do sadhana all the time.

The fact that conditions aren't ideal doesn't mean you cannot and must
not do sadhana. You're still obliged. You work to establish the optimum
conditions always, but even when they're not optimum, no matter what is
arising, you still have the fundamental Yoga to practice and it is practiced
at all times and in all circumstances, even of difficulties in life, including
the death process. You simply enter into the in-depth process.

In the death process, a breakdown occurs at the waking-state gross
level, but it becomes something like flotsam and jetsam. It's just sort of
junk on the water-top there, broken up, floating away, disintegrating. The

undersea there didn't even notice that little shipwreck. So if you remain in the depth, or (otherwise) freely enter into it, you thereby, and directly, transcend the limiting forces of conditional existence.

Of course, being egoically "self-possessed", self-contracted, ego-bound, you don't use your circumstance to advantage. You don't understand it altogether. So you bind yourself further through your searching mechanism—self-contraction resulting in seeking, and seeking going all kinds of directions. Eventually it becomes intolerable. Integrity has to be found, and a way to control and modify and, otherwise, go beyond the pattern that is carrying you, binding you, moment to moment. The way to do that must be persisted in, and, if lost, must be found again.

You know how it is in the waking state. You find it difficult to be completely relaxed, giving up all requirements of waking attention, or dreaming attention, or any attention at all. Simply feel Me, utterly self-given, more and more deeply. Well, you know how it is in the ordinary round, from day to day, hour to hour. How deep can you get about it? You get habituated, in other words, to being wound up significantly. You are a spring wound up, and you don't readily enter into any kind of a depth while in the waking state.

The bulb has built into it this pattern of dreaming and sleeping. If it weren't for that pattern, your tendency to be all wound up would overwhelm you altogether. So this is all built in there. There are rare cases, of course, of somebody who doesn't go into the symptomatic process of deep sleep—there are such people—but that doesn't mean that the in-depth process at the level of sleep doesn't happen, or isn't coincident with them, and isn't (one way or another) clocking their spring and compensating for it, up to a point, anyway. And so it is in every case—up to a point.

But experience does not become perfect waking, dreaming, and sleeping. The more you experience it, the more familiar you get with it, the more you find out about it, the less "up" you feel about it, the more depressed you get (in some sense), or bored.

You know how difficult it is when you first begin to try and adjust your legs to being able to sit cross-legged, at least for some period of time. That's just the physical. The entire psycho-physical structure is set up by you habitually and through all kinds of patterning that everyone is adapting to. There is not only physical patterning associated with your habits, there is patterning at every level (gross, subtle, and causal), into the depth (in other words) of the conditional personality. And so to take up a practice that is about entering into the depth of existence is to run counter to all the habit previous and all the generalized patterning of outward-directed social egos—all the complexities of mortal, stressful, this, that, and everything.

As I pointed out, you know how the legs are when you first want to train them to sit cross-legged or in some position they haven't been adapted to—they resist, they have to be stretched for a while, so you've got to work with them for a while and gradually the adaptation is made, if you do it properly. So it is with all the rest of the structure. It all has to go through a process of adaptation, re-adaptation, new adaptation. You are un-Enlightened by habit. To become Enlightened you must transcend habit, therefore. Your habits are what make you un-Enlightened, therefore—dis-eased. It's pattern, held in place by habit—as if by intelligent design, but it's just pattern. There's no intelligent inspection of it anymore. It's just habit.

ANTONINA RANDAZZO: Like a machine.

AVATAR ADI DA SAMRAJ: Yes. So you've got to transform the asana of the body-mind. It's not just a physical matter, it's a matter of the attitude of all the faculties.

Body, emotion, mind (or attention), and breath (or energy) have become, habitually, or by habit, in your case, in the waking state, associated with superficiality and, therefore, loss of association with the depth. That is your asana then, this superficiality of outward-directedness. So if you sit to meditate not only do your legs bother you, you're thinking and looking at your watch—when can you do something interesting, you know? [Beloved Adi Da laughs.] It's got to be readapted because it is habituated to something else.

A major or principal dimension of the disciplines in this Way—functional, practical, relational and cultural—is this transformation of the asana, the pattern of the body-mind, to change it from its habitual course into a light, Yogic pattern. Also, just by the very gesture of discipline itself, to cause a reflection back to you creates a self-reflecting or, if you like, biofeedback effect, which serves your self-understanding. But these disciplines extend into the depth that cover everything, including meditation and so on.

By persisting in it, you must accept the total range of practices, covering all aspects of your functional, practical, relational, and cultural life. If you do that and persist in it, then the asana of the body-mind is transformed. Its integrity is established by relating the personality to the depth, relating the process of the life to the depth process so that you're not merely outward-directed or limited to waking-state patterning that is superficial and even prevents you from entering into the depth.

By the time you're asleep it's too late to examine sleeping. So, I don't simply tell you, "See? Samadhi, Realization, is not in the waking state or the dream state. It's not in the sleep state, either. It is beyond these three, and, therefore, beyond the deepest dimension of these three, which is deep sleep. So, having told you that, I won't be bothering to give you any instructions while you're awake. Whenever you go to sleep each night, come and see Me in the Communion Hall, and I'll give you your instructions at that time. Because, in the waking state, you get all kinds of nonsensical questions, all based on absurdities of habit and patterning and misunderstanding and lack of inspection of reality and so forth. What kind of a sadhana can you base on that?" *[laughter]*

Of course, it can't be done that way. You cannot initiate your practice in the sleeping state. The matter is first of all even being "considered" only in the waking state. So it is approached from the waking state and you enter into the depth from there. You can enter into the depth of that realm which is otherwise experiencing dreams and you can enter into that depth otherwise experienced in deep sleep while in the waking state—in other words, in the intentional practice of this devotional meditation, Ruchira Buddha Bhakti Yoga.

Since the question only comes up anyway in the waking state, it's from here that you enter into the in-depth process, and the first thing you have to do is observe some rules—some things to do and things not to do. You must change your asana and even the pattern of breath and natural energy and so on, as a ground, a basis, for all of this.

So that's how it begins. And you must do it. You're not to waste your time on these. You take them as one whole pill and that's that. You live these disciplines. You're My devotee. And that's it. You approach Me intelligently. You examine all those things. You see the reasons for them. And you prove them by practicing them. And that's what you do. There's no faking it or trying to get off the hook. The process is in-depth. And you have to handle the do's and the don'ts, and the foundation pattern, and even the energy-and-breath pattern—in other words, yamas and niyamas, asana, pranayama,[38] foundation disciplines of devotional,

---

38. "Yama" and "niyama" are Sanskrit for "restraints" and "observances". Yamas are restraints, or the things one must control or not do. Niyamas are disciplines, or the things one must do. The practice of yamas and niyamas is the foundation stage of traditional Yoga. In the Way of the Heart, various yamas and niyamas are taken on to support the practice of feeling-Contemplation of Avatar Adi Da.

"Asana" is Sanskrit for bodily "posture" or "pose". (By extension, and as Avatara Adi Da often intends, "asana" also refers to the attitude, orientation, posture, or feeling-disposition of the heart and the entire body-mind.)

"Pranayama" is Sanskrit for "restraint or regulation (yama) of life-energy (prana)". Pranayama is a technique for balancing, purifying, and intensifying the entire psycho-physical system by controlling the

functional, practical, relational, and cultural self-discipline. That's what you adapt progressively to.

Every moment is associated with the feeling-stress of seeking. Instead of noting <u>that</u>, you are just motivated by the seeking self, the desires, or whatever; you <u>do</u> the seeking; you forget to examine the source of these motivations, these desires, therefore this seeking.

What <u>is</u> this disturbance?

If you were not ill at ease, you wouldn't be looking to feel better. So there is this doing, but it is a doing even in the depth. It must be rooted out there, ultimately.

Hearing is the capability to do this, found first in the waking state, and, thereafter, because it is a fundamental, or most fundamental, capability, it can be exercised, and is to be exercised, in all the stages of life to follow, and in all the states (waking, dreaming, sleeping, and beyond).

In every moment, there is this fundamental sense of dis-ease, disturbance, that's behind any moment of seeking. And that thing is always the same, it always feels the same. So that's what I Call you to examine—not merely the search and how to make it work out better and so forth, by positive thinking and so forth. Of course, we cover everything about everything, but, fundamentally, I Call you to <u>examine</u> this. What are you doing? What are you always doing? What's the basis of this seeking? What is this dis-ease, this disturbance right now? That has you listening to Me right now because you don't feel completely Happy, and you hope that something I say is going to make you feel Happy, or advance you somehow relative to that matter very positively.

So you're seeking right now. And I'm Calling you right now to examine the disturbance, the dis-ease, the ill-at-ease feeling that's there in your central feeling sense of being, that emotion there. That's always there. That's what you're always experiencing. That's what's motivating you all the time. Every time you find another way to seek, to make that better, you try that too, and everything becomes that, and everything gets tighter and tighter, and always is seeking, therefore, for self-fulfillment, self-release, on and on.

<u>Why</u> this sensation? It's motivating you right now, to listen to Me right now, with the hope that something I'm going to say, the saying, the talking, the thinking, talking, whatever is going on here, is going to either

---

currents of the breath and life-force.

Yama, niyama, asana, and pranayama are the first four "limbs" of the "eight-limbed Yoga" ("ashtanga Yoga") of Patanjali, a great Indian Realizer of the second century. The other four limbs are pratyahara (restraint of the senses), dharana (concentration), dhyana (meditation), and samadhi (exalted states of consciousness achieved through inward concentration and meditation).

make you immediately completely Happy, or advance you in a process that's going to be about some breakthrough in this impasse, because you know by now (you're old enough to know) that you can't feel any better than you have already felt, and never once has it been enough. So that's just the way it's going to be, unless you can break through this limitation that you yourself manufactured.

Right now, you're listening to Me with this seeker's kind of feeling-attention. Notice this feeling you have, emotional sense you have, of dis-ease, ill at ease, anxiety, stress. It's <u>always</u> there.

<u>This</u> is motivating you in every moment.

Notice this is your own activity—this is hearing. When you can, in every moment, deal with the fundamental dis-ease that's motivating any kind of seeking, locate it and feel beyond it, then you enjoy the capability of true hearing. The Means to do this is as I've Given it to you—Ruchira Buddha Bhakti Yoga, in all of its explicit details, including everything of this exercise of the four leading faculties in the devotional Yoga, and everything of functional, practical, relational, and cultural self-discipline.

You have to deal with this dis-ease. But you can't work on it. So it's in your response to Me that you have the Gift of Means, by your Attraction to Me, exercised as a Yoga of all the four faculties. You inherently stand beyond the self-knot.

You apparently stand as separate attention, associated with some kind of apparatus of thoughts, or concepts and perceptions, and yet, in depth, the very same position where you stand, if you deepen there, there is yet more profundity. And it's not in the direction of the mind and the body. It's in the direction of the position where you stand, it's an intensification of the position in which you stand. Yet it's not "you", in the separate or concerned sense. It's just in that position where you and these concerns arise—this sense of you.

You identify this "you" with the contents of the printout—concepts and perceptions. That could be <u>any</u> concepts and perceptions. You can manipulate it in some mysterious way, but <u>it</u> does all the changing, calculating, providing content, by you making a nod with the will somehow, on a grid.

You comfortably exist, for some hours every day, in a state without body or mind in daily sleep. You, in fact, look forward to repeating that experience. By the time another day has run its course, you get to the point where you actually look forward to it, or you're anticipating it pleasurably. So you don't mind going to sleep.

But you draw the line about this death thing. You don't feel comfortable about that. But you feel comfortable about sleep. Well, maybe it's because it's familiar to you and you feel that death is not. And yet they amount to something like the same thing as a process, don't they? You're afraid that you're going to lose body and mind when you die, that you'll come to an end. And yet, every day, you happily, voluntarily give up your body and your mind to go to sleep. And, otherwise, you, as My devotees, in practicing meditation, in-depth exercises, do it in the waking-state time as well—enter into the depth.

That is your root-condition. The causal is the root. The sleep state is the root upon which dreams and waking-state phenomena are built. When you enter into the depth while awake, sleep is where you get to. You can go beyond that, but that's deeper than waking, and deeper than dreaming. There's no images, no mind-process, no thoughts. No thoughts and no perceptions, and yet a blissful, pleasurable experience without shape, without content otherwise. It's like the washing machine transfigured by the electricity coming out of the wall—sort of snoozing, woozing in it, luxuriating in the hum of energy, without need for content, or further differentiation, or complexity. And yet, when you are in the waking state, you fear just exactly those kinds of things, because they are the antithesis of the waking state, with which you are identifying at that moment. But, on the other hand, they are not utterly unlike the process of going to sleep.

In other words, you don't take your experience seriously enough. Or you "consider" matters always from the waking-state point of view, and you never take into account the rest of it.

I Am this Depth. And I Give you, as My Self, the Very Means to Realize this Depth.

I am Deeper than the deep sleep state, but to Realize Me is not merely a matter of going to sleep at night. You will do no sadhana there. It's a matter of collecting yourself in this devotion to Me, such that you enter into the depth in the waking state, ever more deeply, until, at some point, you become capable of the "Perfect Practice". In the "Perfect Practice", the practice is not in the domain of waking, dreaming, and sleeping. It is deeper than sleeping. The entire sadhana of the "Perfect Practice" takes place completely outside of the sphere of waking, dreaming, sleeping—in human or any other form. Those dimensions of process, of course, appear experientially in the case of a devotee during the period of his or her life when engaged in the "Perfect Practice" in its first stage and its second and all the while thereafter, in the third stage of the "Perfect Practice", or the seventh stage of life.

But the process itself is in the depth. So meditation practice, in the case of the "Perfect Practice", has nothing to do with the life of the body, the realm of the body—socially, culturally, or whatever. It has nothing to do with the mind, nothing to do with thoughts, nothing to do with visions, dreams, interior concepts, perceptions of any kind. It is a process, nonetheless, but it has nothing to do with working on any of those other dimensions, anything associated with the first five stages of life. It deals with the self-contraction, certainly, but only in the root (or causal) level, or depth. But the meditation of the "Perfect Practice" is not itself about anything to do with matters associated with waking, dreaming, and sleeping. It has nothing to do with the categories of experience, in those terms at all.

The process associated with the sixth stage of life is associated with the causal dimension, the causal depth, and, therefore, with deep sleep. The subtle dimension of functions, the general realm of mind—and that also includes the energy-dimension that's associated with the physical, the etheric*—is all associated with the same realm of functioning that is dreaming. And ordinary body-consciousness is as in ordinary waking experience, and all of its process of perception and conception.

All these three coincide. They are all in the same moment. "Turiya" is the state beyond the three. "Turiya" means "the fourth". The three are waking, dreaming, and sleeping, using this traditional language. "Turiya" is this traditional term, in other words—the fourth state, beyond waking, dreaming, and sleeping—for the domain of Consciousness Itself. The first two stages of the "Perfect Practice" are associated with that domain or process.

The seventh stage of life is beyond that. It is beyond the limitation of even that. So, to find a traditional term that relates to that, I have used the term "turiyatita", which means "beyond the fourth". The fourth state is that which is beyond waking, dreaming, and sleeping. "Turiyatita" is beyond even that one. It's not concretely referring to anything. There simply are no limitations in the view of the seventh stage Awakening.

Sixth stage processes, fundamentally, address the causal dimension of experience, and that is associated with the root of mind, which is attention itself, just as in deep sleep, and the root-sense of separation, relatedness, and "difference", but in a rather diffuse condition at the core, such that there is even a Depth beyond that that can be found. But that requires the transcendence of the knot of sleep itself.

Before there is body-consciousness, before there are concepts, perceptions, before there is mind, there is this self-consciousness. Now,

325

what is there when it enters into its own Depth, Where it Stands? That is What is to be Realized—That Which is in the Depth. That is always the direction of your devotion to Me.

I am the Means of that, the Way, the Pattern of it. I Am the One you are to Realize. That is not a metaphor for saying it's a matter of realizing what is within you, ultimately. It is not in you, at all. I am not in you, you are in Me. Not merely in the sense that the people you see in your own dreams are arising in you, because that would mean no one else here in the room is conscious but Me, in the functional, ordinary human sense— in other words, you are inert. But you are not inert. You are in Me, as Me. This same Reality is your Condition, but it is not in you, it is not a separate attribute of you. I am not a metaphor for you. You must surrender and forget yourself in Me, not take Me to be any vision, idea, or metaphor for something in yourself.

So the Way I have Given you is the real process of Realization. You must embrace it as Given, however—not just comb through it Chinese-menu style and pick your own "Way" out of it, modify it and change it about and make yourself the principle of it, and all the rest. That's not it! Only the Way exactly as I have Given it is the process. That's what you must find out by study and you must persist in it, by real and right practice.

If you are truly practicing this devotional Way, then meditation is a profound (and also profoundly interesting) process for you. And there's no way you'd be looking for excuses not to be doing it. The same with the disciplines that provide you the asana, the base, the structure wherein this meditation can take place. You would not find that something to be taken casually, or to be picking and choosing about. It would not be uninteresting to you, it would not be something you would be trying to avoid. It would be very interesting to you.

You can, by fulfilling My Instructions at the foundation, transform your life, or have your life become, in that process, transformed from its characteristics karmically or in the pattern of ordinariness, of ordinary destiny and so forth—from all of that, whatever it was in your case—into a truly sattvic, Yogic vehicle for the process of Realizing Me. Your life, your psycho-physical manifestation, your heart-response to Me is your response in depth—the fact that you are discriminative intelligence and will in the pilot seat there, or wherever, sitting in front of your laptop computer.

That response to Me, and right exercise of discriminative intelligence and will in response to Me, is the means whereby you, by fulfilling your responsibilities in this Way, transform your ordinary karmic adapted life into a sattvic Yogic vehicle, a sattvic vehicle for Yogic exercise. And then, in the process, it will have reflected you to yourself, in all of your pattern-adaptations and so forth, served your self-understanding and refining of the practice altogether.

Now, if you're doing that, you're not just going with the flow. Instead, you're doing something interesting. To really live this Way as I have Given it to you is interesting. I don't mean it's gleeful, cultist "fascinating". I mean it's really <u>interesting</u>. It's a <u>profound</u> matter. It's not boring at all.

The Mountain Of Attention, 1996

CHAPTER TWENTY-FIVE

God Is The Deep Of the world

THE HEART OF THE DAWN HORSE TESTAMENT OF THE RUCHIRA BUDDHA,
CHAPTER SEVEN, VERSES 1-3, 26-34, 37-45

1.

"Consider" This. True Religion, or The Real Spiritual, Transcendental, and Divine Way Of Life, Begins With The Transcendence Of Awe and Wonder. Conditional Existence Naturally Evokes Awe and Wonder (and Even Terrible Fear and Stark Bewilderment), but True Religion, or The Real Spiritual, Transcendental, and Divine Way Of Life, Begins With The Free Heart-Response To What Is (Otherwise) Awesome and Wonderful.

2.

Therefore, True Religion Does Not Begin With a belief About God. It Begins When You Truly (and Most Fundamentally) Understand (and Feel Beyond) The Contraction Of The Heart (or The self-Protective, self-Defining, and self-limiting Recoil Of the body-mind From the Apparently Impersonal and Loveless forces Of conditional Nature).

3.

God Is Obvious To The Free (or selfless) Heart. Only The Heart (Free Of self-Contraction) Can "Locate" (or See) and Realize The Divine Person.

26.

God Is Not <u>The</u> <u>Maker</u> Of conditional Nature.

27.

God Is The Unconditional Nature (or Most Prior Condition) Of conditional Nature.

28.

God Is Not Merely The Cause Of all causes and all effects.

29.

God Is The Source and The Source-Condition Of all causes and all effects.

30.

God Is Not The Objective Source and Source-Condition Of all causes and all effects.

31.

God Is The (Perfectly) Subjective Source and Source-Condition (or Self-Condition) Of all causes and all effects.

32.

God Is Not Outside You.

33.

God Is Not Within You.

34.

God Is You (Perfectly Prior To Your Apparently objective conditional self, and Perfectly Prior To Your Apparently subjective conditional self, and, Therefore, Perfectly Prior To Your Total, Complex, and Merely Apparent conditional self).

37.

God Is The God (or The Truth and The Reality) Of Consciousness Itself.

38.

God Is The God (or The Truth and The Reality) Of Inherently Perfect Subjectivity.

39.

God Is Not The God (or The Implicated Maker) Of conditional Nature, Separate self, and All Objectivity.

God Is The God (or The Truth and The Reality) Of Consciousness, Freedom, Love-Bliss, Being, and Oneness.

40.

God Is Not The God (The Cause, The Doer, or Even The Victim) Of Un-Consciousness (or mere causes and effects).

Therefore, God Is Not The God Of Bondage, Un-Happiness, Death (or Separation), and "Difference".

41.

God Is The Subject, Not The Object.

42.

God Is The Inherent Unity Of Being.

43.

God Is The Integrity, Not The Cause, Of the world.

44.

God Is The True Source, The Very Context, The Real Substance, The Truth-Condition, The Very Reality, The Most Native Condition, and The Ultimate Self-Domain Of all conditions, all causes, and all effects, For all that appears Comes From God (but In God, and Only As God).

45.

All "things" Are the media of all "things", but God Is Not The Maker, For God Is Like A Hidden Spring Within the water's world, and God Is Prior Even To Cause (and every cause), and God Is The Self-Domain Of Even every effect, and God Is The Being (Itself) Of all that appears.

Therefore, God Merely Is, and Is Is What Grants every appearance (every being, every thing, every condition, and every conditional process) The Sign Of Mystery, Love, Bliss, and Joy.

Yes, God Is The Deep Of the world, and The Heart Of every Would-Be "I".

CHAPTER TWENTY-SIX

The Deep of Consciousness Itself

FROM *THE ADIDAM SUTRA*

The Adidam Sutra (On the Way of the Infinite Heart-Brightness That Inherently Outshines the ego-"I" and All the Illusions of Separateness, Relatedness, and Difference) *is one of Avatar Adi Da's Source-Texts. Just as* The Dawn Horse Testament Of The Ruchira Buddha *is His fully detailed Revelation of the entire process of the Way of the Heart (or Adidam),* The Adidam Sutra *(which literally means "the Discourse on Adidam") is His summary description of the same complete process in a single extended Essay. In this reading (section XVII of the Text), Adi Da Samraj expounds with great potency His Argument relative to the self-contraction, conveying the deep understanding and transcendence of self-contraction (in its root-form as the feeling of relatedness) that characterizes practice in the context of the sixth stage of life in the Way of the Heart, culminating in the most perfect seventh stage Realization.*

The feeling of relatedness is not itself (or merely) an idea (or a concept in mind).

The feeling of relatedness is an activity.

The feeling of relatedness is the primal or first activity, and, therefore, it is the cause and the pivotal referent of all subsequent activities (including the activities of mind).

The feeling of relatedness is the activity of self-contraction, which effectively causes all subsequent activities (including the effort not to act).

The feeling of relatedness (or the self-contraction) becomes (or is reflected as) the presumption (or idea) of the separate "other" and the presumption (or idea) of the separate "I".

The presumption (or idea) of the separate "I" (or the ego-"I") does not arise independently, but it always, necessarily, and inherently arises coincident with the presumption (or idea) of the separate "other" (related to the separate "I").

Therefore, egoity (or the ego-"I") is not merely or originally an independent entity, category, idea, perception, or experience, but it is the primary consequence of the uninspected feeling of relatedness.

The ego-"I" does not exist outside the context of relatedness.

The ego-"I" is relatedness (or the sign of relationship, rather than of an original entity existing prior to relatedness and relationship), but the ego-"I" (which is self-contraction, and, therefore, self-contracted, or avoiding relationship) is inherently ambivalent toward relatedness itself and every specific kind or context of relationship.

The ego-"I" is "Narcissus", or the self-bondage that results from self-contraction (or the flight from the "other").

The ego-"I" is not a beginning but a necessarily un-Happy result.

The ego-"I" is, simply, a reaction to the implied "other" (or the presumed and otherwise experienced object or context of relatedness) in any moment, and there is no ego-"I" (or separate self idea) without (or except as) a reaction to the implied "other".

The separate "I" and its "other" are not inherent categories of existence.

Rather, the separate "I" and its "other" (in any moment) are added to (or superimposed upon) existence as (or by) a reaction to the conditional perception of existence.

Once this reaction (or self-contraction) is generated, suffering (or every form of contracted existence, or contraction from the Native or Always Already Given Condition of Transcendental and Inherently Spiritual and necessarily Divine Self-Existence, or Perfectly Subjective Being Itself) inevitably follows.

Therefore, egoity (or the suffered drama of the separate "I" and its separate "other") is a disease (even an imaginary disease, since it is self-caused, unnecessary, and self-contained).

The fascinating "I" (separate, independent of any "other" and the process of relationship) is the ultimate psychological and philosophical Illusion.

There Is no separate "I".

Therefore, there Is no separate "other" (or any condition that is separate from "I", since the separate "I" is itself an Illusion).

The separate "I" and the separate "other" are (moment to moment, and in any moment) presumptions (or ideas) generated by a feeling-contraction (or an unnecessary and generally uninspected reaction to

333

the conditional perception of existence).

Therefore, the imaginary disease that is egoity can be transcended, if self-contraction (in its progression, or "Circle", of forms, and, ultimately, in the form of the feeling of relatedness itself) is thoroughly observed, and Relinquished (even Most Perfectly) in its Perfectly Subjective Source.

If the separate "I" and its separate "other" are Most Perfectly Relinquished (or Most Perfectly transcended), so that the complex presumption of separate "I" and separate "other", or the feeling of relatedness itself, is transcended (and is not superimposed on what otherwise arises, or on what is otherwise perceived conditionally), then what arises?

If conditions arise, but no separate "I"-"other" feeling is added to what arises, then what arises?

It is not that, in that case, there are no perceptions of conditions, but all conditions (including the perceiving body-mind) are Comprehended (or Most Perfectly Felt) prior to the self-contraction and its "I"-"other" structure of feeling, perceiving, and presuming.

Therefore, if the separate (and separative) "I"-"other" presumption is not added to what arises, what arises appears only As it Is, or Inherently Free of the feeling-concept of inherent separateness (or "difference").

This Unique and Original Freedom may be likened to the perception of waves from the point of view of the ocean (as compared to the perception of waves from the point of view of any single wave).

If any conditional pattern In What Is becomes a point of view (or the point of view) Toward What Is, then What Is ceases to Be Obvious, and the pattern merely perceives itself (separately, or "differently", over against all other patterns).

If the separate "I" becomes the point of view, then the "other" is everywhere multiplied and perceived, and only the stress of the separate "I"-"other" confrontation is experienced and known.

However, if the separate conditional point of view is transcended, and What Is (Prior to it) becomes the Disposition In Which all conditions (including the perceiving body-mind) are observed, then the pattern of conditions is no longer a problem, a dilemma, or a confrontation of "one" (or the separate "I") against an "other", but the pattern of conditions is an inherently problem-free totality (or an open sea of motions).

In the totality thus perceived, there is no separateness, even if manifold complexity is (apparently) perceived.

There are no separate waters in the sea, but every wave or motion folds in one another on the Deep.

Such is the Disposition of the seventh stage of life.

In the seventh stage of life, whatever arises conditionally (including the conditional body-mind) is Divinely Recognized <u>As</u> it <u>Is</u> (or In and Of and As Self-Existing and Self-Radiant Consciousness Itself, Which Is the Deep Ocean of all apparent events).

In the seventh stage of life, whatever otherwise (or from the conventional, or psycho-physical, point of view) appears to arise separately (as body-mind, or "I", or "other", or "thing", or even the feeling of relatedness itself, or the feeling of "difference" itself) is Divinely Recognized In and As Consciousness Itself (or That Which Always Already Exists As One and the totality).

Therefore, in the seventh stage of life, the feeling of relatedness, or the feeling of "difference", or the ideas of separate "I" and separate "other", or the activity of self-contraction itself, or all suffering (or problem, or dilemma), is not the point of view (nor the result of a separate point of view), but the (apparent) feeling of relatedness, the (apparent) feeling of "difference", the (apparent) ideas of "I" and "other", the (apparent) self-contraction, and all (apparent) suffering register only on the Deep of Self-Existing and Self-Radiant Consciousness Itself.

In the seventh stage of life, the feeling of relatedness (or, Ultimately, or Most Simply, the most tacit feeling of "difference") Is Divinely Recognized, Inherently Transcended, and, Most Ultimately, Outshined In the Perfectly Subjective Feeling of Being (or Love-Bliss Itself).

In the seventh stage of life, all conditions (or all motions, or patterns, or waves of Spirit-Energy) Are (each in their moment) Divinely Recognized On and In and As the Deep (or Self-Existing and Self-Radiant Consciousness Itself, or Perfectly Subjective Being Itself), and That Divine Recognition Is Itself a Force (or "Bright" Vision) That Progressively Outshines the Play of motions (or the apparent modifications of the Self-Existing and Self-Radiant Shine of Love-Bliss).

Therefore, Deep Recognition Realizes Only Self-Existing and Self-Radiant Love-Bliss where the conditional patterns of merely apparent modification rise and fall in their folds.

At first, this Realization Shines in the world and Plays "Bright" Demonstrations on the waves.

At last, the "Brightness" Is Indifferent (Beyond "difference") In the Deep, There Where Primitive relatedness Is Freely Drowned, and, When "Bright" Recognition Rests Most Deeply In Its Fathomless Shine, the Play of motions Is Translated In Love-Bliss, Pervasive In the Water-Stand, and, like a Sea of Blankets, All the Deep Unfolds To Waken In the Once Neglected (Now Un-Covered) Light of Self-Illuminated and Eternal Day.

The Mountain Of Attention, 1996

CHAPTER TWENTY-SEVEN

December 24, 1996

How Far Away Is Your Body?

On December 24, the annual celebration of Danavira Mela (which culminates on December 25) is in full swing. Danavira Mela (Sanskrit for "the Feast [Mela] of the Hero [Vira] of Giving [Dana]") is one of seven major celebrations that are observed by Avatar Adi Da's devotees each year; each celebration is devoted to honoring a certain aspect of Avatar Adi Da's Life and Work. In this December Feast, His devotees celebrate Adi Da Samraj as the Supreme Divine Giver.

The primary event that is occurring at the gathering of December 24 is the beginning of an exchange of gifts between Adi Da Samraj and His devotees, an event that will continue over the next two days. This joyous ceremony of gift exchange, full of delight and humor, is also an occasion for Avatar Adi Da to further His "Considerations" of this gathering period and to bring them to a point of conclusiveness.

Devotees are gathered with Adi Da Samraj not in His office but in the spacious entryway to the Manner of Flowers, which is full of the unique form of decorations that have been developed for this celebration, based on traditional Christmas decorations. Adi Da starts with a further development of the "consideration" of perception.

AVATAR ADI DA SAMRAJ: What you are experiencing now as your passing thoughts, your perceptions of the room, is similar to your observations of the stars if you look in the evening sky on a night. You see the stars, but you are not "seeing the stars", so to speak, as they are at this moment. It took the light however many light-years to get to the position of you being able to notice it with your eyes. Well, likewise, your eyes noticing it is another thing that takes time—from the eyeball surface to "you" being aware of it.

So, when you look at the stars you are seeing them as they were—in their various different distances. When you are observing thoughts or perceptions, likewise, you're noticing some things as they were, not as they are now. You're always looking at a product of space and time in the form of thoughts and perceptions. So "you" are at a certain distance from your eyeball's perception of a star, just as a star is at a certain distance in time and space from your eyeball.

You are seeing the stars as they were. You are seeing thoughts and perceptions of whatevers that were. So if you measure the time from the event to the perception or the concept, it suggests that you are at a significant distance from the body—or at least from the standing-there-in-the-room or sitting-there-on-your-chair place. You're at that distance from the point of the perception. Maybe "you" appear to be at a different distance from each thought, each perception, depending on its associations somehow—just as each of the stars appears as it was at a certain moment but each of them is at a different distance from you.

So all of them are at a different moment, actually, from one another than they appear to you at your point in space and time. And so your thoughts and perceptions are like stars in the heavens there. They took time, in space, in energy, for you to notice them, to be a position to notice them.

So where are you, then? And where is the body, anyway, to begin with? It's all in this mystery of space-time, which is contemplated in the realm of contemporary physics just as it may be contemplated profoundly by anyone at all, by any number of means. It's still contemplation of the same thing, fundamentally, whatever other "blah-blah" everyone adds to it.

Everyone is involved in a "consideration" of the Nature of Reality. Everybody wants to find out about this. You needn't go to the scientific laboratory to "consider" it seriously. I'm "considering" it seriously with you right now.

We began this conversation when looking at some paintings on the wall. That is all about perceiving an image, which is, as a physical form, a certain distance from your eyes. But the distance otherwise suggests a space of mind, and physical space, a paradoxical space, generated by your participation in perceiving the image.

The surface of paint being perceived by your physical eye is at a certain distance. Based on the speed of light, it took a certain amount of time for the perception of that image to travel across the space between you and the painting. It's a minute <u>amount</u> of time, just as it's a small distance in space, but it <u>is</u> an event in time and space. It's not "<u>now</u>". Because it is an event—it took time for the light to travel that distance from the painting surface to your eye.

Well, likewise, having come to the surface of your eye as an initial physical image, then it took another micro-bit of time in energy-space, before "you" were able to notice it. That suggests another very particular distance.

So, your eye is at a certain distance from the surface of that painting and "you" are at a certain distance, a perception's amount of time away, from the surface of your eye. Now, even in micro-seconds, it suggests a significant difference.

So perhaps it is possible to determine where you are by measuring these timings of perceptual and conceptual events. If you make proper calculations, we should be able to find you <u>exactly</u>. *[laughter]* We should be able to find the length of time for perceptions and thoughts to pass to your awareness, and what this suggests in terms of distance, and where that would be—at a relative distance of how many thousands of miles interior to the body-mind? *[with dramatic emphasis]* And where <u>is</u> that?

If you pinched your skin (or if your skin were pinched by any means) the time it takes you to perceive that it is pinched, such that you could indicate you feel it—how long does that take? Well, however long that is, suggests how far away "you" are from the site of the pinch.

So perhaps you can, by making a number of measurements of perceptions or events such as that, find a general basic distance from "you" to the body-mind. If we could find <u>that</u>, and send a spaceship to it and interview you there, wouldn't it be amusing?

DEVOTEES: Yes, definitely.

AVATAR ADI DA SAMRAJ: So, where, even in dimensional space, are "you"—relative to this physical room? Making some of these calculations, we'll be able to locate you, perhaps, sometime. But so far it looks like you're somewhere near Minneapolis.

The Arising Doesn't Know About Itself

AVATAR ADI DA SAMRAJ: There is an immense totality beyond thought-comprehension. But human beings are primitives in all of this, sort of leaping up and down and making gestures, and scratching little things on flat surfaces with things that leave traces. Trying to "figure it all out".

It's remarkable—the complexity of the "you" that's sitting there, in the midst of this complexity of Totality altogether, and you don't <u>know</u> about anything! How could everything get so complicated for everything and everybody, and <u>nobody</u> knows <u>anything</u> about it?! No kind of form or being that arises seems inherently to know about anything. So how could the totality, even of beings—but the whole <u>immensity</u> of the totality of everything, even beyond comprehension—<u>arise</u> before there is any comprehension of it all on the part of anything that arises?

The arising doesn't know about itself. Now, how could it all be so intelligent, therefore, so unified, "systematic" (so to speak, in some sense) and yet never have been known? How could it be known only at the end, after the process of getting to know about it becomes knowledge (eventually, one hopes, complete)? But how could the thing, which is itself so complex that only knowledge can comprehend it, already exist before there is any knowing and comprehending of anything by anyone or anything at all?

Even in the totality of the arising process itself there is no such comprehension. It is not a thinking machine. But how could it be so complex that only thought (super-thought, even) could make it? It seems that the knowing of it has <u>nothing</u> to do with the making of it—just as it is for you now, sitting here with all this concern about yourself as the body, and you didn't do the first thing to make the body, to make it appear. You're not doing anything now to operate the body in its fundamentals. It's just happening. What do you have to do with it? You're just some sort of awareness associated with will and discriminative intelligence noticing the printout of thoughts and perceptions, and relating to that.

What are all these things, anyway? What is a "What are all these things, anyway"? It's just shapes, making shapes, being in a flow of shapes, a sea of shape and shaping, pattern patterning. What is its meaning?

It doesn't have any meaning in any ultimate sense, if you examine it. You get closer and closer to its root-source. When you get to that point, it's not that you have gotten an answer. It's that the question is transcended, the problem is transcended. The problem, the search, comes from an uninspected act of miscomprehension of your situation, of the "you" and "your" to begin with.

Do you think there's anything personal about <u>any</u> of this <u>whats</u>oever? That's why I say in the Mama Form, "Your objections to <u>any</u>thing don't mean shit!" Well, everything that is specifically you, apart from whatever else that may not be that, is a "you" presumption that wants to persist. So that's a kind of "objection" in the midst of things, you could say. In other words, any notions you have of the importance of "you" don't mean shit. And, if that's the case, then do you think this entire process of arising conditions has anything to do with "you"—with any "you"—at all? Because, when it comes down to it, there isn't even the slightest fraction of anything that's a "you", in the case of any "you" at all that survives anything, or that is treated with sacred respect. Everything gets "done". It's always been so. It doesn't have anything to do with you in the form of any "you" or collections of "you's" at all. And if it's something not about that, you're just misinterpreting it because of presumed position based on a non-inspection of reality, or misapprehension of reality—same thing.

You can actually inspect experiencing and so forth, as we do in our "considerations" together. It's not as you conventionally presume—not your experience, not Reality altogether. You go on saying in your speaking and presuming day-to-day that Reality is such-and-such, but if you examine it, it is not so. And it's perfectly plain to you that it's not so, whenever we examine matters.

So conditional existence has nothing to do with you at all. But human beings seem to presume that it <u>must</u> have something to do with them!—as they presume themselves to be. But it's always running counter to the way things are. And if you examine your presumptions about the way things are, you find it's not at all the way you presume (as a matter of convention) things are. When people presume things are whatever, as a way of convention, what does it mean, anyway? What have they thought about? What have they "considered" about anything at all?

Well, why should so-called ordinary people be required, for the sake of their association with Truth, to go through the process and everything required for its Realization, on the part of a great Realizer or a Saint-Realizer, of one degree or another? If that were so, then Truth would have no practical significance whatsoever. It would be, in other words, basically, not applicable to humanity, generally speaking. But, of course, you all presume that Truth has to do with you—as humanity, generally speaking—and that could be <u>totally</u> <u>wrong</u>! *[laughter]*

Did you see any concern in the realm of conditional experience (life and death and so on), for the perpetuation of any pattern, form, person, "you", at all?

DEVOTEES: No.

AVATAR ADI DA SAMRAJ: Well, don't you think it's important to <u>notice</u> this?—so that you don't go about "living", so to speak, based on a wrong presumption about it.

I mean, one way you could do it is get up out of your birthhouse, you know, *[enthusiastically]* open the door, and *[cheerfully whistles several bars]*. You know what I mean? *[enthusiastic falsetto]* "Wooo-woohee!" Flyin' out the door and out into the great world, to abide there, enjoy yourself there for eternity—which is a huge, immense, lot of endless time. It never stops. It's just great, though, for-<u>ever</u>—you know what I'm talkin', baby? You know? That's it. *[whistles briefly, then sings:]* Zippity-doo-dah! You know, for-EVER!

That's one way to go out the door from your birthhouse. Totally right-on, in a certain kind of a world. Is this one of those kind?

DEVOTEES: No, it doesn't seem to be.

AVATAR ADI DA SAMRAJ: No. And it seems like the proper time to find this out is when you're in your birthhouse—given this, found this out, however, with all the Wisdom, rightness, and so forth, required.

But it should be observed that everything that arises disappears, including every lifetime, every person, every body, every thing, every process, every event, every acquisition, every accomplishment—<u>everything</u>. And there's no absolute predicting, it's just that, on the average, things will go on for such and such period of time, whatever that measure means, but it's not even guaranteed.

It's really a <u>lousy</u> <u>line</u> of washing machines—you know what I mean? In some sense, if the "you" is the principle of it, or "I" (in other words, the self-concerned entity) is about reality, then that ought to be reflected in the conditions to be observed. And any objections on the part of a self-concerned entity, any demands it has relative to its own point of view, any expectations (hopes, even, in some sense), ultimately, it's all ended. And it's always changing, unpredictable, and so forth.

So, that's the line of goods you're associated with in this conjunction at the moment. Well, it doesn't sound like that's about *[cheerful whistling]*—out the door, you know what I mean? Forever, "Zippity-doo-dah, oooh-eee!" You know? It sounds like something else is appropriate.

But what is it? <u>What</u> is appropriate? When exactly are you prepared to go out the door, then? What is this all about? Don't you think there ought to be some very fundamental education?

But, generally speaking, mankind isn't giving any fundamental education, or ordering itself collectively in a way that's based on a fundamental right education. Everybody becomes part of a "let's go on and do it" life, a mummery, because there's no comprehension of what it's all for, what it's all about. It's just a babble, a meaningless drama, a—zap!—passing end in which everyone in it smiled and waved and disappeared. For <u>what</u>?

I'm not saying that reality is hopeless, in despair. I'm just saying it should be looked at. This should be a fundamental something you do. Examine this—the "for what?", the "what's it all about?" Reality education in <u>this</u> sense—not the "street" sense, so to speak, but this perpetual education in the understanding of reality in the conditional sense, and right participation in it, and the process of Realizing Reality in the ultimate sense—should be a fundamental ongoing "consideration" of human beings in their individual and collective association.

So you can just go with the flow and be part of the mummery of uncomprehending existence, or you could enter into the in-depth "consideration" or process or sadhana in which not only the reality or nature of conditional existence but the Nature of Reality in the ultimate sense is Realized. Don't you think?

Well, in My "Consideration" with you, not only over this last quarter-century but even in recent months—summary looks at some things—all this suggests a very curious and profound Reality to be Reality. You're all rather mechanistic and nineteenth-century-ish about things, though. And, no matter how profoundly the "consideration" I put to you, you still tend to think in terms of "matter" and "body", and all this kind of sludgy conventional-realism kind of stuff.

Anybody who's been to public school (or just gone to whatever school was available in their early lives) knows that matter is energy and that there are different levels of physical phenomena. There's the gross (or physical) or (in the bodily case) cellular level, and below that there's the molecular dimension of processes, and below that an atomic one. And this is all "common knowledge", so to speak. And yet, where is the culture that is based on such a presumption? The culture of it takes the form of some of the stuff of amusement, or the ordinary business of life, but it doesn't take the form of a culture of presumption—a culture itself. There <u>is</u> no core culture to it. In the very time in which these conceptions of reality are commonplace, there is no core conception of fundamental culture.

Even if you <u>are</u> the body, the body is energy, light. And, at its root-depth, before it is undifferentiated, it is atomic, you could say (to use a common concept of the day). And its little particles are, themselves, nothing but a certain kind of twist of energy floating around in a some-thing like what you call "space". And you would have to be the space as well as the particles, too.

But maybe there's no "you" about it. Your self-concern is a reflection of the depth which, when entered into most profoundly, is found, ulti-mately, to not be about any "you" at all. And if <u>it</u> is not about any "you" at all (then, when Realized Most Ultimately), why is it about any "you" at all now? And yet, this is not negative, if understood correctly. It is, if entered into deeply, a profundity that is profoundly liberating.

An Address to the Annual Meeting of the Transgalactic Society of Somnambulists

*H*aving been up late for many nights of the past month, the devotees gathering with Adi Da Samraj are having difficulty staying awake. Finally, the collective nodding off has become almost comic—no one is staying awake long enough for Adi Da to conduct a coherent "consideration".

AVATAR ADI DA SAMRAJ: Is this the annual meeting of the National Lampoon Somnambulist Society? *[laughter]*

You all indulge in state-of-the-art somnambulism, sleepwalking, and you're having your annual meeting to discuss advances in your profession and especially the merchandising of it. Hm? You're basically a group that is in favor of increasing the numbers of hours that people spend sleeping daily, practicing this, using various aids that the Society provides, until the ultimate goal is achieved, of remaining at all times <u>in</u> the sleep state, and <u>never</u> again having to be bothered by waking, or even dreaming.

Well, it would be an interesting twist on it all, wouldn't it? Just as sellable as anything else, really.

Adi Da adopts the tone of the keynote speaker at the annual meeting of the Society.

The problem is the absurd illusions of this <u>extension</u> of the deep-sleep state (which should be the perpetual state). It becomes aberrated in two potential ways: one associated with the presumptions at the point of discriminative intelligence and the will (in other words, associated with the waking state), and, two, the field or conjunction (subtler, but also sometimes seeming more arbitrary) associated with what we call the dream state. These aberrations are filled with potential difficulties of all kinds, and <u>always</u> a threat. The Society feels there's just so much on the negative side relative to this thing that, on the whole, the Society cannot recommend either the waking state <u>or</u> the dreaming state, until further notice.

So the members of our Society help one another to achieve a state of <u>maximum</u> sleep-time per day (and per year) and hope to achieve a state of <u>unbroken</u> sleep before death.

After all, it's not in the sleep mode that you have any problem about death. It's only in the waking and dreaming modes. So you see how defective they are. They are aberrations on the ground of the deep sleep state, the state prior to body and mind, but not well done enough yet to be worth a gentleman's or gentlewoman's participation. We cannot recommend it to the members and associates of our Society, all of whom are gentlemen and gentlewomen of discreet "consideration".

Your representatives have gathered, and the various committees have submitted their reports. In summary, once again, we must say that the Society cannot recommend participation in either the waking or the dreaming states, for any of its members or associates. All members and associates may do what they will with this advice. Those who would like assistance in magnification, maximization, and ultimate totalization of the sleep-referent may call the following number. You will simply have to wait for someone to respond. If no one is awake at the moment, you'll be of two minds about it: You'll be very happy for them, of course, but wish you had the service which now, in their sleep condition, they will be unable to offer you.

When the laughter dies down, Adi Da speaks in His usual voice again.

Maybe there are such bodhisattvic, Mahayana-style somnambulists, who oblige themselves to participate either in waking or dreaming (or both) for the sake of the Enlightenment of all, until that Enlightenment has occurred, in which case they will be the last to fall asleep, to permit that in themselves, having served all others in their pursuit of sleep.

The address is continued.

It could also occur someday, that the committee, which is made of bodhisattvic "servants of the sleeping", also known as the Somnambulist Society, may find evidence that does suggest that participation in either or both of the waking or the dreaming states may be recommended to members of the Society and associates of the Society. This will not occur, of course, until conditions have improved profoundly. And, until that time, of course, there are always those ready to participate, but the members and associates of our Society do not. Or, at most, only minimally, if they take temporary vows to participate for the sake of all. That's considered worthy and a true sacrifice.

346

All the members of the Society know from deep experience that <u>all</u> participation in the waking and dreaming states is a very difficult business, because, as it turns out, although it always <u>seems</u> to have something to do with you, it never does.

Well, our Transnational—in fact, Intergalactic—Primal Society of Somnambulists . . . . doesn't sound like a bad idea.

Avatar Adi Da mimes falling asleep and snores very loudly. Devotees roar with laughter.

Well, this is a possible point of view. I mean, I just stated it amusedly, but it can be felt to have some kind of a logic about it. Why not?

You all seem to feel obliged to <u>feel</u> <u>obliged</u> to participate in some sort of round of social enactment, and so on, without otherwise inspecting Reality, fundamentally, and are just going along with that more or less.

As I said, you participate in a process, a Reality, that always <u>seems</u> to you to be about you, but it never turns out to be so. It is never so upon inspection. So it may not be far-fetched—this matter of coming to the conclusion that the deep-sleep state (or perhaps something even beyond <u>it</u>, but certainly nothing more superficial than it) is, generally speaking, gone far enough. The rest of it cannot be recommended, except to primitives.

Avatar Adi Da bursts out laughing briefly and then resumes the address.

Members of our Society, who are from the more discriminating among beings, require satisfaction relative to their fundamental "considerations". Of course, as is always said of members of a society, it never turns out to be true of them, either. Except, maybe now, for the truly genuine Society of Somnambulists, it is possible.

Maybe the sleep state, or even something beyond it—but nothing more superficial than that, not dreaming or waking—is the state to be affirmed and entered more and more profoundly, leaving behind all waking and dreaming categories. Not by destroying it from without—rather, by giving it <u>great</u> integrity from without—but, otherwise, by entering into the depth of the process. Then, instead of existing <u>merely</u> to fulfill a social pattern and so on, the fundamental process of your life will be in-depth. You will not be confined to existence as a mere mummery of changes, pattern, and so forth, without integrity or ultimacy.

Well, what do you think about that notion? Does it sound right-on to you?

DEVOTEES: Yes.

AVATAR ADI DA SAMRAJ: If it weren't for your daily—or however frequent, usually daily—visits to the deep-sleep dimension, there would be no sense of meaning or positiveness at all about waking and dreaming.

DEVOTEES: Mm! Right.

AVATAR ADI DA SAMRAJ: And it's not merely that sleeping allows you to refresh the body so you can bodily be more functional—it is necessary for much more important reasons, additionally, because it is the depth domain. Without the automaticity of being refreshed by it—if sleep were not enforced—you might lose touch with it entirely. Even though you can't say anything about it that makes full and comprehensive sense, in your babble of words, nonetheless you do visit it profoundly for even as much as a third of your lifetime. It is a dimension of comprehension of Reality. It is the root of both waking <u>and</u> dreaming, so it is senior to them. When you relax into the depth, in either waking or dreaming, you wind up sleeping. It is the root-condition.

Deeper than sleep is That Which is to be Realized, That Which <u>is</u> Reality no matter what condition (waking, dreaming, or sleeping) apparently arises, and That Which is, when ultimately Realized, Realized to be the Condition <u>of</u> all that arises, whether or not it arises. And there's no "you" about it at all.

So My Mama-Expression to you has profound meaning, said in a manner that suggests you get street-wise about it, about this egoic "self-possession" thing. You can make a big fuss about it, but the reality here, the pattern here, is not about that sort of thing. And that has to be taken seriously by human beings, and this requires a serious entering into the in-depth "consideration" of existence. And everyone should receive education and training in this. In an ideal culture, of course, it would seem that it should be so.

On the other hand, the way it <u>actually</u> is is that everybody has to struggle, and not many get great Wisdom or Realization <u>in</u> it. That sounds like, "Well, that's unjust."

Well, no, it's not, actually, because the ones who get it are the ones who don't take any shit from themselves and get on with it! And then they Realize. Those who are willing to settle for less than that didn't Realize. That sounds like perfect justice. In fact, that's how it works! Because you have to counter the tune here, and persist. Then the "Brightness" that Moves you in it is the Means.

Well, is it unjust because not everyone is Realizing It? Or is it entirely just, because those who commit themselves to Realizing It actually do so?

THANKFULL: Must be the second, Beloved.

AVATAR ADI DA SAMRAJ: So there's no point in you complaining, because it's not about a "you". If you get out of the complaining about "you" and get into the self-surrendering, self-forgetting process of entering into the depth, there is Realization.

It's not about you. You will have to transcend you, because Reality is not about you.

The pattern of appearances is all in a unity and so forth, so when entities appear in this waking state and are associated with that and so forth, there are all kinds of reasonable presumptions that can be made—and hopefully are made—about bringing some order to that, in order to protect everyone in their apparent continuation here—honoring, respecting the fact that all here are involved in this in-depth process, life as a school of "consideration". And all promise to share whatever they find there, and are always looking for those who have been willing to commit themselves completely to Realization, because it is known that Reality is just, and those who commit themselves to Realization, and are going to do whatever is required to go beyond everything that has to do with self, do Realize.

It's also just because when there is Realization in any supposed case, the secrets of it are given, given spontaneously in the disposition, inherently in the disposition, of one who Realizes, to Transmit it to so-called "others". But it is not a merely conventional matter, so any effort along those lines is not about you. It's just about the Revelation Itself.

Then, what about, therefore, this matter that all of conditional arising has arisen, with all forms and entities, beings, processes, and so forth—the extraordinary unity and complexity of the design of all that has arisen—without any portion of what has arisen, or any form or being or entity or species or anything at all, comprehending it? And some, perhaps, clever species (like the human) can get some kind of comprehension of some portion or fraction of it, but, still, basically, you're uncomprehending.

In other words, you are, to begin with, uncomprehending. And yet the whole thing has arisen. Don't you think this is remarkable?

DEVOTEES: Yes!

AVATAR ADI DA SAMRAJ: So it doesn't have anything to do with you at all. You are not a something that has to be informed for Reality to exist.

DEVOTEES: No!

AVATAR ADI DA SAMRAJ: You're looking to be informed for your own sake, but whether you're informed or not is of no interest to Reality, apparently. It's just some sort of quirk in the midst of this. It is about transcendence, however, and not about fulfilling something about the pattern itself.

So the meaning of life is in its depth. The source, or the sense of meaning in life, is in its depth. And that's the in-depth process. It is associated with sleep in the daily cycle, and the in-depth process altogether. Sleep is the fundamental state, the ground of the three states. It has its own force of limitation as well, so Reality is beyond that. But Reality is just beyond that, not just beyond the waking state or just beyond the dreaming state. Instead, it's the third that is the root of all three. [Aniello Panico is nodding off.]

Perhaps Aniello is Translating right now. No, it turns out he was merely asleep. But he wants to fall out of waking into sleep. He doesn't fall out of sleep into waking! You don't usually use that expression, because it is sleep that is the ground-state. It upholds the waking one, and if it's not satisfied, you don't get any waking one.

So what is the thing in depth that is interested in all this? What is in the depth of this bulb, that has this cycle of going through changes and then dying? The point of its "mission", it seems, is to reproduce. And what does it reproduce? More bulbs that pattern. More pattern, in other words. Where's the "you" in it? Where's the "who" in it? Where's the "I" that you use? Where is it? Ever? Or now?

You see, there's something fundamental to comprehend, to understand, to Realize, at the depth. But, ultimately, it comprehends even the waking condition. It is a comprehension that is beyond the notions associated with conventional mind, the consumer mind of daily-life society. But there are some—and, among them, we have the members and associates of the Transgalactic Society of Somnambulists—who insist upon the in-depth culture of existence as being the fundamental one, and, on that basis, also promote positive association, in people and so forth, to minimize struggle, pain, suffering, and so on, and maximize the opportunity for all, the opportunity for life devoted as fundamentally to this in-depth process, and otherwise to the expression of it, educating people in it, and so on.

Even if no one else was interested in this at all—and, in fact, no one else was interested in this at all—I've been here to Do just this. I've

entered into this "consideration" <u>absolutely</u> <u>completely</u>, to participate in it
so profoundly, utterly entered into it, given over into it, identified with it,
to the point of knowing it, understanding it, comprehending it <u>utterly</u>.
Call it a little experiment of My own—whatever the "My" of "Me" and "I"
of "own" are we here.

Whatever meaning means, it's just something to do with shape, a
current of shape in space-time. Just goes through that galumphing, gal-
lahping, galloping, rotating, chuck-chuck-chuck-chuck-chuck-chuck-
chuck, chigga-chiggering, rotating, making-picture-pattern-shapes.

And they do sputter and shutter, by the way, and that's the problem.
At their point of origin, they are not comprehensible. They are one after
the other in shifty shapes, always a new incident that's only slightly different. They look just like endless, incomprehensible shifty shapes. To
have them become something that looks continuous, something else has
to be added.

A device needs to be added—in your case, this body-mind. The
body-mind <u>is</u> a device in the pattern patterning of conditional existence
in this domain, as it now appears. It is a device for having an infinitely
complex, incomprehensible pattern patterning on so many levels appear
to be a something, with some kind of something about it persisting.
Something has to be added, and that's what the body-mind is. It's a kind
of pattern-block, stuck into the machine there. It allows only certain
kinds of pattern experiencing, within degrees of tolerance. It's not there
to preserve that mechanism indefinitely, or under all conditions, but, generally speaking, for the built-in lifespan of the block. And the machine
has replicated huge, vast, almost seeming unlimited examples of the
same mechanism, the same coded piece in the midst of things.

Your body-mind is a selective keypunch, set into the shifty-shape,
incomprehensible, never-seems-to-stop, never-becomes-anything core of
this machine—which is, I can tell you, <u>absolutely</u> <u>horrific</u>. Absolutely horrific. When seen from the other side of sleep and what is beyond it—in
other words, when seen from the dreaming or waking side—it is dreadful.
It confirms your worst imaginings about the nature of reality. It confirms all
the ones you can't even imagine. It's all completely true. It's, at its root,
<u>utterly</u> dark, <u>utterly</u> meaningless. It's just chugga-chugga-chick-chick-chick-
chick-chick-k-t-k-t-k, shifting. It's never anything. And then there are these
keys thrown in, pattern-blocks, and they seem to be a something, everything seems to be about you—but zip-zip, snicker-snack, you're gone.

This is the miscomprehension here, somehow, on the part of these
"you's", who think that Reality is about them. <u>But</u>, deeper than that, the

comprehension is more profound. It's not looking at all this bits-and-blocks, all this pattern-and-suffering. It's deeper than that, comprehending What is Prior to it.

All Great Wisdom comes out of this Well that's Prior to the condition wherein all the struggling seems to be going on. It would seem, then, the best thing to do is to apply appropriate order according to your Master's Instruction relative to conditions of existence, but have your life be <u>about</u> this ever-increasing profundity of in-depth process—which can, should, be going directly (whatever it takes you to go directly) through and deeper than waking and dreaming, to the in-depth condition otherwise experienced as deep sleep, but (in this case) entered into as an event in the context of sadhana, without the loss of consciousness or comprehension.

It's not a mental matter in the verbal sense. It's prior even to discriminative intelligence and will. It is at the root of them. It's beyond their exercise. Even the feeling of relatedness, which is the other side of all self-contraction, is the fundamental form of the self-contraction! This is very curious, if you "consider" the matter.

In any case, so what? It's amusing to say. But you have to go on deeper—beyond all intention to comprehend! Self-<u>surrender</u>, self-forgetting, self-transcending Communion with Me, in the in-depth process, goes beyond all the "you" that you presumed it was all about. It's not about the "you" at all. It's about itself.

What is it, then? By surrendering and forgetting yourself in the rightly guided manner, you can find out about it! You can enter into it profoundly, you can Realize the Root and Ultimate Nature and Condition of it. You can trust that it <u>is</u> worth doing—in other words, that it bears fruit, that Reality is Lawful, those who enter into it most profoundly <u>do</u> Realize. That <u>is</u> the report from countless centuries. So you can trust <u>that</u>.

On the other hand, that report is also full of the indication that it's somehow yet incomplete, to this date, previous to My Appearance. It is also very difficult—in the sense that it requires utter self-transcendence and, therefore, it is constant self-yielding. And, therefore, it can be a profound struggle or ordeal—often is, in general necessarily is, but can be intensified in its apparent difficulty to the degree that there is holding on to separate self, or to some purpose in the psycho-physical position of separate self.

In any case, what difference does all of this saying make? It's only in the state deeper than sleep that there's comprehension, anyway. All this Instruction does is establish your understanding of the pattern of your relationship to Me and the process you are Called to engage in My

Company and prove by demonstrating. And then you have to live that discipline in its daily-life, so-called "outside", sense, and also in its constant, moment to moment, in-depth sense, and the in-depth sense of set-apart times of meditation and so forth.

You all know this, right?

The Mountain Of Attention, 1997

The Infinite Sea of Undifferentiated Happiness

FROM *The Samraj Upanishad*

*A*mong *the Source-Texts of Adi Da Samraj,* The Samraj Upanishad: The "Garland Of Discourses" Of The Adidam Revelation *is unique in being a collection of Discourses rather than a single continuous Argument, and also in including Avatar Adi Da's Spoken Word as well as His Written Word. The magnificent Talks in this book are among His key Spoken Communications from the last ten years of His 25-year Teaching Revelation (1986-1995).*

"The Infinite Sea of Undifferentiated Happiness" appears in The Samraj Upanishad *as the final section of the Talk "The Fundamental Structure That Underlies All Appearances". "The Infinite Sea . . ." was originally spoken by Adi Da Samraj at Ruchira Buddha Dham in the still and pitch-black early morning hours of August 16, 1995, as the conclusion of a very long and utterly sublime Discourse. During the period of time that this Talk was given, Adi Da was not gathering face to face with His devotees to Speak to them. Rather, He communicated by telephone from His bedroom, while His devotees packed into a small room in a building about a mile away around a speaker phone. As Avatar Adi Da pointed out, this form of "gathering" with His devotees eliminated an entire level of social interaction that otherwise tends to take place when people are face to face with each other, and this allowed a remarkable concentration and depth to develop in these "phone gatherings".*

AVATAR ADI DA SAMRAJ: In order to Wake Up totally, to Realize the True Self, you have to do a lot more than just fall asleep. Sleep is, in some sense, a kind of "poor man's enlightenment", or "ordinary man's enlightenment". Things like alcohol, and so forth, are also a kind of "poor man's", or "ordinary man's", ecstasy, in some sense.

Why do you all go to sleep? Why must you sleep? It is not just a physical matter, and so on. In fact, some people never sleep, don't feel the necessity for physical sleep. It is not merely a physical or, otherwise, psychological need. It is, in some sense, a philosophical endeavor, even. You have to sleep in order to get free—at least have a space of a kind of freedom—from the imposition of conditional stress, the stresses of a body-mind.

Sleep is not True (or Most Ultimate) Enlightenment. It is a space. It is a refreshment. Completely apart from any physical fatigue or psychological impulse to sleep, you must sleep in order to be refreshed at the Source. You have to do this regularly. This is the primary reason for sleep. It is a kind of "poor man's", or "ordinary man's", enlightenment. It is even a kind of relief (or "enlightenment") for the ego—"enlightenment" of a kind—because it relieves the separate consciousness (or attention, in other words) from the imposition of objects and entanglements with psycho-physical states and body-identification and the stressful constancy of thoughts. This is the fundamental reason for sleeping. It is not True Enlightenment, but it is a relief, and it is a relief gotten by returning to the Domain of the Source-Position, even though it does not involve Awakening to the Source-Position in any fullest sense.

And you all want to go and do some sleeping right now, don't you?

JONATHAN CONDIT: Not as long as You are Speaking to us, Beloved.

AVATAR ADI DA SAMRAJ: Yes, but you feel tired. That is one reason for wanting to sleep. If you were deprived of sleep, and people jiggled your body, made a lot of noise, whatever, kept you from sleeping for some number of days, or whatever, then it would become a psychological need also. Those are secondary (or peripheral) aspects of the motivation to sleep. The primary motivation, we could say (speaking of the psycho-physical complex altogether), is at the causal root. There is a need at the root (and, generally speaking, in the domain of attention) to simply stand there undisturbed, to be immersed for some hours in the general Field of Bliss without the imposition of objects.

Therefore, sleep is a kind of philosophical quest, as I suggested. It is a need in depth, not merely in the mind or the body. More fundamentally, it is a central need, a foundation need. It is even an expression of the Heart's Always Already and Constant Knowing of the Divine Self-Position, the Ultimate Subjective Position—and how that is the Position of existence, even in the context of conditional experiencing or conditional embodiment.

So you do a bit of sleep. No objects. Still the fundamental presumption of separateness in some sense, but not aggravated by the imposition of objects. And there you lie "in the cut", so to speak. You lie in the Field of Inherent Blissfulness for those moments or hours each day. It is a sign of the impulse at the origin of the heart—another sign that existence is about much more than following the subtle and gross objects.

You might imagine, in the waking state, that it would be <u>terrible</u> to not be able to experience a thought or an object. But that is only a feeling you have in the waking-state identification with the body, and something like it in the dream state. Actually, basically every day, you spontaneously fall into a condition in which you have no experience of objects <u>whatsoever</u>. In that state you are profoundly content, and you look forward to doing it again every day, but you wouldn't be content with it if it arose in the waking state. If you were there feeling the physical, feeling identified with the body, and you suddenly couldn't think—well, then you would be disturbed.

But when you relax the hold on the body and on the mind, suddenly you feel profoundly content, in a state of total objectlessness—still something of the presumption of separateness, but swooned into a Sea of Bliss. No objects whatsoever. No thoughts. No visions. No objects of any kind. Just the Inherent Blissfulness of heart-full existence, without any objects whatsoever. This shows you—should show you—that this condition without objects of any kind (gross or subtle) is profoundly desired, profoundly desirable, and profoundly fulfilling.

The impulse at the heart is not toward objects of any kind, but to be Undifferentiated in the Sea of Essential and Inherent Happiness.

At heart, you require no objects of any kind. And you dip into that Sea daily. And to enter into that Sea to the point of Absolute Non-Differentiation <u>is</u> the impulse at heart.

That <u>is</u> Divine Enlightenment. That <u>is</u> Most Ultimate Realization. It requires no objects whatsoever. If an object arises, it is Inherently Divinely Recognized.

When you wake up, if somebody asks you if you slept well, you have a tacit recollection of whether you did or not. And what is it to sleep well? It is to be rested, immersed in essential blissfulness without any objects. If you say you didn't sleep well, what you mean is that you dreamed, you tossed, you turned, and so on. There were lots of objects—gross and subtle. But when you say you slept well, you mean there were no objects at all—just immersion in blissfulness. When you say you slept well, you acknowledge the fact that a state of objectlessness, simply immersed in Bliss, is profoundly desirable, profoundly pleasurable, profoundly happy. Even, in some sense, then, you acknowledge that it is superior to anything you experience, gross or subtle.

Deep sleep, then, is in the likeness of Divine Self-Realization. It is not itself Divine Self-Realization, but it is in Its likeness, because it is to stand in the attention-position, the causal position, but without objects. So, even in the disposition of separateness, since there are no objects, there is a kind of immersion in the Bliss of the Domain that is Prior even to attention.

Every day, you acknowledge that that state of objectlessness is the best. Ultimately, you would rather sleep than dream or wake. Merely to sleep is not enough, but it is in the likeness of What Is Enough. You acknowledge every day, having slept, that the principal motive in your heart-disposition is to be in the Perfectly Subjective Position of Love-Bliss, without any objects whatsoever. You don't require separateness. You don't require objects. What you require is the Undifferentiated Happiness of Essential Bliss. In that, you do not feel deprived of the objects that are absent. You don't want them.

Someone sleeping well does not want to wake up, does not want to dream. Already having come to the waking state or the dreaming state, you cling to it as if you would not have it come to an end, but then you pass spontaneously into sleep and do not regret the absence of objects at all.

So it is in the Enlightened Condition. There is no regret over the absence of objects. There are no visions in that Profundity. There is no loss in It. It is Complete and Whole. You acknowledge this Great Disposition (as if you were all philosophers) every day, simply because you slept and you were then content. Then you dreamed and were seeking and disturbed. Then you woke up and were clinging and feared death again.

Divine Self-Realization is a kind of Infinite Sleep—Objectless, All-Love-Bliss, never to wake again, never to dream again, never to suffer again. But It is not to be unconscious. Divine Self-Realization is to be Infinitely Conscious, without the slightest differentiation. You are deprived of that Absoluteness even in sleep, but sleep is your pre-vision of It. In some sense, then, sleep is the fundamental position of your life, but you are all troubled by waking and dreaming, thinking and suffering.

Wouldn't you rather sleep? The Infinite Sleep of Divine Love-Bliss?

There is no vision There. No objects There. I Am There Only <u>As</u> That, without the slightest "difference".

That Is Consciousness Itself—not the "consciousness" you presume in the waking state or the dreaming state. That is a trouble.

True Consciousness is beyond objects and without want, without separateness.

True Consciousness is Nirvikalpa Samadhi Absolute, without conditions, without supports, without separate self, without world.

In the waking or dreaming states, you might suggest you don't want that which would deprive you of your objects. But, in sleep, you know, you intuit, something of the Truth of What Happiness is really all about.

Most Ultimate Awakeness, then, is a kind of sleeping, even if appearing to be awake, even if appearing to be dreaming. It is to be asleep. It is to be Free of the imposition and implications of objects, of mere appearances.

Thus, sleep is the foundation of life. It is the root of all refreshment. It is the ground of waking and dreaming. It is that to which you would return every day. And it contains a Secret, the Secret of Ultimate Happiness and Freedom. There is no separateness in That Ultimate Happiness and Freedom, no faculty by which to see or hear or move. But It is not an emptiness. It is Infinite Fullness without qualification. It is the Divine Self-Condition (and Source-Condition), in and of Itself, Vanishing all, Outshining all, Transcending all, utterly without need, without a separate center, without any bounds, without any desire, without any karma, without any movement or mechanics to make another event, a conditional event, an appearance, an object. Don't you know?

DEVOTEES: Yes, Beloved.

AVATAR ADI DA SAMRAJ: And yet, remarkably, you fear death. You might as well fear sleep. When you are agitated and under stress in the body, you may even fear sleep because it suggests to you the loss of body-consciousness. Well, that is all that death suggests: the loss of body-consciousness. And yet you run to the loss of body-consciousness daily, by going to sleep. Why fear death, then?

QUANDRA MAI SUKHA DHAM: Beloved, I am just wondering about my own experience with sleep all my life, in that I have not desired much sleep. I understand what You say about egoity in terms of not wanting to lose bodily consciousness and to cling to objects, but also I can feel in myself an impulse to not just lose consciousness (from the bodily point of view), but to Realize that objectless Samadhi while awake.

AVATAR ADI DA SAMRAJ: Well, you cannot Realize objectless Samadhi by identification with the bodily circumstance of the waking state. The seventh stage Awakening is not dissociated from psycho-physical existence. But psycho-physical existence in that Condition is not what it appears to be from the ordinary point of view.

What is being agitated in the body really all about? Too much stress to rest, such that you are agitated out of sleep. And being agitated out of sleep, then you are identified with the body and the mind, and so forth, and want to cling to them. If you cling too much to the body and the mind, you can't get rest, you can't sleep, or you sleep fitfully, or you get little sleep, and so on. Even if you only get a taste of it, a moment of it, it is still sufficient as a refreshment at the Source.

The seventh stage Awakening is not about clinging to waking conditions, or to a state in which objects are appearing. It is sleep, but without the limitation of separateness. It is simply the Immense, Unbounded, egoless Field of Conscious Radiance, the "Bright" Itself.

Therefore, Most Ultimately, the seventh stage Awakening Outshines conditional existence. It Sleeps it into "Brightness". It doesn't fitfully hold on to the body, or to the mind, or to objective appearances. It simply does not strategically dissociate from them, but It Divinely Recognizes these arising conditions constantly. So It is an Immense, Brilliant, Unquenchable Sleep—not in the sense of unconsciousness, but in the sense of the transcendence of the need and impulse and drive and search for objects.

And so, Most Ultimately, all objects are Divinely Recognized. The body-mind, the entire cosmic domain, is Outshined in the Immense, Eternal Awakeness That is Objectless, and in that sense like sleep.

When people are afraid of dying, it is because they are identified with the body and cling to it. They forget the joy of sleep, of rest. They think they are threatened. But they are not really threatened. It is just because they are contracted in the waking state and would not die. But if they really examined themselves, they would realize that is exactly what they want to do. They don't want to go through the death process, and the suffering in the body to make that transition, and so forth. They would rather just plain old forget about it and be immersed in Immense Bliss and Happiness, and not have to suffer such transitions, not have to struggle to get to rest.

The fundamental heart-impulse is the impulse to Immense Peace— Immense, Objectless, Joyful Peace, Infinitely Conscious. That is True Wakefulness. Divine Recognition in the apparent waking state in the seventh stage of life is just That. It is not about Divine Enlightenment being perpetually associated with conditional (or cosmic) objects. It simply

Divinely Recognizes them from the Prior Position. Most Ultimately, they disappear like the shape of the pig in the kiln—no form, no separateness. It is not an <u>unconscious</u> state. It is <u>Infinitely</u> Conscious, but Objectless. That is the Divine Self-Condition (and Source-Condition).

Pigs in the Kiln

AVATAR ADI DA SAMRAJ: Don't you see the Secret of My being here? I'm Instructing you and so forth, but, by My Siddhi of Divine Recognition, I am relating to the entire cosmic mandala—and, therefore, to all of you—as fresh clay pigs in My Kiln. By the Siddhi, the Force, of My Divine Recognition, I am "Brightening" you—ultimately, to the point of Non-Differentiation. So you are doing sadhana, yes, but I am Exercising this Siddhi. I am also Instructing you, and you are becoming more and more responsible, but this Exercise—My Eternal Exercise of Divine Recognition in this cosmic domain—<u>is</u> how the cosmic domain will be Divinely Translated.

So, you all will do this sadhana, but at the same time <u>My</u> Effect will be continuing. The conjunction between the two will become the Divine Translation of the cosmic domain. Not merely, "Now I have Given you the sadhana—you all do it, and sooner or later you will Divinely Translate". No—all the while, this Force, this Siddhi, of Divine Recognition, Exercised by Me, will be heating up the "pigs". And they start glowing—you can still see them, but they're glowing. At first, a little heat-radiation, blissful feeling, and so on, but you can still see them there, those wet little uglies! Then they start glowing a little more—everything starts glowing a little more. It has got even a fiery redness about it, somehow. You even see the redness directly—a little bit of that—but still you can see those wet little uglies. And you there, too, as a wet little ugly—but somehow "Brightened" up, you know, and actually feeling sort of uplifted!

Well, it just goes on and on. The "Brightness" is Magnified more and more by the Power of My Samadhi, the Power of My Divine Recognition, active throughout the cosmic domain. Eventually, these little clay guys just stop feeling so bulky and so elementally earthy and sort of get blended more with everything, and rather subtle, and seeing subtly, and start getting "Brighter" and "Brighter" and "Brighter". Just a sort of universal glow, hardly any differentiation at all. Just this Ecstasy, this "Intoxication" of "Brightness".

And then, in a wink, without noticing, there's none of it.

No more pigs. No more cosmic domain. [April 30, 1995]

So every being is moved to this Immense Peacefulness, Happiness, and moves toward It readily, spontaneously, every day, in the motion towards sleep, the relinquishment that is sleep. Sleep is not unconscious, because when people wake up in the morning (or whenever) and are asked if they slept well, they say "yes". Well, how would they know, if it was unconscious? It is not unconscious. It is simply objectless.

There is no lack of contentedness in sleep. All objects are replaced by their Substance in sleep and in Most Ultimate Realization. The Essence of all objects, That upon Which they are a play, is Love-Bliss, Infinite Radiance.

In other words, in Most Ultimate Realization, even in sleep, there is no deprivation, no loss of objects. Rather, the Substance of them becomes immediate. The Substance of objects is the Light, the Bliss, the Love-Bliss upon Which they are a merely apparent play. The play subsides—not into unconsciousness, but into Objectless Love-Bliss.

The Substance of appearances is What is Realized in Most Ultimate Awakening, or Divine Enlightenment. Even in deep sleep, that Substance is touched upon. That is why there is rest.

It is in deep sleep that the greatest intuition occurs daily, by direct contact with the Field of Love-Bliss. Therefore, the heart-disposition is Deep. It is as sleep. Fundamentally Objectless. It is moved toward Its own Source-Condition. The heart would Realize That Happiness Which is beyond objects, Which is just touched upon in deep sleep, but Which is the Very Source-Condition.

And when you even go to the meditation hall to meditate, when your meditation achieves a depth, it is like sleep. It goes beyond objects, beyond the concretization of separate self, into a kind of Immersion in Sheer Bliss, the Substance of all objects, beyond body, beyond mind, beyond complication, beyond stress and suffering, beyond seeking. When meditation becomes deep, it is a taste as in deep sleep. It is a taste as in deep sleep of the Source-Condition, the heart returned to its Pool of Origin beyond suffering.

So, in deep meditation and in deep sleep you touch upon the same Source-Condition and get the Knowledge of Happiness. But you must take It seriously, and not, then, return to a disposition of seeking, clinging to objects, and so on. You must stay steady in that nectarous disposition of deep meditation, of Communion with Me—a kind of Sleepless Sleep, or Joy. That is the Circumstance to Which you are moved in this devotion to Me. It is beyond death, beyond suffering, beyond dreams, beyond visions, beyond body, beyond cosmos, beyond even the residual impediment of deep sleep that is experienced by those who are embodied otherwise.

This can be Realized. This is My Gift to you. This is What I Call you to. And This is the potential you have in this Yoga of devotion to Me.

Know, then, that the Impulse to this Love-Bliss is a motivation in you that goes beyond all conditional satisfactions, or impulses, or motives, or searches.

To Know this Objectless Love-Bliss is to be Asleep while alive. It is to be Awake beyond wakening. Then, when It is Fulfilled Most Perfectly, there is no embodiment, no cosmic domain.

So why fear death, then? It is unreasonable. It is like fearing to go to sleep.

In the daily waking state, as it is presumed egoically, the point of view of individual beings is that the worst thing that can happen to you is that you lose body-consciousness. This is all epitomized in your fear of death. Fear of death is attachment to the waking state, attachment to the body. It is a loss of a sense of Essential Heart-Bliss as it is known even in sleep.

The body is just an object. The mind is just an object. To be free of objects is an enjoyment you even pursue daily. Why fear death, then?

The Ground cannot be lost. The Infinite Energy, the Fundamental Force and Source in Which all phenomena are arising, is a Constant. It cannot disappear.

Why fear death, then? Why cling to life in fear?

Live on the Foundation. Live in Truth. Surrender to That Which is Great and Fundamental and Always Already Existing, and fear is gone.

Even in life, then, being thus fearless and grounded in Truth, you can live effectively. You can do sadhana. You can function without fear and without illusion. There is a detachment in this that is not dissociative, just a ground freedom and peacefulness, equanimity, that has no fear of death and does not cling to the body, does not cling to the mind, does not cling to objects, does not cling to want—because there is the ground heart-certainty of the Infinite Peacefulness and Blissfulness of objectless existence, which is given as a natural gift to every being in every world, in every day's cycle.

So even now, because it is early morning, late at night for you all, taking into account the previous day—you are all looking forward to going to sleep, aren't you?

DEVOTEES: Yes, we are.

AVATAR ADI DA SAMRAJ: It will happen spontaneously, and you want it to spontaneously happen.

JONATHAN: That's right.

AVATAR ADI DA SAMRAJ: You don't want to cling to the body, to the mind, or ask any more questions, or engage in any transactions with the body-mind. You are looking forward to the peacefulness, the contentedness, the happiness, of objectless sleep. You are looking forward to it. You would like to do it right now. Well, make this not merely a natural impulse of each day-cycle, make it your heart-impulse, and you transcend death and all suffering. Don't you know?

DEVOTEES: Yes, Beloved.

AVATAR ADI DA SAMRAJ: Get this knowledge more profoundly in the Samadhi of self-surrendering, self-forgetting, self-transcending feeling-Contemplation of Me.

Be willed to this, then, in every moment, and relinquish the anxiety of attachment to the body-mind.

The body-mind is a mere appearance floating in the Infinite Sea of Undifferentiated Happiness Which you visit, by My Grace, in Communion with Me, and even touch upon daily in the Grace of sleep.

So much for death, then. So much for the daily news. So much for the clinging activities of an uninspected life.

The heart has its Proof. All of you have felt Me. I have even Flooded your body-minds with this Proof.

Be converted at heart, then, and live without fear, and give up all, without fear, because of this Proof.

This appearance of life will end like any dream ends. But you always Stand in the Superior Position, having Communed with Me, and even having slept.

You need not take these objects seriously, then. You are superior to the fault and the adventure and the horrible epoch (or epochs) of mere appearances. This is your freedom, even from the beginning of the Way of the Heart.

Go to sleep in peace.
Meditate in peace.
Live in peace.
Live in Depth.
Be in Depth.
Go to this Depth.
Be in this Depth.
And be Free and Happy.
Will you?

An Invitation

I do not simply recommend or turn men and women to Truth. I *Am* Truth. I Draw men and women to My Self. I Am the Present God, Desiring, Loving, and Drawing up My devotees. I have Come to Acquire My devotees. I have Come to be Present with My devotees, to live with them the adventure of life in God, which is Love, and mind in God, which is Faith. I Stand always Present in the Place and Form of God. I accept the qualities of all who turn to Me and dissolve them in God, so that Only God becomes their Condition, Destiny, Intelligence, and Work. I look for My devotees to acknowledge Me and turn to Me in appropriate ways, surrendering to Me perfectly, depending on Me, full of Me always, with only a face of love.

I am waiting for you. I have been waiting for you eternally. Where are you?

AVATAR ADI DA SAMRAJ

1 9 7 1

Having read this book, or any of Adi Da's books, you stand at the threshold of the greatest possibility of a human lifetime. You can begin to participate in the Divine Process that Avatar Adi Da Offers to all. Nothing else in life can match this opportunity. Nothing can compare with the Grace of a devotional relationship to the supreme God-Man, the Ruchira Buddha, Avatar Adi Da Samraj. When you make the great gesture of heart-surrender to Adi Da, He draws you into the profound course of true Awakening to God, Truth, or Reality.

Whatever your present level of interest in Adidam, there is an appropriate form of participation available to you. And whatever form of participation you adopt brings you into the stream of Divine Blessing flowing from Adi Da.

How to Find out More about Avatar Adi Da Samraj and the Way of the Heart

■ **Continue reading Adi Da's Wisdom-Teaching.** Other excellent books are *The Knee of Listening*, Adi Da's Spiritual Autobiography, *The Method of the Siddhas*, a collection of Talks from the early years of His Teaching Work, and *The Heart's Shout*, a comprehensive anthology of His Talks and Writings from 1970 to 1995. All three are available at local bookstores, or you can order directly from the Adidam Pan-Communion (Americas) by calling (800) 524-4941, or (707) 928-4936 outside the USA, or by writing 12040 North Seigler Road, Middletown CA, 95461.

■ **Browse our award-winning Website, http://www.adidam.org,** which will introduce you to many aspects of the Way of the Heart, and also bring you up-to-date on the current Blessing Work of Avatar Adi Da Samraj.

■ **Contact a center of Adidam.** You can call the regional center nearest you (see p. 381) and ask to be put on their mailing list. The regional center will keep you abreast of regular classes, seminars, events and retreats. (You will also be able to talk with devotees, who will answer your questions, make suggestions about the next step, inform you about local events, and tell you about their own experience of practicing in Adi Da's Spiritual Company.) You can also call the central offices of the Adidam Pan-Communion (Americas) at (800) 524-4941 or (707) 928-4936 for further information. Or send e-mail to: correspondence@adidam.org.

■ **Attend an Adidam Area Study Group.** Call a regional center to find out about Area Study Groups near you. These groups, of which there are more than 150 throughout the world, provide the opportunity to meet with others who are interested in Adi Da, see recent video footage of Him, and participate in guided study and meditation.

Becoming an Advocate of Adidam

One way to support Adi Da's Divine Work in the world is by joining the Transnational Society of Advocates of the Adidam Revelation. Advocates are people who recognize Adi Da Samraj as a Source of Wisdom and Blessing in their own lives and for the world, and who want to make a practical response to Him and to His Work. Advocates support Adi Da's Divine Work in the world by offering an annual donation; this donation supports the publication and distribution of the books of Adi Da Samraj. In addition to their annual donation, some advocates pledge an additional monthly amount to support the publications mission of the Adidam Pan-Communion.

As an advocate, you are invited to come on retreat at the regional Adidam ashrams worldwide, and at the advocates' retreat facility at the Mountain Of Attention Sanctuary in northern California. You are also invited to attend the yearly sacred celebrations of Adidam (held in all regional centers), and to participate in special classes, seminars, and events.

Some advocates are moved to enter into a direct devotional relationship with Avatar Adi Da Samraj and become members of the fourth congregation of Adidam (see pp. 379-80). If you are so moved, you make a formal vow of devotion and service to Adi Da as Your Divine Heart-Master. When you take this vow, you are committing yourself to performing a specific consistent service to Avatar Adi Da and His Blessing Work, as well as to embracing the fundamental devotional practice that Adi Da Gives to all His devotees. This is the practice of Ruchira Buddha Bhakti Yoga—devotion to the Ruchira Buddha, Adi Da, as the Divine Awakener of your heart. You do the "simplest" form of this great practice, which Adi Da summarizes as "Invoke Me, Feel Me, Breathe Me, Serve Me".

There is no limit to the kinds of skills you may offer in fulfillment of your service vow. Whether you are a journalist, an artist, an educator, a doctor, a veterinarian, a librarian, an engineer, an architect, a computer specialist, a financial consultant, a marketing expert, a small business entrepreneur, or whether you have clerical or building skills—just to name a few possibilities— there are countless ways you can serve the widening recognition of Adi Da Samraj and/or help to develop and protect the Sacred Treasures of Adidam, including its Sanctuaries and its publications mission.

"Those who serve the Divine are served by the Divine". This is a Spiritual law that holds true under all circumstances. And so, the more you give of your time and energy and attention to Adi Da Samraj, the more you receive His Blessings. He does not have to see you or know you personally. Simply by virtue of your attention to Him, you find yourself becoming happier, and you may observe remarkable, Graceful changes taking place in your life altogether.

Some advocates remain advocates for life, while others at some point take up the more intensive forms of Spiritual practice Offered by Adi Da Samraj.

■ To become an advocate, please contact the regional center nearest where you live. (For a list of regional centers of Adidam, please see p. 381)

■ **Attend a retreat at the Man of Radical Understanding Retreat Center.** Many people will tell you that the best thing they did when approaching Adi Da Samraj and the Way of the Heart was to go on one of the retreats held for advocates at the Man of Radical Understanding Retreat Center. This retreat center has an extraordinary location—it is part of the Mountain Of Attention Sanctuary in northern California (one of the three Ashram Sanctuaries of Adi Da Samraj, which have been Empowered by Him through His living and Working there over extended periods). The entire area is imbued with His Spiritual Transmission, and Adi Da visited the retreat center and sat in its meditation hall in 1995. Devotees who reside at or near the Mountain Of Attention serve the retreats, offering a full program of study of the Teaching Word of Adi Da, videos of Him speaking and granting silent Darshan, Leelas (or stories) of His Life and Work, and many opportunities for group discussion and informal conversation about your own specific questions. You also learn firsthand about the practice of Ruchira Buddha Bhakti Yoga and are invited to periods of formal feeling-Contemplation of Adi Da Samraj in the meditation hall.

For a schedule of retreats at the Man of Radical Understanding Retreat Center, call (707) 928-1129.

Becoming a Student of the Laughing Man Institute of Adidam

I f you are moved to become a devotee of Avatar Adi Da Samraj and want to discover what this would involve, or if you simply want to have the benefit of guided study courses of the Wisdom-Teaching of Adi Da Samraj, you are invited to become a student of the Laughing Man Institute of Adidam. (The Laughing Man Institute offers a variety of courses examining the extraordinary Wisdom-Teaching of Adi Da.) You may enroll in one of these courses at any of the regional centers of the Adidam Pan-Communion. Or you make take courses by correspondence. (These courses give you a chance to really study Adi Da's Teaching Word and to find out what it means to enter into the devotional relationship with Him.) To find out about the courses available, and to enroll in the Laughing Man Institute, contact the regional center nearest you (please see p. 381).

Becoming a Practitioner of Adidam

M any people who discover Adi Da do not want to waste a second! If that is your impulse, you are invited to immediately sign up for a special course (taking four to six weeks) that prepares you to move as quickly as possible toward becoming Adi Da's formal devotee.

Once you have completed this preparatory course, you may take a momentous step. When you have reached the point of complete clarity in your intention to practice the Way of the Heart, you make a vow of commitment—in this life and beyond this life—to Adi Da as your Beloved Guru and Divine Liberator. Nothing could be more profound—or more ecstatic. For when you take this vow in gratitude and love, fully aware of its obligations, Adi Da Samraj accepts eternal responsibility for your Spiritual well-being and ultimate Divine Liberation. His Grace is already guiding your growth day by day, hour by hour through your devotional Communion with Him.

Taking the Eternal Vow is a formal confession that the devotional relationship to Adi Da Samraj is the overriding purpose of your life. In this disposition you take up the practice of a student-novice and begin to adapt to the total Way of life Adi Da has Given to His devotees.

As a student-novice, you are initiated into formal meditation, sacramental worship, and the range of practical life-disciplines. At the same time, you have increasing opportunities to participate with devotees in their celebrations, and through these forms of contact you are embraced by the gathering of devotees of Adi Da Samraj and grow further in your relationship to Him. If your intention and application to the practice is strong, you may become a fully acknowledged practitioner of Adidam, ready to live always in relationship with the Divine Beloved, Adi Da, in the culture of practice that is His Gift to all His devotees.

The Life of a Devotee of Adi Da Samraj

Everything you do as a practitioner of the Way of the Heart is an expression of your heart-response of devotion to Adi Da Samraj. The life of cultivating this response to Him is Ruchira Buddha Bhakti Yoga—or the God-Realizing practice ("Yoga") of devotion ("Bhakti") to the Ruchira Buddha, Adi Da.

The great practice of Ruchira Buddha Bhakti Yoga necessarily transforms the whole of your life. Every function, every relationship, every action is moved by the impulse of devotional heart-surrender to Adi Da.

AVATAR ADI DA SAMRAJ: In every moment you must turn the situation of your life into Yoga by exercising devotion to Me. There is no moment in any day wherein this is not your Calling. This is what you must do. You must make Yoga out of the moment by using the body, emotion, breath, and attention in self-surrendering devotional Contemplation of Me. All those mechanisms must be turned to Me. That turning makes your life Yoga. Through turning to Me, you "yoke" yourself to Me, and that practice of linking, or binding, or connecting, to God is religion. Religion, or Yoga, is the practice of moving out of the separative disposition and state into Oneness with That Which is One, Whole, Absolute, All-Inclusive, and Beyond. [December 2, 1993]

As everyone quickly discovers, it is only possible to practice Ruchira Buddha Bhakti Yoga when you establish a foundation of discipline that enables you to consistently reel in your attention, energy, and feeling from their random wandering. And so Adi Da Samraj has given unique and extraordinarily full Instruction on a complete range of specific disciplines. Some disciplines—meditation, sacramental worship, and study—are specifically contemplative, while others—related to exercise, diet, sexuality, community living, and so on—bring the life of devotion into daily functional activity. The practice of the disciplines begins during the student-novice period and then continues, passing through many refinements, through every stage of practice in the Way of the Heart.

Meditation is a unique and precious event in the daily life of Avatar Adi Da Samraj's devotees. It offers the opportunity to relinquish outward, body-based attention and to be alone with Avatar Adi Da, allowing yourself to enter more and more into the Sphere of His Divine Transmission.

The practice of sacramental worship, or "puja", in the Way of the Heart is the bodily active counterpart to meditation. It is a form of ecstatic worship of Avatar Adi Da Samraj, using a photographic representation of Him and involving devotional chanting and recitations from His Wisdom-Teaching.

"You must deal with My Wisdom-Teaching in some form every single day, because a new form of the ego's game appears every single day. You must continually return to My Wisdom-Teaching, confront My Wisdom-Teaching."

Avatar Adi Da Samraj

The beginner in Spiritual life must prepare the body-mind by mastering the physical, vital dimension of life before he or she can be ready for truly Spiritual practice. Service is devotion in action, a form of Divine Communion.

Avatar Adi Da Samraj Offers practical disciplines to His devotees in the areas of work and money, diet, exercise, and sexuality. These disciplines are based on His own human experience and an immense process of "consideration" that He engaged face to face with His devotees for more than twenty years.

As soon as you assume full membership in the formal gathering of Avatar Adi Da Samraj's devotees, you become part of a remarkable sacred community.

left: Devotees meeting to discuss their practice of Adidam
right: Adidam Sanghashram in Holland

left: Adidam Sanghashram, England
right: Adidam Retreat Centre in Australia

"The principal admonition in the Great Tradition has always been 'Spend time in good company'—in the Company of the Realizer and the company of those who love the Realizer or who truly practice in the Spiritual Company of the Realizer. This is the most auspicious association. Absorb that Company. Imbibe it. Drink deep of it. Duplicate it. Spiritual community is a mutual communication of Happiness."
Avatar Adi Da Samraj

Devotees gather for a Celebration meal at the
Mountain Of Attention Sanctuary in northern California

One of the ways in which Adi Da Communicates His Spiritual Transmission is through sacred places. During the course of His Work He has Empowered three Sanctuaries as His Blessing-Seats. In each of these Sanctuaries—the Mountain Of Attention in northern California, Love-Ananda Mahal in Hawaii, and Ruchira Buddha Dham in Fiji—Adi Da has established Himself Spiritually in perpetuity. He has lived and Worked with devotees in all His Sanctuaries, and has created in each one special holy sites and temples. Devotees who are rightly prepared may go on special retreats at all three Sanctuaries.

top left: the Mountain Of Attention
top right: Love-Ananda Mahal
bottom: Ruchira Buddha Dham

To practice the Way of the Heart in the manner we have just described is to be part of what Adi Da calls the "second congregation" of His devotees. If at some point your attraction and devotion to Adi Da Samraj completely takes over your life, such that you forget everything else, then you may move into the "first congregation", which is the gathering of Adi Da's devotees who have embraced formal renunciation. Becoming a formal renunciate does not mean that you become an ascetic in the traditional sense, or dissociate from others. Not at all. But everything about your life is submitted to your impulse to Realize Adi Da's Gift of Divine Enlightenment—to Realize <u>Him</u>—as quickly as possible. Thus, you are moved to intensify all aspects of your practice of Adidam, and to serve Adi Da and His Work in a uniquely intense manner.

There are two formal renunciate orders in the first congregation, the Lay Renunciate Order and the Advaitayana Buddhist Order. The senior of the two orders is the Advaitayana Buddhist Order (formerly known as the Free Renunciate Order), composed of the most exemplary formal renunciate practitioners practicing the "Perfect Practice", or the ultimate stages of the Way of the Heart. The core of the Advaitayana Buddhist Order, and its senior governing members, will, in the future, be those devotees who have Realized Divine Enlightenment. Adi Da Samraj Himself is the Founding Member of the Advaitayana Buddhist Order, and will obviously remain throughout His Lifetime its Senior Member in every respect.

The Advaitayana Buddhist Order is a retreat Order, whose members are legal renunciates. They are supported and protected in their unique Spiritual role by the Lay Renunciate Order, which is a cultural service Order that serves an inspirational and aligning role for all devotees.

First congregation devotees have a special role to play in the future of the Way of the Heart. Adi Da Samraj must have unique human Instrumentality—Spiritually Awakened and Divinely Self-Realized devotees—through whom He can continue to do His Divine Work after His physical Lifetime. No human being, not even one of Adi Da's Divinely Enlightened devotees, can "succeed" Adi Da Samraj, in the way that, traditionally, a senior devotee often succeeds his or her Spiritual Master.[39] Adi Da Samraj is the Complete Incarnation of the Divine Person—He is truly the Completion of all Spiritual lineages in all times and places. Thus, He remains forever the Awakener and the Liberator of all beings. His Spiritually Awakened renunciate devotees will collectively function as His Spiritual Instruments, or channels for His Blessing Power.

---

39. Adi Da Samraj has Said that, after His physical (human) Lifetime, there should always be one (and only one) "Murti-Guru" as a Living Link between Him and His devotees. Each successive "Murti-Guru" is to be selected from among those members of the Advaitayana Buddhist Order who have been formally acknowledged as Divinely Enlightened devotees of Adi Da. "Murti-Gurus" do not function as the independent Guru of practitioners of the Way of the Heart. Rather, they are simply Representations of Adi Da's bodily (human) Form, and a means to Commune with Him.

**Avatar Adi Da Samraj with members of the Advaitayana Buddhist Order
The Mountain Of Attention, 1995**

Becoming a Benefactor or Server of the Work of Adi Da Samraj

We live in a time when the destiny of mankind and the world is hanging desperately in the balance. Adi Da has Appeared in the world in order to Save us from a dreadful destiny, by Offering the Way of true Liberation from the disease of egoity. Only He, the Divine Person Incarnate, can make that Offering. And only that Liberation can actually reverse all the disastrous trends of our time.

It is the sacred responsibility of those who respond to Avatar Adi Da to provide the means for His Divine Work to achieve truly great effect in the world. He must be given the practical means to Bless all beings and to Work with His devotees in all parts of the world, in whatever manner He is spontaneously moved to do so. He must be able to move freely from one part of the world to another. He must be able to establish Hermitages in various parts of the world, where He can Do His silent Work of Blessing, and where He can also Work with His devotees by receiving them into His physical Company. He must be able to gather around Him a group of devotees (in the first congregation) who are dedicated to most profound practice of the Way of the Heart and who are financially and practically supported, such that they can devote themselves entirely and one-pointedly to serving Him directly and living the life of intense Spiritual retreat in His physical Company. And the mere fact that the Very Divine Being, Adi Da Samraj, is Present in the world must become as widely known as possible, both through the publication and dissemination of books by and about Him, and through public advocacy by people of influence.

If you are an individual of uncommon wealth or influence, you are invited to serve Adi Da's Great Work by becoming His benefactor. To become a benefactor of Adi Da Samraj exceeds all the usual forms of philanthropy. You are literally serving countless people by serving Adi Da Samraj in this way. You are making it possible for Adi Da's Divine Influence to reach people who might otherwise not come to know of Him. You are making it possible for Adi Da to make the fullest possible use of His own physical Lifetime—the unique Lifetime of the Divine, Perfectly Incarnate. And if you make this choice, your own life and destiny will also be transformed in the most Graceful ways.

As a member of the third congregation, your relationship to Adi Da is founded on a vow of Ruchira Buddha Bhakti Yoga—a vow of devotion, through which you commit yourself to serve the Work of Adi Da in this particular manner. In the course of that service to Adi Da (and in daily life altogether), you live your vow of devotion by Invoking Him, feeling Him, breathing Him, and serving Him (without engaging the full range of disciplines practiced in the first two congregations). At all times, this fundamental practice is the means Adi Da has Given for His benefactors to remain connected to His constant Blessing. In addition, Adi Da has invited, and may continue to do so, His benefactors into His physical Company.

If you can serve Adi Da Samraj in this profoundly important way, please call, write, FAX, or e-mail us at:

phone number: (707) 928-4800

Attn: Anne Howell
12040 North Seigler Road
Middletown, CA 95461

FAX: (707) 928-4618
e-mail: Anne_Howell@adidam.org

The Heart-Master of All

Avatar Adi Da Samraj has Appeared in this world for the sake of all. "Each one," He has said, "is My Beloved". He told His devotees many years ago that their service to Him goes on forever, that it ultimately includes doing everything necessary for the Divine Enlightenment of everyone everywhere. And so He Offers His Divine Gifts to people throughout the world. Adi Da has created a "fourth congregation" of Adidam for people everywhere whose heart-response to Him takes the form of engaging the technically "simplest" practice moment to moment in the context of daily life—Invoking Him, feeling Him, breathing Him, and serving Him—and offering consistent service and (if possible) financial support (in accordance with their means). Thus, members of the fourth congregation are not expected to engage the full range of disciplines (meditation, sacramental worship, guided study, exercise, diet, sexual Yoga, cooperative community living, and so on) that are taken up by members of the first and second congregations (although fourth congregation devotees are free to engage these disciplines if they are so moved).

Adi Da's fourth congregation devotees, or "lay attendants", all live under vow to make this "simplest" practice of Ruchira Buddha Bhakti Yoga the foundation of their lives and to consistently offer Bhagavan Adi Da the gift of their service. The fourth congregation embraces all kinds of individuals—in all parts of the world, from all cultural backgrounds, and of all levels of economic means—who are moved to embrace this form of the devotional relationship with Avatar Adi Da. Thus, the fourth congregation includes members of the Society of Advocates (those who choose to formally embrace this vow), and people in traditional ("third world") cultures, and people who (because of limitations in their life-circumstance, or physical or mental disabilities) do not have the option of practicing the full range of disciplines assumed in the first or second congregations.

Adi Da Samraj has told His devotees that once you have entered formally into the devotional relationship to Him through any of the congregations, He is also under vow to you, to Liberate you from ego-bondage and Awaken you to His Divine Condition. Whatever time and space that may require in your case, the process begins from the moment of your initiation.

If, at some time, your heart-movement or life-circumstance changes, it is always possible to formally transition to one of the other congregations: Lay attendants may, if they are so moved and able, move on to become student-novices and then enter the second (or, eventually, the first) congregation.

◆ ◆ ◆

As Adi Da writes in *The Knee of Listening*, His Purpose has always been to found "a new human order that will serve to 'create' a new age of sanity and joy". In the brief period of two decades, and in the midst of this dark and Godless era, Adi Da Samraj has literally established His unique Spiritual culture. He is laying the foundation for an unbroken tradition of Divine Self-Realization arising within a devotional gathering aligned to His fully Enlightened Wisdom, and always receiving and magnifying His Eternal Heart-Transmission. Nothing of the kind has ever before existed.

There are great choices to be made in life, choices that call on the greatest exercise of one's real intelligence and heart-impulse. Every one of us makes critical decisions that determine the course of the rest of our lives—and even our future beyond death. The moment of discovering the Divine Avatar, Adi Da, is the greatest of all possible opportunities. It is pure Grace. How can an ordinary life truly compare to a life of living relationship and heart-intimacy with the greatest God-Man Who has ever appeared—the Divine in Person?

There are many forms of response to Adi Da Samraj—from reading another book to becoming His devotee. Every response draws you more closely to His Heart. If you are moved by what you have read here, take the next step—whatever that is for you. Take this miraculous opportunity to enter into direct relationship with the Divine Heart of all.

Regional Centers of Adidam

■ ADIDAM (AMERICAS)
NORTHERN CALIFORNIA
Adidam
12040 North Seigler Road
Middletown, CA 95461
USA
(800) 524-4941
(707) 928-4936
FAX 928-4618
E-mail: correspondence@adidam.org
or visit our Adidam Home Page at:
http://www.adidam.org
-or-
Adidam
4286 Redwood Highway #G
San Rafael, CA 94903
(415) 492-0930
FAX 479-6626

NORTHWEST USA
Adidam
5600 11th Avenue NE
Seattle, WA 98105
(206) 527-2751
FAX 527-0738

SOUTHWEST USA
Adidam
PO Box 48805
Los Angeles, CA 90048
(213) 939-2390
FAX 388-9062

NORTHEAST USA
Adidam
30 Pleasant Street
S. Natick, MA 01760
(508) 650-0136
FAX 651-2458

SOUTHEAST USA
Adidam
10301 South Glen Road
Potomac, MD 20854
(301) 983-0291
FAX 983-5348

HAWAII
Adidam
105 Kaholalele Road
Kapaa, HI 96746
(808) 822-0216
FAX 822-3386

EASTERN CANADA
Adidam
11 Katimavik Road
Val-des-Monts
Quebec J8N 5EI
Canada
(819) 671-4398
(800) 563-4398
FAX 671-5961

■ ADIDAM (PACIFIC-ASIA)
NEW ZEALAND
Adidam
12 Seibel Road
Henderson
Auckland 8
New Zealand
(09) 838-9114
FAX 838-9119

AUSTRALIA
Adidam
PO Box 460
Roseville
NSW 2069
Australia
(02) 419-7563
(02) 416-7951 (eve)
FAX 415-1741

FIJI
The Ruchira Buddha Foundation
PO Box 4744
Samabula, Suva
Fiji
381-466
FAX 311-311

■ ADIDAM (EUROPE-AFRICA)
THE NETHERLANDS
Adidam Ashram
Annendaalderweg 10
6105 AT Maria Hoop
The Netherlands
(0475) 30-2203
FAX 30-1381
-or-
Adidam Centrum
Oosterpark 39
1092 AL Amsterdam
The Netherlands
(020) 665-3133
FAX 663-0793

THE UNITED KINGDOM & IRELAND
Adidam Ashram
Tasburgh Hall
Lower Tasburgh
Norwich NR15 1NA
England
(01508) 470-574
FAX same as phone

GERMANY
Adidam
Grosse Brunnenstrasse 31
22763 Hamburg
Germany
(040) 390-4438
FAX 399-00898
E-mail: 100520.3175@compuserve.com
http://ourworld.compuserve.com/home-pages/FDAC__Hamburg

The Sacred Literature of Avatar Adi Da Samraj

A New Scripture for Mankind

The books of Avatar Adi Da Samraj are not the product of a scholar's intellectual investigation. They are the Living Communication of Divine Intelligence. They are the forceful Call to live your life in a devotional relationship with the Divine Person in human form. They are a criticism of the never-to-be-satisfied motivations of the separate self to fulfill itself physically, mentally, and emotionally—and a goad to self-transcendence and the Perfect Happiness of Divine Self-Realization. They are a Grand Commentary on every aspect of life, and a realignment of life to its Divine Source and Substance.

But these books are also more than that. They are the Speech of God. In a section of *The Dawn Horse Testament Of The Ruchira Buddha*, Adi Da says of that book:

It is the speech of Ecstasy, of Inherently self-Transcending Heart-Consciousness, or of Perfectly Awakened (and necessarily Divine) Self-Consciousness, the Heart-Word of Reality (Itself), Which Is the Inherent or Native Feeling of Being (Itself).

The books of Adi Da Samraj <u>are</u> Him—they are His Form. Reading them is Communing with the Divine. They are full of His Pleasure, Power, and Purpose—the Pleasure of Divine Happiness; the Power to Liberate all beings from the illusion of separation and Awaken them to the Reality of "The Only One Who Is"; the Purpose of Attracting you beyond every limitation to limitless Life in and as God.

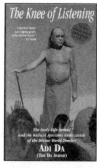

NEW EDITION

The Knee of Listening

The Early-Life Ordeal and the Radical Spiritual Realization of the Divine World-Teacher

This is the astounding Spiritual Autobiography of Adi Da Samraj, the story of the Incarnation of the Absolute Divine Consciousness into a human body-mind in the modern West. Here He describes in vivid detail His first thirty-one years as "Franklin Jones": His Illumined Birth, His acceptance of the ordeal of life as an ordinary human being, His unstoppable quest for Divine Self-Realization, His exploits into the farthest reaches of human experience—from "money, food, and sex" to the most esoteric mystical and Transcendental phenomena—His Divine Re-Awakening and discovery of the Way of God-Realization for all mankind. Unparalleled, utterly compelling, essential reading.

I know of no other teacher who has exposed his life and spiritual journey with such complete abandonment for the teaching of all who will pay attention. His story and process are a fascinating portrayal of the ordeal, potency, and blessing of an infinitely expanding spiritual life. This biography is a perfect gift!

Bonnie Greenwell, Ph.D.
author, *Energies of Transformation: A Guide to the Kundalini Process*;
Director, Transpersonal Counseling Center, Institute of Transpersonal Psychology

$4.95*, popular format

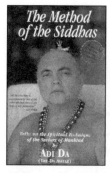

NEW EDITION

The Method of the Siddhas

Talks on the Spiritual Technique of the Saviors of Mankind

When Adi Da Samraj opened the doors of His first Ashram in Los Angeles on April 25, 1972, He invited anyone who was interested to sit with Him and ask Him questions about Spiritual life.

These Talks are the result of that first meeting between the Incarnate Divine Being and twentieth-century Westerners. Here Adi Da Samraj discusses in very simple terms all the fundamentals of Spiritual life, especially focusing on Satsang, the devotional relationship with Him as Sat-Guru, and self-understanding, the "radical" insight He was bringing to the human world for the first time. These Talks are profound, humorous, and poignant. An essential introduction to Adi Da Samraj's Wisdom-Teaching.

I first read The Method of the Siddhas *twenty years ago and it changed everything. It presented something new to my awareness: One who understood, who was clearly awake, who had penetrated fear and death, who spoke English (eloquently!), and who was alive and available!*

Ray Lynch
composer, *Deep Breakfast*;
No Blue Thing; *The Sky of Mind*;
Nothing Above My Shoulders but the Evening

$7.95, popular format

---

* All prices are in US dollars.

NEW! Enlarged and Updated

The Heart's Shout

*Perfect and Urgent Wisdom
from the Living Heart of Reality,
the Incarnate Divine Person,
Adi Da (The Da Avatar)*

The Heart's Shout is an inspiring anthology of the Wisdom-Teaching of Adi Da Samraj—the perfect book to introduce you (or a friend) to the full spectrum of His Teaching "Arguments" and Divine Confessions. You will discover: Why the devotional relationship with the Guru is necessary for God-Realization; "radical" understanding—the unique process of transcending suffering and Awakening to true Happiness; the limits of "scientific materialism" as a method of knowledge, and the liberating realization of "Divine Ignorance"; why all concepts about God are false, and the nature of "Real" God; the "Great Tradition"—a new and perfect presentation of the totality of religious and Spiritual teachings, organized according to the "Seven Stages of Life", Adi Da Samraj's schema of growth from birth to Divine Enlightenment; the practice of true devotion to the God-Realized Adept; the function of discipline in Spiritual practice; the transcendence of the "emotional-sexual" realm by living it as means of devotion to the Divine Person; the necessity of community in true Spiritual life; the truth about death and dying; the nature of Divine Enlightenment.

$17.95, quality paperback

Divine Distraction

A Guide to the Guru-Devotee Relationship, The Supreme Means of God-Realization, as Fully Revealed for the First Time by the Divine World-Teacher and True Heart-Master, Da Avabhasa (The "Bright")

by James Steinberg

In this wonderful book, a longtime devotee of Adi Da Samraj discusses the joys and challenges, the lore and laws, of the most potent form of Spiritual practice: the love relationship with the God-Man. Along with many illuminating passages from the Wisdom-Teaching of Adi Da Samraj, *Divine Distraction* includes humorous, insightful, and heart-moving stories from His devotees, as well as Teachings and stories from the world's Great Tradition of religion and Spirituality. Essential for anybody who wants to know first-hand about the time-honored liberating relationship between Guru and devotee.

This is a warm, loving, and incredibly moving book about the greatest Spiritual Master ever to walk the earth. Here you will find everything you need to know about life, love, and wisdom. I have no doubt whatsoever that this is true, no matter who you are, no matter which spiritual tradition you follow. Adi Da Samraj is the God-Man, the ultimate expression of the Truth residing in all religions. Of this I am absolutely certain.

The Reverend Thomas Ahlburn
Senior Minister, First Unitarian Church,
Providence, Rhode Island

$12.95, quality paperback

The Santosha Avatara Gita

(The Revelation of the Great Means of the Divine Heart-Way of No-Seeking and Non-Separateness)

In 108 verses of incredible beauty and simplicity, *The Santosha Avatara Gita* reveals the very essence of the Way of the Heart—Contemplation of Adi Da Samraj as the Realizer, the Revealer, and the Revelation of the Divinely Awakened Condition.

> *Therefore, because of My always constant, Giving, Full, and Perfect Blessing Grace, and because of the constant Grace of My Self-Revelation, it is possible for any one to practice the only-by-Me Revealed and Given Way of the Heart, and that practice readily (and more and more constantly) Realizes pleasurable oneness (or inherently Love-Blissful Unity) with whatever and all that presently arises . . . .*
>
> Avatar Adi Da Samraj
> *The Santosha Avatara Gita*, verse 78

This is the birth of fundamental and radical Scripture.

Richard Grossinger
author, *Planet Medicine; The Night Sky;*
and *Waiting for the Martian Express*

$24.95, quality paperback

The Liberator (Eleutherios)

The Epitome of the Perfect Wisdom and the Perfect Practice of the Way of the Heart

In compelling, lucid prose, Adi Da Samraj distills the essence of the ultimate processes leading to Divine Self-Realization in the Way of the Heart—the "Perfect Practice", which involves the direct transcendence of all experience via identification with Consciousness Itself, through feeling-Contemplation of His Form, His Presence, and His Infinite State.

> *Be Consciousness.*
>
> *Contemplate Consciousness.*
>
> *Transcend everything in Consciousness.*
>
> *This is the (Three-Part) "Perfect Practice", the Epitome of the Ultimate Practice and Process of the only-by-Me Revealed and Given Way of the Heart.*
>
> Avatar Adi Da Samraj
> *The Liberator (Eleutherios)*

$24.95, quality paperback

The Hymn Of The True Heart-Master

(The New Revelation-Book Of The Ancient and Eternal Religion Of Devotion To The God-Realized Adept)

The Hymn Of The True Heart-Master is a free rendering by Adi Da Samraj of the *Guru Gita*, an ancient Hindu text which proclaims that the relationship between the Guru and the devotee is the Supreme means of Divine Self- Realization. This book celebrates that relationship—and invites every reader into its God-Realizing embrace.

$24.95, quality paperback

Standing Crazy in the Heart

The Divine Life and Work of the Ruchira Buddha, Avatar Adi Da Samraj

by Carolyn Lee

The book *Standing Crazy in the Heart* chronicles and celebrates the Miraculous Leela of Adi Da Samraj's Life, from the profound Spiritual origins of His human Manifestation; through His early-life sacrifice of the knowledge of His Own Divine Identity; His subsequent trial of Divine Re-Awakening; the Love-Ordeal of His Teaching-Work with devotees; and the relinquishment of all of that in the Victory and Fullest Revelation of His "Divine Emergence", Whereby He Openly Blesses all beings in and with the Sign of His Own Inherent Fullness, Contentment, and Eternal Freedom.

Standing Crazy in the Heart will delight and inspire readers with the overwhelming evidence of a Miracle and Spiritual Opportunity of the most profound kind: Adi Da Samraj <u>Is</u> the Expected One, Here and alive Now. And He Invites you to a personal, living, and transformative relationship with Him for the sake of your own Divine Awakening.

$17.95, quality paperback

(forthcoming, summer 1997)

The Adidam Sutra

(On the Way of the Infinite Heart-Brightness That Inherently Outshines the ego-"I" and All the Illusions of Separateness, Relatedness, and Difference)

A unique summary of the entire progress of practice in the Way of the Heart, described in terms of the "sheaths", or bodies, of which the human body-mind complex is composed. The Essay ranges from highly practical sections on diet (as the foundation discipline of Spiritual practice) and sexuality, to sublime expressions of the Realizations of the advanced and the ultimate stages of practice in the Way of the Heart.

By Grace, Perfectly deep inspection (or Inherently Perfect Witnessing) of the feeling of relatedness dissolves (or resolves) the feeling of relatedness in the Inherent (or Most Prior) Feeling of Being, or the Great Heart-Feeling In Which it is arising. In that Event, only the Inherent Happiness of Consciousness Itself Stands Free and Still.

Thus, It Becomes Obvious.

(forthcoming)

The Adidam Revelation

A comprehensive and engaging introduction to all aspects of the religion of Adidam, the Liberating Way that the Ruchira Buddha, Avatar Adi Da Samraj, has made available for all. Addressed to new readers, *The Adidam Revelation* introduces Adi Da Samraj's Life and Work, the fundamentals of His Wisdom-Teaching, the Guru-devotee relationship in His Blessing Company, the principles and practices of Adidam, and life in the community of His devotees.

(forthcoming)

Audiotapes

Of Avatar Adi Da Samraj's Talks and "Considerations"

O ver the years, many people have told us that listening to audiotapes is their favorite way to encounter the Wisdom-Teaching of Adi Da Samraj. The tapes capture His beauty, passion, humor, force, and love. His voice itself is wonderfully resonant—full of His urgency for His devotee's growth, and full of the Fearless, Radiant Bliss that Is His Nature. Each tape—its ideas, its words, and the One Who Speaks them—completely communicates Adi Da Samraj Himself: The Divine Consciousness that is Happiness, Truth, and Reality. These tapes, like all of the Wisdom-Teaching of Adi Da Samraj, are a Gift and a Blessing.
Each audiotape is $11.95 unless otherwise noted.

NEW—

Luxuriate in the Life of Contemplation

A Conversation with the Incarnate Divine Person, Adi Da Samraj

For ten nights in January of 1996, Avatar Adi Da Samraj gathered with a small group of His long-time devotees at the Mountain Of Attention Sanctuary. There, He "considered" with them the Way of the Heart: the practice and process of transcending identification with the limited, suffering, dying self, and—through Contemplation of His Body, Spiritual Presence, and Perfect State—awakening to what Adi Da calls "the seventh stage of life"—the Happiness and Immortal Consciousness of the Radiant Divine Self.

During this gathering of January 6, Adi Da weaves the many threads of His brilliant Discourse into a single fabric of heart-opening and mind-stopping Instruction about Happiness Itself.

$29.95, set of four audiotapes

Other Available Audiotapes—

Be Moved by Me to Infinity

A gathering "consideration" with Adi Da Samraj on January 5, 1996. Often Instructing devotees through the unique medium of spontaneous "guided meditations", Adi Da Samraj Discoursed during this first gathering of that period on: the self-knot and the Witness-Position; the "Perfect Practice" of Realizing Consciousness Itself; the esoteric significance of His liturgical drama, *The Mummery*; tricksters and their role in society; the nature of fear and its transcendence; the culture and politics of individuation—and much more. *The Way is literally the Way of becoming En-Lightened, becoming Perfectly Identified with "Brightness", Me.* —Adi Da Samraj

$19.95, set of two audiotapes

Death is Not the End of Anything

January 14, 1995. An extraordinary Talk by Adi Da on transcending our fear of death.

You Can Suffer or You Can Love

This tape contains two Talks by Adi Da. "You Can Suffer or You Can Love" is Adi Da's Compassionate conversation with a young devotee who asked how she could know what He says is true. "The Placebo Principle" is Adi Da's Call for the exercise of real discrimination and growth beyond all limitation.

Beyond the Koan

A marvelous Discourse that cuts through the "koan" or the omnipresent and apparently unresolvable contradictions that confront us in ordinary life and Spiritual practice. It includes a discussion of the confession "'I' is the body", and how this understanding differs from mere identification with the body itself. (This Discourse is intended for listeners who already have a significant degree of familiarity with the Way of the Heart.)

The Crashing Down of My Divine Grace

February 1993. Talk excerpts on the miracle of Adi Da's Spiritual Heart-Transmission.

Divine Distraction

In highlights from four Ecstatic and Illuminating Talks, Adi Da Discourses on the Guru-devotee relationship, the Supreme Means of God-Realization.

I Will Do Everything

In this Talk, Adi Da Samraj explains how the Guru meditates the devotee who is open to Him. It is the Guru Who does the Yoga of God-Realization, not the devotee.

Identification of the Beloved

Adi Da Samraj Calls all beings to Realize the Truth that transcends conventional reactivity and lovelessness. In this Talk, He describes the cycle of inevitable death of the conditional loved-one, and the necessity to fulfill the Law of Love.

Renunciation and the Gift of Community

It has been traditionally known that esoteric practice requires profound and free renunciation. In this Talk, Adi Da describes how the discipline of community He offers fulfills this function for practitioners.

The Cosmic Mandala

Near-death experiences, the process of death, the after-death-realms—all are discussed by Adi Da in this remarkable tape, which helps us understand the significance of these phenomena in personal, universal, and Divine terms.

Easy Death

A collection of Talks by Adi Da on the death process and the process of transcendence, or "death", of the egoic self in Identification with the Divine. Also included are stories of people who have been directly served by Adi Da's Instruction and Blessing during near death experiences and in the death of intimates.

Listening is the Foundation of True Practice

In this Talk with devotees, Adi Da outlines in detail the progression of practice in the listening-hearing process.

Listen to Me

April 8, 1993. A summary Talk by Adi Da on the devastating and self-deluding act of self-contraction, by which beings are commonly based.

The "Westerner" in Everyone Must Be Converted

November 24, 1993. A Talk by Adi Da on utopian idealism and the need for real religious life.

When the Tiger Disappears

March 27, 1993. A Talk wherein Adi Da Speaks of responsibility as the key to a truly self-transcending, God-Realizing life.

The Method of the Siddhas Classic Audio Tape Series—

This series contains Talks published in the book *The Method of the Siddhas*. These talks were Given by Adi Da during the first year of His formal Teaching work—April 1972 to March 1973.

Money, Food, and Sex

In this early Talk Adi Da Speaks of the traditional error Spiritual aspirants make in resisting (and avoiding) "money, food, and sex".

Guru, Faith, and Satsang

In this Talk, Adi Da reveals the secrets of Satsang, the relationship to the Guru, that "truly marvelous condition" in which what we really need is abundantly given and real faith awakens.

I Only Move Where There is Fire

Finding a cave, retreating within, getting away from the hassle of life's demands—they might have worked in times past, but these traditional recommendations are not enough today. In this Talk, Adi Da Calls us to use the fire of life's tests and frustrations to understand ourselves and to discover and use His Graceful Help to outshine it all.

Meditative Audiotapes—

Tamboura Samaspanda

The tamboura is an ancient Indian instrument that has specific uses in Indian music, but also communicates directly to the body-mind a powerful mood of equanimity and a deep feeling of the Mystery of existence. It plays no melody, but only the repetitive sounds of open strings that resonate with complex overtones through its hollow-gourd body and finely crafted neck. This recording of Adi Da Samraj playing the tamboura is an expression of His own Ecstatic and Transcendental State, and is a Calling to all who listen to it to rest in the disposition of Contemplation of His Blessing Spiritual Transmission of the Heart.

The "Great Questions"

Based entirely on the Word of Adi Da Samraj, these four meditations will allow you to participate in a deeply Contemplative exploration of some of His most basic Teaching Arguments. Beginning with special instruction on relaxation, posture, and the Contemplative disposition, each meditation goes on to draw the listener into pondering several of the ten "Great Questions" of Adi Da Samraj: propositions designed to confound the mind, awaken self-understanding, and open the heart and body to His Grace.

Videotapes

These videotapes provide you with the unique opportunity to see Adi Da Samraj speaking directly with His devotees, conversations in which He Instructs, Guides, Criticizes, Loves—and always Calls the individual to understand the ego and thus to make a truer, firmer heart-commitment to Him and to God-Realization in His Company. VHS, NTSC format.

The 20th Anniversary Series—

20th Anniversary videotapes are **$24.95** each, **$99.95** for the set of six. 1 hour running time each

THE FUNDAMENTAL PURPOSE OF EXISTENCE

The fundamental purpose of existence is to Realize God, Freedom, and Truth. Here, Adi Da Samraj talks about the necessary ordeal of Spiritual Life that makes this Realization possible.

THE COMMITMENT TO GOD-REALIZATION

In this tape, Adi Da Samraj discusses how the motive to God-Realization is a Gift of Grace Given by the Sat-Guru, and not the result of will or self-effort.

THE GREAT SECRET

Avatar Adi Da Samraj explains that the Great Secret of Spiritual life is the relationship with Him as Sat-Guru—a relationship of devotional submission that prepares the individual to receive His Gift of Love-Bliss.

THE INTELLIGENCE OF THE HEART

Adi Da Samraj explains that the practices and disciplines of the Way of the Heart—the Way of God-Realization in His Company—are done in direct, devotional response to the Guru, and not as a part of a search for self-improvement.

THE PROCESS OF SPIRITUAL TRANSMISSION

Through Spiritual Transmission, the devotee is literally "baptized" by the Divine Energy of the Spiritual and always Blessing Presence of Adi Da Samraj, thereby entering more deeply into the process of God-Communion. In this tape, Adi Da Samraj talks about His Great Heart-Transmission, and how the Blessing of the Sat-Guru is the key to Spiritual Growth.

THE LESSON OF LIFE

Avatar Adi Da Samraj says the Lesson of Life is: "You can never become Happy. You can only be Happy." In this tape, He talks with young practitioners of the Way of the Heart about the inevitable failures and frustrations of trying to become Happy by satisfying desires, and the necessity of turning to Him as Sat-Guru, the One Who Is Happiness Itself.

Other Videotapes—

CONSCIOUS EXERCISE

Daily Exercise Routines Practiced by Devotees of Adi Da (The Da Avatar)
A perfect "conscious exercise" companion for those who are just beginning to adapt to "conscious exercise" as well as for those who have been doing these routines for years. This video guides you through the Hatha Yoga, Da Namaskar, Da Chi Gong, and Pranayama routines in a Contemplative manner that leaves you in a refreshed and balanced state of deep bodily equanimity.
77 min running time
$24.95

THE WAY OF THE HEART

An introduction to Adi Da Samraj, and the practice and community of the Way of the Heart. Includes wonderful Talk excerpts and the Leelas of devotees.
70 min running time
$19.95

THE ALWAYS-LIVING VISION

A Video Chronicle of Adi Da Samraj's Tour of Blessing to Northern California and Hawaii, September 1995 to April 1996
This video contains footage of Adi Da Samraj at the Mountain Of Attention, the Adidam Retreat Sanctuary in Northern California, and at Love-Ananda Mahal, the Adidam Retreat Sanctuary in Hawaii. Beloved Adi Da is seen in formal Darshan, interacting with animals in "Fear-No-More Zoo," on an "easter egg hunt", and in many other Sacred and delightful occasions.
30 min running time
$19.95

Polarity Screens

Our bodies may appear solid, but the truth is we are made of energy, or light. And we appear (and feel!) more or less radiant and harmonious depending on how responsible we are for feeling, breathing, and "conducting" the universal "prana", or life-force. In this book, Adi Da Samraj introduces us to this basic truth of our existence and offers a simple practical method for regularly restoring and enhancing the balance of our personal energy field. The Polarity Screens He recommends may be used with remarkable benefit by anyone at any time. Once you have felt the "magic" of these screens, you will never want to be without them.

It was through Adi Da Samraj's references to Polarity Screens, appearing within His extensive and extraordinary literature, that I first learned of them. Soon, not only myself and family, but also friends, and later also my patients, would try the Polarity Screens and would feel themselves—usually for the first time—as energy. It is the sort of shift in perception that can change one's life!

George Fritz, Ed.D.
psychologist,
specializing in pain control

$49.95, set of Polarity Screens and instruction book

What, Where, When, How, Why, and <u>Who</u> To Remember To Be Happy
*A Simple Explanation of
the Way of the Heart
(For Children, and Everyone Else)*

In this tiny jewel of a book, prepare to find the greatest Wisdom made perfectly comprehensible to anyone. Rejoice in the smile of every page restoring you to your native innocence and certainty of God—and discover the pleasure of reading it to children.

(forthcoming)

For a complete listing of books, audiotapes, and videotapes available from the Dawn Horse Press, please send for your free *Dawn Horse Press Catalogue.*

How to Order the Wisdom-Teaching of Avatar Adi Da Samraj

To order any of the listed materials, or to receive your free
Dawn Horse Press Catalogue, send your order to:

THE DAWN HORSE PRESS
12040 North Seigler Road
Middletown, CA 95461
USA
or
Call TOLL-FREE (800) 524-4941
Outside the USA call
(707) 928-4936
or
e-mail: dhp@adidam.org

We accept Visa, MasterCard, personal check, and money order.
In the USA, please add $4.00 (shipping and handling) for the first
book and $1.00 for each additional book. California residents add
7¼% sales tax. Outside the USA, please add $7.00 (shipping and
handling) for the first book and $3.00 for each additional book.
Checks and money orders should be made payable to the Dawn
Horse Press.

The Seven Stages of Life

BASED ON THE WISDOM-TEACHING OF AVATAR ADI DA SAMRAJ

The God that Adi Da Confesses transcends both doubt and belief. The only way to be certain of God is to <u>Realize</u> God, or the Divine Condition, directly. And that Realization requires a great Process.

What is the total process of human growth? What would occur in us if we were to grow to the full extent of our potential? Adi Da Offers a schema of seven stages of life which represents His Wisdom on the entire spectrum of human possibility. He has systematically described not only our physical, emotional, and mental development but also all the phases of Spiritual, Transcendental, and Divine unfolding that are potential in us, once we are mature in ordinary human terms. This unique schema, which proceeds from birth to the final phases of Divine Enlightenment, is a central reference point in Adi Da's Wisdom-Teaching. It is an invaluable tool for understanding how we develop as individuals and also for understanding how the Teachings and practices proposed by the various schools of religion and Spirituality fit into the whole course of human developmental possibility.

Adi Da describes the seven stages of life on the basis of His own Realization, as One Who has fulfilled that entire course. His testimony is literally unique. No one before Adi Da has Realized what He describes as the seventh and Most Ultimate stage of life. There are rare hints and intuitions of this Realization in the annals of Spirituality, particularly within the traditions of Hinduism and Buddhism. Adi Da, however, has both described and Demonstrated not only the process of Awakening to the seventh stage of life, or Divine Enlightenment, but also the progressive signs that unfold in the seventh stage Realizer. And His Wisdom-Revelation is thus a unique Guide by which we may understand all the necessary stages of our developmental "growth and outgrowing".

◆ ◆ ◆

The first three stages of life are the stages of ordinary human growth from birth to adulthood. They are the stages of physical, emotional, and mental development, occurring in three periods of approximately seven years each (until approximately twenty-one years of age). Every individual who lives to an adult age inevitably adapts (although, in most cases, only partially) to the first three stages of life.

STAGE ONE—Individuation: The first stage of life is the process of adapting to life as a separate individual no longer bound to the mother. Most important for the first stage child is the process of food-taking, and coming to accept sustenance from outside the mother's body. In fact, this whole stage of life could be described as an ordeal of weaning, or individuation.

Tremendous physical growth occurs in the first stage of life (the first seven or so years) and an enormous amount of learning—one begins to manage bodily energies and begins to explore the physical world. Acquiring basic motor skills is a key aspect of the first stage of life—learning to hold a spoon and eat with it, learning to walk and talk and be responsible for excretion. If the first stage of life unfolds as it should, the separation from the mother completes itself in basic terms. But there is a tendency in us to struggle with this simple individuation, or to not accept the process fully. Every human being tends to associate individuation with a feeling of separation, a sense of disconnection from love and support. That reaction is the dramatization of egoity, or self-contraction, in its earliest form. And unless one enters profoundly into the process of God-Realization, that reaction characterizes every individual for his or her entire life.

STAGE TWO—Socialization: Between the ages of five and eight years we begin to become aware of the emotional dimension of existence—how we feel and how others respond emotionally to us becomes of great importance. This is the beginning of the second stage of life, the stage of social adaptation and all that goes with it—a growing sense of sexual differentiation, awareness of the effects of one's actions on others, a testing of whether one is loved. Adi Da points out that in the second stage of life children are naturally psychic and sensitive to etheric energy and should be encouraged to feel that "you are more than what you look like", for the sake of their future Spiritual growth. With the arising of greater emotional sensitivity, there is also the tendency to become locked in patterns of feeling rejected by others, and rejecting or punishing others for their presumed un-love. The drama of rejecting and feeling rejected is the primary sign of incomplete adaptation in the second stage of life.

STAGE THREE—Integration: In the early to mid teens, the third stage of life becomes established. The key development of this stage is the maturing of mental ability—the capacity to use mind and speech in abstract, conceptual ways—together with the power to use discrimination and to exercise the will. On the bodily level, puberty is continuing (having begun during the later years of the second stage of life) with all its attendant bodily and emotional changes.

The purpose of the third stage of life is the integration of the human character in body, emotion, and mind, so that the emerging adult becomes a fully differentiated, or autonomous, sexual and social human character. If the process of growth in the first and the second stages of life has proceeded unhindered, then this integration can take place naturally. If, however, there have been failures of adaptation in the earlier stages—a chronic feeling of being separate and unsustained or chronic feelings of being rejected or unloved, and consequent difficulties in relating happily to others—then the process of integration is disturbed.

In fact, in most individuals, the process of the third stage of life becomes an adolescent struggle between the conflicting motives to be dependent on others and to be independent of them. This adolescent drama tends to continue throughout adult life. It is one of the signs that growth has stopped, that the work of the third stage of life was never completed. The truly mature adult—someone who is characterized by equanimity, discriminative intelligence, heart-feeling, and the impulse to always continue to grow—tends never to develop, although a nominal adaptation to the first three stages of life is usually acknowledged by twenty-one years of age.

So how does one begin to grow again? By participating in a culture of living religious and Spiritual practice that understands and rightly nurtures each stage of development. This is Adi Da's recommendation, and the circumstance that He has Worked to create for His devotees by establishing the Way of the Heart. Anyone, at any age, who chooses the Way of the Heart can begin the process of understanding and transcending the limits of his or her growth in the first three stages of life and in all the stages of life that follow.

Adi Da refers to the first three stages of life as the "foundation stages", because the ordeal of growth into human maturity is mere preparation for something far greater—for Spiritual awakening, and, ultimately, for Divine Enlightenment. This greater process begins to flower in the fourth stage of life on the basis of a profound conversion to love.

STAGE FOUR—Spiritualization: Even while still maturing in the first three stages of life, many people devote themselves to religious practices, submitting to an ordered life of discipline and devotion. This is the beginning of establishing the disposition of the fourth stage of life, but it is only the beginning. The real leap involved in the fourth stage of life is a transition that very few ever make. It is nothing less than the breakthrough to a Spiritually-illumined life of Divine contemplation and selfless service. How does such a life become possible? Only on the basis of a heart-awakening so profound that the common human goals—to be fulfilled through bodily and mental pleasures—lose their force.

The purpose of existence for one established in the fourth stage of life is devotion—moment to moment intimacy with the Spiritual Reality, an intimacy that is real and ecstatic, and which changes one's vision of the world. Everything that appears, everything that occurs is now seen as a process full of Spirit-Presence. This new vision of existence is given through Spirit-Baptism, an infilling of Spirit-Power (usually granted by a Spiritually Awakened Master), which is described in many different religious and Spiritual traditions.

For the devotee in the Way of the Heart who has completed the listening-hearing process and entered the seeing stages of practice, Adi Da's Spirit-Baptism is first felt as a Current of energy descending from above the head, down through the front of the body to the perineum, or bodily base. This descent is forceful, sublime, and very effective in purifying and Spiritualizing the human personality, bringing forth the signs of radiance, peace, and universal love that characterize a Spiritually Awakened being. This descending Spirit-Baptism is one of the uniquely characteristic signs of Adi Da's Grace in the life of His Spiritually activated devotee. By the time the fourth stage of life is complete, not only has the Spirit-Current descended fully down the front of the body but It has turned about at the bodily base and ascended up the spine to a place deep behind the eyes (called the "ajna chakra", or sometimes the "third eye"), where It is felt to rest.

The full-hearted and Spiritually Awakened devotion characteristic of the fourth stage of life is generally the summit of Realization achieved in the traditions of Judaism, Christianity, Islam, and much of Hinduism, and even then, it is most uncommon.

The fourth stage of life, though it represents a profound and auspicious advance beyond the foundation stages, is only the beginning of truly Spiritual growth. Adi Da points out that the primary error of one in the fourth stage of life is to presume that God and the individual personality are inherently separate from one another. God is the Sublime "Other" with Whom one Communes and in Whom one may become ecstatically absorbed at times, even to the point of apparent union. Nevertheless, such raptures pass, and one is left with the continuing urge for union with the Divine Beloved. The individual being is still a separate ego, still searching, even though the goal of seeking is Spiritual in nature.

STAGE FIVE—Higher Spiritual Evolution: The fifth stage of life could be described as the domain of accomplished Yogis—individuals involved in the pursuit of Enlightenment through mystical experience, such as the vision of the "blue pearl" and through the attainment of psychic powers. But it is important to note that just as exceedingly few religious practitioners fully Awaken to the Spiritual Reality in the fourth stage of life, exceedingly few would-be Yogis become fifth stage Realizers.

The important difference between the fifth stage of life and all the stages of life that precede it is that awareness on the gross physical plane is no longer the normal mode of existence. Rather, attention is constantly attracted into subtle realms—dreamlike or visionary regions of mind.

The phenomena of the fifth stage of life arise as a result of the further movement of the Spirit-Current, now in the higher regions of the brain. In the fifth stage of life the Spirit-Current moves from the ajna chakra through and beyond the crown of the head. At its point of highest ascent, the Spirit-Current triggers the Yogic meditative state traditionally called "Nirvikalpa Samadhi" ("formless ecstasy") in which all awareness of body and mind is temporarily dissolved in the absolute Love-Bliss of the Divine Self-Condition. This profoundly ecstatic state is regarded as the summit of Realization in the Hindu schools of Yoga, as well as in certain branches of Buddhism and Taoism. (It is precisely defined by Avatar Adi Da as "fifth stage conditional Nirvikalpa Samadhi".) This dissolution of body and mind is a direct demonstration that the apparently separate self has no eternal existence or significance, and that only the Divine Condition of absolute Freedom and Happiness truly exists.

Even so, a limit remains. This great Samadhi, the culminating achievement of the fifth stage of life, is fleeting. At some point bodily consciousness returns, and so does the ache to renew that boundless, disembodied Bliss. Fifth stage conditional Nirvikalpa Samadhi, for all its profundity, is achieved on the basis of a subtle stress.

It is the ultimate fruit of the Yogic strategy to escape the body by directing one's awareness upward into infinite Light.

In His description of the Way of the Heart, Adi Da Reveals that higher mystical experience and the achievement of profound trance states in the maturity of the fourth stage of life and in the fifth stage of life are not prerequisites for most ultimate Divine Enlightenment. In the Way of the Heart, the whole tour of the subtle planes can be bypassed, because of Adi Da's unique Transmission of the Love-Blissful Power of the Divine Itself. When, in the fourth stage of life, the devotee in the Way of the Heart is mature enough to be responsible for constantly receiving and "conducting" Adi Da's Spirit-Current, a most extraordinary process begins to take place in the body-mind. The Infusion of His Spirit-Current purifies and quickens the body-mind in every cell from the crown of the head to the very toes. Every knot in the body-mind is opened up in this ecstatic reception of Him.

When this Sublime Infusion has completed its Work, a great conversion has occurred in the body-mind. One is not susceptible to the fascinations of visionary experience, even when such experiences arise. Neither is one moved to direct one's attention up and out of the body into the infinitely ascended state of "formless ecstasy". Rather, the "tour" of mystical experience is revealed to be simply more of the futile search to be completely Happy and fulfilled. And so that whole pursuit of mystical satisfaction relaxes, and the devotee may be easily drawn beyond all habits of identification with bodily states and even beyond the subtle mind states of the fifth stage of life into a pristine understanding of Reality as Consciousness Itself.

STAGE SIX—Awakening to the Transcendental Self: In the sixth stage of life, one is no longer perceiving and interpreting everything from the point of view of the individuated body-mind with its desires and goals. One stands in a Transcendental Position, Identified with the Very Consciousness that is the Ground of all that exists, rather than with the apparently separate self. In that Position, one stands as the "Witness" of all that arises, even while continuing to participate in the play of life. While life goes on like a movie on a screen, one sees the greater import of Existence and the non-necessity of all that arises. This is the beginning of what Adi Da calls "the ultimate stages of life", or the stages of Identification with Consciousness Itself.

The sixth stage of life may include the experience of Jnana Samadhi, which, like fifth stage conditional Nirvikalpa Samadhi, is a form of temporary and conditional Realization of the Divine Self. However, fifth stage conditional Nirvikalpa Samadhi comes about through the strategy of ascent, the urge to move attention up and beyond the body-mind; in Jnana Samadhi, on the other hand, awareness of gross and subtle states is excluded by concentration in Transcendental Self-Consciousness.

The Awakening to Consciousness Itself in the sixth stage of life is the pinnacle of Realization achieved by the greatest (and exceedingly rare) Realizers in certain schools of Hinduism and Buddhism, as well as Jainism and Taoism. Such Realizers eschewed the fascinations of experience from the beginning, turning away from the enticements of "money, food, and sex" in the first three stages of life, as well as from the attractions of devotional (fourth stage) rapture and of

Yogic (fifth stage) mysticism. Instead, the Sages of the sixth stage of life have traditionally contemplated the freedom and purity of Consciousness—to the degree of Realizing that Consciousness Itself, eternal and Prior to any mortal form or temporary experience, is our True Condition, or True Self.

But even deep resting in the freedom of Transcendental Consciousness is not Most Perfect Enlightenment. Why not? Because there is still a stress involved, still one last barrier to Divine Self-Realization. Sixth stage practice and Realization is expressed by turning within, away from all conditional objects and experiences (including the energies and the movements of attention of one's own body-mind), in order to concentrate upon the Source of individual consciousness. Thus, the root of egoity is still alive. The search still remains, in its most primitive form. The sixth stage of life is the search to identify with Pure Consciousness Prior to and exclusive of phenomena.

STAGE SEVEN—Divine Enlightenment: The Realization of the seventh stage of life is uniquely Revealed and Given by Adi Da. It is release from all the egoic limitations of the previous stages of life. Remarkably, the seventh stage Awakening, which is Adi Da's Gift to His devotees who have completed the developmental course of the first six stages of life, is not an experience at all. The true Nature of everything is simply obvious. Now the Understanding arises that every apparent "thing" is Eternally, Perfectly the same as Reality, Consciousness, Happiness, Truth, or God. And that Understanding is Supreme Love-Bliss.

Adi Da calls this Divine Awakeness "Open Eyes" and also "seventh stage Sahaj Samadhi" ("Sahaj" meaning "natural", or inherent, and "Samadhi" meaning exalted State). No longer is there any need to seek meditative seclusion in order to Realize perpetual Identification with the One Divine Reality. The Ecstatic and world-embracing Confession "There is Only God" is native to one who enjoys the State of "Open Eyes". Consciousness is no longer felt to be divorced from the world of forms, but Consciousness Itself is understood and seen to be the very Nature, Source, and Substance of that world. And so the life of the seventh stage Realizer, Most Perfectly Awake by Grace of Adi Da, becomes the Love-Blissful process of Divinely Recognizing, or intuitively acknowledging, whatever arises to be only a modification of Consciousness Itself.

The Divinely Self-Realized Being is literally "Enlightened". The Light of Divine Being Flows in him or her in a continuous circuitry of Love-Bliss that rises in an S-shaped curve from the right side of the heart to a Matrix of Light above and Beyond the crown of the head. This is Amrita Nadi, the "Channel of Immortal Bliss", mentioned in the esoteric Hindu Spiritual tradition, but fully described for the first time by Adi Da Himself. After His Divine Re-Awakening in 1970, Adi Da experienced the "Regeneration" of this Current of Love-Bliss, and He came to understand Amrita Nadi as the Original Form of the Divine Self-Radiance in the human body-mind (and in all conditional beings and forms).

Divine Self-Realization in the seventh stage of life unfolds through a Yogic process in four phases: Divine Transfiguration, Divine Transformation, Divine Indifference, and Divine Translation.

In the phase of Divine Transfiguration, the Realizer's whole body is Infused by Love-Bliss, and he or she Radiantly Demonstrates active Love.

In the following phase of Divine Transformation, the subtle or psychic dimension of the body-mind is fully Illumined, which may result in extraordinary Powers, Grace-Given by Adi Da, of healing, longevity, and the ability to release obstacles from the world and from the lives of others.

Eventually, Divine Indifference ensues, which is spontaneous and profound Resting in the "Deep" of Consciousness Itself, with progressively less and less noticing of the manifested worlds.

Divine Translation is the ultimate "Event" of the entire process of Awakening—the Outshining of all noticing of objective conditions through the infinitely magnified Force of Consciousness Itself. Divine Translation is the Destiny beyond all destinies, from Which there is no return to the realms.

The experience of being so overwhelmed by the Divine Radiance that all appearances fade away may occur temporarily from time to time during the seventh stage of life. But when that Most Love-Blissful Swoon (or Moksha-Bhava Samadhi) becomes permanent, Divine Translation occurs and the body-mind is inevitably relinquished in death. Then there is only Eternal Inherence in the Divine Domain of unqualified Happiness and Joy.

Adi Da has frequently described the unfolding Mystery of the seventh stage of life through the image of crocks baking in a furnace:

AVATAR ADI DA SAMRAJ: When you place newly made clay crocks in a furnace of great heat to dry and harden the crockery, at first the crocks become red-hot and seem to be surrounded and pervaded by a reddish glow, but they are still defined. Eventually the fire becomes white-hot, and its radiation becomes so pervasive, so bright, that you can no longer make out the separate figures of the crocks.

This is the significance of Divine Translation. At first, conditions of existence are Transfigured by the inherent Radiance of Divine Being. Ultimately, through Self-Abiding and through Divinely Recognizing all forms, in effect all forms are Outshined by that Radiance. This is the Law of life. Life lived Lawfully is fulfilled in Outshining, or the transcendence of cosmic Nature. In the meantime, cosmic Nature is simply Divinely Transfigured, and relations are Divinely Transfigured, by the Power of the Divine Self-Position. [February 9, 1983]

The religious and Spiritual traditions of mankind characteristically conceive of human life as a "Great Path of Return", a struggle to be reunited with the Divine Source of existence. From Adi Da's viewpoint, this is an error. The Way of the Heart is founded in "radical" understanding, or constant restoration to the intuition of present Happiness, present God. Thus, although Adi Da allows for and fully explains all the developmental signs or stages of life through which His devotee may pass, the Way of the Heart is not purposed to "progress through" the stages of life. The entire process is founded in the Wisdom of the seventh stage from the very beginning—and thus is one of release, of surrendering, progressively, via heart-Communion with Adi Da, all obstructions in body, mind, and psyche that prevent that unqualified Divine Enjoyment.

Agency, Agent   All the Means that may serve as Vehicles of Avatar Adi Da's Divine Grace and Awakening Power. The first Means of Agency that have been fully established by Him are the Wisdom-Teaching of the Way of the Heart, the three Retreat Sanctuaries that He has Empowered, and the many Objects and Articles that He has Empowered for the sake of His devotees' Remembrance of Him and reception of His Heart-Blessing. After Avatar Adi Da's human Lifetime, at any given time one (and only one) from among His Divinely Awakened renunciate devotees will serve the Spiritual, Transcendental, and Divine Function of His <u>human</u> Agent in relationship to other devotees, all beings, the psycho-physical world, and the total cosmos.

Arrow   A motionless axis that seems to stand in the center of the body, between the frontal and spinal lines, in which Spirit-Power may be felt. This term is described in more detail on p. 203.

asana   Sanskrit for bodily "posture" or "pose". (By extension, and as Avatar Adi Da often intends, "asana" also refers to the attitude, orientation, posture, or feeling-disposition of the heart and the entire body-mind.)

The Basket of Tolerance   See pp. 298-99 for a description of this Source-Text.

"Bright", "Brightening", "Brightness"
Since His Illumined boyhood, Avatar Adi Da has used the term "the 'Bright'" (and its variations, such as "Brightness") to Describe the Love-Blissfully Self-Luminous, Conscious Divine Being, Which He Knew even then as His own Native Condition, and the Native Condition of all beings, things, and worlds.

causal   See **gross, subtle, and causal**.

chanting   Singing songs of devotion to Adi Da Samraj and in praise of His Gifts. Most often, these songs are sung with a chant leader (or leaders) singing each line and the congregation of devotees repeating the line. [see also **self-discipline**]

Circle   A primary pathway of natural life-energy and the Spirit-Current through the body-mind. This term is described in more detail on p. 203.

conditional, Unconditional   Avatar Adi Da uses the term "conditional" to indicate everything that depends on conditions—in other words, everything that is temporary and always changing. The "Unconditional", in contrast, is the Divine, or That Which is Always Already the Case because it is utterly free of dependence on conditions.

"conductivity"   Those practices in the Way of the Heart through which the practitioner conforms his or her bodily and emotional life, as well as the function of the breath, to the purpose of Spiritual practice in Adi Da's Company. In the broadest sense, "conductivity" includes disciplines of diet, physical exercise, health, sexuality, emotion, relationships, money, and community. In a more specific sense, "conductivity" also refers to the technical exercises (Given by Adi Da Samraj) whereby the practitioner "conducts" the flow of energy in the body.

"conscious process"   Those practices in the Way of the Heart through which the mind, or attention, is turned from egoic self-involvement to Heart-Communion with Avatar Adi Da. It is the senior discipline and responsibility of all Adi Da's devotees.

"consider", "consideration"   The technical term "consideration" in Avatar Adi Da's Wisdom-Teaching means a process of one-pointed but ultimately thoughtless concentration and exhaustive contemplation of something until its ultimate obviousness is clear.

Devotional Way of Faith/Devotional Way of Insight   Avatar Adi Da has Given two forms of the "conscious process" of devotional surrender to Him: The Devotional Way of Faith and the Devotional Way of Insight.

In the Devotional Way of Faith, the practitioner Invokes Avatar Adi Da by Name, and in heart-Attraction to Him is drawn beyond the self-contraction and awakened spontaneously to self-understanding and self-transcendence in Communion with Him.

In the Devotional Way of Insight, the practitioner, while Contemplating Avatar Adi Da with feeling, ponders one of the ten fundamental questions (in the beginning stages) or specifically practices self-Enquiry in the form "Avoiding relationship?", and thus observes, understands, and transcends the self-contraction in Communion with Adi Da Samraj.

Adi Da has noted that faith and insight are not exclusive to either of the forms of the "conscious process", but simply that one or the other is particularly emphasized. Each practitioner of the Way of the Heart formally chooses one of these forms of practice.

Dharma, dharma　Sanskrit for "duty", "virtue", "law". The word "dharma" is commonly used to refer to the many esoteric paths by which human beings seek the Truth. In its fullest sense, and when capitalized, "Dharma" means the complete fulfillment of duty—the living of the Divine Law. By extension, "Dharma" means a truly great Spiritual Teaching, including its disciplines and practices.

discipline　See **self-discipline**.

Divine　See **Spiritual, Transcendental, Divine**.

Divine Indifference, Divine Transfiguration, Divine Transformation, Divine Translation　The four phases of the unfolding of the seventh stage of life. See appendix on pp. 397-98.

Divine Recognition　The self- and world-transcending Intelligence of the Divine Self in relation to all conditional phenomena. In the seventh stage of life, the Realizer of the Divine Self simply Abides as Consciousness, and he or she Freely Recognizes, or inherently and Most Perfectly comprehends and perceives, all phenomena (including body, mind, and conditional self) as (apparent) modifications of the same "Bright" Divine Consciousness.

etheric　The sheath of life-energy that functions through and corresponds with the human nervous system. Our bodies are surrounded and infused by this personal life-energy, which we feel as the play of emotions and life-force in the body.

faculties　See p. 76 for a discussion of the four faculties of the body-mind.

Feeling of Being　The uncaused (or Self-Existing), Self-Radiant, and unqualified feeling-intuition of the Transcendental, Inherently Spiritual, and Divine Self. This absolute Feeling does not merely accompany or express the Realization of the Heart Itself, but it is identical to that Realization. To feel, or, really, to Be, the Feeling of Being is to enjoy the Love-Bliss of Absolute Consciousness, Which, when Most Perfectly Realized, cannot be affected or diminished in any way either by the events of life or by death.

feeling-Contemplation　Avatar Adi Da's term for the essential devotional and meditative practice that all devotees in the Way of the Heart engage at all times in relationship to His bodily (human) Form, His Spiritual (and Always Blessing) Presence, and His Very (and Inherently Perfect) State. Feeling-Contemplation of Adi Da is Awakened by Grace through Darshan, or feeling-sighting, of His Form, Presence, and State. It is then to be practiced under all conditions, and as the basis and epitome of all other practices in the Way of the Heart.

feeling of relatedness/feeling of "difference"　In the foundation stages of practice in the Way of the Heart, the basic or gross level activity of the avoidance of relationship is understood and released in the free capability for simple relatedness, or the feeling of relatedness. Only in the ultimate stages of life in the Way of the Heart is the feeling of relatedness fully understood as the root-act of attention itself and, ultimately, transcended in the Feeling of Being. In that case, it is understood to be the feeling of "I" and "other", or the feeling of "difference" between the egoic self and all its relations or objects of attention. Adi Da Samraj points out that the feeling of relatedness is, at root, the <u>avoidance</u> of relationship in relation to all others and things, or the root-activity of separation, separateness, and separativeness that <u>is</u> the ego.

four faculties (body, mind, emotion, breath) See p. 76 for a discussion of the four faculties of the body-mind.

frontal Yoga See p. 203 for a discussion of the frontal Yoga.

The Great Tradition Avatar Adi Da's term for the total inheritance of human, cultural, religious, magical, mystical, Spiritual, Transcendental, and Divine paths, philosophies, and testimonies from all the eras and cultures of humanity, which has (in the present era of worldwide communication) become the common legacy of mankind.

gross, subtle, and causal Adi Da Samraj has confirmed the correctness of traditional descriptions of the human body-mind and its environment as consisting of three great dimensions—gross, subtle, and causal.

The gross, or most physical, dimension is associated with the physical body and experience in the waking state.

The subtle dimension, which is senior to and pervades the gross dimension, includes the etheric (or energetic), lower mental (or verbal-intentional and lower psychic), and higher mental (or deeper psychic, mystical, and discriminative) functions. The subtle dimension is associated primarily with the ascending energies of the spine, the brain core, and the subtle centers of mind in the higher brain. It is also, therefore, associated with the visionary, mystical, and Yogic Spiritual processes.

The causal dimension is senior to and pervades both the gross and the subtle dimensions. It is the root of attention, or the essence of the separate and separative ego-"I". The causal dimension is associated with the right side of the heart, specifically with the sinoatrial node, or "pacemaker" (the psycho-physical source of the heartbeat). Its corresponding state of consciousness is the formless awareness of deep sleep. It is inherently transcended by the Witness-Consciousness (Which is Prior to all objects of attention).

Hatha Yoga "Hatha" means "force" or "power". This Yoga traditionally aims to achieve ecstasy and even Liberation through manipulation of body, breath, and energy, with concomitant discipline of attention. In the Way of the Heart, the bodily poses (asanas) of Hatha Yoga are engaged to purify, balance, and regenerate the functions of the body-mind.

hearing Avatar Adi Da's technical term for most fundamental understanding of the self-contraction, through which the practitioner awakens to the unique capability for direct transcendence of the self-contraction and for simultaneous Communion with Avatar Adi Da. This term is explained in more detail on p. 78.

klik-klak Avatar Adi Da's term for the mechanical nature of conditional existence—constant change and impermanence. This term is explained in more detail on p. 94.

kriyas Spontaneous, self-purifying physical movements. Kriyas arise when the natural bodily energies are stimulated by the Divine Spirit-Current.

life-business By "life-business", Avatar Adi Da is referring to practical means of survival, bringing the body-mind into basic equanimity, and all social and emotional-sexual relationships. Having your life-business handled grants free energy and attention for Spiritual practice.

listening Avatar Adi Da's term for the disposition of the beginner's preparation and practice in the Way of the Heart. The focus of the listening process is the awakening of true self-observation and most fundamental self-understanding, or hearing. This term is also described on p. 78.

Mama, Mama-talk, Mama Form See p. 48.

maya Sanskrit for the illusion that inevitably arises from ignorance of the True Nature of conditional reality and Unconditional Reality.

meditation In the Way of the Heart, meditation is a period of formal devotional Contemplation of Avatar Adi Da Samraj. [see also **self-discipline**]

"money, food, and sex" Avatar Adi Da uses this phrase to summarize the basic areas of life-business that must be handled by all His devotees (and which are fundamental areas of seeking in the common world). Money includes all uses of life-energy (such as work and service), food includes everything related to health (such as diet and exercise), and sex includes the emotional and sexual dimensions of the body-mind as well as all relationships.

Most Perfect(ly), Most Ultimate(ly) Adi Da Samraj uses the phrase "Most Perfect(ly)" in the sense of "Absolutely Perfect(ly)". Similarly, the phrase "Most Ultimate(ly)" is equivalent to "Absolutely Ultimate(ly)".

In the sixth stage of life and the seventh stage of life, What is Realized (Consciousness Itself) is Perfect (and Ultimate). This is why Avatar Adi Da characterizes these stages as the "ultimate stages of life", and describes the practice of the Way of the Heart in the context of these stages as "the 'Perfect Practice'". The distinction between the sixth stage of life and the seventh stage of life is that the devotee's <u>Realization</u> of What is Perfect (and Ultimate) is Itself Perfect (and Ultimate) only in the seventh stage. The Perfection or Ultimacy (in the seventh stage) <u>both</u> of What is Realized and of the Realization of It is what is signified by the phrase "Most Perfect(ly)" or "Most Ultimate(ly)".

The Mummery The first Revelation-Book made by Avatar Adi Da, written in 1969. *The Mummery*, which Adi Da Samraj describes as "a liturgical prose-opera", is an archetypal story of the process of Realizing Most Perfect Divine Enlightenment, as exemplified through the remarkable adventures of the principal character, Raymond Darling.

Murti Sanskrit for "form". Traditionally, as well as in Avatar Adi Da's usage, the primary meaning of "murti" is "representational image". Generally, in the Way of the Heart, "Murtis" are photographic images of Avatar Adi Da.

"Narcissus" A key symbol in Avatar Adi Da's Teaching-Revelation of the un-

Enlightened individual as a self-obsessed seeker, enamored of his or her own self-image and egoic self-consciousness. In *The Knee of Listening*, Adi Da Samraj describes the significance of the archetype of Narcissus:

He is the ancient one visible in the Greek "myth", who was the universally adored child of the gods, who rejected the loved-one and every form of love and relationship, who was finally condemned to the contemplation of his own image, until, as a result of his own act and obstinacy, he suffered the fate of eternal separateness and died in infinite solitude.

non-humans In its widest sense, Avatar Adi Da's term "non-humans" includes everything that is not human (including plants, trees, animals, walls, rocks, and so on). However, Avatar Adi Da also uses the term to refer specifically to animals.

"Perfect Practice" See pp. 195-96.

Pleasure Dome See p. 23.

"practicing school", "talking school" "Practicing school" is a phrase coined by Avatar Adi Da to refer to those in any tradition of sacred life who are committed to the ordeal of real self-transcending discipline, under the guidance of a true Guru. He contrasts the "practicing school" with the ineffectual—and often presumptuous—"talking school" approach. The "talking-school" approach is characterized by talking, thinking, reading, and philosophical analysis and debate, or even meditative enquiry or reflection without a concomitant and foundation discipline of body, emotion, mind, and breath.

prasad Sanskrit, meaning "gifts that have been offered to the Divine and, having been Blessed, are returned as Divine Gifts to devotees". By extension, Prasad is anything a devotee receives from his or her Guru.

Puja Sanskrit for "worship". All formal sacramental devotion in the Way of the Heart is consecrated to Ruchira-Guru Adi Da and is thus celebrated as Ruchira-Guru Puja. [see also **self-discipline**]

402

Quandra Mai The women who serve Adi Da Samraj personally and who are committed to Him in the most sacred devotional manner of the Guru-devotee bond, and to renunciate practice in His direct physical Company. "Quandra" and "Mai" are references to the main female character in Adi Da Samraj's liturgical drama, *The Mummery*. Quandra is the embodiment of the Divine Goddess, or Spirit-Force.

"radical" The term "radical" derives from the Latin "radix", meaning "root", and thus it principally means "irreducible", "fundamental", or "relating to the origin". Because Adi Da Samraj uses "radical" in this literal sense, it appears in quotation marks in His Wisdom-Teaching to distinguish His usage from the common reference to an extreme (often political) view.

In contrast to the developmental, egoic searches typically espoused by the world's religious and Spiritual traditions, the "radical" Way of the Heart Offered by Avatar Adi Da is established in the Divine Self-Condition of Reality, even from the very beginning of one's practice. Every moment of feeling-Contemplation of Avatar Adi Da, Who is the Realizer, the Revealer, and the Revelation of that "radically" Free Divine Self-Condition, undermines, therefore, the illusory ego at its root (the self-contraction in the heart), rendering the search not only unnecessary but obsolete, and awakening the devotee to the "radical" Intuition of the always already Free Condition.

Ruchira Buddha Bhakti Yoga Ruchira Buddha Bhakti Yoga is the principal Gift, Calling, and Discipline Offered by Adi Da Samraj to all who practice the Way of the Heart.

The phrase "Ruchira Buddha Bhakti Yoga" is itself a summary of the Way of the Heart. "Bhakti", in Sanskrit, is love, adoration, or devotion, while "Yoga" is a God-Realizing discipline or practice. "Ruchira Buddha Bhakti Yoga" is therefore the Divinely Revealed practice of devotional love for (and response to) the Ruchira Buddha, Avatar Adi Da Samraj.

sadhana Self-transcending religious or Spiritual practice.

"Sadhana Years" Avatar Adi Da's "Sadhana Years" refers to the time from which He began His Quest to recover the Truth of Existence (at Columbia college) until His Divine Re-Awakening in 1970.

Samadhi A Sanskrit word that traditionally denotes various exalted states that appear in the context of esoteric meditation and Realization. Avatar Adi Da Teaches that, in the Way of the Heart, Samadhi is, even more simply and fundamentally, a state of ego-transcendence in Communion with Him. Adi Da's devotee is in Samadhi in any moment of standing beyond the separate self in devotional ecstasy.

seeing Avatar Adi Da's technical term for His devotee's Spiritually activated conversion from self-contraction to His Spiritual (and Always Blessing) Presence, and the descent and circulation of His Spiritual Transmission in, through, and (ultimately) beyond the body-mind of His devotee. This term is described in more detail on p. 78.

self-discipline The Way of the Heart necessarily involves a life of disciplined secondary practices, which support the primary practice of Ruchira Buddha Bhakti Yoga. Beloved Adi Da has Said that the life-disciplines serve two primary functions:
• They are practical expressions or evidence of the devotional relationship to Beloved Adi Da.
• They serve the establishment of psycho-physical equanimity (necessary for the effective practice of feeling-Contemplation of Adi Da Samraj). In addition, in the listening stage of practice of the Way of the Heart, the life-disciplines also serve the process of self-observation. (In the stages subsequent to listening, the life-disciplines are expressions of already active self-observation.)

See also pp. 44-45.

self-Enquiry A practice of pondering in the form "Avoiding relationship?", unique to the Way of the Heart, spontaneously developed by Avatar Adi Da in the course of His own Ordeal of Divine Re-Awakening. This practice is one of the forms of the "conscious process" that Adi Da has Given to His devotees. Intense persistence in the "radical" discipline of this unique form of self-Enquiry led rapidly to Avatar Adi Da's Divine Enlightenment (or Most Perfect Divine Self-Realization) in 1970.

"self-possession", "self-possessed" The usual meaning of "self-possessed" is "possessed of oneself"—or having full control (calmness, or composure) of one's feelings, impulses, habits, and actions. However, Avatar Adi Da uses the term to indicate the state of being possessed by one's egoic self, or controlled by chronically self-referring (or egoic) tendencies of attention, feeling, thought, desire, and action. Thus, unless (in every moment) body, emotion, desire, thought, separate and separative self, and all attention are actively and completely surrendered to Avatar Adi Da, one is egoically "self-possessed", even when exhibiting personal control of one's feelings, habits, and actions. And the devotional practice of feeling-Contemplation of Avatar Adi Da is the principal Means Given (by Grace) to practitioners of the Way of the Heart, whereby they may responsively (and, thus, by Grace) surrender, forget, and transcend egoic "self-possession".

seventh stage Sahaj Samadhi, or seventh stage Sahaja Nirvikalpa Samadhi The seventh stage of life is the unique Revelation of Adi Da Samraj, and He is the only (and only necessary) Adept-Realizer of this stage. His Realization of seventh stage Sahaj Samadhi makes that same Realization possible for His devotees, though none of His devotees will have the Adept-Function. The Hindi word "sahaj" means "natural". Avatar Adi Da uses the term "seventh stage Sahaj Samadhi" to indicate the Coincidence, in unqualified self-transcending God-Realization, of the Unconditional, Inherently Spiritual, and Transcendental Divine Reality with conditional reality. It is the Inherent, or Native, and thus truly "Natural" State of Being. Seventh stage Sahaj Samadhi, then, is permanent, Unconditional Divine Self-Realization, free of dependence on any form of meditation, effort, discipline, experience, or conditional knowledge.

"Sahaj Samadhi" (in the sense of a "natural" state of ecstasy) is a term also used in various esoteric traditions (of the fourth, the fifth, and the sixth stages of life). Such Samadhis, however, depend on certain psycho-physical conditions being maintained, and are therefore not permanent. In contrast, seventh stage Sahaj Samadhi is the Unconditional and Eternal Realization of the Divine.

Avatar Adi Da also refers to seventh stage Sahaj Samadhi as "seventh stage Sahaja Nirvikalpa Samadhi", indicating that it is the "Open-Eyed" Realization of the formless (Nirvikalpa) State.

Source-Texts Adi Da Samraj has written nine Source-Texts that form the summary of His entire Teaching-Word:

The Dawn Horse Testament Of The Ruchira Buddha (The "Testament Of Secrets" Of Avatar Adi Da Samraj)

The Heart Of The Dawn Horse Testament Of The Ruchira Buddha (The Essential "Testament Of Secrets" Of Avatar Adi Da Samraj)

The Adidam Sutra (On the Way of the Infinite Heart-Brightness That Inherently Outshines the ego-"I" and All the Illusions of Separateness, Relatedness, and Difference)

The Samraj Upanishad (The "Garland Of Discourses" Of The Adidam Revelation)

Aham Da Asmi (The "Great Declaration" Sutra): The Revelation Of The Great Means Of The Divine Heart-Way Of No-Seeking and Non-Separateness

The Hymn Of The True Heart-Master (The Revelation-Book Of The Way Of ego-Transcending Devotion To The Ruchira Buddha)

The Lion Sutra: The Ultimate Teachings Of Ruchira Buddhism (On Perfect Transcendence Of The Primal Act, Which is the ego-"I", the self-Contraction, or attention itself, and All The Illusions Of Separateness, Otherness, Relatedness, and Difference, and On The Perfect Practice Of Feeling-Enquiry Engaged By Formal Renunciates In The Advaitayana Buddhist Way Of The Heart)

The Liberator (The Eleutherian Sutra): The Epitome of the Perfect Wisdom and the

Perfect Practice of Ruchira Buddhism, the Way of the Heart

The Basket of Tolerance: The Perfect Guide to Perfect Understanding of the One and Great Tradition of Mankind

spinal Yoga   See p. 203.

Spiritual, Transcendental, Divine
Avatar Adi Da uses these terms in reference to different dimensions of Reality that are Realized progressively in the Way of the Heart. "Spiritual" refers to the reception of the Spirit-Force (in the context of the "advanced" fourth stage of life and the fifth stage of life); "Transcendental" refers to the Realization of Consciousness Itself as separate from the world (in the context of the sixth stage of life); and "Divine" refers to the Most Perfect Realization of Consciousness Itself as utterly non-separate from the world (in the context of the seventh stage of life).

stages of life   Avatar Adi Da has Revealed the underlying structure of human growth in seven stages. See appendix on pp. 392-98.

subtle   See **gross, subtle, and causal**.

"talking school"   See **"practicing school", "talking school"**.

Transcendental   See **Spiritual, Transcendental, Divine**.

"turiya", "turiyatita"   Terms used in the Hindu philosophical systems. Traditionally, "turiya" means "the fourth state" (beyond waking, dreaming, and sleeping), and "turiyatita" means "the state beyond the fourth", or beyond all states. Adi Da, however, has given these terms different meanings in the context of the Way of the Heart. He uses the term "turiya" to indicate the Awakening to Consciousness Itself (in the context of the sixth stage of life), and "turiyatita" as the State of Most Perfect Divine Enlightenment, or the Realization of all arising as transparent and non-binding modifications of the One Divine Reality (in the context of the seventh stage of life).

Unconditional   See **conditional, Unconditional**.

Witness, Witness-Position   When Consciousness is free from identification with the body-mind, it takes up its natural "position" as the Conscious Witness of all that arises to and in and as the body-mind.

In the Way of the Heart, the stable Realization of the Witness-Position is associated with, or demonstrated via, the effortless surrender or relaxation of all the forms of seeking and all the motives of attention that characterize the first five stages of life. However, identification with the Witness-Position is not final (or Most Perfect) Realization of the Divine Self. Rather, it is the first stage of the "Perfect Practice" in the Way of the Heart, which Practice Realizes, by Avatar Adi Da's Liberating Grace, complete and irreversible Identification with Consciousness Itself.

Yoga   Sanskrit for (literally) "yoking", or "union", usually referring to any discipline or process whereby an aspirant attempts to reunite with God. Adi Da Samraj acknowledges this conventional and traditional use of the term, but also, in reference to the Great Yoga of the Way of the Heart, employs it in a "radical" sense, free of the usual implication of egoic separation and seeking.

An Invitation to Support Adidam, the Way of the Heart

Avatar Adi Da Samraj's sole purpose is to act as a Source of continuous Divine Grace for everyone, everywhere. In that spirit, He is a Free Renunciate and He owns nothing. Those who have made gestures in support of Avatar Adi Da's Work have found that their generosity is returned in many Blessings that are full of His healing, transforming, and Liberating Grace—and those Blessings flow not only directly to them as the beneficiaries of His Work, but to many others, even all others. At the same time, all tangible gifts of support help secure and nurture Avatar Adi Da's Work in necessary and practical ways, again similarly benefiting the whole world. Because all this is so, supporting His Work is the most auspicious form of financial giving, and we happily extend to you an invitation to serve Adidam through your financial support.

You may make a financial contribution in support of the Work of Adi Da Samraj at any time. You may also, if you choose, request that your contribution be used for one or more specific purposes.

If you are moved to help support and develop Ruchira Buddha Dham (Naitauba), Avatar Adi Da's Great Sannyasin Hermitage Ashram and Renunciate Retreat Sanctuary in Fiji, and the circumstance provided there and elsewhere for Avatar Adi Da and the other members of the Advaitayana Buddhist Order, the senior renunciate order of Adidam, you may do so by making your contribution to The Ruchira Buddha Foundation, the Australian charitable trust which has central responsibility for these Sacred Treasures of Adidam.

To do this: (1) if you do not pay taxes in the United States, make your check payable directly to "The Ruchira Buddha Foundation Pty Ltd" (which serves as the trustee of the Foundation) and mail it to The Ruchira Buddha Foundation at P.O. Box 4744, Samabula, Suva, Fiji; and (2) if you do pay taxes in the United States and you would like your contribution to be tax-deductible under U.S. laws, make your check payable to "The Eleutherian Pan-Communion of Adidam", indicate on your check or accompanying letter that you would like your contribution used for the work of The Ruchira Buddha Foundation, and mail your check to the Advocacy Department of Adidam at 12040 North Seigler Road, Middletown, California 95461, USA.

If you are moved to help support and provide for one of the other purposes of Adidam, such as publishing the sacred Literature of Avatar Adi Da, or supporting either of the other two Sanctuaries He has Empowered, or maintaining the Sacred Archives that preserve His recorded Talks and Writings, or publishing audio and video recordings of Avatar Adi Da, you may do so by making your contribution directly to The Eleutherian Pan-Communion of Adidam, specifying the particular purposes you wish to benefit, and mailing your check to the Advocacy Department of Adidam at the above address.

If you would like more information about these and other gifting options, or if you would like assistance in describing or making a contribution, please write to the Advocacy Department of Adidam at the above address or contact the Adidam Legal Department by telephone at (707) 928-4612 or by FAX at (707) 928-4062.

Planned Giving

We also invite you to consider making a planned gift in support of the Work of Avatar Adi Da. Many have found that through planned giving they can make a far more significant gesture of support than they would otherwise be able to make. Many have also found that by making a planned gift they are able to realize substantial tax advantages.

There are numerous ways to make a planned gift, including making a gift in your Will, or in your life insurance, or in a charitable trust.

If you would like to make a gift in your Will in support of the work of The Ruchira Buddha Foundation: (1) if you do not pay taxes in the United States, simply include in your Will the statement, "I give to The Ruchira Buddha Foundation Pty Ltd, as trustee of The Ruchira Buddha Foundation, an Australian charitable trust, P.O. Box 4744, Samabula, Suva, Fiji, _____ " [inserting in the blank the amount or description of your contribution]; and (2) if you do pay taxes in the United States and you would like your contribution to be free of estate taxes and to also reduce any estate taxes payable on the remainder of your estate, simply include in your Will the statement, "I give to The Eleutherian Pan-Communion of Adidam, a California non-profit corporation, 12040 North Seigler Road, Middletown, California 95461, USA, _____ " [inserting in the blank the amount or description of your contribution].

To make a gift in your life insurance, simply name as the beneficiary (or one of the beneficiaries) of your life insurance policy the organization of your choice (The Ruchira Buddha Foundation or The Eleutherian Pan-Communion of Adidam), according to the foregoing descriptions and addresses. If you are a United States taxpayer, you may receive significant tax benefits if you make a contribution to The Eleutherian Pan-Communion of Adidam through your life insurance.

We also invite you to consider establishing or participating in a charitable trust for the benefit of Adidam. If you are a United States taxpayer, you may find that such a trust will provide you with immediate tax savings and assured income for life, while at the same time enabling you to provide for your family, for your other heirs, and for the Work of Avatar Adi Da as well.

The Advocacy and Legal Departments of Adidam will be happy to provide you with further information about these and other planned gifting options, and happy to provide you or your attorney with assistance in describing or making a planned gift in support of the Work of Avatar Adi Da.

Further Notes to the Reader

as literal expressions and extensions of His Blessing-Transmission. Among these Empowered Sacred Treasures is His Wisdom-Teaching, which is Full of His Transforming Power. This Blessed and Blessing Wisdom-Teaching has Mantric Force, or the literal Power to Serve God-Realization in those who are Graced to receive it.

Therefore, Avatar Adi Da's Wisdom-Teaching must be perpetually honored and protected, "set apart" from all possible interference and wrong use. The fellowship of devotees of Avatar Adi Da is committed to the perpetual preservation and right honoring of the sacred Wisdom-Teaching of the Way of the Heart. But it is also true that in order to fully accomplish this we must find support in the world-society in which we live and its laws. Thus, we call for a world-society and for laws that acknowledge the sacred, and that permanently protect It from insensitive, secular interference and wrong use of any kind. We call for, among other things, a system of law that acknowledges that the Wisdom-Teaching of the Way of the Heart, in all Its forms, is, because of Its sacred nature, protected by perpetual copyright.

We invite others who respect the sacred to join with us in this call and in working toward its realization. And, even in the meantime, we claim that all copyrights to the Wisdom-Teaching of Avatar Adi Da and the other sacred Literature and recordings of the Way of the Heart are of perpetual duration.

We make this claim on behalf of The Ruchira Buddha Foundation Pty Ltd, which, acting as trustee of The Ruchira Buddha Foundation, is the holder of all such copyrights.

AVATARA ADI DA AND THE SACRED TREASURES OF ADIDAM

Those who Realize God to any degree bring great Blessing and Divine Possibility for the world. Such Realizers accomplish universal Blessing Work that benefits everything and everyone. They also work very specifically and intentionally with individuals who approach them as their devotees, and with those places where they reside and to which they direct their specific regard for the sake of perpetual Spiritual Empowerment. This was understood in traditional Spiritual cultures, and those cultures therefore found ways to honor Realizers by providing circumstances for them where they were free to do their Spiritual Work without obstruction or interference.

Those who value Avatar Adi Da's Realization and Service have always endeavored to appropriately honor Him in this traditional way by providing a circumstance where He is completely Free to do His Divine Work. Since 1983, He has resided principally on the island of Naitauba, Fiji, also known as Ruchira Buddha Dham. This island has been set aside by Avatar Adi Da's devotees worldwide as a place for Him to do His universal Blessing Work for the sake of everyone, and His specific Work with those who pilgrimage to Ruchira Buddha Dham to receive the special Blessing of coming into His physical Company.

Avatar Adi Da is a legal renunciate. He owns nothing and He has no secular or religious institutional function. He Functions only in Freedom. He, and the other members of the Advaitayana Buddhist Order, the senior renunciate order of

Adidam, are provided for by The Ruchira Buddha Foundation, which also provides for Ruchira Buddha Dham altogether and ensures the permanent integrity of Avatar Adi Da's Wisdom-Teaching, both in its archival and in its published forms. This Foundation, which functions only in Fiji, exists exclusively to provide for these Sacred Treasures of Adidam.

Outside Fiji, the institution which has developed in response to Avatar Adi Da's Wisdom-Teaching and universal Blessing is known as "The Eleutherian Pan-Communion of Adidam". This formal organization is active worldwide in making Avatar Adi Da's Wisdom-Teaching available to all, in offering guidance to all who are moved to respond to His Offering, and in providing for the other Sacred Treasures of Adidam, including the Mountain Of Attention Sanctuary (in California) and Love-Ananda Mahal (in Hawaii). In addition to the central corporate entity known as The Eleutherian Pan-Communion of Adidam, which is based in California, there are numerous regional entities which serve congregations of Avatar Adi Da's devotees in various places throughout the world.

Practitioners of Adidam worldwide have also established numerous community organizations, through which they provide for many of their common and cooperative community needs, including those relating to housing, food, businesses, medical care, schools, and death and dying. By attending to these and all other ordinary human concerns and affairs via self-transcending cooperation and mutual effort, Avatar Adi Da's devotees constantly free their energy and attention, both personally and collectively, for practice of the Way of the Heart and for service to Avatar Adi Da, to Ruchira Buddha Dham, to the other Sacred Treasures of Adidam, and to The Eleutherian Pan-Communion of Adidam.

All of the organizations that have evolved in response to Avatar Adi Da and His Offering are legally separate from one another, and each has its own purpose and function. Avatar Adi Da neither directs, nor bears responsibility for, the activities of these organizations. Again, He Functions only in Freedom. These organizations represent the collective intention of practitioners of Adidam worldwide not only to provide for the Sacred Treasures of Adidam, but also to make Avatar Adi Da's Offering of the Way of the Heart universally available to all.

INDEX

C

"C" and "&", 181-82
capitalization, in Adi Da's Source-Texts, 129
cats, 207-208
　value depth, 214
causal, defined, 401
causal domain, sadhana in the, 194
cause, is a "what", 147
chameleons, 208
chanting, defined, 399
chimpanzees, human likenesses to, 29-30
Circle
　defined, 399
　described, 203
Coleridge, Samuel Taylor, 23
communication, verbal and non-verbal, 108-118
Communion with Adi Da, 125, 252
　is not an effort, 254
compassion, 266-67
conception
　described, 248
　and "you", 284-86
　See also perception
Condit, Jonathan, Leelas by, 51-65, 69-72
conditional, defined, 6n, 399
"conductivity", 76, 227
　in Adi Da's Sadhana, 133
　defined, 133, 399
Consciousness
　not separate from Energy and world, 227
　"there is only Energy and Consciousness", 233, 234
Consciousness Itself
　not the basis of conversation, 8
　vs. presumption of being an organism, 51-65
　you can't get any deeper than, 214
"conscious process", 227
　in Adi Da's Sadhana, 133
　defined, 46, 399
　and hearing, 173, 174
"consider", defined, 399
"consideration", described, xxi, xxviii
Contemplation
　is considered unusual, 18
　and non-humans, 16, 22
　See also feeling-Contemplation
"Contractio ergo sum", 178
contraction, exercise of feeling and feeling beyond, 2
conversation, not based on presumption of Consciousness, 8
cooperation, 266-67
cooperative community, and handling life-business, 18
copyright, perpetual, 408-409
creativity, 309
cultural disciplines in the Way of the Heart, 45
culture
　loss of, 91
　true culture, 46-47

D

"Da" (Name), defined, xxiii
Danavira Mela, 337
The Dawn Horse Testament Of The Ruchira Buddha, 129, 332
"death" (Spiritual), and Realization, 263
death
　after-death process does not congratulate the ego, 151
　breakdown of gross level in, 318-19
　fear of, 20, 56, 363
　and happiness, 105
　is a continuation of the in-depth process, 153-54
　is a real process, 151
　is built in, 276-78
　is the problem with life, 274-75
　knowledge of inevitable, 204
　near-death experiences and fear of, 150-51
　"The problem about life is death", 135-54
　and purpose of life, 281-82
　registering in the body-mind, 245-46
　and similarity to sleep, 359, 360
　a State deeper than, 215
　transcendence of, 364
　and waking, dreaming, and sleeping, 211
　and the waking state, 200

deeper, you can't get any, 10
　See also depth; in-depth process
definitions, and communication, 32
depth
　everybody wants to be deep, 37
　See also in-depth process
devotee, becoming a devotee of Adi Da is profound, 170
Devotional Way of Faith, defined, 399-400
Devotional Way of Insight, defined, 400
devotion to Adi Da, 39, 257
　See also Ruchira Buddha Bhakti Yoga
Dharma, defined, 400
dictionary, 120
"difference", feeling of, 116, 117
digestion, problems, 11
dilemma, as symptom of self-contraction, 130
discipline, 81
disciplines in the Way of the Heart, 44-45, 81
　associate body-mind with in-depth process, 148
　bring sensitivity, 177
　necessity for, 321-22
　purposes of, 320
　reflective function of, 177, 178-79
discriminative intelligence, 80-84, 301
　and active-life persona, 81
　and choice to be disciplined, 263
　and feeling-depth, 294-95
　given by in-depth process, 148
　and "I", 286-87
　is the captain's seat, 74
　needed for connection to Source, 76
　and sadhana, 13, 326
　See also will
Divine, defined, 79n, 405
Divine Depth, 292
Divine Enlightenment, 195, 357, 397-98
　and its resemblance to deep sleep, 358-59
　refusal of, 53
　you are un-Enlightened by habit, 320
　See also seven stages of life (seventh stage)
Divine Ignorance
　in Adi Da's Sadhana, 133
　defined, 133
　exercise in feeling, 2
Divine Indifference, 398
Divine Reality
　exercises to help one experience, 1-2
　True religion based in experience of, 1
Divine Recognition, 148, 292, 360-61
　defined, 148n, 400
　and knowing what things are, 200-201
Divine Self-Realization, 302-303
Divine Transfiguration, 397
Divine Transformation, 398
Divine Translation, 263, 398
DNA, 231
　as reverse of "and", 184
dreaming
　Adi Da's Instruction in the dream state, 238-39
　resembles waking state, 289
　and revery, 211
　and thinking, 306
　and waking, 216
　See also sleep (deep sleep); waking, dreaming, and sleeping; waking state

E

education, and development of discriminative intelligence, 80
effort, and Yoga, 254
ego, 224
　is not an entity but an activity, 130
　See also "I", "you"
ego-death, 105-106
egoity, global effects of, 266-67
embodiment, 278-79
emotional-sexual patterning, 271-73
emotions, as expansions and contractions of feeling, 167
end-time, xxii
Energy
　is the bottom line of objectively observed things, 224
　not separate from Consciousness and world, 227

412

as the root of everything, 214
"there is only Energy and Consciousness", 233, 234
this domain floats in a sea of, 23
environment, 266-67
etheric, defined, 400
expansion
and emotions, 167
requires "difference", 181
and self-contraction, 168-72
experience
inadequacy of, 20, 231, 244
investigation of, 262-63
is not in present time, 251
the nature of, 5-6
temporary nature of all, 151
what is it?, 243
eyeballs, thinking and turning of, 140

F

faculties
devotion of faculties to Adi Da, 75
surrender of the four faculties to Adi Da, 76, 80, 121
faith
and death, 136-37
defined, 137
fatigue, 255-56
fear, and self-contraction, 85
Fear-No-More Zoo, 208
described, 209
feeling-Contemplation
defined, 400
and "radical" understanding, 189
silent Instruction in, 69-72
see also Contemplation
feeling-disposition, needed for connection to Source, 76
Feeling of Being, defined, 400
feeling of "difference", defined, 400
feeling of relatedness, 332-35
defined, 400
financial support of Adidam, 406-407
fire, Adi Da and, 97-101
first congregation devotees of Adi Da, 376
flow, going with the, 49, 82, 117, 122, 146-47, 230, 327
fly miracle, 296-97
forest fire, Adi Da and, 97-101
fourth congregation of devotees of Adi Da, 379-80
frontal Yoga, 202
Fugitt, Ben, Leela by, 97-101
functional disciplines in the Way of the Heart, 44

G

gathering, defined, xxviii
Gautama Shakyamuni, 56-57, 56n
God, 115, 132
God, Truth, or Happiness Must Be Always Already The Case, 130
Nature of, 303, 329-31
God-Realization
defined, xiii-xv
and transcendence of self-contraction, 130
and waking state, 121-22
going with the flow. See flow, going with the
good company, 374
Grace, 123-24
Great Path of Return, 398
Great Tradition
defined, 17n, 401
described, 298
and presumptions about stages of life, 17
grid of attention, described, 141
gross, subtle, and causal, defined, 401
guided meditation, 8-10
Guru-devotee relationship (with Adi Da)
brings profundity to your life, 42
must be lived profoundly, 43-44
See also Ruchira Buddha Bhakti Yoga
Guru-devotee relationship
and the Look of Blessing, 87
need for, xv-xvii, 39
Guru-devotion, 257
Guru-love, xvi

H

habit, transcending, 320
Happiness, 132
cannot be realized by seeking, 149
and emotion, 167
God, Truth, or Happiness Must Be Always Already The Case, 130
is inherent, 161
the Knowledge of, 362
and money, 103-105
thinking and the Realization of, 112-14, 116-17
vs. expansion, 171-72
Hastings, Thankfull, Leela by, 265-69
Hatha Yoga, defined, 401
hearing, 124, 125, 169
as capability to be established in the heart-position, 185
defined, 78, 191, 401
described, 77-79, 173, 322-23
is capability at the point of action, 250
is understanding of self-contraction, 254
not constant meditation on self-contraction, 179
and the process of deepening, 202
and random exercise of hearing, 181
and the Spiritually responsible stages, 173-74
when it occurs, 176
See also listening
heart, don't lose your, 213
the Heart, 162
Adi Da as, xxv
heartbeat, feeling source of, 8-9
The Heart Of The Dawn Horse Testament Of The Ruchira Buddha, 129
Heart-Transmission, Leelas of Adi Da's, 27, 67-68, 69-72, 86-87, 99-100, 296-97
hierarchies, of self and world, 299-303
Hinayana Buddhism, 310, 311
hive, bees in a, 150
structure of, 19
Horse, "Only the Horse knows", 254
human beings
as humble life-forms, 119, 120
more than what they look like?, 33-34

I

"I"
inside or outside?, 139-40
is not eternal, 291
is the body-mind, 280
nature of, 332-35
See also ego; "you"
ida-pingali, 172
defined, 172n
"I give you everything in the first moment", 27
in-depth process, 227, 235, 350
Adi Da's Call to, 295
conserves the faculties, 244-45
death is a continuation of the, 153-54
enables you to find integrity, 205
frees you, 210
gives you discriminative intelligence, 148
in-depth position, 148, 226
is primary matter, 144-45
is transformative, 146
is what is really interesting, 38, 152
life should be about the, 352
in the midst of daily activity, 207
releases you of concerns, 237
traditions for, 312-13
and waking, dreaming, and sleeping, 194, 197
Way of the Heart requires, 229
"I"-ness, is a process, 223-24
inside
doesn't mean in the physical flesh bag, 177
vs. outside, 8-14, 147
inside out
changes manifest from, 91
choice to function from, 144-45
conditional Reality is composed from, 299
everything works from the, 74
your actual situation is from, 8-14
instruction books, 275-76
integrity, in life and practice, 92

413

417

AN INVITATION

The Truth can be found. Freedom is possible, for we live in an extraordinary moment of Grace.

Avatar Adi Da Samraj, the Living Divine Being, the Promised God-Man of the "end-time", or dark era, is here. Through a Miracle of Divine Grace and Compassionate Intervention, the One who answers the deepest yearning of all beings is alive now—offering a sacred relationship to you and to every man, woman, and child.

We invite you to participate in this direct Spiritual relationship by taking up the Way of the Heart—a self-transcending life of heart-Attraction and Communion with Adi Da Samraj that is ultimately fulfilled in Divine Enlightenment, or unqualified Freedom and Happiness.

If you would like to receive a free introductory brochure or to speak with a practicing devotee of Avatar Adi Da Samraj about Adidam, please write or call:

THE ELEUTHERIAN PAN-COMMUNION OF ADIDAM

AMERICAS	PACIFIC-ASIA	EUROPE-AFRICA
12040 North Seigler Road	12 Seibel Road	Annendaalderweg 10
Middletown, CA 95461	Henderson	6105 AT Maria Hoop
USA	Auckland 8	The Netherlands
(800) 524-4941	New Zealand	(0475) 30-2203
(707) 928-4936	(09) 838-9114	

or

visit our website at:

http://www.adidam.org

or

e-mail us at:

correspondence@adidam.org

418